Countering Economic Crime

Economic crime is a significant feature of the UK's economic landscape and yet despite the government's bold mission statements 'to hold those suspected of financial wrongdoing to account' as part of their 'day of reckoning' and 'serious about white-collar crime' agenda, there is a sense that this is still not being done effectively.

This book examines the history of the creation of the UK's anti-economic crime institutions and accompanying legislation, providing a critique of their effectiveness. The book analyses whether the recent regulatory regime is fit for purpose as well as being appropriate for the future. In order to explore how the UK's economic crime strategies could be improved, the book takes a comparative approach, analysing policy and legislative responses to economic crime in the United States and Australia in order to determine whether the UK could or should import similar structures or laws to improve the enforcement of UK economic crime.

Dr Axel Palmer holds a PhD specialising in economic crime and is a Visiting Lecturer at the Department of Law, University of the West of England, UK. He is a former Head of Debt Management and a Head of Litigation at a major bank. His research interests are in the field of economic crime, encompassing fraud, bribery and corruption.

The Law of Financial Crime

Series Editor: Nicholas Ryder

Available titles in this series include:

Fighting Financial Crime in the Global Economic Crisis
Nicholas Ryder, Umut Turksen and Sabine Hassler

The Financial War on Terror
A Review of Counter-Terrorist Financing Strategies Since 2001
Nicholas Ryder

The Financial Crisis and White Collar Crime - Legislative and Policy Responses
A Critical Assessment
Edited by Nicholas Ryder, Jon Tucker and Umut Turksen

Countering Economic Crime
A Comparative Analysis
Axel Palmer

Forthcoming titles in this series include:

Stemming Terrorist Finance
The Regulation of Hawala and Alternative Remittance Systems
Karen Cooper

Regulatory Responses to Fraud and Market Manipulation in the Financial Markets
An Analysis of United Kingdom and the United States of America
Rinita Sarker

Countering Economic Crime

A Comparative Analysis

Dr Axel Palmer

Routledge
Taylor & Francis Group
LONDON AND NEW YORK

First published 2018
by Routledge

2 Park Square, Milton Park, Abingdon, Oxfordshire OX14 4RN
52 Vanderbilt Avenue, New York, NY 10017

Routledge is an imprint of the Taylor & Francis Group, an informa business

First issued in paperback 2020

British Library Cataloguing in Publication Data
A catalogue record for this book is available from the British Library

Library of Congress Cataloging in Publication Data
A catalog record for this book has been requested

ISBN: 978-1-138-24108-4 (hbk)
ISBN: 978-0-367-59450-3 (pbk)

Typeset in Galliard
by Taylor & Francis Books

Contents

Acknowledgements

This monograph is the culmination of several years of hard work. I would like, especially, to thank my colleague and friend Nicholas Ryder who has provided unwavering support and guidance not only to encourage me to develop this area of research but also to review all the text (in many iterations) to bring this monograph to fruition. The final, and most important, acknowledgement goes to my wife, Helen. Without her love, support and understanding this book would not have been possible, and it is to her that I dedicate this book.

Foreword

The extent and cost of economic crime in all its manifestations are finally being recognised. According to the University of Portsmouth, fraud costs the UK economy nearly £200bn a year. The victims range from vulnerable individuals whose savings are plundered by boiler rooms and other investment scams to anyone who has a bank account that is capable of being hacked; from businesses at all levels to – as Dr Axel Palmer's opening paragraph recognises – the national economy. Fighting fraud must therefore be a national priority: to protect individuals and ensure that the UK has a robust economy. Dr Palmer's book charts the recent history of attempts made by successive governments and law enforcement to police fraud, compares this with other jurisdictions, and sets out his views on what a truly effective UK counter-fraud regime would look like.

Anyone who has been engaged in countering economic crime in the last three decades since the Roskill Fraud Trials Commission Report will have the same degree of scepticism about the chances of success of any system put in place to fight fraud in the UK criminal justice system. As is recorded in a quotation from Lord Roskill towards the end of this book, '[t]he public no longer believes that the legal system in England and Wales is capable of bringing the perpetrators of serious frauds expeditiously and effectively to book'. The range of views about the effectiveness of the various systems adopted over the years to prevent, discourage, disrupt, investigate and prosecute criminal fraud offences, and the priority that should be accorded to this work, is wide. How much police and prosecutorial resource should be devoted to fraud cases when terrorism, historic and current sex abuse, domestic violence, hate crime and the physical protection of people and property (to name but a few) demand law enforcement attention? At the time of the Roskill Report in 1986, nearly every police force in England and Wales had a dedicated fraud squad. By 2008 very few remained and the expertise of the officers working in them had dissipated: the Metropolitan Police Fraud Squad (SCD 6) was a relatively pale shadow of its former self. In the last ten years the City of London Police Fraud Squad has become the 'Lead Force' for economic crime, and has developed and expanded encouragingly, yet the depletion of regional forces has continued.

New counter-fraud legislation has been introduced. The Fraud Act 2006 and the Bribery Act 2010 have both improved and updated the statute book.

Manipulating benchmarks like LIBOR has been made a specific offence. Further improvements are planned in the Criminal Finances Bill, particularly in relation to money laundering. Dr Palmer advocates a new offence of reckless risk-taking on the financial markets. At the same time, the Deferred Prosecution Agreement has been imported from the United States to encourage businesses to self-report wrong-doing in return for a reduced penalty, and the Senior Managers Regime is being brought into force by the financial regulator in order to increase the accountability of directors.

Fraud reporting has undergone significant change. For the average fraud, a telephone call or online report to Action Fraud has taken the place of a direct report to the local police. Such reports rarely result in any direct action being taken: no policeman will arrive at your door to take a statement and start an investigation. The details will instead be used for intelligence purposes. One positive consequence is that there is a better measure of the cost of fraud, and trends and priorities can be assessed.

There is also the problem of changing times and perspectives. When the economy is flourishing, attention tends to wander away from fraud and the resources devoted to it are reduced. When the going gets tough, politicians will call for assertive action against big business and banks – as it did in the wake of the global financial crisis – to appease a public thirst for revenge against the people who, as far as they can see, have escaped unscathed from the serious consequences of their actions. Then, within a few years, imperatives will change again, focusing instead on the need to adopt lighter-touch regulation to allow our financial institutions and big businesses to recover and flourish. In place of this see-saw approach, long-term consistency is needed.

On a broader front there is the question of whether the 'alphabet soup' of counter-fraud agencies – the Serious Fraud Office, the police, the Financial Conduct Authority, the Competition and Markets Authority, Revenue and Customs, NHS Protect, and many others – with the Crown Prosecution Service acting as the prosecuting agency for some of the above, should be replaced by a one-stop shop that would comprise all the existing agencies under one roof. The Home Office and Ministry of Justice are in the process of reviving a plan under which an Economic Crime Agency will take on all counter-fraud work. Dr Palmer is a strong advocate of the Economic Crime Agency approach, and many will agree that a joined-up agency would have many advantages.

Dr Palmer's book provides a very timely and thorough analysis of the current state of play in the fight against economic crime.

David Kirk
Chairman, Fraud Advisory Panel

Abbreviations

AFP	Australian Federal Police
AML	anti-money laundering
APRA	Australian Prudential Regulation Authority
ASIC	Australian Securities and Investment Commission
AUSTRAC	Australian Transaction Reports and Analysis Centre
BBA	British Bankers' Association
CCA	Consumer Credit Act
CCFI	consumer credit financial institutions
CDPP	Commonwealth Director of Public Prosecutions
CEO	chief executive officer
CFO	chief financial officer
City	City of London
CMA	Competition and Markets Authority
COLP	City of London Police
CPS	Crown Prosecution Service
CRO	Civil Recovery Order
CTF	counter-terrorism financing
DANY	Manhattan District Attorney's Office
DoJ	Department of Justice
DPA	Deferred Prosecution Agreement
DPP	Director of Public Prosecutions
ECA	Economic Crime Agency
ECC	Economic Crime Command
ERRA	Enterprise and Regulatory Reform Act
EU	European Union
EURIBOR	Euro Inter-Bank Offered Rate
FATF	Financial Action Task Force
FBI	Federal Bureau of Investigation
FCA	Financial Conduct Authority
FCPA	Foreign Corrupt Practices Act
FFETF	Financial Fraud Enforcement Taskforce
FinCEN	Financial Crimes Enforcement Network
FSA	Financial Services Authority

FSMA	Financial Services and Markets Act
FX	foreign exchange
G20	Group of Twenty
HMRC	HM Revenue and Customs
ICC	International Chamber of Commerce
ICIJ	International Consortium of Investigative Journalists
LIBOR	London Inter-Bank Offered Rate
LIFFE	London International Financial Futures and Options Exchange
LSE	London Stock Exchange
MCLOC	Model Criminal Law Officers Committee
MLR	Money Laundering Regulations
MoJ	Ministry of Justice
NCA	National Crime Agency
NFA	National Fraud Authority
NHS	National Health Service
NPA	Non-Prosecution Agreement
NSW	New South Wales
OAS	Organization of American States
OECD	Organisation for Economic Co-operation and Development
OFT	Office of Fair Trading
OLAF	European Anti-Fraud Office
OTC	over the counter
PEP	politically exposed person
POCA	Proceeds of Crime Act
PPI	payment protection insurance
PRA	Prudential Regulation Authority
RBA	Reserve Bank of Australia
RICO	Racketeer Influenced and Corrupt Organisations
SAR	Suspicious Activity Report
SEC	Securities and Exchange Commission
SFO	Serious Fraud Office
SIB	Securities and Investment Board
SME	small and medium-sized enterprises
UK	United Kingdom
UN	United Nations
UNCAC	United Nations Convention against Corruption
UNODC	United Nations Office on Drugs and Crime
US	United States of America
VAT	value-added tax

1 Introduction

Introduction[1]

Economic crime is an important feature of the United Kingdom's (UK) economy, yet it attracts less attention from the media, government and law enforcement agencies when compared to violent crime,[2] despite fraud alone amounting to £193bn a year,[3] underlining the classic polarity between 'blue collar' and 'white collar' crime.[4] This book is focused on economic crime in the UK and considers whether the current anti-economic crime legislation and enforcement agencies are positioned to meet their objectives.[5] However, since economic crime afflicts all countries,[6] in order to ensure that the UK measures are appropriate, it is

1 The law is at 31 December 2016.
2 Edwin H Sutherland, *White Collar Crime: The Uncut Version* (Yale University Press 1983) 56.
3 Total UK fraud losses estimated to be £193bn. University of Portsmouth, 'Annual Fraud Indicator 2016' 6, 15 www.port.ac.uk/media/contacts-and-departments/icjs/ccfs/Annual-Fraud-Indicator-2016.pdf Accessed 12 September 2016. KPMG estimate that the value of fraud cases reaching the courts exceeded £1bn in 2016. KPMG, 'Value of UK fraud breaks £1 billion barrier for the first time in five years' https://home.kpmg.com/uk/en/home/insights/2017/01/uk-fraud-value-reaches-1bn-first-time-five-years.html Accessed 25 January 2017.
4 J Kelly Strader, *Understanding White Collar Crime* (LexisNexis 2002) 11.
5 Serious Fraud Office: 'The SFO's purpose is to investigate and, where appropriate, prosecute cases of serious or complex fraud, bribery and corruption. In addition, the SFO recovers the proceeds of those crimes it investigates and assists overseas jurisdictions in their investigations into serious or complex fraud, bribery and corruption.' Serious Fraud Office, 'Annual report 2015–16' 3 www.sfo.gov.uk/publications/corporate-information/annual-reports-accounts/ Accessed 3 March 2017. Financial Conduct Authority: 'We want consumers to use financial services with confidence and have products that meet their needs, from firms and individuals they can trust. To achieve this, we regulate firms and financial advisers so that markets and financial systems remain sound, stable and resilient.' Financial Conduct Authority, 'About us' www.fca.org.uk/about Accessed 14 January 2017.
6 Some 178 countries feature in Transparency International. Transparency International, 'Corruption Perceptions Index 2016' www.transparency.org/news/feature/corruption_perceptions_index_2016?utm_medium=email&utm_campaign=CPI%202016%20General%20Mailer&utm_content=CPI%202016%20General%20Mailer+Version+A+CID_310d39acff23636ebb54eda828e1e89d&utm_source=Email%20ma

important to take advantage of experience in some other jurisdictions by comparing and contrasting their government policy and regulatory responses (both legislation and agencies). For reasons that will be explained below, this research has chosen to compare the UK's approach with those of the United States (US) and Australia. This book employs doctrinal and comparative methodologies and will define 'economic crime' before examining and analysing government policy, legislation and anti-economic crime institutions, and the contemporary landscape.

What is economic crime?

The field of economic crime embraces fraud, bribery, corruption and financial regulation, yet Levi shows they are investigated individually rather than the field as a whole.[7] Economic crime is a subset of the field of financial crime, which also includes money laundering, terrorist financing and market abuse – all of which are sometimes called 'white collar crime'. The terms are used interchangeably and even the International Monetary Fund accepts the lack of international definition of financial crime,[8] though their broad view of 'any non-violent crime resulting in a financial loss'[9] closely echoes Sutherland, who highlighted the perceptions that offenders in this category receive more lenient sentences than other spheres of criminality.[10]

The expression 'white collar crime' was first used by Sutherland in 1939.[11] He was examining sociological differences amongst criminals and defined this category as 'a comparison of crime in the upper or white-collar class, composed of respectable or at least respected business and professional men, and crime in the lower class, composed of persons of low economic status,'[12] and according to

rketing%20software&utm_term=SEE%20RESULTS Accessed 25 January 2017. Some 193 countries are members of the United Nations. United Nations, 'At a glance' www.un.org/en/aboutun/index.shtml Accessed 3 November 2016.

7 M Levi, 'Fraud on trial: What is to be done?' (2000) 21(2) Co Law 54, 55. M Levi, 'The Roskill Fraud Commission revisited: An assessment' (2003) 11(1) JFC 38. T M Honess, M Levi and E A Charman, 'Juror competence in serious frauds since Roskill: A research based assessment' (2004) 11(1) JFC 17. R Wright, 'Fraud after Roskill: A view of the Serious Fraud Office' (2003) 11(1) JFC 11(1) 10.

8 International Monetary Fund, 'Financial system abuse, financial crime and money laundering – background paper' 5 www.imf.org/external/np/ml/2001/eng/021201.pdf Accessed 3 November 2016.

9 International Monetary Fund, 'Financial system abuse, financial crime and money laundering – background paper' (n 8) 5.

10 *R v Dougall* [2010] EWCA Crim 1048; *R v Innospec* (unreported) (Lord Judge). Edwin H Sutherland, *White Collar Crime: The Uncut Version* (n 2) 56.

11 B George, 'Edwin Hardin Sutherland: Sociological Criminologist' (1951) 16(1) American Sociological Review 2–9. For a discussion on nineteenth-century 'attempts (…) being made in the public domain to orient financial crimes alongside and against "ordinary crime" a century earlier than Sutherland's famous work', see Sarah Wilson, *The Origins of Modern Financial Crime* (Routledge 2014) 75–85.

12 Edwin H Sutherland, 'White collar criminality' (1940) Am Soc Rev 1. Later, Sutherland refined the definition as 'committed by a person of respectability and high social

Strader included crimes committed by corporations and other legal entities in his definition,[13] which he conceded was 'arbitrary and not very precise'.[14] He concluded that the impact of white collar crime was greatly underestimated in society.[15]

Sutherland drew attention to crimes being a 'lower class' activity with a low incidence in the 'upper class'.[16] He identified 'robber barons', 'merchant princes' and 'captains of finance' from past eras before concluding that 'white collar crime' is found in every occupation,[17] citing a range of activities which 'Al Capone called "the legitimate rackets"'.[18] Furthermore, whilst asserting that 'white collar crime is real crime', Sutherland noted the poor criminal conviction rates by explaining preferences of victims for civil damages recovery or restitution or salvage because criminal prosecution would interfere with obtaining financial recompense.[19] In modern times, Sutherland's definition might appear out-dated because, as Strader notes, white collar crimes 'such as securities fraud and tax fraud are committed not just by people of "high social status" but by people of divergent backgrounds'.[20] However, notwithstanding the blurring of Sutherland's definition, the perpetuation of the term, 'white collar' remains 'a convenient moniker for distinguishing such crime in the public mind from "common" or "street" crime'.[21] The US Department of Justice defines white collar crime as:

> Non-violent crime for financial gain committed by means of deception by persons whose occupational status is entrepreneurial, professional or semi-professional and utilizing their special occupational skills and opportunities; also, nonviolent crime for financial gain utilizing deception and committed by

status in the course of his occupation'. As cited in Sarah Wilson, '"Collaring" the crime and the criminal? "Jury psychology" and some criminological perspectives on fraud and the criminal law' (2006) 70(1) J Crim L 75–92.

13 Strader, *Understanding White Collar Crime* (n 4) 1.

14 Edwin H Sutherland, 'Crime and business' (1941) 217 Annals Amer Acad Pol & Soc Sci 112.

15 Strader, *Understanding White Collar Crime* (n 4) 1. Although Sutherland does not explain why the impact of white collar crime was underestimated in society, Payne does detail the consequences. 'Crime, by its very nature, has consequences for individuals and communities. White-collar crime, in particular, has a set of consequences that may be significantly different from the kinds of consequences that arise from street crimes. In particular, the consequences can be characterized as (1) individual economic losses, (2) societal economic losses, (3) emotional consequences, (4) physical harm, and (5) "positive" consequences.' Brian K Payne, *White-collar Crime* (Sage 2013) 37.

16 Sutherland, 'White collar criminality' (n 12) 1. Crimes include: 'murder, assault, burglary, robbery, larcency [sic], sex offences, and drunkenness, but exclude traffic violations.'

17 Sutherland, 'White collar criminality' (n 12) 1.

18 Sutherland, 'White collar criminality' (n 12) 1.

19 Sutherland, 'White collar criminality' (n 12) 1.

20 Strader, *Understanding White Collar Crime* (n 4) 1.

21 Strader, *Understanding White Collar Crime* (n 4) 1.

> anyone having specialist technical and professional knowledge of business and government, irrespective of the person's occupation.[22]

Or, as the US Federal Bureau of Investigation (FBI) put more succinctly, 'lying, cheating, and stealing'.[23] An alternative approach to a definition is that it may be more convenient to define white collar crime by what it is not: Strader suggests that the prime characteristics of white collar crime do not include violence, drugs, vice, common theft or challenges to national security such as immigration and human rights.[24]

Public attitude to white collar crime is another consideration.[25] Sutherland noted that, clearly, crimes such as murder and rape attracted as much public resentment as felonies but other crimes were categorised as misdemeanours, into which category white collar crime tended to be consigned. Furthermore:

> The differential implementation of the law as it applies to large corporations may be explained by three factors: namely, the status of the businessman, the trend away from punishment and the relatively unorganised resentment of the public against white collar crimes.[26]

The importance of public attitude is that it drives government policy. For example, the financial resources of the police are constrained and 'the allocation of resources is being prioritised towards financial intelligence and money laundering and away from fraud'.[27] Doig identifies the competing priorities: 'this is clearly a consequence of the wider public order, public safety and financial confiscation agendas pursued by successive governments.'[28] The outcome of the maxim 'what gets measured gets done' is that 'investigating and prosecuting fraud does not count in terms of measuring the delivery of these agendas or league tables of performance'.[29]

White collar crime law enforcement

Strader notes that a principal difficulty with white collar crime is that it is often very difficult to detect, relying on circumstantial evidence and complex paper trails

22 Bureau of Justice Statistics, US Department of Justice, 'Dictionary of Criminal Justice Data Terminology' 215 www.ncjrs.gov/App/publications/abstract.aspx?ID=76939 Accessed 14 January 2017.

23 Federal Bureau of Investigation, 'White collar crime' www.fbi.gov/about-us/investigate/white_collar/whitecollarcrime Accessed 14 January 2017.

24 Strader, *Understanding White Collar Crime* (n 4) 1.

25 Michael Levi, 'Suite revenge? The shaping of folk devils and moral panics about white-collar crimes' (2009) Brit J Criminol 48.

26 Sutherland, *White Collar Crime: The Uncut Version* (n 2) 56.

27 Attorney General's Office, *Fraud Review – Final Report* (Attorney General's Office 2006) 130.

28 Alan Doig, *Fraud* (Willan 2006) 133.

29 Doig (n 28) 133.

with only the occasional obvious clues of a 'smoking gun'.[30] This is compounded by investigations that can last for years followed by lengthy trials.[31] In the US, government agencies have sought opportunities to stretch existing laws.[32] For example, in the US PNP case,[33] prosecutors were able to extend their charges for securities and tax fraud to other charges. There, PNP, having been charged with tax fraud, were also charged with 'mail fraud'. This was purely because it had used the US Postal Service as part of the fraud by putting the tax returns in the post, something which would have been avoided by hand delivery.[34] Strader explains the consequences:

> because it charged mail fraud, the government could bring charges under the RICO statute,[35] with mail fraud as the principal predicate acts. And because RICO contains forfeiture provisions, the government could, and did, assume control over PNP's assets prior to trial.[36]

Blakey and Gettings observe that RICO was the end product of a long process of legislative effort to develop new legal routes by adapting the use of existing legislation to deal with 'organized crime'.[37] This case illustrates that as white collar crime changes, prosecutors have to respond and in the US, prosecutors looked to adapt existing legislation, unlike the UK approach to create new legislation, and 'whatever its weaknesses, RICO gives the government an effective threat against sophisticated crime (…) At least for a while, for white-collar criminals as well as gangsters, RICO appears to be evening up the odds'.[38] However, Strader reports difficulties created by 'vagueness of many white collar statutes',[39] providing scope for prosecutors to

30 Strader, *Understanding White Collar Crime* (n 4) 1. 'Compare a domestic violence incident to white-collar crime, (…) police are called, they arrive at the scene and they immediately question participants about the incident. Records (…) might be gathered at a later date. If a banking employee is suspected of embezzling the bank, however, the investigators will wait until they have reviewed the records before interviewing participants. In many white-collar crime cases, multiple suspects might be involved (…) Common strategies for gathering evidence in white-collar crime cases include: audits, record interviews, undercover strategies, whistleblowers and technological devices.' Payne (n 15) 304, 305.

31 Strader, *Understanding White Collar Crime* (n 4) 1.

32 For example: Mail Fraud Statute 1872, Wire Fraud Statute 1952, Racketeer Influenced and Corrupt Organizations Statute 18 U.S.C.§§ 1961–1964 (2006).

33 9 *United States v Regan*, 37 F.2d 823, 826–27 (2nd Cir. 1991).

34 J Kelly Strader, 'White collar crime and punishment: Reflections on Michael, Martha and Milberg Weiss' (2007) 15 Geo Mason L Rev 94.

35 The Racketeer Influenced and Corrupt Organizations [RICO] Statute 18 U.S.C.§§ 1961–1964 (2006), www.law.cornell.edu/uscode/text/18/part-I/chapter-96 Accessed 14 January 2017.

36 Strader, 'White collar crime and punishment' (n 34) 61.

37 G Robert Blakey and Brian Gettings, 'Racketeer Influenced and Corrupt Organizations (RICO): Basic concepts – criminal and civil remedies' (1980) 53 Temp LQ 1012.

38 Blakey and Gettings (n 37) 1012. 'RICO: The enforcer', *Newsweek*, 20 August 1979, at 82, col 3.

39 'Stating that it refused to engage in the exercise of defining federal "common-law crimes," the court concluded that it would "resist the incremental expansion of a

overreach themselves 'in instances of ambiguous harm and unproven legal theories'.[40] The conclusion that 'more carefully crafted statutes would begin to solve this problem',[41] is based on the reasoning that:

> Apart from being incomprehensible, the RICO statute's potential application is nearly boundless, principally because of its inclusion of the mail and wire fraud statutes as predicate acts. These statutes can be used just about anytime anyone puts anything in the mail, makes an interstate phone call, or sends an email in suspicious circumstances.[42]

The US system, discussed in Chapter 4, has a tradition of multiple statutes to criminalise different varieties of fraud which looks complicated when compared with the Fraud Act 2006 and Bribery Act 2010.

Criminal 'upperworld' and sentencing[43]

In parallel with examining white collar crime, this book also considers the belief held at large[44] that white collar criminals are treated differently from other criminals. Lord Judge CJ provides a reminder of the status of fraudsters, as not being some superior species of criminal:

> For all the respectable and reputable fronts that many fraudsters and corrupt businessmen may present, they are criminals. What is sometimes described as white collar crime or commercial crime taking the form of fraud and corruption in particular is crime. And it is not victimless: sometimes identified individuals are victims, and at others, unnamed, unknown individuals in the entire community are victims, and sometimes the community itself is the victim.[45]

statute that is vague and amorphous on its face and depends for its constitutionality on the clarity divined from a jumble of disparate cases." This conclusion is all the more valid because the mail and wire fraud statutes are applied in circumstances where there is no discernable harm.' Strader, 'White collar crime and punishment' (n 34) 61, 96 (footnote omitted).

40 Strader, 'White collar crime and punishment' (n 34) 61, 96.

41 Strader, 'White collar crime and punishment' (n 34) 61, 96.

42 Strader, 'White collar crime and punishment' (n 34) 61, 94.

43 Gus Russo, 'Target criminal "upperworld"' *Baltimore Sun* 11 June 2002 http://articles.baltimoresun.com/2002-07-11/news/0207110056_1_ethos-tax-evasion-dapper Accessed 14 January 2017.

44 'Attending cases in court, (...) Particularly noticeable is the absence of corporate offenders and the prevalence of small shop keepers, restaurateurs, market traders and second hand car salesmen.' Hazel Croall, 'Who is the white-collar criminal?' (1989) 29 Brit J Criminology 164.

45 Lord Judge CJ, *R v Dougall* [2010] EWCA Crim 1048 13 May 2010 www.bailii.org/cgi-bin/markup.cgi?doc=/ew/cases/EWCA/Crim/2010/1048.html&query=dougall&method=boolean Accessed 14 January 2017.

Lord Judge warned that, in fraud and corruption cases, the prosecutors should not believe that these are 'more respectable than other forms of crime',[46] or that these criminals 'should not be ordered to serve prison sentences because such sentences should be reserved for those they regard as common criminals'.[47] Nevertheless, the reasons why there is an actual or apparent disparity in sentencing are worthy of examination.

Suggestions of underlying reasoning include that: white collar crime is less important; white collar crime is different from other crimes and requires different measures; or the legislators and judges come from the same social demographic groups as the perpetrators and are inherently biased. This was a view supported by Leong, who noted that:

> the definition of white-collar crime is criticised for being too narrow as it does not include the differential associations between the 'upperworld' of corporations and the 'underworld' of criminal organisations. At the same time, it is criticised for being too broad as an all-encompassing category. In fact, the distinction between organised crime or 'business in crime' and the activities of white-collar offenders blurs, and organised crime often uses and abuses legitimate corporate enterprises.[48]

This is an interesting distinction between the familiar organised crime 'underworld' criminal activities and 'upperworld' criminality, an expression coined by 'Albert Morris in his textbook *Criminology* in 1934',[49] since 'hardly a day goes by without new scandals coming to light concerning insider trading, money laundering or leveraged buy-outs'.[50]

Robb analyses Sutherland's definition of white collar crime as being undertaken 'in the course of his occupation' and contrasts that:

> non-occupational crimes committed by members of polite society, such as murder or rape, would not be considered white collar crimes. Likewise work-related crimes such as larceny by domestic servants or the theft of building materials by construction workers cannot be categorized as white-collar crimes because they were carried out by lower-class persons.[51]

Croall observes that the label of 'white-collar crime', having entered the *lingua franca*, is 'traditionally associated with high status and respectable offenders'.[52] Furthermore, these are considered to be the 'crimes of the powerful' and

46 Lord Judge CJ (n 45).
47 Lord Judge CJ (n 45).
48 A Leong, 'Definitional analysis: The war on terror and organised crime' (2004) 8(1) Journal of Money Laundering Control 22.
49 George Robb, *White-Collar Crime in Modern England* (CUP 1992) 193.
50 George Robb (n 49) 7.
51 George Robb (n 49) 4.
52 Croall (n 44) 157.

corporate crime.[53] However, this stereotype, while convenient when applied to some major cases, does not cover the whole spectrum: 'some white-collar offences are committed by offenders clearly not of "high status and respectability".'[54] Croall considers that much crime labelled as 'white-collar' is perpetrated by many who 'could not be described as "powerful", high status, or even respectable'.[55] These include 'crimes against the consumer', committed in the course of trade and business by small businesses and where 'large legitimate corporations (…) are the *victims* of such frauds rather than the perpetrators'.[56] Croall identifies areas such as food fraud,[57] weights and measures, trade descriptions and consumer credit.[58]

The essential element in this upperworld is that of trust, as Robb notes where 'white-collar crime can be further defined as breaches of trust within business or professional communities or between those communities and the general public'.[59] Sutherland recognised this by observing that 'embezzlement is usually a violation of trust by an employee at the expense of the employer, while most other white collar crimes are violations of trust by businessmen at the expense of consumers, investors and the state'.[60] Thus, the positioning of white collar crime in this book is that, in relation to economic crime, the 'upperworld' is inhabited by respectable people of authority within business, even if not themselves of high social status.

Fraud, bribery and corruption definitions

Fraud is difficult to define. Although the Fraud Act 2006 is modern legislation, interestingly, it does not define 'fraud', merely stating that 'a person is guilty of fraud if he is in breach of any of the sections listed'.[61] Furthermore, there is no universal definition at common law.[62] The City of London Police defines fraud as

53 Croall (n 44) 157.
54 Croall (n 44) 157.
55 Croall (n 44) 157.
56 Croall (n 44) 157, 164. Croall considers 'crimes against the consumer', including health, safety and economic interests. The type of offender is seen as 'small shopkeepers, restaurateurs, market traders and second hand car salesmen'. 'Many offences, even if detected, are unlikely to be reported. Frequently, there is only a minimal effect on individual consumers, and they may seem too trivial to warrant further action (…) The deficiencies of cheap goods bought at a sale or market stall may be dismissed as a "bad buy".'
57 *Financial Times*, 'Horsemeat report calls for "food fraud" unit' www.ft.com/cms/s/0/ecc37282-3409-11e4-8832-00144feabdc0.html#axzz3D6kg3eVz Accessed 17 January 2017.
58 Croall (n 44) 157.
59 George Robb (n 49) 4.
60 E H Sutherland, 'Crime and business' (1941) 217 Annals Amer Acad Pol & Soc Sci 112.
61 Fraud Act 2006, s 1.
62 Alan Doig and Michael Levi, 'Inter-agency work and the UK public sector investigation of fraud, 1996–2006: Joined-up rhetoric and disjointed reality' (2009) 19(3) Policing and Society 199–215.

'when trickery is used to gain a dishonest advantage, which is often financial, over another person'.[63] However, the Serious Fraud Office (SFO) defines it as 'abuse of position, or false representation, or prejudicing someone's rights for personal gain'.[64]

Bribery has been described as 'a princely kind of thieving'[65] and has been unlawful since the Magna Carta declared 'to no one will we sell, to no one deny or delay right or justice'.[66] The Bible also states 'and you shall take no bribe, for a bribe blinds the clear-sighted and subverts the cause of those who are in the right'.[67] Notwithstanding this lineage, as the Law Commission observes, 'most people have an intuitive sense of what "bribery" is. However, it has proved hard to define in law'.[68] The modern-day cliché is a brown-paper bag stashed with cash, but bribes are usually more subtle than that, suggested Benstead.[69] Although accepting that 'at common law, bribery and corruption were criminal offences',[70] in *R v J*, Lord Thomas CJ observed that a 'single definition is not easy'[71] and then followed the Law Commission's stance in using a general statement from *Russell on Crime*:

> Bribery is the receiving or offering [of] any undue reward by or to any person whatsoever, in a public office, in order to influence his behaviour in office, and incline him to act contrary to the known rules of honesty and integrity.[72]

There are three principal statutes, dating to 'the end of the nineteenth century and beginning of the twentieth century (…), without abolishing the common law offence',[73] but they have different variations in their definitions of the term 'reward'. In the Public Bodies Corrupt Practices Act 1889, the nature of 'reward' is defined as: 'any gift, loan, fee, reward, or advantage whatever as an inducement.'[74] In the Prevention of Corruption Act 1906, the word consideration

63 City of London Police, 'What is fraud and cybercrime?' www.actionfraud.police.uk/what-is-fraud Accessed 18 October 2016.
64 Serious Fraud Office, 'What is fraud?' http://webarchive.nationalarchives.gov.uk/20130704104410/http://www.sfo.gov.uk/fraud/what-is-fraud.aspx Accessed 18 October 2016.
65 A T Denning, 'The independence and impartiality of the judges' (1954) 71 S African L J 345.
66 Magna Carta 1215, translation para 40 www.nationalarchives.gov.uk/museum/item.asp?item_id=3 Accessed 14 January 2017.
67 *The Holy Bible*, English Standard Version (HarperCollins 2007) Exodus 23:8.
68 Law Commission, *Reforming Bribery* (Law Com No 313, 2008).
69 John Benstead, 'Biting the bullet' (2010) 160 NLJ 1291.
70 *R v J, B, V and S, and D* [2013] EWCA Crim 2287.
71 *R v J* (n 70).
72 J W C Turner, *Russell on Crime*, 12th edn (Stephens & Sons 1964) 381.
73 *R v J* (n 70).
74 Public Bodies Corrupt Practices Act 1889, s 1. 'Advantage' includes 'any office or dignity, and any forbearance to demand any money or money's worth or valuable thing, and includes any aid, vote, consent, or influence, or pretended aid, vote, consent, or influence, and also includes any promise or procurement of or agreement or endeavour to procure, or the holding out of any expectation of any gift,

appeared in 'any gift or consideration as an inducement or reward'[75] (with 'consideration' being 'valuable consideration of any kind');[76] and then simplified in the Prevention of Corruption Act 1916 as 'any money, gift, or other consideration'.[77] The quantum of the reward is explained as: the amount of the reward 'must be more than a trivial amount'.[78] A public officer was 'an officer who discharges any duty in the discharge of which the public are interested, more clearly so if he is paid out of a fund provided by the public'.[79] According to the World Bank, bribery is 'the abuse of public office for private gain'.[80] It estimates that bribery costs the world around $1tn a year[81] and believes that 'corruption is a product of bad governance and the weaknesses inherent in public sector institutions'.[82] Transparency International 'defines corruption as the abuse of entrusted power for private gain. It hurts everyone whose life, livelihood or happiness depends on the integrity of people in a position of authority'.[83]

Rationale for selecting jurisdictions

Economic crime is a major drain on the UK economy and yet attracts little public attention.[84] Transparency International details an annual index showing the perceptions of corruption in 178 countries: the UK, Australia and the US being in 10th, 13th and 18th positions, respectively, well behind the Scandinavian countries and New Zealand at the head.[85] The UK cannot respond to the threats of

loan, fee, reward, or advantage, as before defined.' Public Bodies Corrupt Practices Act 1889, s 7.

75 Prevention of Corruption Act 1906, s 1.1.

76 Prevention of Corruption Act 1906, s 1(2).

77 Prevention of Corruption Act 1916, s 2.

78 Paul Cohen and Arthur Marriott, *International Corruption* (Sweet & Maxwell 2010) 3.

79 *R v Whitaker* [1914] 3 K.B. 1283.

80 World Bank, 'Helping countries combat corruption: The role of the World Bank, corruption and economic development' www1.worldbank.org/publicsector/anticorrupt/corruptn/cor02.htm Accessed 14 January 2017.

81 William Christopher, 'Trillion dollar bribery' (2011) 161 NLJ 25.

82 Indira Carr, 'Fighting corruption through the United Nations Convention on Corruption 2003: A global solution to a global problem?' (2005) 11(1) Int TLR 24, 28.

83 Transparency International, 'Corruption Perceptions Index 2016' (n 6).

84 Jonathan Fisher, *The Times* 11 March 2010 www.thetimes.co.uk/tto/law/article2464153.ece Accessed 18 October 2016. In 2013–14, the 'horsemeat' scandal did attract headlines and a government report. 'Professor Chris Elliott, (…) has recommended that the Food Standards Agency establish a national food crime unit to protect the sector from organised criminal gangs, who were "adulterating, tampering, stealing and counterfeiting" food within the supply chain.'*Financial Times*, 'Horsemeat report calls for "food fraud"' (n 57). HM Government, 'Elliott Review into the Integrity and Assurance of Food Supply Networks – Final Report' www.gov.uk/government/uploads/system/uploads/attachment_data/file/350726/elliot-review-final-report-july2014.pdf Accessed 14 January 2017.

85 On a scale of 100 (very clean). In 2015, all four Scandinavian countries are in the top five, whereas the last are Somalia, Afghanistan and North Korea. Transparency International, 'Corruption Perceptions Index 2016' (n 6).

economic crime in isolation because there are global issues. Since 1986, as the UK emerged from economic recession, there have been many vicissitudes in the global economic environment, together with the global political change occasioned by the terrorist attacks in September 2001 (9/11) in the US, which resulted in President George W. Bush engaging in the 'financial war on terror'.[86] In response to these events, US resources were diverted away from financial crime and towards anti-terrorism.[87] This was followed by the 2008 financial crisis which brought poor financial practice and fraud to the surface.[88] As a response to fraud emanating from the financial crisis, President Barack Obama introduced the Financial Fraud and Recovery Act 2009 which increased resources to the Department of Justice (DoJ) by $330m, whereas in the UK, the government planned reductions in the SFO's budget by 40% to £30m.[89]

It is because the UK is not the only country to face issues over the management, prevention and control of the elements of economic crime that, in order to inform the discussion, it is instructive to review how two other countries, the US and Australia, dealt with the same issues. These countries were chosen for comparison because the former is the UK's most significant trading partner outside Europe[90] and the latter is regarded as having more successfully

86 'On 24 September 2001 President George Bush proclaimed that "we will starve terrorists of funding", thus instigating the "financial war on terrorism".' Nicholas Ryder, *Financial Crime in the 21st Century* (Edward Elgar 2011) 51 (footnotes omitted).

87 Nicholas Ryder, *The Financial Crisis and White Collar Crime – The Perfect Storm* (Edward Elgar 2014) 37. US Department of State, 'President freezes terrorists' assets' http://2001-2009.state.gov/s/ct/rls/rm/2001/5041.htm Accessed 14 January 2017. R Suskind, *The One Percent Doctrine* (Simon & Schuster 2006) 142, as cited in S Eckert, 'The US Regulatory Approach to Terrorist Financing' in T Biersteker and S Eckert (eds), *Countering the Financing of Terrorism* (Routledge Cavendish 2008) 22.

88 '[Y]ou only find out who is swimming naked when the tide goes out.' Warren Buffett, Chairman's Letter to Shareholders, Berkshire Hathaway 2001, www.berkshirehathaway.com/letters/2001pdf.pdf Accessed 14 January 2017.

89 'The Serious Fraud Office investigates the most serious and complex cases of fraud, bribery and corruption. The quantity of such work is unpredictable. The SFO has a core budget which is supplemented as necessary by additional funding agreed with the Treasury. This includes "blockbuster" funding, which enables us to take on very big cases where the annual expenditure is expected to exceed an agreed percentage of our core budget. The current "blockbuster" funding arrangement was agreed in October 2012.' The SFO core budget showed actual reductions from £53.2m in 2008/09, to £29.6m in 2013/14. The core budget for 2016/17 is £35.7m. In 2013/14, additional blockbuster funding of £24m was made available, with £24.5m in 2014/15 and £28m in 2015/16. Serious Fraud Office, 'About us' www.sfo.gov.uk/about-us/ Accessed 6 December 2016. Nicholas Ryder, 'White collar crime and the global financial crisis; How long will we have to wait for the day of reckoning?' (2013) 57 Criminal Law News 5, 11.

90 Note: The European Union was not selected for comparison, primarily because EU directives to establish a common regime across member states are absent, through lack of political will, as evidenced by complaints of patchy adoption of international corruption conventions. 'Several EU Member States have ratified all or most of the

withstood the effects of the financial crisis than other leading industrial nations.[91]

Differing political philosophies, especially in the UK and the US, provide a logical sequence for examining governmental action. In the UK, the incoming Conservative government in 1979 faced a change in world financial markets, heralding a radical structural change known as the 'Big Bang'. The following Labour government in 1997 was determined to overhaul financial regulation, putting in place a 'super-regulator' and system whose shortcomings were exposed in the 2008 financial crisis. This was followed by a Conservative-Liberal Democrat coalition government from 2010, with a mission to replace the failed system, and then the Conservative government from 2015 facing economic difficulties.

In the US, the Clinton Administration of 1993 gave way to George W Bush in 2001, who was immediately faced with the 9/11 terrorist attacks and responded by giving priority to the fight against terrorism in his 'war on terror'. At the end of the Bush Administration was the 2008 financial crisis, which engulfed the US and UK and provided President Obama with the challenge to deal with its consequences. Meanwhile, in Australia, the financial crisis was demonstrated not to be a global phenomenon, partly attributed to a 'twin peaks' model of financial regulation which it had adopted to advantage and which was then adopted by the UK, its progenitor.

The importance of placing the UK into an international context provides the opportunity to evaluate the outcome of the comparative research in order to inform the discussion as to the most appropriate economic crime model that should be adopted by the UK. The spectrum of possibilities of the most appropriate economic crime model ranges between endorsement of the UK's current model, wholesale changes to adopt either of those of the US or Australia, or a hybrid model.

existing international anti-corruption instruments. However, three EU Member States (Austria, Germany, Italy) have not ratified the Council of Europe's Criminal Law Convention on Corruption, twelve have not ratified its additional Protocol (Austria, the Czech Republic, Estonia, Finland, Germany, Hungary, Italy, Lithuania, Malta, Poland, Portugal, Spain) and seven have not ratified the Civil Law Convention on Corruption (Denmark, Germany, Ireland, Italy, Luxembourg, Portugal and the UK). Three Member States have not yet ratified the UN Convention against Corruption (The Czech Republic, Germany, and Ireland). Five EU Member States (Cyprus, Latvia, Lithuania, Malta, and Romania) have not ratified the OECD Anti-Bribery Convention.' EU, 'Commission steps up efforts to forge a comprehensive anti-corruption policy at EU level' 3 June 2011 http://europa.eu/rapid/pressReleasesAction.do?reference=MEMO/11/376&format=HTML&aged=0&language=EN&guiLanguage=en Accessed 17 January 2017.

91 Michael Levi and Russell G Smith, 'Fraud Vulnerabilities and the Global Financial Crisis' in *Trends and Issues in Crime and Criminal Justice* (Australian Institute of Criminology No. 422) July 2011 www.aic.gov.au/publications/current%20series/tandi/421-440/tandi422.html Accessed 17 January 2017.

UK contemporary landscape

Having established the parameters of this book, it is appropriate to place events and policies in context. The government change in 1979 highlighted dissatisfaction with the workings of 'the City', and especially the inability of juries to convict people accused of major fraud, and caused the commissioning of two major studies: the 'Roskill' Report[92] (Roskill) and the 'Gower' Report[93] (Gower). The former reviewed the workings of fraud trials and the latter the role of investor protection. Both reports influenced government policies and resulted in major changes, such as the establishment of the SFO, and the creation of the 'City' regulator.[94] These reports provided a convenient base because they were broadly concurrent and appeared early in the life of the then new Conservative government. These reports represented two separate streams of research and subsequent legislation. However, these streams became intertwined because of the issues of fraud, insider dealing and market abuse in the City. The confluence of these streams came in with the new millennium which heralded the possibility of synergy between two ineffective regimes because the new City regulator was given a statutory object to reduce financial crime.[95]

The changes in the fields of economic crime and City regulation reflected the differing views of governments, initially over a 31-year period, split into three sections:

1 Conservative government from 1979 to 1997;
2 Labour government from 1997 to 2010; and,
3 Conservative-Liberal Democrat coalition government from 2010 to 2015, then Conservative government from 2015 onwards.

Fraud

Roskill represents a key stage in examining the arena of fraud. Levi's view of government attitude to fraud prior to 1979 was of 'benign neglect',[96] identifying cynicism in the City questioning whether juries could understand the cases put at trial.[97] A consequence of this was that 'commercial fraud was a subject of concern principally to a small group of academics'.[98] Levi observed that for politicians and

92 *Fraud Trials Committee Report* (HMSO 1986). City of London, hereinafter the City.
93 L C B Gower, *Review of Investor Protection* (HMSO 1984).
94 First, the Securities and Investment Board in 1986, then the Financial Services Authority in 2000; then the Financial Conduct Authority in 2013.
95 Financial Services and Markets Act 2000, ss 2(2) and 6(3). E Z Lomnicka, 'Reforming UK financial services regulation: The creation of a single regulator' (Sept 1999) JBL 480, 482. Iain MacNeil, 'The trajectory of regulatory reform in the UK in the wake of the financial crisis' (2010) 11 EBOR 483.
96 M Levi, 'Fraud in the courts. Roskill in context' 1986 26(4) Br J Criminal 394.
97 Levi, 'Fraud in the courts' (n 96) 394.
98 Levi, 'Reforming the criminal fraud trial: An overview of the Roskill proposals (1986) 13(1) J L & Soc'y 117.

criminologists 'street and household crime constituted "the crime problem" over which they would do battle'.[99] This has echoes of Sutherland's discussion.[100]

Roskill's initial conclusion,[101] congruent with Levi's analysis, was that:[102]

> The public no longer believes that the legal system in England and Wales is capable of bringing the perpetrators of serious frauds expeditiously and effectively to book. The overwhelming weight of the evidence laid before us suggests that the public is right.[103]

The Roskill Report was commissioned because 'informed sources state that the aim was to get rid of the reputational problem caused by "failures" to convict'.[104] Roskill is discussed in detail in Chapter 2.

Financial markets regulation

The regulation of UK financial services has progressed from 1979 but, unlike the SFO, the regulatory framework has continued to develop. Part of this process of change which brought in new regulators in 1986, 1997 and 2013, was because formal regulation was a new feature and 'the international regulatory framework (…) is complex, particularly on resolution that crosses regulatory boundaries'.[105] The way in which the City worked in 1979 was a mix of non-intervention or self-regulation,[106] with Irving,[107] McRea and Cairncross,[108] and Fisher and Bewsey[109] putting into perspective the regulatory landscape based on the Prevention of Frauds (Investments) Act 1958. The main study was by Gower.[110]

The regulation of investments and markets proved to be problematic, as demonstrated by the frequent changes in the structure and institutions,[111] because, according to Cohrs, 'the global financial institutions became experts in "global regulatory arbitrage". While there are still some large gaps between policy

99 Levi, 'Reforming the criminal fraud trial' (n 98) 117.
100 Sutherland, 'White collar criminality' (n 12) 1.
101 Roskill (n 92) 1.
102 M Levi, 'Blaming the jury: Frauds on trial' (1983) 10 J L & Soc'y 257.
103 Roskill (n 92) 1.
104 Levi, 'The Roskill Fraud Commission revisited: An assessment' (2003) 11(1) JFC 38.
105 Michael Cohrs, Speech to the University of the West of England. 'Broken glass – moving towards sustainable financial regulation' 13 November 2012 www.bankofengland.co.uk/archive/Documents/historicpubs/news/2012/106.pdf Accessed 18 February 2017.
106 Editorial, 'How many regulators?' (1996) 17(2) Co Law 34.
107 Joe Irving, *The City at Work* (Andre Deutsch 1981).
108 Hamish McRea and Frances Cairncross, *Capital City. London as a Financial Centre* (Eyre Methuen 1974).
109 J Fisher and J Bewsey, *The Law of Investor Protection* (Sweet & Maxwell 1997).
110 Gower (n 93).
111 Financial Services Act 1986, Financial Services and Markets Act 2000, Financial Services Act 2010.

makers in different countries on regulatory topics, we are making progress on closing down regulatory arbitrage'.[112]

The Bank of England

The historic role of the Bank of England is of considerable importance because the Bank of England has had an historically pivotal position as central bank, banking regulator and financial markets regulator. McRea and Cairncross note that the 'paradoxical Old Lady [the Bank of England] is the link between the City and the government (…) [this] is an inherent contradiction (…) it is the government's arm in the City, and the City's representative in the government – the gamekeeper and the poacher, the foreman and the shop steward'.[113] The Bank of England is a traditional-looking institution: 'the Bank's tall, windowless walls built (…) in 1828, give it the look of an elegant fortress (…) guarded by pink coated doormen',[114] providing an emblematic view of the City's premier club. The Bank of England, established in 1694 by Royal Charter, operated as a private institution until 1946.[115] Over time, according to Galpin, it 'had taken on a regulatory role and it could act flexibly and with understanding, which made it all the more acceptable to those whose affairs it chose to monitor'.[116] Ritchie notes that 'the twin aims of the Bank's controlling activity in the City are regulation of institutions and implementation of policy',[117] which includes managing the government's debt, issuing notes and coin, acting as banker to the government, acting as banker to commercial banks, managing the country's gold and currency reserves, and controlling the monetary system of the UK.[118] The hallmark of these supervisory arrangements was its flexibility;[119] however, as Fisher and Bewsey comment, 'the secondary banking crisis of the 1970s had effectively undermined confidence in the informal system of supervision and the 1979 Banking Act was introduced'.[120] Thus, after almost three centuries the Bank was given statutory authority for authorisation and supervision of banks.[121] However, this development did not take place in a vacuum, when the rapidly changing regulatory environment necessitated a review, leading to the Banking Act 1987.[122]

112 Cohrs (n 105).
113 McRea and Cairncross (n 108) 193.
114 McRea and Cairncross (n 108) 194.
115 Bank of England, 'History of the Bank of England' www.bankofengland.co.uk/about/Pages/history/default.aspx Accessed 24 November 2016. Bank of England Act 1946.
116 Rodney D Galpin, 'A Central Banker's View' in *The Banks and Risk Management* (The Chartered Institute of Bankers 1988) 5.
117 Nicholas Ritchie, *What Goes on in the City?* (Woodhead Faulkner 1986) 22, 25.
118 Ritchie (n 117) 25.
119 Galpin (n 116) 5.
120 Fisher and Bewsey (n 109) 201.
121 Banking Act 1979. Fisher and Bewsey (n 109) 201.
122 Fisher and Bewsey (n 109) 201.

Between 1946 and 1979, the Bank of England's main concern was the provision of liquidity to the UK banking system, which it undertook through dealings with merchant banks. Thus, the Bank of England had regular contact with a privileged few banks through which it exercised supervision, although as Robb comments:[123]

> The Bank of England Act 1946 gave the Bank powers to 'request information from and make recommendations to bankers' and, if authorised by the Treasury, to 'issue directions to any banker for the purpose of securing that effect is given to any such request or recommendation'. No such directions were ever issued.[124]

The clear inference of this is that the Bank of England enjoyed informal power because 'before the introduction of the first Banking Act in 1979 there was no statutory requirement that a bank or similar deposit-taking institution be authorised to accept deposits or undertake banking business in the UK'.[125] Existing legislation was the Protection of Depositors Act 1963, but this 'prescribes the conditions under which companies may advertise for deposits from the general public'.[126] In 1971, the Bank of England initiated reforms through 'Competition and Credit Control',[127] which had the objective of engendering competition between the banks and, at the same time, providing greater control over monetary policy.[128] Unsurprisingly, as Crockett notes, 'the new arrangements were arrived at by voluntary agreement with the banks'.[129] As Robb describes, 'the status of a banking institution was based in practice on what became known as "ladder of recognitions", depending on its position under various statutes'.[130] At the top of the ladder was '[a]uthorised status under the Exchange Control Act 1947' and at the bottom 'recognition under Income and Corporation Taxes Act 1970'.[131] The

123 Victoria Robb, 'The Genesis of Regulation' in *Financial Stability Review – Autumn* 1997 (Bank of England) 29 www.bankofengland.co.uk/archive/Documents/historicpubs/fsr/1997/fsrfull9710.pdf Accessed 18 October 2016. For a description of how the money markets worked at that time, see Ritchie (n 117) 29–37.

124 Victoria Robb (n 123) 29.

125 Victoria Robb (n 123) 29.

126 Andrew Crockett, *Money: Theory, Policy and Institutions* (Nelson 1973) 130.

127 Bank of England, 'Competition and credit control' September 1971 www.bankofengland.co.uk/archive/Documents/historicpubs/qb/1971/qb71q2189193.pdf Accessed 5 March 2017.

128 Crockett (n 126) 192.

129 Crockett (n 126) 193.

130 Victoria Robb (n 123) 30.

131 'The status of a banking institution was based in practice on what became known as "ladder of recognitions", depending on its position under various statutes. 1 Authorised status under the Exchange Control Act 1947 – the Bank and the Treasury were responsible for establishing a list of banks authorised to deal in foreign exchange. This was regarded as the highest accolade a bank could attain. 2 Companies Act 1948 exemption from disclosure of certain information in company accounts. 3 Exemptions from the Protection of Depositors Act 1963 restrictions on advertising for deposits. 4

Bank of England's 1971 reforms[132] looked to take advantage of circumstances which Crockett describes as 'particularly propitious for a new initiative. The recently elected Government had a commitment to greater competition; there was a slackening in loan demand and little risk that an easing in restrictions would lead to unmanageable growth in borrowing'.[133] Such optimism proved to be short-lived, because government action to control the growth of money supply[134] by increasing interest rates led to problems such as those experienced by London and County Securities.[135] Other fringe lenders also faced difficulties and the Bank of England decided that it was important to rescue those in the sector suffering liquidity (as opposed to solvency) problems.[136]

The Bank of England mounted a rescue operation, establishing the 'Control Committee of the Bank of England and the English and Scottish Clearing Banks' – a joint liquidity support facility that subsequently became known as the 'Lifeboat'.[137] The Lifeboat was managed by the Bank of England and the risks were shared amongst the committee, the Bank of England's exposure being capped at 10%. This was all handled without statutory underpinning.[138]

The role of the Bank of England had evolved over time but the basic tenet was that it exercised its influence without any real form of statutory underpinning. Indeed, it successfully used the 'Governor's eyebrows' not only to regulate but, as with the 'Lifeboat', cause commercial organisations to risk their own capital to support the Bank of England's rescue plan. This is important in the research into economic crime because of the way it held sway over UK institutions.

The three decades after the end of the Second World War were labelled as those of 'the welfare state', which took 'cradle-to-grave' responsibility for British citizens.[139] During this time, there had been little legislative activity in relation to

Companies Act 1967, section 123 certificate – issued by the Board of Trade to institutions it considered to be *bona fide* carrying on the business of banking. This certificate secured exemption from the Moneylenders Acts. 5 Recognition under Income and Corporation Taxes Act 1970 – granted by the Inland Revenue to *bona fide* banking businesses allowing them to pay and receive interest gross of tax. Some of the "lesser" recognitions only required decisions about the type of business carried on (eg section 123 certificates) rather than fitness and properness and sound-ness of the institution.' Victoria Robb (n 123) 30.

132 Bank of England, 'Competition and credit control' (n 127).

133 Crockett (n 126) 195.

134 Money Supply: 'the total amount of money in circulation or in existence in a country.' Oxford Dictionaries, http://oxforddictionaries.com/definition/english/money%2Bsupply?q=money+supply Accessed 18 October 2016.

135 Victoria Robb (n 123) 30.

136 Victoria Robb (n 123) 30.

137 'Secondary Banking Crisis 1973–75' (Lifeboat). Bank of England, 'The secondary banking crisis and the Bank of England's support operations' www.bankofengland.co.uk/archive/Documents/historicpubs/qb/1978/qb78q2230239.pdf Accessed 17 October 2016. Richard Dale, 'Bank crises management: The case of the United Kingdom' (1995) 10(8) JIBL 326–333.

138 Dale (n 137) 326–333.

139 Simon Jenkins, *A Short History of England* (Profile Books 2011) 310.

economic crime, save for the Prevention of Fraud (Investments) Act 1958. However, at the end of the 1970s, and following the 'winter of discontent',[140] a general election brought in a Conservative government with a radically different view, 'that the curse of the British economy lay in restrictive trade practices of every sort, and an overdependence by everyone on the state',[141] and introduced many reforms to the regulation of finance, some of which dated back to the Second World War.[142]

The government noted that the general approach to investor protection was light regulation.[143] In the fraud arena, issues surrounding the failure to convict such criminals for economic crime emerged.[144] However, investor protection came to prominence through events, rather than being part of a grand political strategy.

In 1979, the government abolished exchange controls.[145] This was a momentous decision since exchange controls, established as a defensive measure in the Second World War,[146] limited investments and travel outside the UK jurisdiction. At a stroke,[147] the dynamics of the markets changed and, as Gower notes:

> faced the UK with the full consequences of the internationalisation of investment business. It made it far easier for the British to invest abroad and for foreign firms, straight or crooked, to induce them to do so. In particular, it led to British institutions, such as insurance companies, unit trusts and pension funds, diversifying their portfolios (…) The weakness of our indigenous financial services industry was highlighted when it became clear that the major part of this lucrative business had been undertaken not by it but by American firms.[148]

One consequence of the internationalisation of the markets was the emergence of firms that did not share the heritage of compliance with City regulation.

The government commissioned 'a review to recommend proposals for a new legislative framework of protection for investors in securities and other forms of property'.[149] Gower differed from Roskill: the former being 'in-house' research;[150] the latter independent.

140 'A strike-bound "winter of discontent" in 1978–9, came close to being a public sector general strike.' Jenkins (n 139) 322.
141 Jenkins (n 139) 325.
142 For example, repeal of Exchange Control Act 1947, Prevention of Fraud (Investments) Act 1939, Bank of England Act 1946, Prevention of Fraud (Investments) Act 1958.
143 Editorial, 'How many regulators?' (1996) 17(2) Co Law 34. Fisher and Bewsey (n 109) 13.
144 Fisher and Bewsey (n 109) vi.
145 Forrest Capie, *The Bank of England: 1950's – 1979* (CUP 2010) 768.
146 Exchange Control Act 1947.
147 The Chancellor of the Exchequer announced an 'immediate easement' of controls on individuals on 12 June 1979. HC Deb 12 June 1979 vol 968 cc244–5.
148 L C B Gower, '"Big Bang" and City regulation' (1988) 51 MLR 7.
149 HC Deb 23 July 1981 vol 9 c194W.
150 Gower was the Department of Trade's 'research advisor on company law, with the assistance of officials' HC Deb 23 July 1981 vol 9 c194W.

Against the background of abolition of exchange controls, which destabilised the markets, and a regulatory scandal involving the Bank of England,[151] the investment markets themselves were under pressure to break down barriers between one class of investment and another,[152] where Gower comments that:

> the main difficulty peculiar to the UK has been that despite a remarkable freedom from inhibiting *legal* regulation (such as the [US] Glass-Steagall Act) there have been restrictive rules of trade and professional associations designed to protect the vested interests of their members.[153]

Gower addressed the question of why investors should need protection:

> It is sometimes argued that investment necessarily entails risk and that investors should realise this and not expect any special protection over and above the general law of theft and fraud. If they get their fingers burnt that is their own fault. However, this robust affirmation of laissez-faire principles has long since been rejected and it has been recognised that it is the investors' own fault only if they were in a position to judge the extent of the risk.[154]

Thus, Gower saw the object of his review as 'to consider whether the existing system of disclosure [with criminal sanctions for failure] plus regulation affords adequate protection in an efficient and economical way'.[155] Gower noted the confusion for dealers in securities who took deposits by their Bank of England licence,[156] and insurance companies regulated by various insurance acts and European Economic Community directives, and a plethora of other legislation, bodies and practitioners.[157]

A key question for Gower was enforcement: 'it is not much use having regulations unless they are enforced.'[158]

151 'Regulatory responsibilities were divided among the Bank of England, the Treasury, the Department[s] of Trade and Industry, and the London Stock Exchange (…)' Henry Laurence, 'Spawning the SEC' (1998) 6 Ind J Global Legal Stud 660.
152 Gower, '"Big Bang" and City regulation' (n 148) 1.
153 Gower, '"Big Bang" and City regulation' (n 148) 1.
154 Gower, *Review of Investor Protection – A Discussion Document* (HMSO 1982) 12.
155 Gower, *Discussion Document* (n 154) 14.
156 Banking Act 1979. Gower, *Discussion Document* (n 154) 24.
157 Insurance Companies Act 1974; Insurance Companies Act 1980; Insurance Companies Act 1981. Directive 73/239/EEC. '3.11 There are a number of other relevant statutes, in particular the Companies Acts, the Industrial and Provident Societies Act 1965, Industrial and Provident Societies Act 1968, the Building Societies Act 1986, The Banking Act 1979, the Insurance Companies Acts, the Policy Holders' Protection Act 1975, and the Insurance Brokers (Registration) Act 1977.' Gower, *Discussion Document* (n 154) 21, 26.
158 Gower, *Discussion Document* (n 154) 48.

> It is not easy to detect any rationale for the choice of one method of regulation than another (...) the practice has been to avoid any form of regulation until some scandal has shown that it cannot be avoided and then to choose statutory Governmental regulation unless there is a traditional self-regulatory agency in existence to which the task may be left. In the last few years, however, there has been a tendency to encourage the creation of new self-regulatory agencies and assign the task to them, either wholly or partly and either by statute or persuasion.[159]

Gower concluded that there was a trend towards more statutory controls: 'these, in the main, have been imposed on bodies which *create* investments rather than on the markets or intermediaries which *sell* them.'[160] Furthermore, the burden placed upon intermediaries was to those 'that did not bear traditional hallmarks of respectability'.[161] As a consequence, 'the result is a regulatory system which is difficult to enforce effectively'.[162]

Gower then considered 'the changing face of the securities industry'.[163] Gower identified the main changes in the previous 50 years as: 'the movement from direct personal investment to indirect investment'; 'the distorting effect of tax considerations'; 'distortions by differing methods of remunerating intermediaries'; 'the growth of firms of investment managers and advisors' and 'multi-purpose firms and multi-national groups'; 'internationalisation of investment'; and the 'influence of EEC'.[164] First, Gower pointed to a change in the way in which people invested. Whereas, people used to invest directly in stocks and shares, Gower observed that indirect investment had branched out from merely investment in 'with profits' insurance contracts to 'a variety of packages such as unit trusts, commodity and futures funds, property or index-linked policies, and occupational pension schemes'.[165] The issue identified was that although the number of investments made *directly* by individual investors had declined, which on the face of it reduced the overall risks, the use of an investment packager or intermediary gave rise to different risks, not covered by existing legislation or regulation.[166] Gower pondered taxation considerations[167] which created distortion in returns and *pace* the fine, upstanding traditions of the City:

159 Such as the Take-over Panel, the Council for the Securities Industry, the Insurance Brokers Registration Council. Gower, *Discussion Document* (n 154) 52.
160 Gower, *Discussion Document* (n 154) 53 (emphasis added).
161 Gower, *Discussion Document* (n 154) 53.
162 Gower, *Discussion Document* (n 154) 53.
163 Gower, *Discussion Document* (n 154) 54.
164 European Economic Community, which became the European Union. Gower, *Discussion Document* (n 154) 54–60.
165 Gower, *Discussion Document* (n 154) 54.
166 Gower, *Discussion Document* (n 154) 55.
167 'For example, one of the great attractions of an investment in a linked-life policy, rather than in the unit trust to which it is linked, is that it attracts life assurance relief.' Gower, *Discussion Document* (n 154) 55.

> it may be more attractive to the investor for his investments to be managed on the basis that the manager is rewarded, not by a fee (which is not tax deductible) but by *whatever he can make on the side* (for example by retaining interest earned on money awaiting investment and any share of brokers' commissions that he may be able to extract).[168]

It may be that Gower, perhaps unwittingly, identified the very issue that came to be seen as the trademark of the City. Rather than *Probus et Fidelis* (integrity and faithfulness),[169] the assumption of 'whatever he can make on the side', perhaps, was a portent of things to come.

Whereas taxation anomalies represent opportunities to be exploited outside the investment itself, the distortion identified by Gower relating to different commissions, acts as a powerful incentive to place an investment in one direction rather than another.[170]

Gradually, it can be seen that Gower had identified a rich seam of self-interest. The report then turned to the increase in the number of investment managers and advisers,[171] which had grown, from being a minor part of, say, a stockbrokers business, it had become significant by 1985. Gower pointed out that investment management was outside the scope of formal regulation.[172] Thus, a relatively new business activity of providing investment management services to private investors took place in an environment hardly touched by regulation or legislation and yet affording opportunity for enrichment 'on the side'.

Gower's conclusion was that:

> It is not surprising that a framework which was erected 50 or more years ago and which has since been plastered over with a patch-work of ad hoc embellishments, but without any examination of its foundations, should have revealed cracks and subsidences (…) The basic question (…) is whether we can continue to maintain the existing framework, merely papering over the cracks, or whether we should undertake a major structural rebuilding.[173]

168 Gower, *Discussion Document* (n 154) 55–56 (emphasis added).

169 Edwin Green, *Debtors to their Profession* (Routledge 2012) 152.

170 For example, 'unit trust managers found that they were losing business to insurance companies because insurance companies paid 3% commission to insurance brokers whilst they paid only 1¼% to their intermediaries'. Gower, *Discussion Document* (n 154) 57. What followed was the market adapting its methods to obtain higher rates because, 'so long as commission rates and commission sharing arrangements continue to differ as between one investment and another, the temptation to temper advice will remain'. Gower, *Discussion Document* (n 154) 57.

171 'Which specialised in managing and advising on investments for individual investors.' Gower, *Discussion Document* (n 154) 57.

172 'Unless the way the business is conducted requires the firm to obtain a licence as a dealer or deposit taker (or both).' Gower, *Discussion Document* (n 154) 57.

173 Gower, *Discussion Document* (n 154) 62.

This analysis is not merely of academic interest, because the contemporary consideration of what constituted a 'security' had a bearing on whether they were covered by the Prevention of Fraud Act or not, and 'if they are not, there may be no control over them'.[174] In a similar way, the 1984 invention of the London Inter-Bank Offered Rate (LIBOR)[175] was later discovered to be 'not designated a qualifying investment for the purpose of the legislation',[176] with the consequence that a criminal prosecution could not be made following the LIBOR scandal.[177]

Cracks in the foundations, included firms 'working around' regulations,[178] the 'failure to treat like with like', for example insurance policies being exempted from the Prevention of Fraud Act while their underlying investments, acquired directly, are not, and the public issue of shares to be traded on the London Stock Exchange (LSE) being regulated by the LSE, but any others being unregulated.[179] The regulations were considered inflexible and lacking 'discretion in many areas, particularly those covered by statutory government regulation',[180] and pointing to the 'grey areas in a rapidly developing field of activity'.[181] The inconsistency of regulation was criticised: 'the present system is in some respects too paternalistic in that it bans activities which are innocuous and even desirable, and (...) is excessively lax in that it fails to regulate activities where the public needs attention.'[182] Furthermore, the way the City worked was to concentrate on the honesty of people employed in investment to the exclusion of competence, where Gower notes:

> statutory licensing schemes which purport to exclude those who are not 'fit and proper persons' generally succeed only in excluding those who are dishonest and, moreover, have been shown to be dishonest by being convicted of serious criminal offences, and that self-regulation all too often achieves no more than weeding out those who are obviously not 'the right sort'. The investor, it can be argued, is entitled to some protection from ignorant fools as well as from convicted crooks and unfortunates who lack wealth and social graces.[183]

174 Gower, *Discussion Document* (n 154) 62.
175 British Bankers Association, 'Welcome to BBALIBOR: Historical perspective' www.bbalibor.com/bbalibor-explained/historical-perspective. Accessed 28 February 2017.
176 House of Commons Treasury Committee, 'Fixing LIBOR: some preliminary findings. Second Report of Session 2012–13'. Criminal enforcement, *Legal lacunae* www.publications.parliament.uk/pa/cm201213/cmselect/cmtreasy/481/481.pdf Accessed 28 February 2017.
177 See Chapter 2.
178 Gower, *Discussion Document* (n 154) 63.
179 Gower, *Discussion Document* (n 154) 63–66.
180 Gower, *Discussion Document* (n 154) 67.
181 Gower, *Discussion Document* (n 154) 67.
182 Gower, *Discussion Document* (n 154) 68.
183 Gower, *Discussion Document* (n 154) 74.

Gower then addressed a 'most fundamental question. Have we achieved a satisfactory balance between Governmental regulation and self-regulation?'[184] From a standpoint of having identified 'certainly a very considerable diversity of regulations and of the agencies which operate them',[185] and, tellingly, for what subsequently transpired 'no country that I know of has found it practicable or desirable to regulate insurance, banking, dealings in commodities and dealings in stocks and shares in precisely the same way and through precisely the same agencies'.[186] Rejecting Wilson's conclusion[187] that the balance between governmental and self-regulation was about right,[188] Gower pointed to a spectrum of controls between 'tight statutory regulation', 'no effective regulation' and a broad middle of 'relatively loose rein', controlled by the Bank of England by its 'statutory authority', or 'subject to its surveillance without such authority', and 'self-regulation under statutory authority' and 'self-regulation without statutory authority'.[189] Gower commented that:

> The ideal would be to weld self-regulation and Governmental regulation into a coherent statutory framework which would cover the whole field that needs to be regulated and which would perform the role which it does best, working harmoniously together.[190]

Thus, the financial services landscape was recognised to be ready for regulatory change and the government's response to Gower was to establish a system of self-regulatory organisations under a new 'Securities and Investment Board, reporting to HM Treasury'.[191] This major change was subsequently regarded

184 Gower, *Discussion Document* (n 154) 75.
185 Gower, *Discussion Document* (n 154) 74.
186 Gower, *Discussion Document* (n 154) 74. What transpired was the creation of a single regulator, the Financial Services Authority, under the Financial Services and Markets Act 2000. 'Businesses to be authorised and regulated under the Act include: Banks, Building Societies, Insurance companies, Friendly societies, Credit unions, Lloyd's, Investment and pensions advisers, Stockbrokers, Professional firms offering certain types of investment services, Fund managers, and Derivatives traders.' Financial Services Act 2000 Explanatory Notes 7, www.publications.parliament.uk/pa/cm201213/cmselect/cmtreasy/481/481.pdf Accessed 28 February 2017.
187 Report of the Committee to Review the Functioning of the Financial Institutions (Wilson Committee) Cmd 7937 (HMSO 1980).
188 Gower, *Discussion Document* (n 154) 77.
189 Gower, *Discussion Document* (n 154) 77.
190 Gower, *Discussion Document* (n 154) 82.
191 Below the SIB were various self-regulatory organisations (SROs): Life Assurance and Unit Trust Regulatory Organisation (LAUTRO); Financial Intermediaries, Managers and Brokers Regulatory Association (FIMBRA); Association of Futures Brokers and Dealers (AFBD); Recognised Investment Exchanges (The Securities Association – formed through the merger of the International Securities Regulatory Organisation and The Stock Exchange); Recognised Professional Bodies (Institutes of Chartered Accountants (England and Wales, Scotland, Ireland)); Chartered Association of Certified Accountants; The Law Societies (England and Wales, Scotland, Northern Ireland); Institute of Actuaries; Insurance Brokers Registration Council; and Recognised

as a failure.[192] The Securities and Investment Board (SIB) was criticised for taking a narrow view of its responsibilities and 'paying little or no attention to its supervisory role towards tackling or even preventing financial crime'.[193]

The government embarked upon 'privatisation'.[194] After a slow start the strategy gathered pace under Lawson, 'a vigorous free-marketeer'.[195] The range of state assets that were privatised indicates 'how far the post-war consensus had extended nationalisation across almost every sector of the economy'.[196] Jenkins noted, ominously, 'then in 1986 Lawson moved into the hitherto sacrosanct territory of financial services',[197] 'because it entailed admitting foreign firms into the most jealously guarded of markets [and] merchant banks'.[198]

The outcome of the Lawson deregulation,[199] known as the 'Big Bang',[200] was that the regulation of the City markets and institutions was relaxed. The explanation of deregulation had less to do with loosening supervision than 'seeking no more than to convey the freedom to compete'.[201] The specialist roles adopted by institutions and their traditional areas of activity became blurred, coinciding with the breakdown of the inherent protectionism of the City, because foreign-owned institutions were allowed access to the City markets.[202] Marr,

Clearing Houses. The SIB was established by the Financial Services Act 1986. Cento Veljanovski, 'Introduction' in Arthur Seldon (ed), *Financial Regulation – or Over-Regulation* (The Institute of Economic Affairs 1988).

192 Lomnicka, 'Reforming U.K. financial services regulation' (n 95) 480. The SIB structure brought issues with rule books, claims of reductions in standards, structural complexity and demarcations between banking and securities industries being hard to delineate, and was concluded to have 'failed to protect investors'. William Blair, 'The reform of financial regulation in the UK' (1998) 13(2) JIBL 43, 45.

193 Nicholas Ryder, 'The Financial Services Authority and money laundering. A game of cat and mouse' (2008) 67(3) CLJ 639.

194 'Privatisation is a term which is used to cover several distinct, and possibly alternative, means of changing the relationships between the government and the private sector. Among the most important of these are denationalisation (the sale of publicly owned assets), deregulation (the introduction of competition into statutory monopolies) and contracting out (the franchising to private firms of the production of state financed goods and services).' J A Kay and D J Thompson, 'Privatisation: A policy in search of a rationale' (1986) 96(3) The Economic Journal 18.

195 Nigel Lawson, Chancellor of the Exchequer. Jenkins (n 139) 330.

196 Jenkins (n 139) 330.

197 Jenkins (n 139) 330.

198 Jenkins (n 139) 330.

199 George Robb (n 49) 34.

200 The proposals were based on the Gower Report. Gower, *Review of Investor Protection* (n 93). The phrase 'big bang' was referred to by Professor Gower during the enactment of the Financial Services Act 1986. Gower, '"Big Bang" and City regulation' (n 148) 1.

201 Galpin (n 116) 8.

202 *The Guardian*, 'Big Bang's shockwaves left us with today's big bust' 9 October 2011. 'Twenty-five years on, Lawson is unrepentant, insisting that the benefits of the Big Bang far outweigh the disadvantages. But even he admits to a certain nostalgia for the old City: "The Stock Exchange was run as a kind of private club: no outsiders could come in and it was riddled with restrictive practices. It was a very charming club – I rather liked it – but there was no way in which it could be a strong player in that

though, traces the genesis to international monetary policy in the 1960s and a change in US government attitude which provided an opportunity for London:

> The influence of the Eurodollar and Eurobond market on the culture of the City and by extension British business life generally can hardly be overstated. From the early sixties, it was internationalising and shaking up London, introducing more aggression, fatter salaries and less of the old school tie.[203]

This was significant because in the 1970s, there was a 'Labour government intent on controlling everything'[204] and, thus, mainstream domestic investment was controlled by HM Treasury, whereas 'in the side streets',[205] 'just a whiff of the can-do, devil-may-care Wild West spirit was suddenly felt in the streets of old London'.[206] This manifested itself in '1982, [when] another slice of American business life came to London in the multi-coloured jackets and raucous bear-pit atmosphere of the new international financial futures market, or LIFFE'.[207] This analysis is not just of historic interest but will be seen to contribute to the genesis of the LIBOR scandal and allied market manipulations revealed in the 2008 financial crisis.

The 'Big Bang' was 'something which has a claim to be the single most significant change of the whole Thatcher era, on a par with confronting the unions or privatisation'.[208] It was, according to Plender:

> A scramble in which most of the City's leading brokers and jobbers paired off with clearing banks, merchant banks and a host of other institutions including foreign banks, (…) [which] committed an estimated £1 billion or so to buying the cream of the London broking and jobbing fraternity (…) Yet the purchasers were making a leap in the dark, because (…) [they did not] know how the regulatory framework might affect future revenues (…) [from] the assets that were being acquired – dealing skills and customer contacts (…) Perhaps most important of all, the buyers were paying large sums for a stake in a monopoly that was waning very rapidly.[209]

This 'leap in the dark' may well be seen to have contributed to the breakdown in City integrity.

business in the modern world".' www.guardian.co.uk/business/2011/oct/09/big-bang-1986-city-deregulation-boom-bust Accessed 28 February 2017.

203 Andrew Marr, *A History of Modern Britain* (Pan 2008) 423.

204 Marr (n 203) 423.

205 Marr (n 203) 423.

206 Marr (n 203) 423.

207 Marr (n 203) 423. The London International Financial Futures and Options Exchange (LIFFE).

208 Marr (n 203) 424.

209 John Plender, 'London's Big Bang in international context' (1987) 63 (1) International Affairs 39.

This major change was viewed as: 'It is no exaggeration to say that the Financial Services Act 1986 has proved to be one of the most controversial pieces of commercial legislation of recent times.'[210]

The controversy was not so much about the Act itself but 'rather it centred around the way in which the Act was interpreted by the Securities and Investment Board'[211] and the detailed mass of regulations and rules which it produced 'had spawned a bureaucratic monster which would wreak havoc with the day to day running of investment business'.[212] Chancellor Lawson admitted that 'what eventually emerged was something far more cumbersome and bureaucratic than I, or, I believe any of us in Government had ever envisaged'.[213]

One feature introduced was a new funding structure for the SIB which Lawrence considered 'was a constitutional novelty'. 'It was financed by levies on the private financial firms it regulated, but was not accountable either to them or Parliament.'[214] This was an attractive mechanism for its financing which has been retained (by both the Financial Services Authority (FSA) and Financial Conduct Authority (FCA)), and which gave it considerable financial resources not dependent upon government departmental budgets. The hybrid nature of the SIB was the result of an 'uneasy compromise' between a strong and central regulator modelled along the lines of the US Securities and Exchange Commission (SEC), Gower's preference,[215] and a government 'known to be ideologically hostile to any extension of government that could be avoided'.[216] The Bank of England's position was that 'it was reluctant to see the establishment of an SEC-type body that would clearly undercut its pre-eminence as the chief overseer of London's financial markets'.[217] The outcome was a body 'deliberately kept less powerful than the Bank of England'.[218] The position of the Bank of England was to return to the fore, or rather rear, in Chancellor of the Exchequer Gordon Brown's 1997 restructuring to create the FSA.

It is ironic that Gower's report was entitled *Review of Investor Protection* and yet by 1994 Ashe reported that:

> It is now widely acknowledged – by investors, politicians of all parties, the industry and trade bodies and regulators – that the standard of protection

210 Joanna Gray, 'Financial Services Act 1986 reforms: Part 1' (1990) 9(7) IBL 370.
211 Gray (n 210) 370.
212 Gray (n 210) 370.
213 Henry Lawrence, 'Spawning the SEC' (1999) 6 Ind J Global Legal Stud 661. Citing Nigel Lawson, *The View from No. 11: Memoirs of a Tory Radical* (Bantam 1992). 'The original bill consisted of 212 sections, 300 pages and 600 amendments. It had been drafted by lawyers and bureaucrats, and practitioners found it a nightmare to understand, let alone implement.' Lawrence (n 213) 661.
214 Lawrence (n 213) 661, 662.
215 Gower, *Review of Investor Protection* (n 93) 188.
216 Lawrence (n 213) 661, 663.
217 Lawrence (n 213) 661, 663.
218 Lawrence (n 213) 661, 663.

> afforded to investors in retails products, and the standard of conduct of firms, advisers, and sales forces in this sector need to be improved.[219]

Thus, with regulations being relatively untouched for half a century, the endeavours to create a new regulatory regime in 1986 led to further significant refinements over the following eight years before Chancellor Brown initiated a wholesale change to reform financial services regulation by the creation of the Financial Services Authority as a 'super'-regulator, taking over all SIB activities and banking supervision from the Bank of England.[220]

However, despite Brown's intention to strengthen regulation, the FSA, too, is considered to have failed.[221] This partly stems from its original brief and partly from the manner in which it had, or had not, discharged its duties. In the field of economic crime, Rider notes that 'the City has always had a mixed take on insider abuse',[222] which is that although officially condemned, City spokesmen have played down the impact and the FSA gave little encouragement to those minded to act.[223] This gave credence to the view that insider dealing may have been regarded as a 'naughty perk of the job'.[224] Ultimately, however, it was the FSA's range of responsibilities which caused its downfall: 'the decision to divide responsibility for assessing systemic financial risks between three institutions [FSA, HM Treasury and the Bank of England] meant that in reality no one took responsibility.'[225]

In 1997, the new Labour government announced an ambitious and ground-breaking new financial regulatory regime, which Ryder notes 'would set basic standards and prevent systematic failure'.[226] This change was not just a matter of political determination to stamp a new regime on the financial markets but 'like all reforms, this one did not take place in a vacuum'.[227] Drawing on Blair, it is clear that global financial markets had been evolving with new technology, market innovation and breakdown of traditional demarcations,[228] which, as former Federal Reserve Chairman Alan Greenspan remarked, 'make it virtually impossible to maintain some of the rules and regulations established for a different economic

219 Michael Ashe, 'The continuing saga of PIA' (1994) 15(7) Comp Law 207.
220 Financial Services and Markets Act 2000. Lomnicka, 'Reforming UK financial services regulation' (n 95) 480, 489.
221 House of Commons Library, Research paper 12/08 www.parliament.uk/briefing-papers/SN05934.pdf Accessed 28 February 2017. 'In the dock: City watchdog accused of incompetence' *The Sunday Times* 1 August 2004 www.thetimes.co.uk/tto/business/industries/banking/article2158333.ece Accessed 28 February 2017.
222 Barry A K Rider, 'Editorial. An abominable fraud?' (2010) 31(7) Co Law 197.
223 Rider (n 222) 197.
224 Jason Mansell, 'Financial Services Authority: can it be saved after the election?' *The Times* 26 March 2010.
225 House of Commons Library, 'Research paper 12/08' www.parliament.uk/briefing-papers/SN05934.pdf Accessed 14 April 2012.
226 N Ryder, 'An unhappy coupling' (2008) 158 NLJ 609.
227 Blair (n 192) 43.
228 Blair (n 192) 43.

environment'.[229] Protection of the City was the *raison d'être* because that is how the UK financial markets are judged internationally.[230] Consequently, effective regulation of the markets was needed to ensure international competitiveness.[231] Thus, to match the expectation of a 'super-regulator',[232] the government heralded the FSA's creation as 'a ground-breaking piece of legislation designed to thwart financial criminals, protect consumers and maintain London's reputation as a global financial centre'.[233]

Brown championed the case for bringing financial regulation under the one roof.[234] He argued that this was necessary because firms organise their affairs on a group-wide basis, and this regulatory structure would be in line with 'the day's increasingly integrated financial markets'.[235] The headlines, naturally, highlighted the prudential and regulatory 'cross-sectorial' roles,[236] which removed banking supervision from the Bank of England, but gave the new unified regulator a wide remit.[237] As Blair observes, the 'setting up of a single regulator would be pointless if the existing structure merely continued under a new nameplate'.[238] The previous approach was based on 'moral persuasion' and voluntary codes, whereas the new structure was defined as 'authorisation, supervision and enforcement'.[239] Whereas previously firms were subject to different disciplinary powers depending upon their individual regulator, the FSA presented a single dedicated unit to undertake investigation, enforcement and disciplinary work,[240] in policing the UK financial services sector.[241]

The UK recognised that financial crime was a threat to national security when it criminalised terrorist financing,[242] because of Northern Irish terrorism,[243] thus being in advance of the US 'financial war on terrorism', which followed the 9/11

229 The Federal Reserve Bank, 'Testimony of Chairman Alan Greenspan H.R. 10, the Financial Services Competitiveness Act of 1997 Before the Committee on Banking and Financial Services, U.S. House of Representatives May 22, 1997' https://federalreserve.gov/boarddocs/testimony/1997/19970522.htm Accessed 26 January 2015.
230 B A K Rider, 'Where angels fear' (2008) 29(9) Co Law 257–258.
231 Blair (n 192) 44.
232 Lomnicka, 'Reforming UK financial services regulation' (n 95) 480, 489.
233 N Ryder and C Chambers, 'The Financial Services Act 2010: How will the FSA rise to meet its new challenges?' FRI 26 May 2010.
234 HC Deb 20 May 1997 vol 294 cc507–24.
235 Blair (n 192) 43, 45.
236 Lomnicka, 'Reforming UK financial services regulation' (n 95) 480, 485.
237 Blair (n 192) 43, 47.
238 Blair (n 192) 43, 47.
239 Blair (n 192) 43, 47.
240 Blair (n 192) 43, 47.
241 This comprised: banks, building societies, friendly societies, credit unions; insurance companies, Lloyd's insurance market; investment and pension advisers, fund managers; professional firms; stockbrokers and derivatives traders. Ryder and Chambers (n 233).
242 Prevention of Terrorism (Temporary Provisions) Act 1989, s 13. Terrorism Act 2000, s 15.
243 Nicholas Ryder, *Financial Crime in the 21st Century* (Edward Elgar 2011) 79.

terrorist attacks.[244] The FSA was given a specific objective to reduce financial crime.[245]

The importance of regulation is underlined by Wright because of the 'threat to the reputation of the UK as an honest trustworthy market where you can safely do business'.[246] Furthermore, the international ramifications are severe: 'a financial services industry which is known to be riddled with crooks, awash with dirty money, is not the place where investors want to do business. It is not a trusted market.'[247] Whilst this may seem an axiomatic truth, in the US there was a view that:

> London had become the money-laundering capital of the world. It is an unenviable reputation to have. London's huge financial markets are not surprisingly a magnet for the launderer; $1,000bn a day is exchanged in the foreign currency markets and the sheer volume of transactions makes it impossible to check every single one. We are also to an extent the victim of our own magnificent reputation: dollars ending up in a bank account in the UK are less likely to be thought to be tainted than if they were put through less reputable offshore banking centres.[248]

This analysis by Wright is important because it provides a contemporary view of the risks to the City from economic crime. The City's 'magnificent reputation' depended upon the integrity of the markets and the informal style of regulation led by the Bank of England, but which were suited to a different economic environment.[249] Thus imposition of greater regulation became an imperative together with a focused approach to dealing with serious fraud in order to protect the City's integrity.
Within weeks of the 2010 General Election,[250] the new chancellor of the exchequer, George Osborne, announced: 'We take white collar crime as seriously as other crime and we are determined to simplify the confusing and overlapping responsibilities in this area in order to improve detection and enforcement.'[251]

244 Ryder, *Financial Crime in the 21st Century* (n 243) 51.

245 The FSA had four equal objectives, one being 'the reduction of financial crime'. The FCA has 'a single overarching strategic objective to ensure that markets function well'. Financial Services and Markets Act 2000, s 6(3). HM Treasury, 'A new approach to financial regulation: Transferring consumer credit regulation to the Financial Conduct Authority' www.gov.uk/government/uploads/system/uploads/attachment_data/file/221913/consult_transferring_consumer_credit_regulation_to_fca.pdf Accessed 28 February 2017.

246 R Wright, 'Keynote address to the 17th International Cambridge Symposium on Economic Crime' (2000) 9(4) JFC 304, 305.

247 Wright (n 246) 304, 305.

248 Wright (n 246) 304, 305. See also, Nicholas Ryder, *Money Laundering – An Endless Cycle* (Routledge 2012) 5.

249 Blair (n 192) 43 (footnotes omitted).

250 UK Parliament, 'General Elections' www.parliament.uk/about/how/elections-and-voting/general/ Accessed 28 February 2017.

251 HM Treasury, 'Speech by the Chancellor of the Exchequer, Rt Hon George Osborne MP, at Mansion House' 16 June 2010 www.gov.uk/government/speeches/speech-

The coalition government announced that it would create an Economic Crime Agency,[252] but in the event the organisation that was created, the National Crime Agency, bore little resemblance to the original proposals. In the arena of fraud, bribery and corruption, there was no attempt to change legislation but the Bribery Act was implemented. Financial regulation, though, was subject to immediate change with the FSA being replaced by the Bank of England, together with a new Prudential Regulation Authority and Financial Conduct Authority. In terms of economic crime, a review of the financial crisis revealed unacceptable practices in banking and financial markets which brought about new legislation in the event of a financial institutions failure[253] and promised 'tough new domestic criminal offences for market abuse'[254] because of issues with manipulation of LIBOR, foreign exchange and other markets.

Neither the 1997 nor 2013 changes were the result of government-sponsored reports: incoming governments had already determined to make changes prior to taking office. Thus, whereas Gower and Roskill provided an opportunity to analyse and comment on proposals, this practice affords the opportunity for retrospective analysis where Wilson and Wilson,[255] and Ryder[256] explore FSA performance, which gives this research an opportunity to consider the effectiveness of its 'credible deterrence' policy. Gray's immediate analysis of the changes described them as controversial.[257] This has assumed greater prominence following the announcement of a review into the way wholesale markets operate.[258]

Contents overview

Analysis of the contemporary landscape shows the progression of financial services regulation from treating the City as a 'club' with rules to being regulated by a powerful City regulator, which the 2008 financial crisis revealed to be ill placed to

by-the-chancellor-of-the-exchequer-rt-hon-george-osborne-mp-at-mansion-house Accessed 28 February 2017.

252 Cabinet Office, 'The Coalition: Our programme for government' www.cabinetoffice.gov.uk/media/409088/pfg_coalition.pdfhttp://www.cabinetoffice.gov.uk/media/409088/pfg_coalition.pdf Accessed 28 February 2017. Jonathan Fisher and Ted Sumpster, 'Fighting fraud and financial crime', Research Note March 2010 https://policyexchange.org.uk/publication/fighting-fraud-and-financial-crime/ Accessed 28 February 2017.

253 Financial Services (Banking Reform) Act 2013.

254 HM Treasury, 'Mansion House Speech 2014' www.gov.uk/government/speeches/mansion-house-2014-speech-by-the-chancellor-of-the-exchequer Accessed 28 February 2017.

255 Gary Wilson and Sarah Wilson, 'The FSA "credible deterrence", and criminal enforcement – a "haphazard pursuit"?' (2014) JFC 4, 5.

256 Nicholas Ryder, *The Financial Crisis and White Collar Crime – The Perfect Storm* (Edward Elgar 2014) 18.

257 Gray (n 210) 370.

258 HM Treasury, 'Fair and effective markets review announced by Chancellor of the Exchequer' 12 June 2014 www.gov.uk/government/news/fair-and-effective-markets-review-announced-by-chancellor-of-the-exchequer Accessed 28 February 2017.

be able to meet its wide remit. The UK has now re-addressed the areas of fraud, bribery and corruption and City regulation, where the 2008 financial crisis can be seen to have provided a jolt to the authorities.

The contents of this book are divided into five further chapters: Chapter 2 sets the scene for economic crime in the UK, focusing on fraud; Chapter 3 looks at UK bribery and corruption. The international comparisons with the US and Australia follow in Chapter 4 and Chapter 5, respectively. The final chapter draws together the themes of the book and makes a number of recommendations.

2 The United Kingdom

Fraud and related offences

Introduction

This chapter sets the scene of the economic crime regime in the UK by reviewing the historical context to the establishment of the three important agencies: the Serious Fraud Office (SFO), the Financial Conduct Authority (FCA)[1] and the Competition and Markets Authority (CMA).[2] This is important because these bodies have failed to live up to the high expectations set at their inception, with the consequence that only the former has not been reformed.[3] Thus, it is essential to understand the background to their creation and the powers they were granted, to establish whether the original concepts were at fault or whether they were overtaken by events. Furthermore, this analysis will provide the bedrock for the analysis of current UK legislative and institutional frameworks.

Economic crime is defined as a crime perpetrated by 'white collar criminals', which has a significant and negative impact upon society.[4] The term 'economic crime' is distinguished from 'financial crime', which Ryder[5] describes as having 'evolved into a multifaceted business or industry with a global reach and is

1 Financial Services Authority (FSA) until April 2013.

2 Previously the Office of Fair Trading (OFT).

3 In June 2010 the Chancellor announced changes to the way that financial services will be regulated. These changes included separating the regulation of prudential and conduct operations – both currently regulated by the Financial Services Authority – to be carried out by two new organisations: the Prudential Regulation Authority (PRA) and the Financial Conduct Authority (FCA). HM Treasury, 'A new approach to financial regulation: Building a stronger system' (Cm 8012). The Office of Fair Trading merged with the Competition Commission to form the 'Competition and Markets Authority (CMA)'. The FCA took over the OFT's consumer credit responsibilities from April 2014. Philip Collins, Chairman, Office of Fair Trading (OFT), 'Looking ahead to change' 18 October 2012, King's College http://webarchive.nationalarchives.gov.uk/20140402142426/http://www.oft.gov.uk/shared_oft/speeches/2012/0812.pdf Accessed 18 October 2016.

4 Fraud amounting to £73bn in the UK. National Fraud Authority, 'Annual Fraud Indicator' March 2012 www.homeoffice.gov.uk/publications/agencies-public-bodies/nfa/annual-fraud-indicator/annual-fraud-indicator-2012?view=Binary Accessed 18 October 2016.

5 Nicholas Ryder, *Financial Crime in the 21st Century* (Edward Elgar 2011) 1.

commonly associated with illegal drugs, human trafficking, organized criminals and terrorists'.[6] These activities, which include money laundering, do not form part of this book. Over time, UK governments have sought to restrict economic crime by enacting laws that criminalise illegal conduct,[7] giving powers to state prosecutors, and creating a body to regulate, control and discipline financial markets – the FCA. This chapter considers the background to the creation of the current institutional framework of the special prosecutor and the financial regulator. This examination illustrates how the endeavours of governments[8] to adapt to changing financial markets and economic conditions had the unforeseen consequences of providing increased opportunity for 'white collar crime' and, according to Wright, leading to London being regarded as the 'financial crime capital' and the UK being condemned for its weak processes and controls.[9]

The history of regulation of the markets shows that as they became more vibrant and varying, governments[10] proposed improvements to reflect the changing environment.[11] This chapter takes as its base the changes occasioned as a consequence of the 1979 general election. The then new Conservative government presaged a challenge to the status quo, resulting in 'privatisation',[12] 'deregulation'[13] and a tougher response to serious fraud.[14] Hitherto, the attitude of

6 Ryder, *Financial Crime in the 21st Century* (n 5) 1.
7 For example: Fraud Act 2006, Bribery Act 2010.
8 Conservative government 1979–97; Labour government 1979–2010; Conservative-Liberal Democrat coalition government 2010–15; Conservative government 2015 onwards.
9 Rosalind Wright, 'Keynote address to the 17th International Cambridge Symposium on Economic Crime' (2000) 9(4) JFC 304–307. The issues of bribery and corruption are considered in Chapter 3.
10 For example: Interdepartmental Committee on Sharepushing (Bodkin Committee) 1937 Cmd 5539. Anderson Committee on Unit Trusts 1936 Cmd 5239. G W Keeton, 'Reports of committees' 1938 1 (March) MLR 313. (The outcome of these reports was the Prevention of Fraud (Investments) Act 1939.) *Report of the Committee to Review the Functioning of the Financial Institutions* (Wilson Committee) Cmd 7937 (HMSO 1980).
11 For example: Report of the Committee to Review the Functioning of the Financial Institutions (Wilson Committee) (n 10); Bodkin Committee (n 10); Anderson Committee (n 10); *Fraud Trials Committee Report* (HMSO 1986) (hereinafter Roskill); Attorney General's Office, *Fraud Review – Final Report* (Attorney General's Office 2006); Financial Services Authority, 'A regulatory response to the global banking crisis March' (Turner Review) www.fsa.gov.uk/pubs/other/turner_review.pdf Accessed 14 January 2017.
12 'Privatisation is a term which is used to cover several distinct, and possibly alternative, means of changing the relationships between the government and the private sector. Among the most important of these are denationalisation (the sale of publicly owned assets), deregulation (the introduction of competition into statutory monopolies) and contracting out (the franchising to private firms of the production of state financed goods and services).' J A Kay and D J Thompson, 'Privatisation: A policy in search of a rationale' (1986) 96(3) The Economic Journal 18–32.
13 'The reduction of government control over an industry.' *Dictionary of Accounting*, s.v. 'deregulation' www.credoreference.com.ezproxy.uwe.ac.uk/entry/acbaccount/deregulation Accessed 18 October 2016.
14 '[T]o protect society from extensive, deliberate criminal deception which could threaten public confidence in the financial system.' Serious Fraud Office, 'SFO Budget

governments of different political hues towards commercial fraud was of 'benign neglect',[15] which had the effect of fostering apathy among City of London (the City) institutions because when cases were prosecuted they failed to achieve the expected convictions, which was attributed to juries not fully understanding the cases.[16] Levi notes that, 'fraud was not part of the law and order agenda',[17] stating that:

> Commercial fraud in Britain was a subject that was of concern principally to a small group of academics. For almost all politicians and criminologists, conservative and radical alike, street and household crime constituted 'the crime problem' over which they would do battle.[18]

It appeared that fraud was ignored because of the profile of fraudsters,[19] leading to a lack of punishment[20] which was attributed to issues with the legal system,[21] and, as will be shown, frustrating the interests of justice.[22]

Fraud

Having established the background to the description of fraud as not being part of the historic law and order agenda, this chapter examines the process for it to become part of that agenda, leading to specific legislation in the UK together with other legislation and identification of regulatory and other bodies. This will show a crowded arena with differing bodies having overlapping responsibilities.[23] In a

2009–2010' www.sfo.gov.uk/about-us/ Accessed 18 October 2016. Kay and Thompson (n 12) 18–32.

15 Michael Levi, 'Fraud in the courts. Roskill in context' (1986) 26(4) Br J Criminal 394.

16 Levi, 'Fraud in the courts' (n 15) 394.

17 Michael Levi, 'Reforming the criminal fraud trial: An overview of the Roskill proposals' (1986) 13 JL & Soc'y 117.

18 Levi, 'Reforming the criminal fraud trial' (n 17) 117.

19 Levi, 'Reforming the criminal fraud trial' (n 17) 118.

20 Roskill (n 11) 1.

21 'At every stage, during investigation, preparation, committal, pre-trial review and trial, the present arrangements offer an open invitation to blatant delay and abuse. While petty frauds, clumsily committed, are likely to be detected and punished, it is all too likely that the largest and most cleverly executed crimes escape unpunished.' Roskill (n 11) 1.

22 Roderick Munday, 'The Roskill report on fraud trials' (1986) 45 CLJ 177. Roskill's remedy was a greater use of 'pre-trial reviews' to allow issues to be more clearly defined to make the trial easier for juries to follow and understand. Roskill (n 11) 82.

23 Button, Shepherd and Blackbourn estimate that there were 15,696 proven fraudsters in the UK in 2014–15, excluding TV Licensing offenders. For an interesting analysis of fraud offenders subject to non-criminal justice (including 600,000 penalty notices issued to persons wrongly claiming exemption from NHS charges), see Mark Button, David Shepherd and Dean Blackbourn, 'The fraud "justice systems": A scoping study on the civil, regulatory and private paths to "justice" for fraudsters' main report'

contrast to bribery and corruption, money laundering, terrorism financing and insider dealing, there are no international conventions dealing with fraud.

Criminalisation

Roskill Report

Fraud is a significant constituent of economic crime, alongside bribery and corruption. Fraud is not a new phenomenon. Indeed, history provides many examples from *The Carriers Case* in 1473,[24] *South Sea Bubble* in 1720,[25] and the share scandals resulting in enactment of the Prevention of Fraud (Investments) Act 1958.[26] More recently, Staple noted that 'there is some evidence to suggest that fraud, at any rate, company fraud, like the economy, is cyclical'.[27] In boom conditions, there is market manipulation and then, when the cycle declines and insolvency approaches, deception emerges alongside false accounting and fraudulent trading.[28] Thus, fraud opportunities are always present but the cycle determines the different types and, on some occasions, whether a fraud has been committed or not can be finely balanced with a small margin between success and failure. Kirk and Woodcock stated that:

> An enterprise, which may be intensely ambitious or of marginally dubious ethical standards, can, with a fair wind, become successful, popularly acclaimed and the recipient of a Queen's Award. With ill fortune (…) the fragility of the original structure may be exposed and either lead to the commissioning of criminal offences, or to the perception that the whole basis of the business was criminally conceived.[29]

Over many years, the response to fraud, and failure to prevent or convict, has been 'something must be done': that is, to set up a committee to examine the claim that 'the system does *not* cope with serious frauds, and since they are serious crimes by any standards, effective ways must be found to bring offenders to court'.[30] Furthermore, Munday comments that 'the length and complexity of some fraud trials (…) aroused concern',[31] although Lord Devlin considered that

November 2016 www.port.ac.uk/media/contacts-and-departments/icjs/ccfs/Fraud-Justice-Systems-2016—Final-Report.pdf Accessed 29 November 2016.

24 Flora Page, 'Defining Fraud: An argument in favour of a general offence of fraud' (1997) 4(4) JFC 288.

25 Patrick Walsh, 'The South Sea Bubble: A parable of our own time' (2009) 17(2) History Ireland 6–7. Described as 'classic market manipulation': Page (n 24) 288.

26 D N Kirk and A J Woodcock, *Serious Fraud: Investigation and Trial*, 2nd edn (Butterworths 1997) 1.

27 George Staple, 'Serious and complex fraud: A new perspective' (1993) 56 (2) MLR 127.

28 Staple (n 27) 128.

29 Kirk and Woodcock (n 26) 3.

30 Kirk and Woodcock (n 26) 7.

31 Munday (n 22) 175.

'what causes disquiet, I submit, is not the element of fraud but the length and complexity of the ensuing trial'.[32]

In the years before structural changes to UK markets and regulation took effect in the mid-1980s,[33] the main issue in the fraud arena was dissatisfaction with the management and outcomes of fraud trials. A 1981 headline in *The Times*, '£2½m trial ends with fees inquiry', typifies the contemporary concerns.[34] In that case, relating to a bogus bank,[35] two trials were involved, both lasting 137 sitting days, with the first trial being halted because of allegations of jury interference. This case highlighted concerns over the length and cost of fraud trials and whether complex fraud trials should be before a jury or a panel of financial experts.[36] Levi explains:

> As the potential social control risks of the democratisation of the jury have become apparent, in Britain at least, juries have been condemned for their alleged lack of commitment to legal values and susceptibility to bribery.[37]

This dates back to 1972 when the need for a juror to be a property owner was abolished, giving rise to Levi's concerns about 'a reduction not only in the moral standards but also the educational level of jurors'.[38] Furthermore, Levi notes prior to 1979, the attitude of government to commercial fraud was of 'benign neglect',[39] where 'fraud was not part of the law and order agenda',[40] and the focus was on street and household crime.[41]

Levi argues that the reason 'the relative immunity from law enforcement agencies has been enjoyed by both professional criminal and criminal professional types engaged in fraud', is because 'criminal types' have been policed more heavily than 'respectable' people.[42] Thus, Roskill observed that 'it is all too likely that the largest and most cleverly executed crimes go unpunished',[43] because the 'system' was 'archaic, cumbersome and unreliable'.[44] Criminals were able to escape without sanction and this was partly due to the manner in which cases were tried. As Munday concludes, 'perhaps the time has come to admit that the criminal trial ought no

32 Lord Devlin, 'Trial by jury for fraud' (1986) 6 Oxford J Legal Stud 313.
33 Creation of the Securities and Investment Board and Serious Fraud Office.
34 *The Times*, '£2½m trial ends with fees inquiry' 2 May 1981 The Times Digital Archive 1798–1985 http://find.galegroup.com/ttda/infomark.do?action=interpret&tabID=T003&prodId=TTDA&userGroupName=uwesteng&docPage=article&searchType=AdvancedSearchForm&docId=CS17402018&type=multipage&contentSet=LTO&version=1.0&finalAuth=true Accessed 18 October 2016.
35 Universal Banking Corporation: *The Times* '£2½m trial ends with fees inquiry' (n 34).
36 *The Times*, '£2½m trial ends with fees inquiry' (n 34).
37 Michael Levi, 'Blaming the jury: Frauds on trial' (1983) 10 JL & Soc'y 257.
38 Levi, 'Fraud in the courts' (n 15) 394.
39 Levi, 'Fraud in the courts' (n 15) 394.
40 Levi, 'Reforming the criminal fraud trial' (n 17) 117.
41 Levi, 'Reforming the criminal fraud trial' (n 17) 117.
42 Levi, 'Reforming the criminal fraud trial' (n 17) 118.
43 Roskill (n 11) 1.
44 Roskill (n 11) 1.

longer to resemble a crafty game where one side's strategy may remain artfully concealed until the last moment to no real end other than to frustrate the interests of justice'.[45]

In a criminal trial for fraud, the fundamental issue that faced prosecutors was the degree of complexity, which gave scope for counsel to extend the length of a trial by examining the *minutiae*, with the twin consequences of greater risk of confusion, or obfuscation, and increased costs.[46] Roskill concluded that 'the present arrangements may even encourage the defence to conduct its case like a prolonged and orderly retreat from the truth'.[47] Although Levi reports that juries can understand non-complex fraud in line with their 'life experience' (such as benefit fraud, cheque and banking fraud), more difficult matters would stretch jurors' comprehension.[48] A response to this was exhortations to judges to shorten summings-up and for prosecutors to limit the number of co-defendants to 'real villains'.[49]

The disquiet about fraud trials centred on the performance of juries rather than the other actors such as judges, counsel, police and prosecutors, to which was added corruption, and not just of jurors.[50] As a response, the government established an independent Fraud Trials Committee which reported in 1986. The Fraud Trials Committee (Roskill), was established[51] 'because the government understand the concern which has been expressed about the range of problems generated by allegations of serious commercial fraud'.[52] The brief given to Roskill was:[53]

> To consider in what ways the conduct of criminal proceedings in England and Wales arising from fraud can be improved, and to consider what changes in existing law and procedure would be desirable to secure the just, expeditious, and economical disposal of such proceedings.[54]

This was a wide remit for the enquiry which should have enabled the committee to make radical recommendations.

Roskill stated that 'much of this report, and the majority of the recommendations, are concerned with changes in the procedures to be adopted'.[55] Although inspired by the need to tackle fraud, Roskill saw that those procedural reforms

45 Munday (n 22) 175, 177.
46 Roskill concluded that 'the average time in fraud cases at all stages is 30 to 40 per cent longer than that found in all cases taken as a whole'. Roskill (n 11) 175.
47 Roskill (n 11) 3.
48 Levi, 'Fraud in the courts' (n 15) 394.
49 Levi, 'Fraud in the courts' (n 15) 394.
50 Levi, 'Fraud in the courts' (n 15) 394.
51 By both the then Lord Chancellor and Home Secretary. HC 8 November 1983 vol 48 col 83–84W.
52 HL 8 November 1983 vol 444, col WA 790.
53 Roskill (n 11) 1, iii.
54 HL 8 November 1983 vol 444, Written Answers, col 790.
55 Roskill (n 11) 1.

would have general application to criminal cases as a whole.[56] These were accepted by the government, which said: 'the report shows that the legal and administrative machinery for this purpose has been creaking badly. We are determined to bring about the changes in law, practice and attitudes which are necessary.'[57] The three key recommendations were: establishment of a 'Fraud Trials Tribunal', being a judge sitting with lay members but not a jury, for serious complex frauds; 'a new unified organisation responsible for all the functions of detection, investigation and prosecution of serious fraud'; and 'an independent monitoring body ("the Fraud Commission")'.[58] The report was welcomed by the Home Secretary;[59] the government viewed the report as radical but stated that measures had already been taken to 'reduce the fragmentation in the investigation and prosecution of complex fraud cases',[60] a theme that remains current. That measure was the establishment of the Fraud Investigation Group by the Director of Public Prosecutions, to concentrate on major frauds. The government also pointed to the forthcoming Financial Services Act 1986, which followed the Gower Report, and established the SIB to regulate investment business and other financial services,[61] and it was clear from the Home Secretary's comments[62] that Roskill's recommendations should include protection for savers and investors. In the field of economic crime, this is still not embedded since overlap with the FCA remains.[63] The Home Secretary observed that 'the committee's message to the House and to the Government is that one cannot send a policeman on a bicycle to catch a runaway car. We have to equip those who chase fraud with the same speed already possessed by the fraudster'.[64] This endorsement provides an entry to the Roskill Report.

As an early indication of the committee's findings, Roskill commenced the summary of the report with:

> The public no longer believes that the legal system in England and Wales is capable of bringing the perpetrators of serious frauds expeditiously and effectively to book. The overwhelming weight of the evidence laid before us suggests that the public is right.[65]

Roskill found that the system of investigation and trial was open to 'blatant delay and abuse' and that whilst 'petty frauds, clumsily committed'[66] would be discovered and punished, the same did not apply to 'large' and 'cleverly executed'

56 Roskill (n 11) 6.
57 HC Deb 14 January 1986 vol 89 cc925–34.
58 Roskill (n 11) 2, 3, 147.
59 Mr Douglas Hurd, Home Secretary. HC Deb 13 February 1986 vol 91 cc1148–85.
60 Hurd (n 59).
61 Financial Services Act 1986 www.legislation.gov.uk/ukpga/1986/60/pdfs/ukpga_19860060_en.pdf Accessed 18 October 2016.
62 Hurd (n 59).
63 Hurd (n 59).
64 Hurd (n 59).
65 Roskill (n 11) 1.
66 Roskill (n 11) 5.

frauds. Roskill highlighted the government's 'vision of an "equity-owning democracy"',[67] and pointed out that if 'ordinary families' invested in the markets then the markets should be properly policed.[68] This was further evidence of Roskill's intention that his report considered financial markets to be within his committee's purview. Tellingly, because subsequent events revealed significant inadequacies, Roskill foreshadowed the forthcoming self-regulation regime with the warning that 'where those mechanisms are abused, the law must deliver retribution, swift and sure'.[69]

At the outset, it might have appeared that the problem with fraud trials would be solved by tackling the issue from the standpoint of reforming or eliminating the involvement of juries.[70] However, as Levi notes, 'the collapse of most of the lengthy trials that had aroused public comment resulted either from judicial directions to acquit on technical/legal grounds, or from factors extraneous to jury competence'.[71] Thus, much of the report and recommendations dealt with procedural changes and called for attitudinal changes by those involved in investigation and the courts, including administration, judiciary and the bar.[72]

By the time Roskill reported, the 'benign neglect' of fraud had been replaced because 'business crime in high places [had] become a central political issue'.[73] The committee's title identifies that fraud *trials* themselves were the concern and 'it seemed that its purpose was to decide principally what should be done about the jury'.[74] However, proposals and submissions made to the committee caused it to 'broaden out into an examination of the policing and prosecutorial processes',[75] which led to prosecutions (or decisions to discontinue). This 'system' is scathingly described by Levi as, 'if "system" is the appropriate word, given the poor communication between the multiplicity of agencies allegedly involved in the control process (…) of dealing with fraud'.[76]

Complex or serious fraud

The committee addressed their attention to the 'largest and most cleverly executed crimes',[77] but failed in their attempt to provide a precise definition of a 'complex fraud case'.[78] In order to differentiate cases, they produced guidelines which would identify a case for special treatment.[79] Their view was that neither

67 Roskill (n 11) 5.
68 Roskill (n 11) 5.
69 Roskill (n 11) 5.
70 Levi, 'Fraud in the courts' (n 15) 394.
71 Levi, 'Fraud in the courts' (n 15) 394.
72 Roskill (n 11) 1.
73 Levi, 'Reforming the criminal fraud trial' (n 17) 117.
74 Levi, 'Reforming the criminal fraud trial' (n 17) 118.
75 Levi, 'Reforming the criminal fraud trial' (n 17) 118.
76 Levi, 'Reforming the criminal fraud trial' (n 17) 118.
77 Roskill (n 11) 1.
78 Roskill (n 11) 133.
79 Roskill (n 11) 133, 153.

quantum nor volume of documentation or number of witnesses alone would denote complexity. Roskill opined that 'complexity' was found:

> In a fraud in which the dishonesty is buried in a series on inter-related transactions, most frequently in a market offering highly-specialised services, or in areas of high-finance involving (for example) manipulation of the ownership of companies.[80]

The relevance is that it was a return to the original perception of the public that juries could not comprehend the issues; that frauds were perpetrated by people who were experts in their field; and that those fields 'bear no obvious similarity to anything in the general experience of most members of the public'.[81] The committee had in mind the London Stock Exchange (LSE), Lloyd's of London, commodities and financial futures markets, having geographic presence or communication links to the City.[82] This then supported a somewhat bizarre view, which Levi reported, that 'criticisms from the City institutions were that there was no point in blaming them for failing to tackle fraud when the juries could not understand the cases brought before them'.[83]

In essence, Roskill recognised the difficulties faced by those unfamiliar with such markets, whom they believed would need educating in order to understand the particular markets and appreciate the alleged dishonesty. Roskill believed this was an 'intellectual challenge, to which only the exceptional could rise', thus, perhaps, being self-serving in the conclusion that the 'non-exceptional' would not be suited to serving on a jury and that trials should be before judges, who could be trained to have the exceptional financial knowledge required.[84] Notwithstanding Roskill's view of juror competency, the use of 'bench trials' is not supported by judges[85] and is undermined by prosecution failings.

Non-jury trials

The right in England and Wales to trial by jury dates back to the Magna Carta in 1215, when it replaced 'trail by ordeal',[86] and any attempt by government to

80 Roskill (n 11) 153. An example of such manoeuvrings can be found in the 'Official Transcript of *R v Cushnie and Clough*' [2005] EWCA Crim 962.

81 Roskill (n 11) 153.

82 Roskill (n 11) 153.

83 Levi, 'Fraud in the courts' (n 15) 394.

84 Roskill (n 11) 153.

85 This is an interesting article which researches attitudes of judges who have conducted serious fraud trials. 'To date little comment has been offered about jury trials in serious fraud cases by the judges who actually try these cases. This article explores the opinions of nine such judges about jury function presently and the prospect of judge only trials in serious fraud cases. The judges conclude that the juries perform well in these cases and identify concerns with and potential problems posed by judge only serious fraud trials.' Robert F Julian, 'Judicial perspectives on the conduct of serious fraud trials' (2007) Oct Crim L R 751, 768.

86 Roskill (n 11) 134.

move away from this form of justice evokes strong feelings and outcry from some sectors of the public, 'on the ground that it would erode a fundamental principle of the justice system – the right to trial by a person's peers'.[87] Roskill reported a 'bitter struggle' between opponents and defenders[88] and would have been well aware of the heat the proposals would generate. Devlin's observation that 'not since the glorious revolution of 1688 has a citizen been imprisoned for any substantial time (…) otherwise than on the verdict of a jury',[89] is an example of the contra view. However, in the review of the contemporary landscape, Roskill pointed to the total number of criminal cases handled each year of some 3,000,000, of which merely 32,000 were tried by a jury.[90] Roskill concluded that:

> In almost every area of the law, society has accepted that just verdicts are best delivered by persons qualified by training, knowledge, experience, integrity or by a combination of those four qualifications. Only in a minority of cases is the delivery of a verdict left in the hands of jurors deliberately selected at random without any regard for their qualifications.[91]

Thus, Roskill advanced the proposition that 'non-jury trials' for serious, complex fraud, far from being an exception to the norm, would be congruent with the overwhelming majority of criminal cases, where the judge or tribunal have to understand or interpret the law and make the decisions themselves. Roskill, in examining the characteristics of a complex fraud case, doubts whether the public appreciate the difficulties faced by the 'average juror' outwith their experience or knowledge, and speculates that the presence on the jury of someone possessed with such knowledge was mere happenstance.[92] Indeed, earlier, Roskill drew attention to something more fundamental and recommended that in any fraud trial 'it is imperative that as a matter of principle that the members of the jury should be able to read and write English without difficulty'.[93] This would appear to be self-evident in relation to all trials and not just for fraud, as was concluded by the Morris Committee in 1965.[94]

Roskill was persuaded that the interests of justice in complex fraud cases would be best served by a non-jury trial. The line of reasoning was that complex fraud cases possessed features of complexity, though 'it is not possible to provide a precise definition'.[95] Thus, because of the presence of such 'complexities', it was

87 *The Times*, 'Right to jury trial faces axe in post-riot reforms' 16 January 2011 www.thetimes.co.uk/tto/news/politics/article3287652.ece Accessed 18 October 2016.
88 Roskill (n 11) 134. J Baldwin and M McConville, *Jury Trials* (Clarendon 1979) 1.
89 'i.e. longer than the short sentence for summary offences.' Lord Devlin (n 32) 313.
90 Roskill (n 11) 134–135.
91 Roskill (n 11) 139.
92 Roskill (n 11) 139–140.
93 Roskill (n 11) 122.
94 'Nor are they prepared to countenance any limitations based on education, intelligence or literacy apart from the basic ability to read, write, speak and understand English without difficulty.' *Report of the Departmental Committee on Jury Service* (1965) Cmnd 2627, para 80.
95 Roskill (n 11) 133.

considered to be asking too much of an 'ordinary' juror to comprehend the issues and evidence, especially given the committee's perceptions in trial of 'defence gamesmanship'.[96] Roskill, therefore, recommended 'trial by judge and two lay members should replace trial by judge and jury'.[97] A further significant issue is that those charged with economic crime are often 'well resourced and lawyered up'[98] because they have access to considerable financial resources to defend themselves, as the SFO found with *Tchenguiz* (see below).

Roskill settled on the proposal of a Fraud Trials Tribunal after considering and eliminating 'special juries' comprising jurors with 'above standard of education, training and experience';[99] trial by single judge; and trial by a panel of judges.[100] Rather scathingly, Lord Devlin described this exercise, which was rooted in the committee's 'bland' terms of reference, as: 'seemingly to line up the existing method of trial by jury alongside any other method the committee can think of and to test them all by what is "just, expeditious and economical".'[101]

The chosen proposal was of a judge sitting with two lay members (assessors or adjudicators), 'who would play an equal part with the judge in deciding questions of fact but the judge alone would deal with questions of law and procedure'.[102] The lay members should have business experience and the 'capacity' to understand complex transactions.[103] Levi[104] referred to rather thin evidence presented by Roskill of lack of jury competence, though acknowledging the difficulties posed by the Contempt of Court Act 1981, which made interviewing jurors unlawful.[105] Evidence from lawyers may have been tainted by their own interests.[106] Nevertheless, Roskill accepted the evidence of witnesses that it was the case that many jurors were 'out of their depth'.[107]

96 Levi, 'Reforming the criminal fraud trial' (n 17) 117.
97 'Fraud Trials Tribunal', Roskill (n 11) 154.
98 'These cases require above all else resilience and focus on the part of the investigating team. Vast quantities of digital data have to be obtained, uploaded, searched and assessed. Witnesses need to be identified and traced. Often, we will need to obtain evidence from jurisdictions where that exercise can be problematic. Those we investigate are well resourced and lawyered-up. Claims of privilege can transcend extravagance and amount to a strategy of deliberate obstruction, a strategy we will always challenge. But individuals, corporates and their lawyers need to understand that we will make progress and we will not go away.' David Green, Serious Fraud Office, 'Cambridge Symposium 2014' www.sfo.gov.uk/2014/09/02/cambridge-symposium-2014/ Accessed 18 October 2016.
99 Roskill (n 11) 144.
100 Roskill (n 11) 146.
101 Lord Devlin (n 32) 313.
102 Roskill (n 11) 146.
103 Roskill (n 11) 149.
104 Levi, 'Reforming the criminal fraud trial' (n 17) 117.
105 Roskill (n 11) 201.
106 For example: 'As lawyers never sit on juries, and often have their cherished arguments rejected by them, they tend to under-estimate the intelligence of 12 random people acting as a group. Swapping them for a number of "experts" closely bound to the City is likely to result in even more leniency towards fraudsters than is currently the inclination of confused but impartial judges and juries.' Page (n 24) 288, 306.
107 Roskill (n 11) 142.

Roskill wanted the courts to assign cases to judges with 'appropriate special experience'[108] as 'a (thinly disguised) reaction to criticism from police, counsel and judges that some judges are not capable of handling fraud trials'.[109] Drawing on Levi, the rationale for this is that the complexity of fraud can be distinguished from other complex criminal cases because 'technology and internationalisation have changed it more radically than other offences, *frequently* creating major jurisdictional and evidentiary problems'.[110] For example, the use of modern communication methods and the easy facility to move monies through the international banking system gives rise to greater reliance on documentary evidence, including audit trails, than in other types of case.[111] Thus, Roskill wanted to combat economic crime by providing specialist courts but defendants would still have access to their own counsel and the tribunal would still have to evaluate evidence so successful prosecutions would not be a foregone conclusion.

Fraud Commission

Roskill proposed 'an independent monitoring body, the "Fraud Commission"',[112] because of their concerns over the fragmented nature of the existing system which led to inefficiencies and lack of cost effectiveness. The remit of the Fraud Commission was proposed to be to study and report on the new system and advise on improvements to policy and procedure.[113] It is a clear conclusion by Roskill that the task of tackling fraud was not aided by the number of bodies involved, leading them to justify the Fraud Commission's role by observing that 'apart from other advantages, we believe that this would provide a degree of co-ordination of the numerous interests involved which is at present lacking'.[114] Congruent with this was an expectation that the Fraud Commission would work closely with other bodies in the same field, including self-regulatory organisations.[115] This recommendation was not implemented because, as Doig shows, 'the objectives of different bodies were so diverse and their accountability mechanisms were so fragmented that it was difficult to see how overall supervision could occur'.[116] The fragmented nature of the anti-economic crime institutions remains a current issue.

Creation of the Serious Fraud Office

Roskill recommended that 'a new unified organisation responsible for all the functions of detection, investigation and prosecution of serious fraud should be

108 Roskill (n 11) 52.
109 Levi, 'Reforming the criminal fraud trial' (n 17) 117.
110 Levi, 'Reforming the criminal fraud trial' (n 17) 117, 128.
111 Levi, 'Reforming the criminal fraud trial' (n 17) 117.
112 Roskill (n 11) 37.
113 Roskill (n 11) 27.
114 Roskill (n 11) 27.
115 Roskill (n 11) 28.
116 Alan Doig, *Fraud* (Willan 2008) 228.

examined forthwith'.[117] The context of this recommendation was that investigations into allegations of serious fraud 'commonly involved long delays', with the consequence that fraudsters may not have been brought to trial or, if they were, the passage of time weakened prospects of successful prosecution.[118] This was because witnesses might not come up to proof or even upon conviction that sentences handed down were 'hopelessly inadequate', based on the lapse of time in bringing a case to trial.[119] Thus, the conclusion reached by Roskill was that the nation's and the City's standing as 'one of the world's great financial centres' was at stake through the lack of detection or prosecution thereby facilitating the growth of fraud.[120]

A particular deficiency that the committee examined was the significant number of different organisations which could be involved: 43 independent police forces,[121] the Department of Trade and Industry, Fraud Investigation Group, the Inland Revenue, and Customs and Excise. Any one of those organisations might initiate enquiries, 'but the resources available to each vary both as regards their powers under existing legislation and the quality and range of their staffs'.[122] Furthermore, in theory, where different departments are involved one department would coordinate; however, Roskill did not find evidence of fully effective coordination,[123] but rather found the 'fragmented nature of the powers of investigation (...) act as a hindrance'[124] and 'traditional divisions are still part of the scene'.[125] These are clear and important conclusions: serious and complex fraud is not served by investigation and prosecution being haphazardly undertaken by a variety of agencies, working without coordination. Indeed, the implication is that the varying bodies work independently on a 'traditional' basis in silos, having little desire to see themselves being part of a team. Roskill's circumlocution cannot disguise this problem: 'we recognise that bringing about changes of this kind would not be easy, because it would involve bringing together under one roof organisations who have for historical reasons worked apart.'[126]

Part of this new model was already in place because, concurrent with Roskill's deliberations, the Director of Public Prosecutions (DPP) had established the

117 Roskill (n 11) 3.
118 Roskill (n 11) 5.
119 Roskill (n 11) 5.
120 Roskill (n 11) 5.
121 In England and Wales, HM Inspector of Constabulary reports (21 July 2014) '[a] less fragmented, more structured approach to effective working between forces or between forces and other organisations is required. In particular, there is now a pressing need for greater clarity as to which policing services are best provided by forces at the local, regional or national level'. HMIC, 'Policing in austerity' 33 www.hmic.gov.uk/wp-content/uploads/policing-in-austerity-meeting-the-challenge.pdf Accessed 18 October 2016.
122 Roskill (n 11) 25.
123 Roskill (n 11) 25.
124 Roskill (n 11) 9.
125 Roskill (n 11) 9.
126 Roskill (n 11) 26.

Fraud Investigation Group, which was a team of lawyers and accountants. Roskill proposed that policing and prosecution of fraud[127] should be undertaken by a 'unified body to investigate and prosecute all frauds',[128] replacing the Fraud Investigation Group. Investigation and prosecution by one body was different from the 'independent' prosecution model established by the Crown Prosecution Service,[129] which was separate from investigation undertaken by the police.[130] Roskill also proposed that the new body should have in its armoury the type of inspectorial powers available to Department of Trade inspectors appointed by the Secretary of State.[131] Roskill proposed that the new body would operate with a 'case controller' from the outset who would control the cases and deployment of officers, including early assignment of prosecuting counsel.[132] The intention was to avoid 'the existing tradition of individual and departmental buck-passing',[133] together with bringing the Bar 'rules of etiquette' into the twentieth century.[134]

Fraud legislation

The UK Attorney General commissioned the Fraud Review, considered a brave initiative with no obvious political gain.[135] The Fraud Review was tasked to 'recommend ways of reducing fraud and the harm it does to society',[136] and positions fraud as it 'may be second only to class A drug trafficking as a source of harm from crime'.[137] However, unlike drug crime, police forces are often reluctant to take reports of fraud and, even if they do, take little action as a result because fraud has not been seen as a national policing priority.[138] Furthermore, it was seen as expensive for the police to

127 Levi, 'Reforming the criminal fraud trial' (n 17) 117.
128 Levi, 'Reforming the criminal fraud trial' (n 17) 119.
129 HM Crown Prosecution Service Inspectorate, 'Review of the Fraud Prosecution Service' 2008 5 www.justiceinspectorates.gov.uk/crown-prosecution-service/wp-content/uploads/sites/3/2014/04/FPS_2008_thm_rpt.pdf Accessed 4 December 2016.
130 Although this unified model was already employed by Inland Revenue, Customs and Excise, and the Department of Trade and Industry (later, Department of Business, Energy and Industrial Strategy).
131 Companies Act 1985, s 432. Inspectors appointed by the Secretary of State have the power to require the production of documents and take evidence from 'officers and agents of the company, and of all officers and agents of any other body corporate whose affairs are investigated'. Evidence may be taken on oath. s 434. Obstruction to be Contempt of Court, s 435. http://legislation.data.gov.uk/ukpga/1985/6/data.htm?wrap=true Accessed 18 October 2016.
132 Levi, 'Reforming the criminal fraud trial' (n 17) 117, 121.
133 Levi, 'Reforming the criminal fraud trial' (n 17) 117, 120.
134 Levi, 'Reforming the criminal fraud trial' (n 17) 117, 121.
135 Roskill (n 11). Attorney General's Office, *Fraud Review – Final Report* (London: Attorney General's Office 2006). Fraud Advisory Panel, 'The Fraud Review: Ten years on' 1 www.fraudadvisorypanel.org/wp-content/uploads/2016/06/The-Fraud-Review-Ten-Years-On-WEB.pdf Accessed 8 September 2016.
136 Attorney General's Office, *Fraud Review* (n 135) 4.
137 Attorney General's Office, *Fraud Review* (n 135) 3.
138 BBC, 'Fraud police chief warns of lack of officers' www.bbc.co.uk/news/uk-29507414 Accessed 10 October 2016.

deal with.[139] This then set the first question to be considered: 'what is the scale of the problem?'[140] The lack of ability to answer the question, because data were not available, led the report to conclude that a body should be created to devise a strategic response: the National Fraud Authority (NFA).[141] The Review also recommended the creation of the National Fraud Reporting Centre[142] to provide a central point for receipt of reports of fraud, together with the National Fraud Intelligence Bureau which would analyse and assess fraud. To complete the organisational changes, the City of London Police (COLP) would become the national lead force, acting as a centre of excellence for fraud investigations and undertaking the more complex investigations.

The second and third questions considered by the review were to determine the appropriate role of government in dealing with fraud and how resources could be spent to maximise value for money across the system.[143] The review noted the range of departments and agencies involved and the range of penalties and remedies they may deploy in the three areas of criminal, civil and regulatory. There were two specific recommendations: to increase the sentencing options available in the Crown Courts; and the establishment of a specialised 'financial court'. The increased sentencing powers included the ability to order compensation to all victims, not just those specified in a particular case, and the ability to make specific orders relating to other advisers such as solicitors and accountants. The 'financial court' proposal recognised the difficulties of trying fraud cases and proposed deploying judges with experience of financial cases to longer, more complex, criminal trials: according to Coolican, 'all matters could be resolved on the basis of a single unified set of evidence at one facts hearing with a variety of outcomes under criminal, civil and regulatory powers'.[144]

The review considered sentencing and concluded that the maximum sentence for serious or repeated fraud should be increased from ten years to 14 years, which would match money laundering penalties.[145] However, the proposal that excited the most comment was 'plea bargaining'.[146] The review proposed a system for reduced sentences in return for a guilty plea and agreement to other sanctions. The rationale for this being the benefits to be gained by reducing the length of trials and shortening investigations.[147]

At that stage there was no formal system in the UK for 'plea bargaining'.[148] Although, clearly, discussions do take place between prosecution and defence legal

139 Fraud Advisory Panel, 'The Fraud Review: Ten years on' (n 135) 2.
140 Attorney General's Office, *Fraud Review* (n 135) 4.
141 Originally 'National Fraud Strategic Authority'.
142 The National Fraud Reporting Centre became established as 'Action Fraud' run by the City of London Police. Action Fraud, www.actionfraud.police.uk/about-us/who-we-are Accessed 24 November 2016.
143 Attorney General's Office, *Fraud Review* (n 135) 4.
144 Tim Coolican, 'Time out for fraud' (2006) 156 NLJ 1460.
145 Proceeds of Crime Act 2002, Part 7. Money Laundering Offences s 328, s 333.
146 Rachel Rothwell, 'New: Plea bargaining' (2006) LS Gaz 27 Jul 6 (3); Kate Hanley, 'Plea bargaining: Striking a bargain' (2006) LS Gaz 14 Sep 20; Coolican (n 144) 1460.
147 Attorney General's Office, *Fraud Review – Final Report* (2006) (n 135) 40.
148 There are provisions in the Serious Organised Crime and Police Act 2005 ss 71–75 for immunity from prosecution or reduced sentences for offenders assisting with investigations or prosecutions.

teams, these provide no certainty, unlike the US model. Hanley observes that 'plea bargaining is as integral to the US legal system as fast-talking, sharp-suited attorneys',[149] and 'if you look at fraud alone, you will see some form of plea bargaining in approximately two-thirds to three-quarters of cases'.[150] As with Roskill, its predecessor by 20 years, implementation of the Fraud Review recommendations was slow, with the NFA and COLP measures being the only concrete achievements, though the NFA was quickly subsumed into the National Crime Agency (NCA).[151] However, in 2016, a newly created Joint Fraud Task Force was charged with taking a strategic approach to fraud.[152] Against this backdrop, it is clear that fraud is a significant and costly matter for government to tackle, as the NFA reported:

> The threats created by fraudsters are serious and real. Serious and organised crime groups are behind much fraudulent activity across the world. Funds generated by fraud are being used to support and expand other serious criminal activity such as people and drug trafficking. Fraud has also featured in terrorist cases both in the UK and abroad.[153]

The UK's fraud policy can be divided into three distinct parts: criminalisation, financial/law enforcement agencies, and the reporting of suspected instances of fraud.[154] This neatly positions the importance of the issues. The 'three distinct parts' to tackling fraud more than suggests that when policies are made they are

149 Hanley (n 146) 20.
150 Hanley (n 146) 20 (Jeff Stone).
151 The Fraud Advisory Panel's view is that 'with the abolition of the National Fraud Authority we lost the only body specifically charged with creating a coordinated, multi-agency, public-private fraud response working to a strongly evidence-based strategy. Recent government pronouncements on cybercrime (Treasury), banking (Home Office), fraud statistics (Culture, Media and Sport), corruption (the prime minister) and public sector fraud (Cabinet Office) do not suggest a coordinated approach'. Fraud Advisory Panel, 'The Fraud Review: Ten years on' (n 135) 6.
152 The Home Office established in 2016 a 'Joint Fraud Task Force', 'a public-private partnership to bring banks, law enforcement and government together to coordinate and strengthen our collective action against fraud'. In November 2016, the Home Secretary 'asked the taskforce to turn their focus onto the strategic issues that will have real impact on the threat. This will include: improving the national, regional and local law enforcement response to fraud; introducing a system to make it much easier for the victims of fraud to have their money repatriated; launching a very visible national fraud prevention campaign to provide targeted advice to protect members of the public; a new collective approach to better support victims of fraud'. Home Office, 'Home Secretary's speech to the FCA's Financial Crime Conference' www.gov.uk/government/speeches/home-secretarys-speech-to-the-fcas-financial-crime-conference Accessed 1 December 2016.
153 Bernard Herdan, Chief Executive, National Fraud Authority, '2009 Annual Report & Accounts' http://webarchive.nationalarchives.gov.uk/20120816224015/http://www.attorneygeneral.gov.uk/nfa/GuidetoInformation/Documents/NFSA%20Accounts%20to%2031%20March%2009.pdf Accessed 18 October 2016.
154 Nicholas Ryder, *Financial Crime in the 21st Century* (n 5) 123.

not fully integrated with each other. Although a generation ago problems were identified by Roskill and a way forward recommended, the fraud policy has evolved in a haphazard form rather than being mapped. This chapter will, first, consider the legal definition of 'fraud'; second, it will review the legislation and consider whether this can be effective; third, it will examine the myriad enforcement agencies, which are ripe for rationalisation; and finally, it will look at the limited way in which fraud is reported.

Fraud is difficult to define. Although the Fraud Act 2006 is modern legislation, interestingly, it does not define 'fraud', merely stating that '[a] person is guilty of fraud if he is in breach of any of the sections listed'.[155] Furthermore, there is no universal definition at common law.[156] The COLP defines fraud as 'when trickery is used to gain a dishonest advantage, which is often financial, over another person'.[157] However, the SFO defines it as 'abuse of position, or false representation, or prejudicing someone's rights for personal gain'.[158] As will be seen, the Fraud Act is closer to the SFO definition and provides a clear criminal offence.

In the financial crime arena, fraud was neglected until the establishment of the SFO[159] and then the Fraud Act. The City Regulator was in a different category because it is a regulator of the financial markets, rather than primarily a prosecutor.[160] However, it has raised its profile 'bringing criminal proceedings for conspiracy', thus developing its role 'as a specialist criminal prosecutor'.[161]

Conspiracy to defraud

The criminalisation of fraud has evolved over time with the various Theft Acts which eventually became seen as being inadequate to deal with complex fraud cases. Indeed, the 'troublesome technicalities'[162] of the Theft Acts left prosecutors falling back on the common law charge of 'conspiracy to defraud'.[163] The Fraud Act has simplified the law by providing a new offence of 'fraud' instead of a variety

155 Fraud Act 2006, s 1.

156 Alan Doig and Michael Levi, 'Inter-agency work and the UK public sector investigation of fraud, 1996–2006: Joined-up rhetoric and disjointed reality' (2009) 19(3) Policing and Society 199–215.

157 City of London Police, 'What is fraud and cybercrime?' www.actionfraud.police.uk/what-is-fraud Accessed 18 October 2016.

158 Serious Fraud Office, 'What is Fraud?' http://webarchive.nationalarchives.gov.uk/20130704104410/http://www.sfo.gov.uk/fraud/what-is-fraud.aspx Accessed 18 October 2016.

159 Criminal Justice Act 1987, s 1.

160 Richard Peat, Ian Mason, and Stuart Bazley, 'The FSA as a criminal prosecutor' (2010) Co Law 31(4) 119.

161 Now under the Serious Organised Crime and Police Act 2005, via the Coroners and Justice Act 2009, s 113.

162 Jonathan Pickworth, 'The Fraud Act 2006: A death knell for conspiracy to defraud – the "prosecutor's darling"?' Euro News (Aug 2009) 64, 1, 2.

163 Common Law (preserved by section 5(2) of the Criminal Law Act 1977). Crown Prosecution Service, 'Sentencing Manual' www.cps.gov.uk/legal/s_to_u/sentencing_manual/index.html Accessed 6 July 2016.

of ineffective deception offences under the Theft Acts (1968–96).[164] The Fraud Act removed such crimes as 'obtaining a pecuniary advantage' and 'procuring execution of a valuable security' from the statute book. In practice, the range of deception offences created 'a hazardous terrain for prosecutors' which, consequently, encouraged reliance on 'conspiracy to defraud',[165] a common law offence which:

> has been described in Parliament as 'repellent'; and the Law Commission has proffered the opinion that it is 'indefensible' and 'so wide that it offers little guidance on the difference between fraudulent and lawful conduct' and has recommended its abolition.[166]

In *R v Eric Evans* the court accepted a further observation from the Law Commission that 'in effect, conspiracy to defraud is a "general dishonesty offence", subject to the irrational requirement of conspiracy'.[167] That case, which was pursued by the SFO, concluded, interestingly, 'that a conspiracy to defraud in which both the object and the means are lawful is unknown to the common law'.[168] This case endeavoured to use the charge of conspiracy to defraud, notwithstanding the availability of the Fraud Act. In the UK, the most significant use of conspiracy to defraud was in the LIBOR cases, considered later when reviewing the SFO.

Sentencing for conspiracy to defraud has also attracted attention following the Court of Appeal's judgment in *R v Levene* and *R v Kallakis and Williams.* [169] In these cases, the Court considered whether the Sentencing Council's guidance on sentencing for substantive fraud offences should apply to conspiracy to defraud, for which there is no specific guidance. Additionally, the Court considered the question of whether sentences should be concurrent or consecutive, and quoted the current guidelines: 'there is no inflexible rule governing whether sentences should be structured as concurrent or consecutive components. The overriding principle is that the overall sentence must be just and proportionate'.[170] In 2014, the Sentencing Council introduced new guidelines (which for the first time

164 David Ormerod, 'The Fraud Act 2006 – Criminalised lying?' (Mar 2007) Crim LR 193–219. Theft Act 1968: s 15, Obtaining property; s15A, Obtaining a money transfer; s 16, Obtaining a pecuniary advantage; s 20(2), Procuring the execution of a valuable security. Theft Act 1978: s 1, Obtaining services; s 2(1)(a), securing the remission of a liability; s 2(1)(b), Inducing a creditor to wait or forego payment; s 2(1)(c), Obtaining an exemption from or abatement of liability.

165 Ormerod (n 164) 193–219.

166 *R v Eric Evans & others T20137190* (Hickinbottom J). Crimeline, www.crimeline.info/uploads/cases/2014/evans.pdf Accessed 24 February 2017 (footnotes omitted).

167 *R v Eric Evans & others T20137190* [149] (n 166).

168 *R v Eric Evans & others T20137190* [149] (n 166).

169 Nicola Finnerty, 'Judges set for fraud crackdown' *The Lawyer* (10 June 2013) 8. *R v Kallakis and another; R v Levene* [2013] EWCA Crim 709. [2013] All ER (D) 201 (May) CA.

170 Kallakis (n 169); *R v Levene* (n 169).

included conspiracy to defraud)[171] and a toughening of their approach to sentencing.[172]

Fraud Act 2006

The importance of tackling fraud is illustrated not just by the financial numbers involved but the significant instances of fraud which caused the collapse of multinational corporations in the UK, including for example BCCI and Barings, and in the US Madoff and Stanford.[173] The 2008 financial crisis has focused attention on the risks in 'Casino' banking, evidenced by Kerviel[174] and Adoboli.[175] However, large as these cases may be, the threat that has overshadowed the global financial markets is mortgage fraud, estimated to cost the UK £1.3bn per annum.[176]

The criminal offences contained within the Fraud Act were seen as being wide enough to meet current and future challenges, by being designed as 'modern and flexible statutory offences of fraud'[177] and being broad enough to cover conduct that can be dealt with by summary disposal, right through to conduct meriting a sentence of ten years' imprisonment and an unlimited fine.

In the Fraud Act, a person is guilty of fraud by: false representation;[178] failing to disclose information;[179] and abuse of position.[180] Conviction on indictment carries a

171 Andrew Ashworth, 'Sentencing for fraud and related offences' (2014) 8 Crim LR 553, 554.

172 'Longer prison sentences for frauds that target the vulnerable and fresh sanctions against money-laundering are recommended in new judges' guidelines issued by the Sentencing Council.' *The Guardian*, 'Jail fraudsters for longer, judges told' www.theguardian.com/law/2014/may/23/jail-fraudsters-longer-judges-sentencing-council Accessed 14 November 2016. *R v Samuriwo* [2016] EWCA Crim 1948, analysed the correct approach in light of new guidelines.

173 Securities and Exchange Commission, 'What is a Ponzi Scheme?' 'A Ponzi scheme is an investment fraud that involves the payment of purported returns to existing investors from funds contributed by new investors. Ponzi scheme organizers often solicit new investors by promising to invest funds in opportunities claimed to generate high returns with little or no risk. In many Ponzi schemes, the fraudsters focus on attracting new money to make promised payments to earlier-stage investors and to use for personal expenses, instead of engaging in any legitimate investment activity.' www.sec.gov/answers/ponzi.htm Accessed 24 November 2016.

174 George Gilligan, 'Jérôme Kerviel the "Rogue Trader" of Société Générale: Bad luck, bad apple, bad tree or bad orchard?' (2011) 32(12) Co Law 355–362.

175 *The Times*, 'UBS trader was only "a gamble away from destroying Switzerland's biggest bank"' 14 September 2012 www.thetimes.co.uk/tto/news/uk/crime/article3538412.ece. BBC, 'UBS "rogue trader": Loss estimate raised to $2.3bn' 18 September 2011 www.bbc.co.uk/news/business-14965438 Accessed 24 November 2016. *R v Kweku Adoboli* www.judiciary.gov.uk/judgments/kweku-adoboli-sentencing-remarks-20112012/ Accessed 17 March 2017.

176 Total UK fraud losses estimated to be £193bn. University of Portsmouth, 'Annual Fraud Indicator 2016' 6, 15 www.port.ac.uk/media/contacts-and-departments/icjs/ccfs/Annual-Fraud-Indicator-2016.pdf Accessed 12 September 2016.

177 Pickworth (n 162) 1.

178 Fraud Act 2006, s 2.

179 Fraud Act 2006, s 3.

180 Fraud Act 2006, s 4.

maximum sentence of ten years' imprisonment, an unlimited fine, or both.[181] Fraud by false representation[182] occurs when '(a) it is untrue or misleading, and (b) the person making it knows that it is, or might be, untrue or misleading'.[183] Thus fraud requires dishonesty, and the intention 'to make a gain for himself or another, or to cause loss to another or expose another to a risk of loss'.[184] It is intention that is key: an actual gain or loss does not have to take place. Dishonesty is not defined in the Act but is defined in *R v Ghosh*, [185] which sets a two-stage test:

> The first question is whether a defendant's behaviour would be regarded as dishonest by the ordinary standards of reasonable and honest people. If answered positively, the second question is whether the defendant was aware that his conduct was dishonest and would be regarded as dishonest by reasonable and honest people.[186]

By representation, the Act 'means any representation of fact or law including a representation of [any person's] state of mind'.[187] It can be express or implied, and could be written, spoken or posted on a website. For example, 'dishonestly using a credit card, phishing on the internet or selling fake designer goods'.[188] To cover 'chip and pin' and similar transactions (and, perhaps, 'future proof' legislation against technological developments), there is a provision to 'ensure that a fraud can be committed where a person makes a representation to a machine and a response can be produced without any need for human involvement'.[189]

Second, 'fraud by failing to disclose information'[190] is where a person 'dishonestly fails to disclose to another person information which he is under a legal duty to disclose'.[191] Again, there has to be an intention to cause gain or loss:

> Such a duty may derive from statute (such as provisions governing company prospectuses), from the fact that the transaction in question is one of the utmost good faith (such as a contract of insurance), from the express or implied terms of a contract, from the customer of a particular trade or market, or from the existence of a fiduciary relationship between the parties (such as that of agent and principal).[192]

181 Fraud Act 2006, s 1(3)(b).
182 Fraud Act 2006, s 2.
183 Fraud Act 2006, s 2(2).
184 Fraud Act 2006, s 2(1)(b)(i) & (ii).
185 *R v Ghosh* [1982] QB 1053.
186 Ministry of Justice, 'Explanatory notes to the Fraud Act 2006' www.opsi.gov.uk/acts/acts2006/en/ukpgaen_20060035_en_1.htm Accessed 18 October 2016.
187 Fraud Act 2006, s 2(3).
188 City of London Police, Economic Crime Department, 'Fraud Act 2006' www.cityoflondon.police.uk/CityPolice/Departments/ECD/Fraud/preventingfraud.htm Accessed 18 October 2016.
189 Fraud Act 2006, s 2(5).
190 Fraud Act 2006, s 3.
191 Fraud Act 2006, s 3(a).
192 Law Commission, *Fraud* (Law Com No 276) para 7.29.

Examples might be the failure of a solicitor to share vital information with a client or non-disclosure of a medical condition when entering into a life insurance contract.[193]

Third, 'fraud by abuse of position',[194] again dishonestly and with intent. This recognises situations where a person 'occupies a position where he is expected to safeguard, or not act against, the financial interests of another person'[195] and covers situations where his 'conduct consisted of an omission rather than an act'.[196] This would apply in circumstances of: employee and employer; director and company; professional and client; agent and principal; business partners; within a family; or in the context of voluntary work.[197] Some examples would include: where someone acts for personal gain against the client's interests; an employee of a software company who clones the company's products; someone employed to care for an elderly person having access to bank accounts and taking funds for their own use; and includes omissions such as not taking up a favourable contract to allow a rival company to do so.[198] *R v Valujevs* provided the courts with their first opportunity to consider fraud by abuse of position and, in particular, the meaning of expectation, confirming that 'the judge and jury must decide whether a reasonable person would uphold such an expectation'.[199]

The Fraud Act has other provisions[200] which replace the quaint-sounding crimes of 'going equipped for stealing' and 'when not at his abode'[201] with 'possession etc. of articles for use in frauds',[202] which is a very far-reaching provision. 'A person is guilty of an offence if he has in his possession or under his control any article for use in the course of or in connection with any fraud.'[203] As the COLP describes, 'any article means anything anywhere',[204] and 'includes any program or data held in electronic form'.[205] The provision is constructed to bring across existing case law from the Theft Act 1968, where 'it is enough to prove a general intention to use'.[206] This provision brings computers and software programs into scope.[207]

193 Ministry of Justice, 'Explanatory notes to the Fraud Act 2006' (n 186).
194 Fraud Act 2006, s 4.
195 Fraud Act 2006, s 4 (1)(a).
196 Fraud Act 2006, s 4 (2).
197 Law Commission, *Fraud* (n 192) 7.38.
198 City of London Police, 'Fraud Act 2006' (n 188).
199 *R v Valujevs* [2015] QB 745. For a detailed discussion, see Jennifer Collins, 'Fraud by abuse of position and unlicensed gangmasters' (2016) 79(2) MLR 341.
200 Fraud Act 2006, s 6–8.
201 Theft Act 1968, s 25.
202 Fraud Act 2006, s 6.
203 Fraud Act 2006, s 6 (1).
204 City of London Police, 'Fraud Act 2006' (n 188).
205 Fraud Act 2006, s 8.
206 Ministry of Justice, 'Explanatory notes to the Fraud Act 2006' (n 186) 25. *R v Ellames* 60 Cr App R 7 (CA).
207 Whether at a home address or public, and examples of use are: a computer program can generate credit card numbers; computer templates can be used for producing blank utility bills; computer files can contain lists of other people's credit card details

The next offence is 'making or supplying articles for use in frauds, knowing that it is designed or adapted for use in a fraud'.[208] This might, for example, include a device to cause an electricity meter to malfunction or a device to obtain satellite TV signal without payment.[209] The first significant case, *R v James McCormick*,[210] was far removed from those prosaic examples. McCormick was convicted and sentenced to ten years' imprisonment for selling fake explosives detectors to Iraq.[211]

One provision retained is 'conspiracy to defraud', which the Law Commission wanted to abolish. It is retained because of serious practical concerns about the ability to prosecute multiple offences in the largest and most serious cases of fraud, and acts as a failsafe to see how the new statutory offences work.[212] In practice, the retention of 'conspiracy to defraud' is considered to be beneficial. The Ministry of Justice (MoJ) review of the Fraud Act, in 2012, concluded that:

> this offence continues to be an effective and essential tool in combating fraud. This is particularly pertinent where there are various levels of criminal activity involved and the court would not otherwise be aware of the full extent of criminality involved.[213]

However, the effectiveness of legislation is in the hands of prosecution agencies that deploy it, principally the SFO and the FCA.[214]

or draft letters in connection with 'advance fee' frauds. Ministry of Justice, 'Explanatory notes to the Fraud Act 2006' (n 186) 28.

208 Fraud Act 2006, s 7.

209 City of London Police, 'Fraud Act 2006' (n 188).

210 Judiciary of England and Wales, 'Central Criminal Court 2 May 2013, Sentencing Remarks of His Honour Judge Hone QC' www.judiciary.gov.uk/wp-content/uploads/JCO/Documents/Judgments/r-v-mccormack-sentencing-remarks-20130502.pdf Accessed 17 October 2016.

211 'The jury found that you knew the devices did not work, yet the soldiers in Iraq and elsewhere believed in them, in part due to your powers of salesmanship and in part the extravagant and fraudulent claims made in your promotional material (…) I am wholly satisfied that your fraudulent conduct in selling so many useless devices for simply enormous profit promoted a false sense of security and in all probability materially contributed to causing death and injury to innocent individuals. It is this exceptional feature which distinguishes your case from the usual case of fraud.' Judiciary of England and Wales (n 210). McCormick was also subject to a confiscation order for £7.9m under Proceeds of Crime Act 2002. Avon and Somerset Constabulary, 'Disgraced Somerset businessman faces huge confiscation order', 15 June 2016 www.avonandsomerset.police.uk/newsroom/disgraced-somerset-businessman-faces-huge-confiscation-order/ Accessed 17 October 2016.

212 Fraud Act 2006. Ministry of Justice, 'Explanatory notes to the Fraud Act 2006' (n 186) 6.

213 Ministry of Justice, 'Post-legislative assessment of the Fraud Act 2006. Memorandum to the Justice Select Committee' (Cm 8372) 10.

214 Nicholas Ryder (n 5) 128.

International conventions

The fraud arena does not benefit from any international conventions, unlike bribery and corruption, discussed in Chapter 3. Some international organisations, such as the United Nations (UN) and the European Union (EU), have their own anti-fraud policies, but these are fraud against the institutions themselves rather than setting policy for member states. For the UN, in their system, some

> organizations have in place a stand-alone corporate anti-fraud policy, which provides direction and serves as a repository for the relevant fraud-related policies and procedures. However, in other organizations, anti-fraud-related policies and activities are spread over an array of different rules, regulations, guidelines and administrative issuances, with different owners and different entities responsible for their implementation. This fragmentation often creates duplication of work and inconsistences, and jeopardizes the effective implementation of the organizations' anti-fraud activities.[215]

The EU has its own anti-fraud office (European Anti-Fraud Office – OLAF).[216] The role of OLAF is to 'investigate fraud against the EU budget, corruption and serious misconduct within the European institutions, and develop anti-fraud policy for the European Commission'.[217] OLAF has had a poor reputation for its anti-fraud performance,[218] however; Transparency International report that although there is a good foundation in the EU system to support integrity and ethics,

> this foundation is often undermined by poor practice, lack of political leadership, failure to allocate sufficient staff and funding, and unclarity about to whom the rules apply. The result is that despite improvements to the overall framework, corruption risks persist at the EU level. The most urgent of these include opacity in EU law-making and in EU lobbying, poorly managed conflicts of interest, weak protection for EU whistle-blowers, and weak sanctions for corrupt companies.[219]

215 United Nations, Joint Inspection Unit, 'Fraud prevention, detection and response in United Nations systems organizations' www.unjiu.org/en/reports-notes/JIU%20Products/JIU_REP_2016_4_English.pdf Accessed 17 October 2016.

216 Decision 1999/352/EC, ECSC, Euratom of 28 April 1999, establishing the European Anti-fraud Office. OLAF is its French abbreviation, for Office de Lutte Anti-Fraude. International Association of Anti-Corruption Authorities, 'European Anti-Fraud Office' www.iaaca.org/AntiCorruptionAuthorities/ByInternationalOrganizations/InterGovernmentalOrganization/201202/t20120215_805457.shtml Accessed 17 October 2016.

217 European Commission, 'European Anti-Fraud Office' http://ec.europa.eu/anti-fraud/home_en Accessed 17 October 2016.

218 Helen Xanthaki, 'What is EU fraud? And can OLAF really combat it?' (2010) 17(1) JFC 133, 138.

219 Transparency International, 'The European Union Integrity System' 8 www.transparencyinternational.eu/wp-content/uploads/2014/04/EU_Integrity_System_Report.pdf Accessed 18 October 2016.

Thus, the absence of any anti-fraud conventions can be explained by the difficulties faced by two international bodies in enforcing common standards within their own organisations, let alone independent countries.

Regulatory bodies

Alongside fraud as a key component of economic crime is protection of investments and markets where the government initiated a separate enquiry into the protection of investors, concurrent with examination of the state's response to fraud.[220] The general approach to financial services regulation in 1981 was non-intervention, or self-regulation.[221] This is not surprising since financial services have a long history, dating back to 'barter markets' around 1,000 AD. [222] These markets and institutions centred on the City have developed their own practices, generally without formal state intervention,[223] as Irving notes:

> The ways in which the City institutions work are governed by a blend of statutory and self-imposed rules. Standards of behaviours have developed over the years with the growth of the City. Reprisals which can follow the breaking of any institution's rules are usually sufficient deterrent (...) The Bank [of England] exercises its supervisory role in different degrees (...) The Bank itself sees no good reason for basically changing the present mixture of statutory and self-regulation (...) Voluntary rules are much easier to introduce and modify than legal ones, and to operate within the strict letter of the law does not amount to the kind of ethical behaviours that the City institutions demand, and the Bank of England expects.[224]

Thus, an era when the most effective regulator was the Bank of England 'Governor's eyebrows'[225] serves as a backdrop to the new landscape for tackling fraud.

The three main bodies that prosecute fraud are the SFO, Crown Prosecution Service (CPS) and FCA. There are other regulations that have involvement but are

220 L C B Gower, *Review of Investor Protection* (HMSO 1984) (hereinafter Gower Report).

221 Editorial, 'How many regulators?' (1996) 17(2) Co Law 34.

222 George P Gilligan, 'The origins of UK financial services regulation' (1997) 18 (6) Comp Law 167–176.

223 '[T]he FSA had been criticised prior to the financial crisis for being too "heavy and intrusive" and was under pressure to become even more "light touch".' Roman Tomasic, 'The financial crisis and the haphazard pursuit of financial crime' (2011) 18 (1) JFC 8 (footnote omitted). Iain MacNeil, 'The trajectory of regulatory reform in the UK in the wake of the financial crisis' (2010) 11 EBOR 483, 484. The investment markets benefited from light regulation by government, as had been the case for centuries, apart from the Prevention of Fraud (Investments) Act 1958. J Fisher and J Bewsey, *The Law of Investor Protection* (Sweet & Maxwell 1997) 13.

224 Joe Irving, *The City at Work* (Andre Deutsch 1981) 26, 27.

225 Attributed to Montagu Norman (Lord Norman), Governor of the Bank of England 1920–44. See also: L C B Gower, '"Big Bang" and City Regulation' (1988) 51 MLR 21.

not central, such as the Bank of England, Prudential Regulation Authority (PRA), CMA, together with policy developers, HM Treasury and the Home Office. This chapter will not consider these bodies in detail.

Serious Fraud Office

The SFO was established in 1987[226] to tackle 'the topmost tier of serious and complex fraud and bribery'.[227] It was created due to disquiet about the prosecution of serious fraud.[228] It has had a troubled life, being perceived as a failing organisation. Early high-profile cases tarnished its reputation, including Guinness, Barlow Clowes, Blue Arrow, Maxwell, Levitt and Saunders.[229] More recently, it has been criticised over its handling of bribery allegations against BAE,[230] the controversial abandonment of investigations into arms sales to Saudi Arabia;[231] and its attempt to 'plea bargain' has brought judicial opprobrium that in economic crime cases the SFO should not believe that these are 'more respectable than other forms of crime', or that these criminals 'should not be ordered to serve prison sentences because such sentences should be reserved for those they regard as common criminals'.[232]

The SFO is judged on its role as a prosecutor. Its mixed success has in recent years shown an increase in activity, reporting an 81% conviction rate, and it states that 'it is stronger, faster and leaner' and 'delivering more for less'.[233] However, in 2014 it was reported that 'the SFO this year reached their lowest level since the financial crisis (…) but the results will come through and we will have to weather the inevitable criticism in the meantime about case numbers and investigation costs'.[234]

For example, in 2011 the SFO made a case for its continued existence as an independent specialist investigator and prosecutor, when the return of Asil Nadir

226 Criminal Justice Act 1987, s 1(1).

227 Serious Fraud Office, 'Ethical business conduct: An enforcement perspective' www.sfo.gov.uk/2014/03/06/ethical-business-conduct-enforcement-perspective/ Accessed 24 November 2016.

228 Roskill (n 11) 1.

229 *Bishopsgate Investment Management Ltd v Maxwell* [1993] Ch. 1; *Re Levitt* [1992] Ch. 457; Re Arrows Ltd (No. 4) [1994] 3 All ER 814; *R v Saunders* [1996] Crim LR 420.

230 *R (on the application of Corner House Research and another) v Director of Serious Fraud Office (BAE Systems plc, interested party)* [2008] All ER 927.

231 James Wilson, 'The Day We Sold the Rule of Law' Halsbury's Law Exchange www.halsburyslawexchange.co.uk/?s=the+day+we+sold+the+rule+of+law Accessed 24 November 2016.

232 Lord Judge CJ, *R v Dougall* [2010] EWCA Crim 1048 13 May 2010 www.bailii.org/cgi-bin/markup.cgi?doc=/ew/cases/EWCA/Crim/2010/1048.html&query=dougall&method=boolean Accessed 24 November 2016.

233 HC Deb 7 February 2017 vol 621 col 50WH.

234 *The Telegraph*, 28 December 2013 'SFO plans fightback in 2014' www.telegraph.co.uk/finance/financial-crime/10540905/SFO-plans-fightback-in-2014.html Accessed 24 November 2016.

to the UK brought echoes of its past difficulties with major cases. Asil Nadir was due to be tried for theft in 1993[235] but fled to Northern Cyprus and could not be extradited. On his return the SFO faced difficulties in prosecution because of failing memory or the death of some witnesses in the intervening 19 years, combined with problems of reassembling evidence, some documents of which were considered a health hazard.[236] Nonetheless, 'the conviction of Asil Nadir of theft on a grand scale from a public company nineteen years after he fled the jurisdiction is a remarkable achievement'.[237] The then director of the SFO stated that its 'cases are high profile and carry high risk'[238] and the significance of the Asil Nadir case is that it provided a reference back to its mixed success in achieving convictions in the early 1990s, when this case should have been tried, and its ultimate success was not a foregone conclusion.

The financial crisis provided the SFO with an opportunity 'to investigate suspected offences committed within the UK jurisdiction in relation to Icelandic Bank Kaupthing prior to its collapse'.[239] The SFO wanted to understand what had 'allowed substantial value to be extracted from the bank in the year prior to its collapse'.[240] The SFO said: 'this is a complex investigation which crosses numerous jurisdictions. We have been working closely with the Icelandic Special Prosecutor's Office to ensure that comprehensive and robust investigations are conducted'.[241] This was just the type of case for which the SFO was established.[242] However, when the SFO announced that it had arrested people in London and Reykjavik, *The Guardian* [243] identified the SFO's target as Kaupthing's 'biggest client Robert Tchenguiz'.[244] The SFO conceded that search

235 *R v Asil Nadir* T19920238.

236 *Financial Times*, 'SFO faced uphill struggle in Nadir case' 22 August 2012 www.ft.com/cms/s/0/9a0dfb06-e53d-11e1-8ac0-00144feab49a.html#axzz2ucpXDq2D Accessed 16 September 2016.

237 'Turkish Cypriot businessman Asil Nadir, jailed in Britain in 2012 for stealing millions from his business empire, was released in Turkey on Friday shortly after he was returned there to complete his sentence, under prisoner transfer agreement.' Reuters, 'Turkey releases Polly Peck fraudster Nadir after repatriation from Britain' 22 April 2016 http://uk.reuters.com/article/uk-turkey-britain-nadir-idUKKCN0XJ0G4 Accessed 24 November 2016. Serious Fraud Office, 'Asil Nadir found guilty' www.sfo.gov.uk/2012/08/22/asil-nadir-found-guilty/ Accessed 16 September 2016.

238 Serious Fraud Office, 'Asil Nadir found guilty' (n 237).

239 Serious Fraud Office, 'Kaupthing hf' 16 December 2009 www.sfo.gov.uk/cases/kaupthing-hf/ Accessed 16 September 2016.

240 Serious Fraud Office, 'Kaupthing hf' 16 December 2009 (n 239).

241 Serious Fraud Office, 'Kaupthing hf' 16 December 2009 (n 239).

242 'The SFO will take on those cases which need the Roskill model of multi-disciplinary, team-based investigation.' Serious Fraud Office, David Green, 'Speech to Cambridge Symposium 2013' www.sfo.gov.uk/2013/09/02/cambridge-symposium-2013/ Accessed 20 March 2017.

243 *The Guardian*, 'SFO focuses on role of Robert Tchenguiz' 11 March 2011 www.theguardian.com/business/2011/mar/11/tchenguiz-kaupthing-serious-fraud-office?INTCMP=SRCH&guni=Article:in%20body%20link Accessed 16 September 2016.

244 *The Guardian*, 'SFO raids offices in Luxembourg over failed Icelandic bank Kaupthing' 29 March 2011 www.guardian.co.uk/business/2011/mar/29/robert-tchenguiz-kaupthing.

warrants were flawed[245] and its actions were subject to adverse judgment of the court because of 'serious mistakes',[246] resulting in the Tchenguiz brothers claiming £300m in damages.[247] With clear echoes of past difficulties, the SFO eventually settled *Tchenguiz* [248] by paying damages and costs totalling £14.25m together with its own costs of £14.3m.[249] The SFO stated that it 'accepts the criticisms of it made by the Divisional court[. T]he outcome of this particular case which concerned events in 2011 does not reflect the quality of the SFO's work in 2013'.[250] This is understandable because 'high-profile' cases are 'high risk' and have the potential to embarrass, as with the earlier cases. This potential for embarrassment was realised when the SFO had to seek additional funding from HM Treasury to cover not only costs relating to the Tchenguiz claim but also 'historic legal liabilities relating to its payment of VAT'[251] and making unauthorised payments to its staff.[252]

The management of the SFO also suffered when the House of Commons Committee of Public Accounts[253] reported that the SFO's internal management had 'showed a disregard for the proper use of taxpayers' money'.[254] The

Financial Times, 'SFO admits Tchenguiz case errors' 22 February 2012 www.ft.com/cms/s/0/01068b74-5d68-11e1-889d-00144feabdc0.html Accessed 16 September 2016.

245 Serious Fraud Office, 'Kaupthing hf' 16 December 2009 (n 239).

246 Serious Fraud Office, 'Annual Report and Accounts 2011–2012' 31 www.sfo.gov.uk/publications/corporate-information/annual-reports-accounts/ Accessed 24 November 2016.

247 'The SFO has so far spent £8.1m defending the £300m claim by the Tchenguiz brothers, due to go to trial in October, the High Court heard', *Financial Times*, 8 April 2014 www.ft.com/cms/s/0/5f0e1f06-bf41-11e3-a4af-00144feabdc0.html#axzz2yUAjxFyc Accessed 24 November 2016.

248 *Rawlinson and Hunter Trustees SA and others v Akers and another* [2014] EWCA Civ 136.

249 Since July 2014 the SFO has paid out £4.5m in full and final settlement of the damages claims, and £9.75m in full and final settlement of its costs liability in respect of those claims. Defending the damages claims cost the SFO a total of £14.3m (plus VAT where non-recoverable) in legal fees and associated expenditure. Serious Fraud Office, 'Annual Report and Accounts 2015–16' 8 www.sfo.gov.uk/publications/corporate-information/annual-reports-accounts/ Accessed 6 September 2016.

250 Serious Fraud Office, 'Annual Report and Accounts 2012–2013' www.sfo.gov.uk/publications/corporate-information/annual-reports-accounts/ Accessed 24 November 2016.

251 *The Times*, 'Fraud Office gets £19m bailout after misleading taxman' 1 March 2014 www.thetimes.co.uk/tto/news/uk/article4019911.ece Accessed 24 November 2016. Written Statement, Serious Fraud Office (Contingencies Fund Advance), HC Deb 30 January 2014 col 39WS.

252 *The Guardian*, 'Ex-chief of Fraud Office apologises over £1m severance payments' 15 March 2013 www.theguardian.com/law/2013/mar/15/fraud-office-chief-apology Accessed 24 November 2016.

253 House of Commons Committee of Public Accounts, 'Serious Fraud Office – redundancy and severance arrangements. Tenth Report of Session 2013–14' 3 www.publications.parliament.uk/pa/cm201314/cmselect/cmpubacc/360/360.pdf Accessed 24 November 2016.

254 House of Commons Committee of Public Accounts, 'Serious Fraud Office – redundancy and severance arrangements. Tenth Report of Session 2013–14' (n 253).

committee concluded that 'the reputation of the SFO has been undermined by a catalogue of errors and poor judgement and the morale of its staff has suffered'.[255] This is underlined by a headline from *The Telegraph*: '"BAE" documents lost by SFO found at cannabis farm.'[256] This was followed by the collapse of another prosecution: 'fresh reversal for SFO as £40m bribery trial collapses.'[257] The SFO had earlier announced that 'Dahdaleh, an international businessman, has been arrested today and charged with corruption offences relating to contracts for the supply of aluminium to Bahrain'.[258] In December 2013, the SFO issued a statement: 'the SFO has today offered no evidence against Victor Dahdaleh, having concluded that there is no longer a realistic prospect of conviction in this case.'[259] This was due to the principal witness changing his evidence and difficulties with two US witnesses who were unwilling to give evidence.[260]

However, what puts this case into sharp relief is a parallel case in the US, where 'Alcoa World Alumina admitted links to what US authorities called a "corrupt international underworld" and agreed to a $384m settlement over charges relating

255 House of Commons Committee of Public Accounts, 'Serious Fraud Office – redundancy and severance arrangements. Tenth Report of Session 2013–14' (n 253).

256 HC Deb 11 September 2013 vol 567 col 707W. *The Telegraph*, '"BAE" documents lost by SFO found at cannabis farm' 13 September 2013 www.telegraph.co.uk/finance/financial-crime/10307238/BAE-documents-lost-by-SFO-found-at-cannabis-farm.html Accessed 24 November 2016. Serious Fraud Office, 'Statement on Data Loss Incident' www.sfo.gov.uk/2013/08/08/statement-data-loss-incident/ Accessed 26 September 2016.

257 *The Telegraph*, 'Fresh reversal for SFO as £40m bribery trial collapses' 10 December 2013 www.telegraph.co.uk/finance/financial-crime/10509552/Fresh-reversal-for-SFO-as-40m-bribery-trial-collapses.html Accessed 24 November 2016.

258 Serious Fraud Office, 'Victor Dahdaleh charged with bribery' www.sfo.gov.uk/press-room/press-release-archive/press-releases-2011/victor-dahdaleh-charged-with-bribery.aspx Accessed 13 January 2014.

259 Serious Fraud Office, 'Statement: R v Dahdaleh' www.sfo.gov.uk/2013/12/10/statement-r-v-dahdaleh-2/ Accessed 24 November 2016.

260 Serious Fraud Office, 'Statement: R v Dahdaleh' (n 259). See *R v J* [2013] EWCA Crim 2287; [2014] 1 Cr App R 21; [2014] Lloyd's Rep FC 87. 'Evidence as to the informed consent of the actual principal might, however, be material to the issue of whether a payment was made corruptly, depending on the facts of the case. The judge's ruling was set aside (see paras 24–25, 32, 44–46 of judgment).' https://login.westlaw.co.uk/maf/wluk/app/document?&srguid=ia744d065000001453d0fdaebac1e09fd&docguid=I988A88705E0511E3ABAE9189C69E07DD&hitguid=I988A88705E0511E3ABAE9189C69E07DD&rank=4&spos=4&epos=4&td=664&crumb-action=append&context=45&resolvein=true Accessed 24 November 2016. 'Dahdaleh was charged under that law because the alleged offences pre-dated the Bribery Act 2010, under which the "principal's consent" defence is no longer available.' Reuters, 'UK bribery trial collapses in blow to anti-fraud agency' 10 December 2013 www.reuters.com/article/2013/12/10/britain-bahrain-trial-idUSL6N0JP2FL20131210 Accessed 24 November 2016. Department of Justice, 'Alcoa World Alumina agrees to plead guilty to foreign bribery and pay $233 million in fines and forfeiture' 9 January 2014 www.justice.gov/usao/paw/news/2014/2014_january/2014_01_09_02.html Accessed 24 November 2016.

to bribery'.[261] The US Department of Justice (DoJ)[262] detailed the outcome of fines and undertakings regarding future conduct but no criminal conviction against an individual, although it did refer to the middleman involved as 'Consultant A', a 'London-based middleman with close ties to certain [Bahrain] Royal Family members as a sham sales agent and agreed to pay him a corrupt commission intended to conceal bribe payments, according to court papers'.[263]

The contrast in outcome of the two matters with similar facts highlights the difference in approach where, until 2014, the SFO had limited room for manoeuvre. The former director commented on the facilities available to SFO:

> My view is that the prosecution-led approach with integrated teams of lawyers and investigators is needed in this very specialist and complex area. This view is shared by other experts in the field. It is the basis upon which the DoJ as well as the [FCA] works.[264]

However, the DoJ have long had the ability to employ 'negotiated outcomes' or a 'plea bargaining' strategy, where such deals are widely used and 'a policy of judicial acquiescence or self-restraint prevails'.[265] Litigation has risks and the outcomes are far from certain, and, as Buchanan observes, 'litigation is expensive. One has to consider not only the costs of the proposed court action but also the prospect of being unsuccessful in court and being ordered to pay the expenses of others involved in the particular court action'.[266] It is understandable that the SFO saw the attractions of 'negotiating outcomes', bringing with them cost savings and certainty advantages. However, two cases where the

261 *Financial Times*, 'Alcoa in $384m deal to settle Bahrain bribery charges' 10 January 2014 www.ft.com/cms/s/0/62b10d60-793e-11e3-91ac-00144feabdc0.html#axzz2ucpXDq2D Accessed 24 November 2016.*The Independent*, 'SFO left shamefaced after US nails City fraudster' 9 January 2014 www.independent.co.uk/news/uk/crime/sfo-left-shamefaced-after-us-nails-city-fraudster-9050099.html Accessed 24 November 2016.

262 'Alcoa World Alumina has agreed to plead guilty in the Western District of Pennsylvania to one count of violating the anti-bribery provisions of the FCPA in connection with a 2004 corrupt transaction, to pay a criminal fine of $209 million, and to administratively forfeit $14 million. As part of the plea agreement, Alcoa Inc. (Alcoa) has agreed to maintain and implement an enhanced global anti-corruption compliance program. In a parallel action, Alcoa settled with the U.S. Securities and Exchange Commission (SEC) and will pay an additional $161 million in disgorgement, bringing the total amount of U.S. criminal and regulatory penalties to be paid by Alcoa and Alcoa World Alumina to $384 million.' Department of Justice, 'Alcoa World Alumina Agrees to Plead Guilty to Foreign Bribery' (n 260).

263 Department of Justice, 'Alcoa World Alumina Agrees to Plead Guilty to Foreign Bribery' (n 260).

264 Richard Alderman, Director, SFO, quoted in the *The Telegraph*: 'Director speaks out over plan to strip Serious Fraud Office of prosecution powers' 19 March 2011 www.telegraph.co.uk/finance/businesslatestnews/8392895/Director-speaks-out-over-plan-to-strip-Serious-Fraud-Office-of-prosecution-powers.html Accessed 24 November 2016.

265 D Corker, 'Time for a serious (SFO) rethink' (2010) 160 NLJ 783, 784.

266 Gillian C Buchanan, 'Funding the cost of litigation' (2014) 161 SPEL 8.

SFO wished to 'plea bargain' caused judicial tensions. First, in *R v Innospec Limited*, the Court of Appeal criticised the SFO for 'usurping' the judge's authority by agreeing punishment. Second, in *R v Dougall*, the judge rejected SFO claims for leniency.[267]

Reporting fraud

The UK does not have a legal requirement to report fraud per se. The NFA admitted that 'not having a centralised body to co-ordinate fraud intelligence (...) has made it easier for criminals to operate undetected and free to re-offend'.[268] The minimal reporting regime and the lack of scope and consistency leave significant gaps in effectiveness. Notwithstanding the Fraud Act, which repositioned the crime of fraud, there is no statutory obligation to report fraud as such, unlike money laundering and terrorist financing. Fraud is only required to be reported if it is part of suspected money laundering or terrorist financing. The NCA and its offspring, the National Fraud Intelligence Bureau, seem to rely on 'best endeavours' and 'encouragement' to report.[269] The key statutory requirement to report fraud is the Proceeds of Crime Act 2002 (POCA) (and the Terrorism Act 2000):[270]

> Persons in the regulated sector are required to make a report in respect of information that comes to them (...) where they *know* or; where they *suspect* or; where they *have reasonable grounds for knowing or suspecting* that a person is engaged in, or attempting, money laundering or terrorist financing.[271]

Consequently, it is quite plain that 'if you have knowledge or suspicion that a money laundering offence is taking place then you must submit a Suspicious Activity Report (SAR) to NCA'.[272] The submission of the SAR should be done in a timely manner, to allow NCA time to react. The form should include Customer Due Diligence,[273] in addition to the grounds for suspicion and any known links to criminality. If an SAR is made before a suspicious transaction is completed, NCA then have seven days to determine whether to give consent or whether to impose

267 *R v Innospec* (2010) Crim LR 665 Crown Ct (Southwark). *R v Dougall* (n 232).

268 National Fraud Authority, 'National Fraud Intelligence Bureau' www.gov.uk/government/organisations/national-fraud-authority/about Accessed 20 March 2017.

269 National Fraud Authority, 'National Fraud Intelligence Bureau' (n 268).

270 Proceeds of Crime Act 2002, s 330; Terrorism Act 2000, s 19.

271 National Crime Agency, 'Submitting a Suspicious Activity Report (SAR) within the Regulated Sector' 2 www.nationalcrimeagency.gov.uk/publications/517-submitting-a-suspicious-activity-report-sar-within-the-regulated-sector/file Accessed 24 November 2016 (emphasis added).

272 National Crime Agency, 'Submitting a Suspicious Activity Report (SAR) within the Regulated Sector' (n 271) 10.

273 National Crime Agency, 'Submitting a Suspicious Activity Report (SAR) within the Regulated Sector' (n 271) 5.

a 31-day moratorium to facilitate further enquiries.[274] Penalties of completing a transaction or 'tipping off' are up to five years' imprisonment and/or a fine.[275] This creates practical difficulties where, for example, a bank is required to process a transaction which, being subject to an SAR, the bank is able neither to process the transaction nor explain why, because

> POCA and the Terrorism Act each contains two separate offences of tipping off and prejudicing an investigation. The first offence relates to disclosing that an internal or external report has been made; the second relates to disclosing that an investigation is being contemplated or is being carried out.[276]

K Ltd v National Westminster Bank demonstrates the issues a bank faces. In this case, NatWest were suspicious of a receipt by K of monies from the Netherlands Antilles and an instruction to transfer the monies the same day to a Swiss bank. Because of their suspicions, NatWest reported to the authorities and refused to honour K's instructions. K applied for an injunction requiring NatWest to explain its reasons. The Court of Appeal stated that since it is unlawful under POCA to honour the mandate, NatWest was not in breach of its contract with K. If the bank has suspicions (not defined) then the customer has no redress during the 31-day moratorium.[277] This does, however, illustrate a practical problem for bankers: what can they say to their customer when they do not comply with their customer's mandate? To make the payment when suspicions have been raised is to facilitate money laundering. To explain the reasons for non-payment to the customer is 'tipping off'. Penalties are up to 14 years' imprisonment for the former and five years for the latter and/or a fine.[278] Or they are in the uncomfortable position of 'stone-walling' the customer by saying they are not in a position to make the payment and leaving the customer to reach their own conclusion as to the underlying reasons.[279]

274 The Criminal Finances Bill was introduced into Parliament in October 2016. This includes proposals to allow a moratorium up to a further 186 days upon application to the Court. Home Office, 'Factsheet – Part 1 Chapter 2 – Power to obtain further information and extend the SARs moratorium period' www.gov.uk/government/uploads/system/uploads/attachment_data/file/564471/CF_Bill_-_Factsheet_4_-_SARs_moratorium_and_Request_Information_Power.pdf Accessed 24 November 2016.

275 Proceeds of Crime Act 2002, s 329. *Squirrell Ltd v National Westminster Bank Plc* [2006] 1 WLR 637.

276 'Suspicious Activities, Reporting and Data Protection' in *Butterworths Banking Law Handbook* http://lexisweb.co.uk/guides/sources/butterworths-banking-law-handbook?contentonly=true. Accessed 17 January 2017.

277 *K Ltd v National Westminster Bank* [2007] 1 WLR 311.

278 Proceeds of Crime Act 2002, Part 7. Money Laundering Offences s 328, s 333.

279 The government introduced the Criminal Finances Bill in October 2016, which contains provisions for: 'Unexplained Wealth Orders, where individuals whose assets are disproportionate to their known income will need explain the origin of their wealth, and, Disclosure Orders will be extended to money laundering investigations and will provide an effective, efficient and flexible means of obtaining information.' There are

There is also an option, rather than a duty, to report acquisitive crime.[280] The police have a duty to record the crime under 'Home Office Counting Rules for Recorded Crime'.[281] The FCA imposes obligations on regulated firms: Principle 11 – 'A firm must deal with its regulators in an open and co-operative way, and must tell the FCA promptly anything relating to the firm of which the FCA would reasonably expect prompt notice.'[282] This requires the firm, taking a 'risk-based approach', to establish systems and controls, policies and procedures 'that enable it to identify, assess, monitor and manage money laundering risk'. Interestingly, 'financial crime' is only mentioned in the heading, since money laundering is the focus.[283]

A further area of reporting relates to higher-risk situations, which include any high-risk customers, encompassing 'politically exposed persons' (PEPs). PEPs 'are individuals whose prominent position in public life may make them vulnerable to corruption'.[284] For example, individuals entrusted with prominent public functions,[285] such as heads of state or government, with the definition extending to immediate family members and close associates.[286] The clear danger is that these persons might be corrupt and involved in money laundering through the UK

also some increased provisions to strengthen capability to recover proceeds of crime. Home Office, 'Factsheet – Criminal Finances Bill' www.gov.uk/government/uploads/system/uploads/attachment_data/file/564464/CF_Bill_-_Factsheet_1_-_The_Bill.pdf Accessed 24 November 2016.

280 Where items are stolen or acquired fraudulently (i.e. theft, burglary, vehicle crime and fraud). The NCA state that it is not a crime-reporting agency and that reports, if any, should be made to Action Fraud. National Crime Agency, 'Submitting a Suspicious Activity Report (SAR) within the Regulated Sector' 9 www.nationalcrimeagency.gov.uk/publications/517-submitting-a-suspicious-activity-report-sar-within-the-regulated-sector/file Accessed 24 November 2016.

281 Home Office, 'Counting Rules for Recorded Crime' http://webarchive.nationalarchives.gov.uk/20110314171826/http://rds.homeoffice.gov.uk/rds/pdfs10/countgeneral10.pdf Accessed 14 January 2017.

282 Financial Conduct Authority, 'Principles of good regulation' www.fca.org.uk/about/principles-good-regulation Accessed 24 November 2016.

283 'A *firm* must notify the *FSA* immediately if one of the following events arises and the event is significant: (1) it becomes aware that an *employee* may have committed a fraud against one of its *customers*; or (2) [by] … a *person* … against it; or (3) … any *person* … acting with intent to commit a fraud; or (4) … identifies irregularities in its accounting or other records, whether or not there is evidence of fraud; or (5) [suspicion of] … one of its *employees['*] … serious misconduct concerning his honesty or integrity.' Financial Conduct Authority, ***Handbook. Supervision. Fraud, Errors and Other Irregularities*** (SUP 15.3.17) www.handbook.fca.org.uk/handbook/SUP/15/3.html?searchtext=suspected%20fraud&searchtype=boolean Accessed 24 November 2016.

284 Financial Services Authority, 'Banks' management of high money-laundering risk situations' 3 www.fca.org.uk/publication/corporate/fsa-aml-final-report.pdf Accessed 24 November 2016.

285 See Third EU Money Laundering Directive. Directive 2005/60/EC.

286 Financial Conduct Authority, 'Politically exposed persons' www.handbook.fca.org.uk/handbook/document/FC1_FCA_20130401.pdf#search='politically%20exposed%20person Accessed 24 November 2016.

banking system.[287] For PEPs, the Money Laundering Regulations of 2007 (MLR2007) require 'Enhanced Customer Due Diligence and Monitoring', for which there are reporting obligations to the FCA (but the onus is on the firm to report in line with its 'risk-based approach').[288] In 2011, the regulator issued a reminder to regulated firms of 'continuing need for vigilance and robust systems and controls' because of political developments in the Middle East.[289]

Fraud reporting in the UK is limited to areas where there is a connection to money laundering or terrorism financing and/or where a party involved is regulated by the FCA. Thus, there can be overlap between reporting to the NCA and the FCA. Outside those reporting structures there is no general reporting requirement, which has the effect that other fraud information is not captured. As a result, anti-fraud agencies and government work in the dark on the basis of incomplete information. By contrast, in the US, the Financial Crimes Enforcement Network (FinCEN) requires full reporting.[290] It is a single reporting centre and, significantly, part of the US Department of the Treasury. In sum, the lack of a statutory coordinated reporting regime in the UK has the twin effect of causing a significant administrative burden, yet allowing much fraud activity to go unreported and consequently unpursued.

LIBOR scandal

The LIBOR scandal has been described as 'the most high profile current issue in the United Kingdom'.[291] The LIBOR scandal is 'allegations that bankers have colluded to manipulate the London inter-bank lending interest rate'.[292] LIBOR was managed by the British Bankers' Association (BBA) and 'used to calculate the interest rates for a range of financial instruments (…) [which were] used as the basis for many types of lending, from syndicated and commercial lending, to calculating rates on residential

287 For example, a significant case was that of General Sani Abacha, the former President of Nigeria, where the regulator identified 42 personal and corporate account relationships linked to Abacha family members and close associates in the UK. These accounts were held at 23 banks, which included UK banks and branches of banks from both inside and outside the European Union and had a turnover amounting to $1.3 billion for the four years to 2000. Financial Services Authority, 'FSA publishes results of money laundering investigation' 8 March 2001 www.fsa.gov.uk/Pages/Library/Communication/PR/2001/029.shtml Accessed 24 November 2016.

288 Financial Conduct Authority, *Handbook. Supervision. Fraud, Errors and Other Irregularities* (SUP 15.3.17) 15.3 (n 283).

289 Financial Services Authority, 'A reminder to FSA regulated firms after recent events in the Middle-East' 18 February 2011 www.fsa.gov.uk/pages/About/What/financial_crime/events_middle-east.shtml Accessed 4 November 2016.

290 Discussed in Chapter 4. Financial Crimes Enforcement Network, US Department of the Treasury, 'Mandatory e-Filing FAQs' www.fincen.gov/mandatory-e-filing-faqs Accessed 24 November 2016.

291 Attorney General's Office, 'Fighting economic crime in the modern world' www.gov.uk/government/speeches/fighting-economic-crime-in-the-modern-world Accessed 24 November 2016.

292 Attorney General's Office, 'Fighting economic crime in the modern world' (n 291).

mortgages'.[293] In July 2012, the SFO announced that it had agreed to investigate manipulation of LIBOR, since when, 13 people have been charged with conspiracy to defraud, of whom five have been convicted, six acquitted and two are facing a retrial.[294] The SFO stated that it would continue to work with the FCA and US agencies.[295]

The LIBOR scandal erupted in June 2012 when the FSA announced a financial penalty of £59.5m had been imposed on Barclays Bank.[296] The FSA described the penalty as being for 'significant failings'.[297] The press and politicians referred to the issue as a scandal.[298] The issue was that LIBOR was 'something of an anachronism, a throwback to a time when many bankers within the square mile [City of London] knew one another and when trust was more important than contract'.[299] As *The Economist* reports, 'what may still seem to many to be a parochial affair involving Barclays, a 300-year-old British Bank, rigging an obscure number, is beginning to assume global significance'.[300] The FSA reported the misconduct of Barclays employees who 'were involved in submitting artificially low estimates for the setting of the LIBOR, before and during the financial crisis'.[301] LIBOR may well be a 'throwback' and the BBA, as discussed later, may well regret its role in managing a benchmark rate[302]

293 Financial instruments such as, 'derivatives based on the BBA LIBOR rates are now traded on exchanges such as LIFFE and the Chicago Mercantile Exchange (CME) as well as over-the-counter.' British Bankers' Association, 'Understanding BBA LIBOR – a briefing by the British Bankers' Association' www.bbalibor.com/news-releases/understanding-bba-libor Accessed 24 November 2016.

294 'Charges have so far been brought against 13 individuals. Of the 13, one individual pleaded guilty in October 2014, the first criminal conviction for a LIBOR offence in the UK. Another individual was found guilty by a jury in August 2015. A trial of six individuals began on 6 October 2015. All six defendants were found not guilty of all charges. A further trial began on 4 April 2016 and concluded with three convictions, one guilty plea and the jury not being able to reach verdicts on two individuals. The investigation into others continues.' Serious Fraud Office, 'LIBOR' www.sfo.gov.uk/cases/libor-landing/ Accessed 18 October 2016.

295 The SFO director comments that international cooperation such as with LIBOR can benefit from different laws where the US has corporate vicarious liability. Serious Fraud Office, 'Cambridge Symposium 2016' www.sfo.gov.uk/2016/09/05/cambridge-symposium-2016/ Accessed 8 September 2016.

296 Financial Services Authority, 'Barclays fined £59.5 million for significant failings in relation to LIBOR and EURIBOR' www.fsa.gov.uk/library/communication/pr/2012/070.shtml Accessed 14 January 2017.

297 Financial Services Authority, 'Barclays fined £59.5 million for significant failings in relation to LIBOR and EURIBOR' (n 296).

298 *The Economist*, 'The LIBOR scandal: The rotten heart of finance' 7 July 2012 www.economist.com/node/21558281 Accessed 24 November 2016. George Osborne MP, HC Deb 2 July 2012 col 616.

299 *The Economist*, 'The LIBOR scandal' (n 298).

300 *The Economist*, 'The LIBOR scandal' (n 298).

301 Greame Baber, 'A critical examination of the legislative response in banking and financial regulation to issues related to misconduct in the context of the crisis of 2007–2009' (2013) 20(2) JFC 237.

302 'Like many of the City's ways, LIBOR is something of an anachronism, a throwback to a time when many bankers within the Square Mile knew one another and when

which was used for purposes outwith its original intention; however, the 'LIBOR issue is serious'.[303]

The reason why LIBOR is serious is that it, alongside the Euro Inter-Bank Offered Rate (EURIBOR), 'are benchmark reference rates fundamental to the operation of both UK and international financial markets, including markets in interest rate derivatives contracts'.[304] The FSA said that 'LIBOR and EURIBOR are by far the most prevalent benchmark reference rates used in euro, US dollar and sterling over the counter (OTC) interest rate derivatives contracts and exchange traded interest rate contracts'.[305] The use made of these data affects 'payments made under a wide range of other contracts including loans and mortgages'[306] and involves 'a wide range of counterparties including small businesses, large financial institutions and public authorities'.[307] The volume of trades is significant.[308]

It became clear that 'since 2009, the FSA and other international regulators have been extensively investigating allegations of widespread attempts in the banking industry to manipulate' LIBOR.[309]

Contemporaneously with Barclays' financial penalty to the FSA, 'Barclays was also fined $200m by the US Commodity Futures and Trading Commission and a further US $160m penalty imposed by the DoJ in respect of attempted LIBOR manipulation

trust was more important than contract. For LIBOR, a borrowing rate is set daily by a panel of banks for ten currencies and for 15 maturities. The most important of these, three-month dollar LIBOR, is supposed to indicate what a bank would pay to borrow dollars for three months from other banks at 11am on the day it is set. The dollar rate is fixed each day by taking estimates from a panel, currently comprising 18 banks, of what they think they would have to pay to borrow if they needed money. The top four and bottom four estimates are then discarded, and LIBOR is the average of those left. The submissions of all the participants are published, along with each day's LIBOR fix.'*The Economist*, 'The LIBOR scandal' (n 298).

303 Baber (n 301) 237.

304 Financial Services Authority, 'Barclays Bank plc – Final Notice' 27 June 2012 www.fsa.gov.uk/static/pubs/final/barclays-jun12.pdf Accessed 18 October 2016.

305 Financial Services Authority, 'Barclays Bank plc – Final Notice' (n 304).

306 Financial Services Authority, 'Barclays Bank plc – Final Notice' (n 304).

307 Financial Services Authority, 'Barclays Bank plc – Final Notice' (n 304).

308 'The notional amount outstanding of OTC interest rate derivatives contracts in the first half of 2011 has been estimated at 554tn dollars. The total value of volume of short term interest rate contracts traded on LIFFE [London International Financial Futures and Options Exchange] in London in 2011 was 477 trillion euro including over 241 trillion euro relating to three month EURIBOR future contract.' Financial Services Authority, 'Barclays Bank plc – Final Notice' (n 304).

309 Other regulators included the US, Canada and Japan. Victoria Callaghan and Zia Ullah, 'The LIBOR scandal – the UK's legislative response' (2013) 28(40) JIBLR 160. 'Regulators around the world have woken up, however belatedly, to the possibility that these vital markets may have been rigged by a large number of banks. The list of institutions that have said they are either co-operating with investigations or being questioned includes many of the world's biggest banks. Among those that have disclosed their involvement are Citigroup, Deutsche Bank, HSBC, JP Morgan Chase, RBS and UBS.'*The Economist*, 7 July 2012 'The LIBOR scandal' (n 298).

and false reporting charges'.[310] The FCA has fined major international banks: Rabobank £105m, UBS £160m, ICAP £14m, Royal Bank of Scotland £87.5m, Lloyds £105m, Barclays £59.5m, Deutsche £227m.[311]

The LIBOR scandal affected the UK and US in particular but a full review will have to wait until the various trials are completed.[312] However, a key issue was not just the ability of the regulator to levy financial penalties but an examination of whether there had been breaches of the criminal law.[313]

The outcome of the SFO review[314] was that it was 'formally accepted on 6 July 2012, and involves an investigation into allegations of attempts by traders and submitters at a number of banks and other financial institutions to manipulate the rate at which LIBOR was set',[315] since when it has charged 13 people with conspiracy to defraud and obtained five convictions.[316] The issue of the relationship between the FSA and SFO was highlighted by the House of Commons Treasury Select Committee, which recommended a 'formal and comprehensive framework'.[317]

The suggestion of a framework between the SFO and FSA (now FCA) emphasises the need for cooperation between two agencies operating under the separate agency model, instead of reaping the benefit of matters being dealt with by one agency.

310 Callaghan and Ullah (n 309) 160. Financial Services Authority, 'Barclays fined £59.5 million for significant failings in relation to LIBOR and EURIBOR' (n 296). Financial Services Authority, 'UBS fined £160 million for significant failings in relation to LIBOR and EURIBOR' http://webarchive.nationalarchives.gov.uk/20130301170532/http://www.fsa.gov.uk/library/communication/pr/2012/116.shtml Accessed 18 October 2016; Financial Services Authority, 'FSA Final Notice 2013: The Royal Bank of Scotland plc' www.fca.org.uk/your-fca/documents/final-notices/2013/fsa-final-notice-2013-the-royal-bank-of-scotland-plc Accessed 18 October 2016; Financial Conduct Authority, 'ICAP Europe Limited fined £14 million for significant failings in relation to LIBOR' www.fca.org.uk/news/icap-europe-limited-fined Accessed 24 November 2016; Financial Conduct Authority, 'The FCA fines Rabobank £105 million for serious LIBOR-related misconduct' www.fca.org.uk/news/the-fca-fines-rabobank-105-million-for-serious-libor-related-misconduct Accessed 24 November 2016.

311 Financial Conduct Authority, '2013 Fines' www.fca.org.uk/news/news-stories/2013-fines; Financial Conduct Authority, '2014 Fines' www.fca.org.uk/news/news-stories/2014-fines; Financial Conduct Authority, '2015 Fines' www.fca.org.uk/news/news-stories/2015-fines Accessed 18 October 2016.

312 For initial analysis, see: Rob Stokes, 'LIBOR Manipulation: The Limits and Potential of Corporate Criminal Liability' in N Ryder, U Turksen and S Hassler (eds), *Fighting Financial Crime in the Global Economic Crisis: Policy, Trends and Sanctions* (Routledge Cavendish 2014) 5.

313 George Osborne MP, HC Deb 2 July 2012, col 612.

314 Serious Fraud Office, 'LIBOR: SFO to investigate' www.sfo.gov.uk/2012/07/06/libor-sfo-to-investigate/accessed Accessed 25 February 2014.

315 Serious Fraud Office, 'Annual Report and Accounts 2012–13' 30 www.sfo.gov.uk/media/256255/30597%20hc%209.pdf Accessed 24 November 2016.

316 Serious Fraud Office, 'LIBOR' (n 314).

317 House of Commons Treasury Committee, 'Fixing LIBOR: Some preliminary findings Second Report of Session 2012–13 Volume I' www.publications.parliament.uk/pa/cm201213/cmselect/cmtreasy/481/481.pdf Accessed 24 November 2016.

A key challenge for the SFO is management of its financial resources, which have recently diminished.[318] Because of financial constraints, the SFO has to rely upon 'blockbuster' funding.[319]

In January 2014, the government announced further resources of £19m,[320] but would not specify the resource allocation.[321] However, the press reported that this was needed for the SFO's inquiry into LIBOR, 'Barclays fundraising from Qatar, a Rolls Royce investigation and to meet costs linked to a £300m damages suit launched by (…) the Tchenguiz brothers'.[322] The latter was settled by the SFO paying damages and costs in 2014.[323] Unhappily for the SFO, the House of Commons Justice Committee has published more information,[324] prompting the headline 'Fraud Office gets £19m bailout after misleading taxman'[325] because 'it wrongly reclaimed

318 House of Commons Justice Committee, 'Serious Fraud Office supplementary estimate 2013–14' 3 www.publications.parliament.uk/pa/cm201314/cmselect/cmjust/1005/1005.pdf Accessed 24 November 2016. Reuters, 'UK fraud prosecutor seeks extra 19 million pounds for Libor, other cases' 30 January 2014 http://uk.reuters.com/article/2014/01/30/uk-sfo-budget-idUKBREA0T14O20140130 Accessed 4 November 2016. 'The Serious Fraud Office investigates the most serious and complex cases of fraud, bribery and corruption. The quantity of such work is unpredictable. The SFO has a core budget which is supplemented as necessary by additional funding agreed with the Treasury. This includes "blockbuster" funding, which enables us to take on very big cases where the annual expenditure is expected to exceed an agreed percentage of our core budget. The current "blockbuster" funding arrangement was agreed in October 2012.' The SFO core budget showed actual reductions from £53.2m in 2008/09, to £29.6m in 2013/14. The core budget for 2016/17 is £35.7m. In 2013/14, additional blockbuster funding of £24m was made available, with £24.5m in 2014/15 and £28m in 2015/16. Serious Fraud Office, 'About us' www.sfo.gov.uk/about-us/ Accessed 6 December 2016.

319 Serious Fraud Office, 'Annual Report and Accounts 2012–13' (n 315) 4.

320 Oliver Heald MP, HC Deb 30 January 2014, vol 574 col 39W.

321 Oliver Heald MP, HC Deb 4 February 2014, vol 575 col 147W.

322 Reuters, 'UK fraud prosecutor seeks extra 19 million pounds for Libor, other cases' (n 318).

323 *Financial Times*, 'The SFO has so far spent £8.1m defending the £300m claim by the Tchenguiz brothers, due to go to trial in October, the High Court heard' 8 April 2014 (n 247). 'The SFO has now agreed to pay Mr Tchenguiz and his business entities the total sum of £3 million plus their reasonable costs in full and final settlement of their civil claims.' Serious Fraud Office, 'The Serious Fraud Office and Vincent Tchenguiz announce settlement of civil claims' www.sfo.gov.uk/press-room/latest-press-releases/press-releases-2014/the-serious-fraud-office-and-vincent-tchenguiz-announce-settlement-of-civil-claims.aspx. 'The SFO has now agreed to pay Mr Robert Tchenguiz, R20 and the Trustee the total sum of £1.5 million in full and final settlement, with costs to be determined by the Court if they cannot be agreed.' Serious Fraud Office, 'The Serious Fraud Office and Robert Tchenguiz announce settlement of civil claims' www.sfo.gov.uk/press-room/latest-press-releases/press-releases-2014/the-serious-fraud-office-and-robert-tchenguiz-announce-settlement-of-civil-claims.aspx Accessed 18 October 2016.

324 House of Commons Justice Committee, 'Serious Fraud Office Supplementary Estimate 2013–14' (n 318) 4.

325 *The Times*, 'Fraud Office gets £19m bailout' (n 251).

VAT between 2009 and 2012 on fees paid to counsel'.[326] These issues are laid at the door of the previous director.[327] With the Solicitor General having described the LIBOR scandal as 'the most high profile current issue in the UK',[328] the shadow Attorney General remarked that 'it was entirely predictable that the scale and pace of budget cuts inflicted on the SFO would make it impossible for the agency to prosecute its workload'.[329] In recognition of this, *The Times* reported that the 'Justice Committee is now to ask (…) if "the current funding arrangements of the SFO are sustainable"'.[330]

The perception of the SFO's workload presents a further difficulty because it does not provide a running commentary on its work, merely providing some occasional comment, such as: 'the biggest is Libor. This investigation employs a team of 60. Charges have been laid against [13] individuals so far. There will be further significant developments in due course.'[331] Such statements are then augmented by further announcements of additional persons charged.[332] The effect of this is that the SFO's director has no opportunity to advance his case, where Reuters report that 'he has staked his reputation on the success of high-profile investigations such as the sprawling global investigation into Libor manipulation'.[333] This then allows a vacuum to be filled by politicians, such as the shadow Attorney General observing:

> this is not a government that takes economic crime seriously, which is why it is allowing the SFO to stagger from crisis to crisis and providing temporary sticking plasters [blockbuster funding] where what is needed is a long-term plan to put it on a sustainable footing.[334]

In 2015, the SFO achieved a landmark conviction in its prosecution of LIBOR cases: Tom Hayes was convicted of conspiracy to defraud and sentenced to 14 years' imprisonment, later reduced to 11 years.[335] However, while the conviction of Hayes represented a high point, the acquittal of six defendants accused of conspiring with him in the Yen LIBOR-setting process was a setback.[336]

326 *The Times*, 'Fraud Office gets £19m bailout' (n 251).
327 House of Commons Justice Committee, 'Serious Fraud Office Supplementary Estimate 2013–14' (n 318) 9.
328 Attorney General's Office, 'Fighting economic crime in the modern world' (n 291).
329 Reuters, 'UK fraud prosecutor seeks extra 19 million pounds for Libor, other cases' (n 318).
330 *The Times*, 'Fraud Office gets £19m bailout' (n 251).
331 Green, Cambridge 2014 (n 98).
332 Green, Cambridge 2014 (n 98).
333 Reuters, 'UK fraud prosecutor seeks extra 19 million pounds for Libor, other cases' (n 318).
334 Reuters, 'UK fraud prosecutor seeks extra 19 million pounds for Libor, other cases' (n 318).
335 Hayes was also ordered to pay a confiscation order of £878,806 at Southwark Crown Court. Serious Fraud Office, 'LIBOR (Yen) Hayes' www.sfo.gov.uk/cases/libor-hayes/ Accessed 23 August 2016.
336 Serious Fraud Office, 'LIBOR (Yen) Interdealer brokers' www.sfo.gov.uk/cases/libor-interdealer-brokers/ Accessed 23 August 2016.

In the third series of cases, four former Barclays Bank employees were convicted of conspiracy to defraud in connection with manipulation of the US dollar LIBOR and were sentenced to imprisonment for much shorter periods than Hayes of between two years and nine months, and six years and six months.[337] The jury could not reach verdicts regarding two further defendants and there was to be a retrial in 2017.[338]

In the meantime, parallel civil proceedings were instituted in *Graiseley Properties Limited v Barclays Bank Plc.*[339] In these cases, 'the Court of Appeal ruled (…) that two businesses bringing separate cases against Barclays and Deutsche Bank could include allegations about manipulation of the Libor lending benchmark in their cases'.[340] However, Barclays settled the case before trial,[341] which had the effect of keeping documentary and witness evidence private. This might have shed light on the commercial issues giving rise to allegations of manipulation, which would have been a helpful insight in parallel with the SFO cases.

In a recent development, the courts considered 'spoofing', a term commonly used to describe the practice of placing and then cancelling orders on a trading exchange for the purpose of manipulating the market. In extradition proceedings brought by the US against Navinder Sarao, where there is a 'spoofing' offence in the US but not the UK, the court held that 'spoofing' would be an offence under the Fraud Act and the Financial Services and Markets Act 2000 (FSMA).[342]

Financial Conduct Authority

The UK's main means of financial regulation lies with specific agencies, which report to sponsoring government departments, where '[t]he FCA was created in

337 Serious Fraud Office, 'LIBOR US Dollar (Barclays)' www.sfo.gov.uk/cases/libor-barclays/ Accessed 23 August 2016.

338 Serious Fraud Office, 'LIBOR US Dollar (Barclays)' (n 337).

339 *Graiseley Properties Limited v Barclays Bank Plc* [2013] EWCA Civ 1372.

340 'The precedent could be damaging for banks because some, including Royal Bank of Scotland and Barclays, have already admitted they manipulated Libor and others are set to follow with their own settlements. Businesses fighting for redress over mis-sold interest rate swaps want to use these admissions of guilt to argue that since Libor was fundamentally flawed, their swaps products should automatically be judged to be faulty. In most cases the price of swaps was linked to Libor. Barclays, which paid £290 million to settle Libor allegations last summer, and Deutsche, which is set to settle in the New Year, have fought two early attempts to link swaps mis-selling to Libor. One case was brought by Guardian Care Homes against Barclays, the other was from Unitech, an Indian property company, against Deutsche.' *The Times*, 'Banks lose bid to dismiss Libor claims' 9 November 2013 www.thetimes.co.uk/tto/business/industries/banking/article3916826.ece Accessed 18 October 2016.

341 *The Times*, 'Settlement keeps Diamond and Ricci out of court' 8 April 2014 www.thetimes.co.uk/tto/business/industries/banking/article4057124.ece Accessed 18 October 2016.

342 Fraud Act 2006 s 2, Financial Services and Markets Act 2000 s 397, Financial Services Act 2012 s 90. *The Government of the United States of America v Navinder Singh Sarao*, Westminster Magistrates Court, 3 November 2016.

2013 in the heat of the conduct crisis. It is a dedicated conduct regulator, part of the twin peaks approach adopted by the UK'.[343]

The FCA embraces a wide-ranging brief encompassing 'consumer protection, competition and market integrity',[344] whereas the SFO's role is in relation to serious fraud and bribery.[345] Both agencies have available to them specific legislation for use in countering economic crime behaviour.

The FCA, formerly the FSA, had a wide range of responsibilities of which economic crime was merely a part. The financial crisis cast light on the performance of the FSA, where the then coalition government considered that it had failed in meeting its objectives. The outcome was the disbanding of the FSA and, notwithstanding the government's initial proposals to create an Economic Crime Agency (ECA), created the new FCA,[346] as 'a dedicated and focused conduct of business regulator'.[347] The government explained that 'effective conduct regulation is vital to securing better outcomes for all consumers and restoring trust in the financial system'.[348]

The coalition government announced the abolition of the 'tripartite' regulatory system. The FCA[349] succeeded the FSA[350] with a role to take 'responsibility for conduct of business (…) with the mandate and tools to be a proactive force for enabling the right outcomes for consumers and market participants, including through the promotion of competition'.[351] The FCA has a limited remit when compared to the FSA, which 'until the financial crisis enjoyed jurisdiction over "virtually everything financial in the UK"'.[352] The challenge for the FCA is to demonstrate that it is not merely a *rebranded* FSA.[353]

343 Financial Conduct Authority, 'Our future mission' 2 www.fca.org.uk/publication/corporate/our-future-mission.pdf Accessed 27 October 2016. For an explanation of twin peaks see Chapter 5.

344 HM Treasury, 'A new approach to financial regulation' (n 3).

345 'We are investigators and prosecutors of the topmost tier of serious and complex fraud, bribery and corruption. We are not a regulator, a deal-maker or a confessor.' Green, Cambridge 2013 (n 242).

346 The FSA responsibilities being split into three: Financial Policy Committee, Prudential Regulatory Authority and Financial Conduct Authority. Financial Services Bill 2012 www.parliament.uk/briefing-papers/RP12-8 Accessed 18 October 2016.

347 HM Treasury, 'A new approach to financial regulation: transferring consumer credit regulation to the Financial Conduct Authority' www.gov.uk/government/uploads/system/uploads/attachment_data/file/221913/consult_transferring_consumer_credit_regulation_to_fca.pdf Accessed 18 October 2016.

348 HM Treasury, 'A new approach to financial regulation: transferring consumer credit regulation' (n 347).

349 *The Telegraph*, 'W, for FSA?' 17 March 2011 www.telegraph.co.uk/finance/newsbysector/banksandfinance/8386709/What-next-for-the-FSA.html Accessed 18 October 2016.

350 HM Treasury, 'A new approach to financial regulation' (n 3) 3.

351 HM Treasury, 'A new approach to financial regulation' (n 3) 3.

352 Gary Wilson and Sarah Wilson, 'The FSA "credible deterrence", and criminal enforcement – a "haphazard pursuit"?' (2014) JFC 4, 5 (footnotes omitted).

353 N Ryder, *The Financial Crisis and White Collar Crime – The Perfect Storem* (Edward Elgar 2014) 18. Wilson and Wilson (n 352) 4, 5.

The change is interesting because the FSA had four equal objectives, one being 'the reduction of financial crime',[354] while the FCA has 'a single overarching strategic objective to ensure that markets function well'.[355] This is supported by three operational objectives: consumer protection; integrity; and competition.[356] The integrity objective means 'protecting and enhancing the integrity of the UK financial system',[357] and includes 'not being used for a purpose connected with financial crime'.[358] Furthermore, the 'integrity' of the UK financial system includes: its soundness, stability and resilience;[359] its not being affected by behaviour that amounts to market abuse;[360] the orderly operation of the financial markets;[361] and the transparency of the price formation process in those markets.[362] The government's intention in creating the FCA was 'delivering a regulatory regime under which the conduct of business of *all* retail financial services is regulated by a single body'.[363] The scale of those responsibilities is regulating over 56,000 firms and 130,000 approved persons.[364]

The FCA is responsible for dealing with financial crime within the regulatory framework, including the MLR2007,[365] the Market Abuse Regime[366] and maintenance of links with the police, SFO and NCA.[367] Furthermore, the FCA operates FIN-NET,[368] the cross-European fraud and financial crime network.

354 Financial Services and Markets Act 2000, s 6.
355 HM Treasury, 'A new approach to financial regulation: transferring consumer credit regulation' (n 347).
356 Financial Services Act 2012, s 1B(3).
357 Financial Services Act 2012, s 1D(1).
358 Financial Services Act 2012, s 1D(2)(b).
359 Financial Services Act 2012, s 1D(2)(a).
360 Financial Services Act 2012, s 1D(2)(c).
361 Financial Services Act 2012, s 1D(2)(d).
362 Financial Services Act 2012, s 1D(2)(e).
363 HM Treasury, 'A new approach to financial regulation: transferring consumer credit regulation' (n 347).
364 Financial Conduct Authority, 'Our future mission' (n 343).
365 The Money Laundering Regulations 2007 SI 2007/2157. FSA, *Handbook SYSC* 6.3 http://fsahandbook.info/FSA/html/handbook/SYSC/6/3 Accessed 18 October 2016.
366 'Certain types of behaviour, such as insider dealing and market manipulation, can amount to market abuse. Types of conduct constituting market abuse are set out in section 118 of the Financial Services and Markets Act 2000 and in the Market Abuse Directive.' Financial Conduct Authority, 'Market Abuse' www.fca.org.uk/firms/markets/market-abuse Accessed 18 October 2016.
367 The Home Secretary announced that it 'will close by 31 March 2014', Rt Hon Theresa May MP, Home Secretary. 'Written Statement to the House of Commons' 2 December 2013 www.gov.uk/government/speeches/national-fraud-authority Accessed 18 October 2016.
368 'FIN-NET is a financial dispute resolution network of national out-of-court complaint schemes in the European Economic Area countries (the European Union Member States plus Iceland, Liechtenstein and Norway) that are responsible for handling disputes between consumers and financial services providers, i.e. banks, insurance companies, investment firms and others. This network was launched by the European

The FCA stated that they would build 'on the FSA's direction [and] would involve retaining "our policy of credible deterrence, pursuing enforcement cases to punish wrongdoing"'.[369] Although Wilson and Wilson note that this is not defined, 'but can be discerned contextually from (…) key FSA publications',[370] the FSA state that it is 'robustly deploying our civil and criminal prosecution powers'.[371] The FCA state that they are 'more committed than ever to showing firms and individuals that they must play by the rules; because if they don't, robust sanctions are a matter of course'.[372]

The FCA Business Plan[373] states that their 'enforcement powers[374] enable them to deter firms and individuals from wrongdoing by making it clear that there are real and meaningful consequences for poor practice'.[375] The FCA's 'credible deterrence' approach enables them to 'take effective, targeted action across the range of our regulatory responsibilities in support of our objectives'.[376] The FCA highlight that they 'have already delivered significant outcomes following intensive work on the attempted manipulation of LIBOR benchmark rate'.[377] This is a surprising claim since this is an area that the FCA did not wish to enforce and which was subject to criticism from the Parliamentary Commission on Banking Standards.[378] Notwithstanding this, in 2014, the FCA published warning notices to two individuals, relating to LIBOR manipulation, stating that it proposed to take unspecified action at some unspecified time.[379] In April 2016, Paul White, an

Commission in 2001.' European Commission, 'Welcome to FIN-NET' http://ec.europa.eu/internal_market/fin-net/index_en.htm Accessed 18 October 2016.

369 Wilson and Wilson (n 352) 4.

370 Wilson and Wilson (n 352) 4, 6.

371 Financial Services Authority, 'FSA Business Plan 2012/13' 6 www.fsa.gov.uk/static/pubs/plan/bp2012-13.pdf Accessed 18 October 2016.

372 Financial Conduct Authority, 'Financial services regulation and enforcement: recent developments and emerging issues' 9 October 2013 www.fca.org.uk/news/speeches/financial-services-regulation-enforcement Accessed 18 October 2016.

373 Financial Conduct Authority, 'Business Plan 2014/15' 13 www.fca.org.uk/news/about-us/business-plan-2014-15 Accessed 18 October 2016.

374 'We use a wide range of Enforcement powers – criminal, civil and regulatory – to protect consumers and to take action against firms or individuals that do not meet our standards. We can take action such as: withdrawing a firm's authorisation; prohibiting individuals from carrying on regulated activities; suspending firms or individuals from undertaking regulated activities; fining firms or individuals who breach our rules or commit market abuse; applying to the Court for injunctions and restitution orders; and bringing criminal prosecutions to tackle financial crime, such as insider dealing or unauthorised business.' Financial Conduct Authority, 'Enforcement' www.fca.org.uk/about/enforcement Accessed 24 November 2016.

375 Financial Conduct Authority, 'Business Plan 2014/15' (n 373) 13.

376 Financial Conduct Authority, 'Business Plan 2014/15' (n 373) 13.

377 Financial Conduct Authority, 'Business Plan 2014/15' (n 373) 13.

378 House of Commons Treasury Committee, 'Fixing LIBOR' (n 317).

379 Financial Conduct Authority, 'Warning Notice 14/1' www.fca.org.uk/static/documents/warning-notice-statements/warning-notice-statement-14-1individual.pdf Accessed 5 March 2017. No action appears to have been taken on Notice 14/1. 'The FCA appears to have issued the warning notices to ensure that it does not fall foul of a three-year limit

RBS LIBOR submitter, was prohibited 'from performing any function in relation to any regulated activity carried on by any authorised or exempt person, or exempt professional firm'. Because of White's serious financial hardship, the FCA did not impose a £250,000 financial penalty.[380] The FCA had earlier banned three other people because they had been convicted of LIBOR offences in the US.[381]

In pursuit of the FCA's credible deterrence approach, they 'have the power to impose fines, withdraw or cancel authorisation, stop firms or individuals from carrying out regulated activities, apply for injunctions and restitution orders, and prosecute certain financial crimes'.[382] Cartwright[383] suggests that the deployment of these powers is to make people 'sit up and take notice',[384] and that it has a clear preference for 'the imposition of a financial penalty as central to its policy of credible deterrence'.[385] In 2014 alone, the FCA fined five banks a total of £1.1bn for foreign exchange failings.[386]

Wilson and Wilson observe that 'no jurisdiction has had a great deal of success in utilising the criminal law in combating sophisticated abuse activity on its capital

on taking action while the Serious Fraud Office pursues individuals in the criminal court.' *The Times*, 'FCA to punish bankers involved in Libor scandal' 4 February 2014 www.thetimes.co.uk/tto/business/industries/banking/article3994517.ece Accessed 24 November 2016.

380 In the second case, Arif Hussein has appealed the decision. Financial Conduct Authority, 'Final Notice' www.fca.org.uk/publication/final-notices/paul-white.pdf; Financial Conduct Authority, 'FCA publishes Decision Notice for former UBS LIBOR trader' www.fca.org.uk/news/press-releases/fca-publishes-decision-notice-former-ubs-libor-trader Accessed 18 October 2016.

381 Financial Conduct Authority, 'FCA bans former Deutsche Bank trader, Michael Ross Curtler, following LIBOR fraud' www.fca.org.uk/news/press-releases/fca-bans-former-deutsche-bank-trader-michael-ross-curtler-following-libor-fraud Accessed 18 October 2016.

382 Financial Conduct Authority, 'Business Plan 2014/15' (n 373) 13.

383 Peter Cartwright, 'Credible Deterrence and Consumer Protection through Imposition of Financial Penalties: Lessons for the Financial Conduct Authority' in N Ryder, U Turksen and S Hassler (eds), *Fighting Financial Crime in the Global Economic Crisis: Policy, Trends and Sanctions* (Routledge Cavendish 2014) 5.

384 Cartwright (n 383) 5 (footnote omitted).

385 Cartwright (n 383) 5. The FCA also has power under Financial Services and Markets Act 2000, s 56 to impose prohibition orders, and made 43 in 2012–13. Financial Services Authority, 'Enforcement Annual Performance Account. 2012/13' http://fca.org.uk/static/documents/annual-report/fsa-enforcement-performance-account-2012-13.pdf Accessed 18 October 2016.

386 'The Financial Conduct Authority (FCA) has imposed fines totalling £1,114,918,000 on five banks for failing to control business practices in their G10 spot foreign exchange (FX) trading operations: Citibank £225,575,000, HSBC Bank £216,363,000, JPMorgan Chase Bank £222,166,000, The Royal Bank of Scotland Plc £217,000,000 and UBS AG £233,814,000.' Financial Conduct Authority, 'FCA fines five banks £1.1 billion for FX failings and announces industry-wide remediation programme' www.fca.org.uk/news/press-releases/fca-fines-five-banks-£11-billion-fx-failings-and-announces-industry-wide Accessed 16 September 2016. Financial Conduct Authority, 'Handbook: Decision Procedures and Penalties Manual' DEPP 6.1.2 www.fshandbook.info/FS/html/FCA/DEPP/6/1 Accessed 18 October 2016.

markets',[387] and that the response to market misconduct was 'moving away from criminal enforcement, on account of this being perceived as costly and ineffectual'.[388] Thus, the 'effectiveness of the policy within the UK can be seen in the FSA's enthusiasm for non-criminal enforcement of market abuse'.[389] Such enthusiasm for financial penalties as a demonstration of the credible deterrence is examined by Cartwright, who rightly points to the unlikelihood of firms undertaking a cost-benefit analysis regarding the adherence to FCA requirements as a conscious decision, but rather that 'many breaches of FSMA occur where firms lack adequate controls, supervision and organisation rather than where they display wilful misconduct'.[390]

The practical implementation of the credible deterrence pre-dates the FCA, where the FSA had been criticised for its performance and 'light-touch' approach and an 'overly close relationship with the City'.[391] However, Tomasic suggests that this was because 'political pressure may also be facilitated by governments which have been competing with each other to create business-friendly financial centres such as London and New York'.[392] This attitude allowed the view to pervade of insider dealing as 'a naughty perk of the job'.[393] However, 'the number of insider trading cases brought by the FCA has risen sharply in the past few years [and] secured 31 convictions since 2009'.[394] In parallel, the increase in the number of fines by the regulator[395] appears to show that their strategy to

387 Wilson and Wilson (n 352) 4, 7.
388 Wilson and Wilson (n 352) 4, 7.
389 Wilson and Wilson (n 352) 4, 7.
390 Cartwright (n 383) 6.
391 Tomasic (n 223) 7, 8.
392 Tomasic (n 223) 7, 8.
393 Jason Mansell, 'Financial Services Authority: can it be saved after the election?' *The Times* 26 March 2010 www.thetimes.co.uk/tto/law/article2467878.ece Accessed 12 August 2016.
394 *Practical Law*, 'Insider dealing: FCA criminal prosecutions tracker' http://uk.practicallaw.com.ezproxy.uwe.ac.uk/5-502-2966?q=insider+dealing#a598239 Accessed 18 October 2016.
395 Financial Services Authority, 'Fines Table' 2002 £7.4m http://webarchive.nationalarchives.gov.uk/20130301170532/http://www.fsa.gov.uk/about/press/facts/fines/2002; 2003 £11.0m http://webarchive.nationalarchives.gov.uk/20130301170532/http://www.fsa.gov.uk/about/press/facts/fines/2003; 2004 £24.8m http://webarchive.nationalarchives.gov.uk/20130301170532/http://www.fsa.gov.uk/about/press/facts/fines/2003; 2005 £17.0m http://webarchive.nationalarchives.gov.uk/20130301170532/http://www.fsa.gov.uk/about/press/facts/fines/2003; 2006 £13.3m http://webarchive.nationalarchives.gov.uk/20130301170532/http://www.fsa.gov.uk/about/press/facts/fines/2003; 2007 £5.3m http://webarchive.nationalarchives.gov.uk/20130301170532/http://www.fsa.gov.uk/about/press/facts/fines/2003; 2008 22.7m http://webarchive.nationalarchives.gov.uk/20130301170532/http://www.fsa.gov.uk/about/press/facts/fines/2008; 2009 £35.0m http://webarchive.nationalarchives.gov.uk/20130301170532/http://www.fsa.gov.uk/about/press/facts/fines/2009; 2010 £89.1m http://webarchive.nationalarchives.gov.uk/20130301170532/http://www.fsa.gov.uk/about/press/facts/fines/2010; 2011 £66.1m http://webarchive.nationalarchives.gov.uk/20130301170532/http://www.

prosecute a steady stream of cases to demonstrate that they 'mean business' is bearing fruit.[396] The total fines were at modest levels until 2010, when they increased from £89.1m to £311.6m in 2012, £474m in 2013, £1.471bn in 2014, £905m in 2015 and down to a much reduced £22m in 2016.[397]

The regulator has successfully prosecuted and imposed record financial penalties for insider dealing offences and breaches of the Market Abuse Regime.[398] Examples include McQuoid and Melbourne,[399] Uberois,[400] Calvert,[401] Ahmad,[402] Rollins[403] and Littlewoods.[404] In 2016, two defendants in Operation Tabernula were convicted in the first FCA/NCA case, with investigation dating back to

fsa.gov.uk/about/press/facts/fines/2010; 2012 £311.6m http://webarchive.nationalarchives.gov.uk/20130301170532/http://www.fsa.gov.uk/about/press/facts/fines/2010; 2013 £1.9m www.fca.org.uk/news/news-stories/2013-fines2013; 2014 www.fca.org.uk/news/news-stories/2014-fines; www.fca.org.uk/news/news-stories/2015-fines; 2015 www.fca.org.uk/news/news-stories/2016-fines Accessed 20 March 2017.

396 Jason D Haines, 'FSA determined to improve cleanliness of markets: custodial sentences continue to be a real threat' (2008) 29(12) Comp Law 370.

397 Financial Services Authority, Fines (n 395).

398 'The FCA, and previously the Financial Services Authority, have secured 28 convictions in relation to insider dealing: Christopher McQuoid and James William Melbourne in March 2009; Matthew and Neel Uberoi in November 2009, Malcolm Calvert on 11 March 2010, Anjam Ahmad on 22 June 2010, Neil Rollins on 21 January 2011, Christian Littlewood and Angie Littlewood on 8 October 2010 and Helmy Omar Sa'aid on 10 January 2011, Rupinder Sidhu on 15 December, and James and Miranda Sanders together with James Swallow in May 2012 and Ali Mustafa, Pardip Saini, Paresh Shah, Neten Shah, Bijal Shah and Truptesh Patel on 27 July 2012, Thomas Ammann on 13 December 2012, Paul Milsom on 7 March 2013, Richard Joseph on 11 March 2013 and Graeme Shelley on 27 March 2014, Julian Rifat on 7 November 2014, Ryan Willmott on the 26 February 2015, Paul Coyle on 3 March 2015 and Damien Clarke on 15 March 2016.' Financial Conduct Authority, 'Insider dealers sentenced in Operation Tabernula trial' www.fca.org.uk/news/press-releases/insider-dealers-sentenced-operation-tabernula-trial Accessed 18 October 2016.

399 Financial Services Authority, 'Solicitor and his father-in-law found guilty in FSA insider dealing case' www.fsa.gov.uk/library/communication/pr/2009/042.shtml Accessed 18 October 2016.

400 Financial Services Authority, 'Former corporate broker intern and father found guilty of insider dealing' www.fsa.gov.uk/library/communication/pr/2009/149.shtml Accessed 18 October 2016.

401 Financial Services Authority, 'Former Cazenove broker sentenced to 21 months in prison for insider dealing' 11 March 2010 www.fsa.gov.uk/library/communication/pr/2010/043.shtml Accessed 19 February 2014.

402 Financial Services Authority, 'Ex-hedge fund trader sentenced for insider dealing' www.fsa.gov.uk/library/communication/pr/2010/104.shtml Accessed 19 February 2014.

403 Financial Services Authority, 'Insider Dealing: Financial Services Authority prosecutes Mr Neil Rollins' www.fsa.gov.uk/library/communication/pr/2009/002.shtml Accessed 18 October 2016.

404 Financial Services Authority, 'Investment banker, his wife and family friend plead guilty to insider dealing' www.fsa.gov.uk/library/communication/pr/2011/002.shtml Accessed 18 October 2016.

2007.[405] The increase in the enforcement activities demonstrates its tougher approach towards insider dealing.

The main engine for the increase in fines is the LIBOR scandal,[406] where Barclays was fined £59.5m.[407] This was followed by UBS £160m,[408] RBS £87.5m,[409] ICAP £14m[410] and Rabobank £105m.[411] These fines amount to £426m but, as a change from the previous regime, the FCA 'must pay to the Exchequer all financial penalties we receive, less the enforcement costs that we incurred in generating these penalties'.[412] Additionally, the FCA say that 'investigations against others [firms] continue',[413] and they have levied their largest (non-LIBOR or foreign exchange – FX) penalty[414] of £137.6m on JPMorgan Chase Bank for misconduct in an activity known as the 'London Whale' trades.[415]

This is an example of the application of the credible deterrence strategy and, tellingly, 'this was not some dim and distant pre-[financial] crisis past when people believed they had conquered the risk. This was in 2011 and 2012'.[416] Furthermore, the FCA stated that 'we engaged with the firm, being very clear about the candour that we expected and the risks we were concerned about, J P Morgan failed to be open and co-operative, even on one occasion deliberately misleading us'.[417] Even though JP Morgan lost $6.2bn,[418] there is no reference to criminal charges against individuals in the UK. However, it has been reported that the DoJ

405 *Practical Law*, 'Insider dealing: FCA criminal prosecutions tracker' (n 394).
406 Attorney General's Office, 'Fighting economic crime in the modern world' (n 291).
407 Financial Services Authority, 'Barclays fined £59.5 million for significant failings in relation to LIBOR and EURIBOR' (n 296). Barclays also paid $160m to the DoJ. Department of Justice, 'Barclays Bank PLC admits misconduct related to submissions for the London Interbank Offered Rate and the Euro Interbank Offered Rate and agrees to pay $160 million penalty' www.justice.gov/opa/pr/2012/June/12-crm-815.html Accessed 24 November 2016.
408 Financial Services Authority, 'UBS fined £160 million for significant failings in relation to LIBOR and EURIBOR' (n 310).
409 Financial Services Authority, 'FSA Final Notice 2013: The Royal Bank of Scotland' (n 310).
410 Financial Conduct Authority, 'ICAP' (n 310).
411 Financial Conduct Authority, 'Rabobank' (n 310).
412 Financial Conduct Authority, 'Business Plan 2014/15' (n 373) 41.
413 Financial Conduct Authority, 'Financial services regulation and enforcement' (n 372).
414 Financial Conduct Authority, 'Financial services regulation and enforcement' (n 372).
415 'The Financial Conduct Authority (FCA) has fined JPMorgan Chase Bank N.A. ("JPMorgan") £137,610,000 ($220 million) for serious failings related to its Chief Investment Office (CIO). JPMorgan's conduct demonstrated flaws permeating all levels of the firm: from portfolio level right up to senior management, resulting in breaches of Principles 2, 3, 5 and 11 of the FCA's Principles for Businesses – the fundamental obligations firms have under the regulatory system.' Financial Conduct Authority, 'JPMorgan Chase Bank N.A. fined £137,610,000 for serious failings relating to its Chief Investment Office's "London Whale" trades' www.fca.org.uk/news/jpmorgan-chase-bank-na-fined Accessed 18 October 2016. See also Chapter 5.
416 Financial Conduct Authority, 'Financial services regulation and enforcement' (n 372).
417 Financial Conduct Authority, 'Financial services regulation and enforcement' (n 372).
418 Financial Conduct Authority, 'JPMorgan Chase Bank' (n 415).

have charged two people with 'conspiracy, falsifying books and records, wire fraud, and causing false statements to be made to the Securities and Exchange Commission (SEC)'.[419] The FSMA 2000 gives the FCA authority to set and enforce regulations, which includes levying significant financial penalties, but the lack of criminal charges in the UK against any individual involved casts doubt on the credible deterrence influencing individuals. Indeed, as Judge Rakoff stated,[420] 'the failure of the government to bring to justice those responsible for such colossal fraud bespeaks weaknesses in our prosecutorial system that need to be addressed'.[421]

The FCA could have considered action against Mark Stevenson, who engaged in market abuse[422] 'for deliberately manipulating a government bond to make money out of the Bank of England's quantitative easing programme'.[423] The FCA said that it regarded this as a *particularly serious* example of market abuse, which sought to profit unreasonably from quantitative easing at the expense of the Bank of England and ultimately the taxpayer.[424] The financial penalty imposed by the FCA was £662,700,[425] although noting that his remuneration for the year in question was £2.367m,[426] and a ban[427] from working in the

419 'Javier Martin-Artajo (…) and Julien Grout, a junior trader, were indicted in the US in 2013 but the Spanish and French authorities have refused to allow extradition. Both deny wrongdoing.' The cases are *SEC v Martin-Artajo*, 13-cv-05677, and *US v Martin-Artajo*, 13-cr-00707, US District Court, Southern District of New York (Manhattan). *The Telegraph*, 'JP Morgan's "London Whale" trader breaks his silence' 23 February 2016 www.telegraph.co.uk/business/2016/02/23/jp-morgans-london-whale-trader-breaks-his-silence/. Reuters, 'U.S. charges two ex-JPMorgan bankers over "London Whale" loss' 14 August 2013 http://uk.reuters.com/article/2013/08/14/us-jpm-whale-charges-idUSBRE97D0QU20130814 Accessed 18 October 2016.

420 US District Court, 'Hon. Jed S Rakoff', www.nysd.uscourts.gov/judge/Rakoff Accessed 18 October 2016.

421 Rakoff (n 420).

422 Financial Conduct Authority, 'FCA Final Notice 2014: Mark Stevenson' www.fca.org.uk/your-fca/documents/final-notices/2014/mark-stevenson Accessed 18 October 2016.

423 *The Times*, 'Bond trader fined and banned for attempt to manipulate stimulus plan' 21 March 2014 www.thetimes.co.uk/tto/business/industries/banking/article4039438.ece Accessed 18 October 2016.

424 Financial Conduct Authority, 'FCA Final Notice 2014: Mark Stevenson' (n 422) 2 (emphasis added).

425 Financial Conduct Authority, 'FCA Final Notice 2014: Mark Stevenson' (n 422) 1.

426 Financial Conduct Authority, 'FCA Final Notice 2014: Mark Stevenson' (n 422) 22.

427 Financial Services and Markets Act 2000, s 56(1). 'The FCA may make a prohibition order if it appears to it that an individual is not a fit and proper person to perform functions in relation to a regulated activity.' Financial Conduct Authority, 'FCA Final Notice 2014: Mark Stevenson' (n 422). The Authority considers that Mr Stevenson deliberately acted to increase the price of the Bond on 10 October 2011 and considers that this amounted to deliberate market abuse. His behaviour is particularly egregious as it took place on the first day of QE2 and effectively sought to deprive the economy from QE's full effect in order to maximise the potential profit from selling the Bond to the Bank of England in the QE2 reverse auction. The Authority considers that, as a

City.[428] This may, or may not, be an appropriate case for criminal sanctions, but although the FCA describe the case as *particularly serious*, that view is not shared by some commentators.[429]

This comment is instructive because it suggests that there is something special about trading in the financial markets that should justify different treatment from other crimes, and it does not show that the credible deterrence policy either acts as a deterrent or has changed perceptions of integrity in the financial markets. This is at the heart of the debate over white collar crime sentencing.[430]

In 2016, the FCA appointed a new chief executive, who commented: 'It is striking to me at least that financial conduct regulation is not supported by a particularly large body of academic and other thinking.'[431] The reason for this comment is that the FCA are undertaking a review of their mission:

> We have an overriding strategic objective set by Parliament to ensure that relevant markets function well. In addition, we have three operational objectives with which to deliver our strategic objective; to protect consumers, protect the integrity of UK markets and enhance competition.
>
> We need to ensure we are a proportionate and effective regulator as financial services adapt to meet new needs in new ways. This is a good opportunity to define the way in which we make our regulatory choices.[432]

Thus, some three and a half years after the FCA was established, it is now consulting on its role and redefinition of its priorities.

The Competition and Markets Authority

The third agency involved in countering economic crime is the CMA[433] which was established by the Enterprise and Regulatory Reform Act 2013 (ERRA),[434] at

result of this behaviour, Mr Stevenson lacks fitness and propriety in terms of his integrity. 'The Authority therefore makes a prohibition order pursuant to section 56 of the Act prohibiting Mr Stevenson from performing any function in relation to any regulated activity carried on by any authorised or exempt person or exempt professional firm. This order takes effect from 20 March 2014.' Financial Conduct Authority, 'FCA Final Notice 2014: Mark Stevenson' (n 422) 18.

428 *The Times*, 'Bond trader fined and banned for attempt to manipulate stimulus plan' (n 423).

429 *The Times*, 'Ian King: Business Editor's Commentary: Market abusers on every side' 21 March 2014 www.thetimes.co.uk/tto/business/columnists/article4040153.ece Accessed 18 October 2016.

430 For a further discussion on the effectiveness of credible deterrence, see: Gauri Sinha, 'Post-crisis Regulation and Prosecutions in Financial Crime: Progress or Paradox?' in N Ryder and others (eds), *The Financial Crisis and White Collar Crime – Legislative and Policy Responses. A Critical Assessment* (Routledge 2017).

431 Financial Conduct Authority, 'Our future mission' (n 343) 2.

432 Financial Conduct Authority, 'Our future mission' (n 343) 4.

433 Enterprise and Regulatory Reform Act 2013, ss 25–28.

434 Enterprise and Regulatory Reform Act 2013, s 25.

which stage the OFT and Competition Commission were abolished.[435] It is a non-ministerial department of the Department for Business, Energy and Industrial Strategy.[436] The government rationale for merging two 'world class'[437] organisations was provided by the CMA: 'competition is a key driver for delivering greater productivity and growth in the UK economy, particularly in the context of the financial crisis and recession and the challenges that lie ahead in sustaining competitiveness.'[438] The CMA is a 'single competition and consumer authority, bringing together most of the OFT's consumer role and all of its competition work together with the Competition Commission'.[439] The OFT's consumer credit activities were transferred to the FCA.[440]

The OFT's[441] 'mission [was] to make markets work well for consumers'.[442] It aimed to achieve this through the enforcement of competition and consumer protection legislation and monitoring of consumer credit.[443]

The establishment of the OFT predated the creation of the FSA/FCA and SFO, and it played a different role in relation to economic crime because of its wider consumer focus. However, the role of the OFT in relation to markets is an example of overlapping jurisdictions of institutions, where 'most obviously, some financial firms presently answer to two different regulators with different powers

435 Enterprise and Regulatory Reform Act 2013, s 26.

436 Competition and Markets Authority, 'What we do' www.gov.uk/government/organisations/competition-and-markets-authority; Department for Business, Energy and Industrial Strategy, 'Works with 47 agencies and public bodies' www.gov.uk/government/organisations#department-for-business-energy-and-industrial-strategy Accessed 24 August 2016.

437 Competition and Markets Authority, 'Speech Redesigning regulatory architecture – the UK experience', Speech given by CMA Chairman David Currie to the Institute of International and European Affairs, Dublin, 22 January 2014 www.gov.uk/government/speeches/redesigning-regulatory-architecture-the-uk-experience Accessed 20 March 2017. 'This included a review of the (already well-regarded) competition framework': Niamh Dunne, 'Recasting competition concurrency under the Enterprise and Regulatory Reform Act 2013' (2014) 77(2) MLR 254, 263.

438 Competition and Markets Authority, 'Speech Redesigning regulatory architecture' (n 437).

439 Competition and Markets Authority, 'Speech Redesigning regulatory architecture' (n 437).

440 HM Treasury, 'A new approach to financial regulation: transferring consumer credit regulation' (n 347).

441 Established by the Fair Trading Act 1973.

442 Office of Fair Trading, 'What we do' http://webarchive.nationalarchives.gov.uk/20140402142426/http://www.oft.gov.uk/about-the-oft/what/ Accessed 18 October 2016.

443 The Office of Fair Trading, 'Frequently Asked Questions'. 'The enforcement of competition law under the Competition Act 1998; the enforcement of consumer protection legislation in matters that affect consumers in general; monitoring consumer credit through a licensing system under the Consumer Credit Act 1974.' http://webarchive.nationalarchives.gov.uk/20140402142426/http://www.oft.gov.uk/about-the-oft/faqs/ Accessed 18 October 2016.

and approaches'.[444] The overlapping responsibilities led to the OFT prosecuting, for example, property sale frauds by prosecuting estate agents,[445] and people involved in motor trade fraud.[446] Lomnicka pointed to a range of anomalies: a residential mortgage to finance a home purchase being regulated by the FSMA while a second mortgage by the Consumer Credit Act 1974 (CCA); payment protection insurance (PPI) premiums covered by the CCA although the writing and issuing of the policies was by the FSMA.[447]

The OFT also required firms that it supervised to register with them under the MLR2007,[448] such firms being estate agents and consumer credit financial institutions (CCFIs) – businesses carrying on consumer credit lending activity which are neither authorised by the FSA nor money service businesses supervised by HM Revenue and Customs (HMRC).[449] This explanation introduces another element, namely that there are some businesses which were neither regulated by the FCA nor OFT but by HMRC, a further regulatory body in the field of financial markets.

A major role of OFT was competition within markets including investigation of cartel offences: 'in its simplest terms, a cartel is an agreement between businesses not to compete with each other. The agreement is usually secret, verbal and often informal',[450] and where the Enterprise Act 2002 makes it a criminal offence for an individual dishonestly to agree with one or more other persons that two or more undertakings will engage in certain prohibited cartel agreements.[451]

Since there were two institutions with an interest in prosecuting fraud (OFT and SFO), it was another example of the anti-economic crime responsibilities being split. Joshua noted that the OFT's first prosecution, against British Airways

444 Eva Lomnicka, 'The future of consumer credit regulation: a chance to rationalise sanctions for breaches of financial services regulatory regimes?' (2013) 34(1) Co Law 13.

445 OFT, 'OFT announces criminal charges in estate agent investigations' http://webarchive.nationalarchives.gov.uk/20140402142426/http://www.oft.gov.uk/news-and-updates/press/2012/80-12 Accessed 18 October 2016.

446 OFT, 'Owner of mileage correction business jailed for car clocking' 22 November 2012 www.gov.uk/cma-cases/mileage-correction-services-provider-investigation-and-conviction Accessed 24 November 2016.

447 Lomnicka, 'The future of consumer credit regulation' (n 444) 13.

448 The Money Laundering Regulations 2007, SI 2007/2157.

449 OFT, 'Anti-Money laundering Registration' www.gov.uk/anti-money-laundering-registration Accessed 20 March 2017. HM Revenue and Customs, 'Guidance. Money laundering supervision: guidance for money service businesses.' The term Money Service Business has a special meaning under the Money Laundering Regulations 2007. Under the regulations, your business is a Money Service Business if it acts as a bureau; transmits money in any way; or cashes cheques that are payable to your customers. https://www.gov.uk/government/publications/anti-money-laundering-guidance-for-money-service-businesses Accessed 25 July 2017.

450 OFT, 'What is a cartel?' 'Typically, cartel members may agree on: prices, output levels, discounts, credit terms, which customers they will supply, which areas they will supply, who should win a contract (bid rigging).' http://webarchive.nationalarchives.gov.uk/20140402142426/http://www.oft.gov.uk/OFTwork/competition-act-and-cartels/cartels/what-cartel Accessed 20 March 2017.

451 OFT, 'What is a cartel?' (n 450).

for airline fuel price fixing, collapsed in 2010 with 'OFT's credibility deservedly in tatters'.[452] This high-profile failure received the same type of press comment as that visited on SFO for its earlier lack of success,[453] and provides support for the central theme that such prosecutions should be in the experienced hands of a single prosecution authority.

This provides the background to the merger of the OFT with the Competition Commission to form the CMA, where some simplification took place with the FCA taking over the OFT's consumer credit responsibilities, though, as Lomnicka describes, 'this will not be a simple process' because of the differing regulations under the FSMA and CCA.[454] Furthermore, the FCA through the Competition Act has investigatory and enforcement powers for breaches of competition law,[455] evidencing another body with a role in enforcing competition.

The CMA was established to be a 'strong, independent competition authority'[456] but, notwithstanding its independence, given a 'steer'[457] by government as to its priorities, in particular: 'securing strong, sustainable economic growth is the Government's central priority and open and fair competition is a vital ingredient in achieving this.'[458] The CMA is given a 'steer'[459] to enforce: 'the CMA should select and conclude an appropriate mix of complex and simpler enforcement cases to maximise its impact, end abuse and create a credible deterrent effect to anticompetitive behaviour across the whole economy.'[460]

The significance of the establishment of the CMA is that it is the single entity to regulate competition and markets and it is a 'unitary body (…) bringing together the OFT's competition and key consumer functions with the functions of the

452 Julian Joshua, 'OFT's credibility is in tatters following the failed BA price-fixing trial' www.lawgazette.co.uk/analysis/ofts-credibility-is-in-tatters-following-the-failed-ba-price-fixing-trial/55531.article Accessed 24 November 2016.

453 *The Daily Telegraph*, 'Soaring ambitions of OFT get shot down' 11 May 2010 www.telegraph.co.uk/finance/comment/damianreece/7707709/Soaring-ambitions-of-OFT-get-shot-down.html Accessed 24 November 2016.

454 Lomnicka, 'The future of consumer credit regulation' (n 444) 13.

455 Financial Conduct Authority, 'Our future mission' (n 343) 7.

456 Department for Business, Innovation and Skills, 'Competition Regime: Response to consultation on statement of strategic priorities for the CMA 1 October 2013. Strategic Steer for the Competition and Markets Authority 2014–17' 10 www.gov.uk/government/uploads/system/uploads/attachment_data/file/245607/bis-13-1210-competition-regime-response-to-consultation-on-statement-of-strategic-priorities-for-the-cma.pdf Accessed 24 November 2016.

457 'The Steer is intended to provide a transparent statement of how the Government sees the competition regime fitting with its broader economic priorities. It sits alongside the CMA's accountability framework and legal duties, particularly the duty to promote competition for the benefit of consumers. The CMA will be asked to have regard to the Steer but the CMA will operate independently and is not obliged to follow the Steer. The CMA will be accountable for its decisions taken in light of the Steer and other considerations.' Department for Business, Innovation and Skills, 'Competition Regime' (n 456) 4.

458 Department for Business, Innovation and Skills, 'Competition Regime' (n 456) 10.

459 Department for Business, Innovation and Skills, 'Competition Regime' (n 456) 4.

460 Department for Business, Innovation and Skills, 'Competition Regime' (n 456) 17.

Competition Commission'.[461] The concentration of resources into one entity is precisely what was proposed in relation to the formation of an ECA. The government rationale is that by 'combining these roles in a single body, the regime will be more coherent and predictable, competition processes more efficient and there will be more flexible allocation of resources'.[462] Clearly, the inference to be drawn is that a multiplicity of bodies is less coherent, less predictable and less efficient because resources cannot be managed to advantage. Furthermore, in pursuance of the CMA's objective to criminalise cartels, the prosecutor no longer has to prove dishonesty.[463]

Unlike conspiracy to defraud, where dishonesty has to be present,[464] the 'removal of the requirement to establish *Ghosh* [465] dishonesty from the criminal cartel offence',[466] in addition to the ERRA,[467] which also addresses the concurrent enforcement powers 'granted to certain sector economic regulators is one of the more remarkable features of UK competition law'.[468] These regulators were established as part of the privatisation[469] of state-owned businesses, such as water, gas and electricity[470] and have their own regulatory powers. The government was keen to see increased enforcement activity, stating that 'the cartel offence should deter the most serious forms of anti-competitive behaviour but there have been only two cases prosecuted, only one

461 Department for Business, Innovation and Skills, 'New competition authority comes into existence' www.gov.uk/government/news/new-competition-authority-comes-into-existence Accessed 18 October 2016.

462 Department for Business, Innovation and Skills, 'Competition Minister Jo Swinson launches shadow Competition and Markets Authority (CMA)' 1 October 2013 www.gov.uk/government/speeches/competition-and-markets-authority-launch Accessed 18 October 2016.

463 Enterprise Act 2002, s 188. 'The criminal cartel offence was created (...) with the intention of criminalising and deterring behaviour by individuals leading to the most serious and damaging forms of anti-competitive agreements, namely "hardcore cartels".' Competition and Markets Authority, 'Cartel Offence Prosecution Guidance, Consultation Document September 2013' www.gov.uk/government/uploads/system/uploads/attachment_data/file/243709/5-cartel-offence-prosecution-guidance-consultation.pdf Accessed 24 November 2016.

464 *R v Eric Evans & others* T20137190 (n 166).

465 *R v Ghosh* [1982] EWCA Crim 2.

466 Dunne (n 437) 254.

467 Enterprise and Regulatory Reform Act 2013.

468 Dunne (n 437) 254.

469 '[P]rivatisation of utilities as vertically (or horizontally) integrated monopolies was routine, particularly in the initial stages, as liberalisation was viewed as a secondary consideration to the need to secure sufficient investment. This had the parallel effect of creating an abundance of new regulatory regimes and agencies to administer competition in privatised sectors, many of which retained natural monopoly segments.' Dunne (n 437) 254, 257.

470 'The Water Services Regulation Authority (Ofwat), the Office of Rail Regulation (ORR), the Gas and Electricity Markets Authority (Ofgem), the Northern Ireland Authority for Utility Regulation (NIAUR), the Civil Aviation Authority (CAA), and Monitor, the newly-established regulator for health services.' Dunne (n 437) 254, 260.

successfully'.[471] Thus, there is increased pressure on sector regulators to use antitrust powers to promote competition: the 'CMA will also have powers to allocate cases, and in certain circumstances, take cases from sector regulators'.[472] The clarity of purpose is plain and within the CMA structure, including the network of statutory regulators, the expectation is that either the regulators use their powers or the CMA will do so. This offers a template which could be used with advantage in relation to an ECA.

An increase in CMA activity has been seen in 2016 in relation to cartels, with ITW being fined £2.3m for breaking competition law by restricting dealers from offering online discounts. In a similar vein, Trod was fined £163,000 for online price fixing, and Ultra £787,000.[473]

The CMA state that they have a further 17 Competition Act cases under investigation.[474] In the previous year, CMA settled two Competition Act cases:

> One case involved an association of estate and letting agents and a local newspaper publisher who had agreed to restrict the advertising of fees or discounts in a local newspaper. The other case involved a membership organisation of private consultant ophthalmologists (specialists in medical and surgical eye procedures) and concerned anti-competitive information exchange and pricing agreements.[475]

The CMA also fined 'a number of pharmaceutical companies a total of £45 million for anti-competitive conduct and agreements in relation to the supply of paroxetine,

471 Department for Business, Innovation and Skills, 'Competition Minister Jo Swinson launches shadow Competition and Markets Authority (CMA)' (n 462) 1. '[T]he CMA found that 4 suppliers of galvanised steel tanks infringed competition law between 2005 and 2012 by engaging in price-fixing, bid-rigging and market sharing by way of customer allocation. The CMA imposed penalties totalling £2.5 million. Three individuals were charged with an offence under section 188 of the Enterprise Act 2002, the criminal cartel offence, with one defendant pleading guilty and two others being acquitted following trial by jury.' Competition and Markets Authority, 'Supply of galvanised steel tanks for water storage: criminal investigation' www.gov.uk/cma-cases/criminal-investigation-into-the-supply-of-galvanised-steel-tanks-for-water-storage Accessed 18 October 2016.

472 Department for Business, Innovation and Skills, 'Competition Minister Jo Swinson launches shadow Competition and Markets Authority (CMA)' (n 462) 1.

473 Competition and Markets Authority, 'Fridge supplier fined £2.2 million for restricting online discounts' www.gov.uk/government/news/fridge-supplier-fined-22-million-for-restricting-online-discounts; Competition and Markets Authority, 'CMA issues final decision in online cartel case' www.gov.uk/government/news/cma-issues-final-decision-in-online-cartel-case; Competition and Markets Authority, 'CMA issues bathroom fittings infringement decision and fine' www.gov.uk/government/news/cma-issues-bathroom-fittings-infringement-decision-and-fine Accessed 27 October 2016.

474 Competition and Markets Authority, 'Fridge supplier fined £2.2 million for restricting online discounts' (n 473).

475 Competition and Markets Authority, 'Sarah Cardell speaks about the CMA's enforcement priorities and approach' www.gov.uk/government/speeches/sarah-cardell-speaks-about-the-cmas-enforcement-priorities-and-approach Accessed 27 October 2016.

an anti-depressant medicine',[476] citing this as evidence of their determination to stifle competition at the expense of customers, in this case the National Health Service (NHS). The CMA also obtained a criminal conviction of a company director who pleaded guilty and received a six-month prison sentence.[477] Notwithstanding these successes, the development of the CMA remains a work in progress, as they comment: 'this twin-track of tough and rigorous enforcement alongside support to businesses is both effective and well-received, although we have a long way to go before we have fully embedded a "competition culture" across all UK businesses.'[478]

The CMA provide discretionary payments to whistleblowers up to £100,000, unlike the FCA, PRA and SFO.[479]

Crown Prosecution Service

The CPS, established in 1986, headed by the DPP is, in volume terms, the main prosecutor of fraud in England and Wales.[480]

The CPS has a Specialist Fraud Division which is a dedicated fraud prosecuting team within the CPS. It has a national remit and the specialist expertise to prosecute the most serious, complex and difficult fraud cases investigated by police forces across England and Wales. This includes the COLP, Metropolitan Police, NCA, Economic Crime Command (ECC) and regional police fraud units.[481] This division also: prosecutes all criminal tax, excise and strategic export cases, which are subject to criminal investigations by HMRC, including examining the 'Panama Papers' data leak;[482] all criminal cases relating to benefits and child maintenance legislation, which

476 Competition and Markets Authority, 'Sarah Cardell speaks about the CMA's enforcement priorities and approach' (n 475).

477 Nigel Snee, the former managing director of Franklin Hodge Industries, pleaded guilty to dishonestly agreeing with others to fix prices, divide up customers and rig bids between 2005 and 2012 in respect of the supply in the UK of galvanised steel tanks for water storage. Competition and Markets Authority, 'Director sentenced to 6 months for criminal cartel' www.gov.uk/government/news/director-sentenced-to-6-months-for-criminal-cartel Accessed 27 October 2016.

478 Competition and Markets Authority, 'Annual Report and Accounts 2015–16' www.gov.uk/government/publications/cma-annual-report-and-accounts-2015-to-2016 Accessed 27 October 2016.

479 The CMA offers financial rewards of up to £100,000. Competition and Markets Authority, 'Rewards for information about cartels' www.gov.uk/government/uploads/system/uploads/attachment_data/file/299411/Informant_rewards_policy.pdf Accessed 30 November 2016.

480 The CPS was established by Prosecution of Offences Act 1985 as an independent prosecution service for police forces in England and Wales. There were some 637,000 prosecutions in 2015 with a conviction rate of 83%. Crown Prosecution Service, 'Annual Report and Accounts 2015–16' 3 http://cps.gov.uk/publications/docs/annual_report_2015_16.pdf Accessed 20 March 2017.

481 Crown Prosecution Service, 'Specialist Fraud Division' www.cps.gov.uk/your_cps/our_organisation/sfd.html#a01 Accessed 18 October 2016.

482 The International Consortium of Investigative Journalists (ICIJ)'s Panama Papers data leak, 8 November 2016. The government task force reported that the taskforce has:

are investigated by the Department of Work and Pensions; NHS fraud; and criminal matters investigated by the Department for Environment, Food and Rural Affairs and the Medicines and Healthcare Products Regulatory Agency.[483]

Other actors: National Crime Agency

The Home Office leads the government response to 'immigration and passports, drugs policy, crime policy and counter-terrorism and works to ensure visible, responsive and accountable policing in the UK'.[484] Of particular relevance to economic crime, the Home Office is responsible for the NCA, which gives this organisation a greater political dimension because the Home Secretary is accountable to Parliament for a department with a broad spectrum of responsibilities, ranging from border policing, organised crime, economic crime, and child exploitation and online protection.[485] The NCA includes the ECC, which straddles fraud, bribery and corruption, and organised crime.[486] Clearly, the ECC name is an unhelpful confusion.[487]

opened civil and criminal investigations into 22 individuals for suspected tax evasion; led the international acquisition of high-quality, significant and credible data on offshore activity in Panama – ensuring the important work of the taskforce was not delayed by the ICIJ's refusal to release all of the information that it holds to any tax authority or law enforcement agency; identified a number of leads relevant to a major insider-trading operation, led by the FCA and supported by the NCA; identified nine potential professional enablers of economic crime – all of whom have links with known criminals; placed 43 high-net-worth individuals under special review while their links to Panama are further investigated; identified two new UK properties and a number of companies relevant to an NCA financial sanctions enquiry; and established links to eight active SFO investigations. Philip Hammond, Chancellor of the Exchequer, 8 November 2016 HCWS 247.

483 Crown Prosecution Service, 'Specialist Fraud Division' www.cps.gov.uk/your_cps/our_organisation/sfd.html#a01 Accessed 18 October 2016.

484 Home Office, 'What we do' www.gov.uk/government/organisations/home-office/about Accessed 24 November 2016.

485 'The NCA has a wide remit. We tackle serious and organised crime, strengthen our borders, fight fraud and cyber crime, and protect children and young people from sexual abuse and exploitation. We provide leadership in these areas through our organised crime, border policing, economic crime and CEOP commands, the National Cyber Crime Unit and specialist capability teams. The NCA works closely with partners to deliver operational results. We have an international role to cut serious and organised crime impacting on the UK through our network of international liaison officers.' National Crime Agency, 'What we do' www.nationalcrimeagency.gov.uk/about-us/what-we-do Accessed 24 November 2016.

486 National Crime Agency, 'Economic Crime Command'. 'Economic crime covers a range of crimes including: Fraud; Intellectual property crime; Identity crime; Counterfeit currency. These crimes cost the UK millions of pounds each year, and prey on the most vulnerable members of society. The Economic Crime command's role is to fight economic crime by undermining criminals and educating those most at risk of attack. We do this by sharing intelligence and knowledge with partners, disrupting criminal activity, and seizing assets.' www.nationalcrimeagency.gov.uk/about-us/what-we-do/economic-crime Accessed 4 November 2016.

487 For a discussion of the National Crime Agency, see: Christopher Recker, 'The National Crime Agency: A Critical Analysis of its Potential Impact on the UK's Financial Crime

Government departments

HM Treasury

HM Treasury 'is the government's economic and finance ministry, maintaining control over public spending, setting the direction of the UK's economic policy and working to achieve strong and sustainable economic growth'.[488] In relation to economic crime, it is responsible for anti-money laundering,[489] anti-terrorism and financial sanctions,[490] 'financial services policy: including (…) financial services regulation, financial stability, and ensuring competitiveness in the City'.[491] HM Treasury is the key driver of financial regulation, explaining its mission as: 'the Government is committed to introducing a new approach to financial regulation – one which is based on clarity of focus and responsibility, and which places the judgement of expert supervisors at the heart of regulation.'[492] HM Treasury asserts that 'responsibility for the overall regulatory framework, and the protection of the public finances remains with HM Treasury and the Chancellor of the Exchequer'.[493]

The first step taken by the government was to make the role of the Bank of England pivotal by forming 'a new macro-prudential body, the Financial Policy Committee, and a new micro-prudential supervisor, the Prudential Regulation Authority (PRA)'.[494] Second, 'responsibility for conduct of business will sit with the new FCA, with the mandate and tools to be a proactive force for enabling the right outcomes for consumers and market participants, including through the promotion of competition'.[495] These new bodies were described as 'regulatory centres of excellence', but there is clear overlap.[496]

Bank of England

The coalition government positioned the Bank of England at the heart of ensuring financial stability for the UK by giving it prime responsibility for management of the economy.[497] In relation to economic crime and regulation, the PRA has a role

Policy' in N Ryder and others (eds), *The Financial Crisis and White Collar Crime – Legislative and Policy Responses. A Critical Assessment* (Routledge 2017).

488 HM Treasury, 'What we do' www.gov.uk/government/organisations/hm-treasury/a bout Accessed 18 October 2016.

489 Nicholas Ryder, *Money Laundering – An Endless Cycle* (Routledge 2012) 79.

490 HM Treasury, 'Financial sanctions: Regime-specific lists and release' www.gov.uk/government/collections/financial-sanctions-regime-specific-consolidated-lists-and-re leases Accessed 18 October 2016.

491 HM Treasury, 'What we do' (n 488).

492 HM Treasury, 'A new approach to financial regulation' (n 3) 3.

493 HM Treasury, 'A new approach to financial regulation' (n 3) 3.

494 HM Treasury, 'A new approach to financial regulation' (n 3) 3.

495 HM Treasury, 'A new approach to financial regulation' (n 3) 3.

496 HM Treasury, 'A new approach to financial regulation' (n 3) 3.

497 'Responsibility for financial stability – both at the macro-level of the financial system as a whole, and the micro-level of individual firms – will rest within the Bank of England, in a new macro-prudential body, the Financial Policy Committee, and a new micro-

because it 'will make judgments about the safety and soundness of individual firms, and will take supervisory and regulatory action to ensure that firms take necessary steps'.[498] This appears to be a more formal approach than the 'Governor's eyebrows'.[499]

Prudential Regulation Authority (PRA)

The PRA, established by the Financial Services Act 2012,[500] is a subsidiary of the Bank of England and 'its core objective will be to promote the safety and soundness of the firms it regulates'.[501] The PRA 'is responsible for the prudential regulation and supervision of banks, building societies, credit unions, insurers and major investment firms'.[502] The PRA has two statutory objectives: 'the promotion of the safety and soundness of PRA-authorised persons';[503] and 'specifically for insurers, to contribute to the securing of an appropriate degree of protection for policyholders'.[504] The PRA has been given statutory power to prosecute senior executives in the event of an institution's failure.[505] The legislative landscape has become more complicated because the Financial Services (Banking Reform) Act 2013, which introduced the new criminal offence[506] of 'relating to a decision causing a financial institution to fail'.[507] If a person is convicted of this offence they could face a custodial sentence up to seven years and/or an unlimited fine.[508]

prudential supervisor, the Prudential Regulation Authority.' HM Treasury, 'A new approach to financial regulation' (n 3).

498 HM Treasury, 'A new approach to financial regulation' (n 3).

499 See Chapter 1. Attributed to Montagu Norman (Lord Norman), Governor of the Bank of England 1920–44. See also: L C B Gower, '"Big Bang" and City Regulation' (n 225).

500 Financial Services Act 2012, s 6.

501 HM Treasury, 'A new approach to financial regulation' (n 3).

502 In total the PRA regulates around 1,700 financial firms. Prudential Regulation Authority, www.bankofengland.co.uk/PRA/Pages/default.aspx Accessed 18 October 2016.

503 Financial Services Act 2012, s 132.

504 Prudential Regulation Authority (n 502). Financial Services Act 2012, s 133.

505 Financial Services (Banking Reform) Act 2013, s 36.

506 The key provisions are: (1) A person ('S') commits an offence if – (a) at a time when S is a senior manager in relation to a financial institution ('F'), S – (i) takes, or agrees to the taking of, a decision by or on behalf of F as to the way in which the business of a group institution is to be carried on, or (ii) fails to take steps that S could take to prevent such a decision being taken, (b) at the time of the decision, S is aware of a risk that the implementation of the decision may cause the failure of the group institution, (c) in all the circumstances, S's conduct in relation to the taking of the decision falls far below what could reasonably be expected of a person in S's position, and (d) the implementation of the decision causes the failure of the group institution.

507 Financial Services (Banking Reform) Act 2013, s 36.

508 Financial Services (Banking Reform) Act 2013, s 36(4). '(a) on summary conviction – (i) in England and Wales, to imprisonment for a term not exceeding 12 months (or 6 months, if the offence was committed before the commencement of section 154(1) of the Criminal Justice Act 2003) or a fine, or both; (ii) in Scotland, to imprisonment for

The power to institute proceedings is vested in the PRA, FCA, secretary of state or DPP.[509] There is no specific role intended for the SFO. However, this new offence is limited because the person committing the offence has to be a senior manager[510] and the financial institution has to have failed by, among others, insolvency.[511] That being so, significant losses caused to an institution either by someone who is not a 'senior manager', or which, though large, do not deal a catastrophic blow to an institution's solvency, would not be encompassed by this statute. Thus, there continues to exist a gap in the regulatory response to economic crime. Some conduct can be dealt with by administrative sanction by the FCA but when David Cameron said that 'those responsible should be held to account',[512] he had in mind prosecution but that would need a change in the law.[513] Thus, the criminal offence of causing an institution to fail[514] or 'reckless banking'[515] should be accompanied by a criminal offence of '[r]eckless risk-taking on the financial markers'.[516] As Fisher comments:

> Whilst it is true that reckless risk-taking on the financial markets does not necessarily involve behaviour which is deceitful, the affirmation of the principle that it is sufficient for the defendant's conduct to imperil the economic interests of another is significant in this context.[517]

Such a criminal sanction would complete the suite of sanctions available where there is conduct that imperils the financial system, and ensure that, in future, questions such as those of Judge Rakoff of 'the financial crisis: why have no high level executives been prosecuted?'[518] would not be for the want of appropriate legislation. This would be a counter-party to the suggested corporate offence of failure to prevent all acts of financial crime by its employees,[519] and would include

a term not exceeding 12 months or a fine not exceeding the statutory maximum, or both; (iii) in Northern Ireland, to imprisonment for a term not exceeding 6 months or a fine not exceeding the statutory maximum, or both.'

509 Financial Services (Banking Reform) Act 2013, s 38.

510 Designated as such by Financial Services and Markets Act 2000, s 59(6A) & (6B).

511 Financial Services (Banking Reform) Act 2013, s 37(9).

512 Conservative Home, 'Cameron: We won't treat the richest any differently from the poorest' http://conservativehome.blogs.com/torydiary/2008/12/cameron-we-wont.html Accessed 24 November 2016.

513 Conservative Home (n 512).

514 Financial Services (Banking Reform) Act 2013, s 36.

515 Jonathan Fisher, 'Risk, Recklessness and Policing the Financial Markets' in N Ryder, U Turksen and S Hassler (eds), *Fighting Financial Crime in the Global Economic Crisis: Policy, Trends and Sanctions* (Routledge Cavendish 2014) 21.

516 Fisher (n 515) 2.

517 Fisher (n 515) 14.

518 Jed S Rakoff, 'The financial crisis: Why have no high-level executives been prosecuted?' *The New York Review of Books* www.nybooks.com/articles/archives/2014/jan/09/financial-crisis-why-no-executive-prosecutions/ Accessed 24 November 2016.

519 'I have suggested that the situation could easily be remedied by an amendment to s.7 of the Bribery Act to create the corporate offence of a company failing to prevent acts

cases such as: Jerome Kerviel's illegal transactions which cost Société Générale £3.7bn;[520] Nick Leeson's unauthorised trading which presaged the collapse of Barings Bank; a UBS trader, Kweku Adoboli, who lost £1.5bn;[521] and JP Morgan's 'London Whale' affair which cost it $6bn.[522]

Markets and banking

In March 2014, the Bank of England launched its new 'strategic plan',[523] which included the creation of a new Deputy Governor for Markets and Banking, who would be responsible for 'efficient and effective financial markets'.[524] Bank of England Governor Mark Carney describes this as an 'extraordinarily important task'.[525] This is an interesting regulatory response which attracts attention because of the Bank of England's role in the foreign exchange markets. It was reported that allegations of manipulation of the foreign exchange markets had come as a surprise,[526] and were very serious, and Martin Wheatley, chief executive of the FCA, 'told a parliamentary hearing that allegations traders had colluded to rig prices in the $5.3tn spot market were "every bit as bad as they have been with Libor"'.[527]

of financial crime by its employees. We need to tackle corporate criminal liability for DPAs to have maximum bite.' Serious Fraud Office, 'Ethical business conduct: An enforcement perspective' (n 227).

520 Gilligan, 'Jérôme Kerviel the "Rogue Trader" of Société Générale: Bad luck, bad apple, bad tree or bad orchard?' (n 174).

521 *The Times*, 'UBS trader was only "a gamble away from destroying Switzerland's biggest bank"' (n 175). BBC, 'UBS "rogue trader": Loss estimate raised to $2.3bn' 18 September 2011 www.bbc.co.uk/news/business-14965438 Accessed 18 October 2016.

522 ASIC, 'Senate inquiry into the performance of the Australian Securities and Investments Commission. Main submission by ASIC, October 2013' 170 www.asic.gov.au/asic/asic.nsf/byHeadline/13-300MR%20ASIC%20lodges%20major%20Senate%20Inquiry%20submission?opendocument Accessed 18 October 2016.

523 Bank of England, 'News Release – Bank of England launches strategic plan' 18 March 2014 www.bankofengland.co.uk//publications/Pages/news/2014/058.aspx Accessed 18 October 2016.

524 Bank of England, 'News Release' (n 523).

525 Bank of England, 'Speech given by Mark Carney' 18 March 2014 www.bankofengland.co.uk/publications/Documents/speeches/2014/speech715.pdf Accessed 18 October 2016.

526 *Financial Times*, 'Forex claims "as bad as Libor", says FCA' 4 February 2014 www.ft.com/cms/s/0/6d2f697a-8da8-11e3-bbe7-00144feab7de.html#axzz2wz74O2Ae Accessed 18 October 2016.

527 *Financial Times*, 'Forex claims "as bad as Libor"' (n 526). 'On 12 November 2014, the FCA reported: The Financial Conduct Authority (FCA) has imposed fines totalling £1,114,918,000 ($1.7 billion) on five banks for failing to control business practices in their G10 spot foreign exchange (FX) trading operations: Citibank N.A. £225,575,000 ($358 million), HSBC Bank Plc £216,363,000 ($343 million), JPMorgan Chase Bank N.A. £222,166,000 ($352 million), The Royal Bank of Scotland Plc £217,000,000 ($344 million) and UBS AG £233,814,000 ($371 million) ("the Banks").' Financial Conduct Authority, 'FCA fines five banks £1.1 billion for FX

Price rigging would suggest fraudulent conduct in a similar manner to the LIBOR cases considered above, where 13 people have been charged by the SFO with conspiracy to defraud. The Bank of England said 'it is a matter of public record that the Bank of England has been conducting an internal review into allegations that Bank of England officials condoned or were informed of manipulation in the foreign exchange market or the sharing of confidential client information'.[528]

The Bank of England initiated an independent inquiry into its role in market manipulation and 'found no evidence to suggest that any Bank official was involved in any unlawful or improper behaviour in the FX market', although it was 'aware of a market practice which (...) could involve collusive behaviour and lead to market participants being disadvantaged and he failed to raise this with the appropriate people'.[529]

The foreign exchange allegations are that the Bank of England 'had concerns about manipulation as early as 2006',[530] at a time when the Bank's role had diminished, because it was part of a 'tripartite' system that had deconstructed 'the old model of central banking',[531] which Governor Carney viewed to be a 'fatally flawed' approach.[532]

Carney's sideswipe was that for over a century the Bank's responsibilities 'remained broad and largely informal until 1997'.[533] This is a significant observation because in 1997, the Labour government took office and downgraded the Bank of England's role,[534] which previously had '*informal* responsibility for a broad range of policy areas'.[535] Carney added that the Bank 'promoted financial

failings' (n 386). Furthermore, the SFO announced in July 2014 that it was investigating the foreign exchange market allegations. This was closed in 2016 because there was insufficient evidence to mount a criminal prosecution. Serious Fraud Office, 'SFO Closes Forex Investigation' www.sfo.gov.uk/2016/03/15/sfo-closes-forex-investigation/ Accessed 9 March 2017.

528 Bank of England, 'News Release – Foreign Exchange – The Perfect Storm' www.bankofengland.co.uk/publications/Pages/news/2014/044.aspx Accessed 24 November 2016. Bloomberg, 'FX Traders Surprised by Scope of Bank of England Probe' www.bloomberg.com/news/2014-09-09/fx-traders-said-to-be-surprised-by-scope-of-boe-probe.html Accessed 24 November 2016.

529 Bank of England, 'Bank of England foreign exchange market investigation a report by Lord Grabiner' www.bankofengland.co.uk/publications/Documents/news/2014/grabiner.pdf Accessed 18 October 2016.

530 *Financial Times*, 'Top barrister chosen to lead Bank of England forex enquiry' 12 March 2014 www.ft.com/content/e2a5e2b6-aa03-11e3-8bd6-00144feab7de Accessed 14 January 2017. See also Ryder, *The Financial Crisis and White Collar Crime* (n 353) 105, where LIBOR manipulation was noted the previous year in 2005.

531 Bank of England, 'Speech given by Mark Carney' (n 525).

532 'While there were enormous innovations of enduring value during this period, the reductionist vision of a central bank's role that was adopted around the world was fatally flawed (...) thus [a] return to a broad role is welcome.' Bank of England, 'Speech given by Mark Carney' (n 525).

533 Bank of England, 'Speech given by Mark Carney' (n 525).

534 Philip Rawlings, 'Reform of bank regulation in the United Kingdom: The opening salvo' (2010) JIBLR 522.

535 Bank of England, 'Speech given by Mark Carney' (n 525) (emphasis added).

stability through its role as the effective lender of last resort, and more generally – through judicious exercise of the Governor's eyebrows – as the institution which managed and resolved financial crises'.[536]

The Bank of England clearly recognise that there are issues with the functioning of core markets, together with a 'host of financial reforms',[537] and 'most fundamentally, given the serious issues raised by the Libor and foreign exchange scandals, changes must be made to both the hard and soft infrastructure of core markets to ensure they are fair, effective and efficient'.[538] However, this adds a further layer of complexity because the Bank of England is itself involved in LIBOR and foreign exchange as well as regulating the markets, where the 'watchdog' is the FCA and the investigative and prosecutorial agency is the SFO. The Bank of England provides market liquidity,[539] which entails being a participant in markets that it regulates. To add to the confusion over roles, the FCA 'was accused of triggering a disorderly market in insurance company shares after revealing that the FCA was launching a review of zombie [insurance] funds and their treatment of 30 million customers'.[540] It was reported that the Bank of England were concerned at the false market in shares[541] because although it was the FCA's 'responsibility to oversee financial markets',[542] the Bank of England 'has responsibility for the stability of the system as a whole'.[543] This demonstrates that there should be one body with ultimate responsibility and that body should be the Bank of England.

Conclusion

The UK's counter-economic crime landscape has been shaped over many years in a haphazard manner, thus exhibiting the disadvantages of responding to events

536 'In the late 19th Century the banking system was relatively unregulated (and partly self-regulated) – the Bank did not have an explicit supervisory infrastructure or system of prudential control until 1979. Nevertheless, the scope of the Bank's responsibilities was arguably as broad then as it is now, albeit that the mix was different.' Bank of England, 'Speech given by Mark Carney' (n 525).

537 Bank of England, 'Speech given by Mark Carney' (n 525).

538 Bank of England, 'Speech given by Mark Carney' (n 525).

539 'Banks and building societies ("banks") make long-term loans but fund themselves through on-demand or short-term deposits, so they are subject to liquidity risk: the risk that a material part of their funding is withdrawn before the assets can be realised at their true economic value.' Bank of England, 'Liquidity Insurance' www.bankofengland.co.uk/markets/Pages/sterlingoperations/liquidityinsurance.aspx Accessed 24 November 2016.

540 *The Times*, 'Hosking on Monday: waiting for the watchdog to fall' 31 March 2014 www.thetimes.co.uk/tto/business/columnists/article4049293.ece Accessed 18 October 2016.

541 *The Sunday Times*, 'FCA ignored warnings of false market' 6 April 2014 www.thesundaytimes.co.uk/sto/business/Finance/article1396697.ece Accessed 18 October 2016.

542 *The Sunday Times*, 'FCA ignored warnings of false market' (n 541).

543 *The Sunday Times*, 'FCA ignored warnings of false market' (n 541).

rather than as a result of creating a formal plan. The UK emerged from the post-war 'welfare state' era with rudimentary protection for investors and an historic overseer in the form of the Bank of England, without powers to regulate and relying on persuasion rather than force of law. Thus, the traditional 'Old Lady' relying on the 'Governor's eyebrows' could not police the attitudes of 'whatever he can make on the side'[544] or a 'naughty perk of the job',[545] and had to give way to greater regulation. This process took 31 years under two long governments and several iterations of regulatory systems, but another new government showed that the lack of a cohesive strategy is still apparent because overlap between prosecutor and regulator remains.[546] The general field of crime is broad but economic crime is a specialised area, based on a contemporary label of white collar but, regardless of neckwear, is not a new phenomenon. However, although the suggestion of this type of crime being undertaken by people of high social status still pervades, it is the paucity of convictions and inadequacy of penalties for such conduct that remain to be addressed. This chapter has demonstrated the history that brought them to the threshold of a new government in 2010, where the SFO had remained unchanged since its inception while the City regulator had mutated. Sadly, the broad conclusions of Gower and Roskill remain valid, leading to the conclusion that further change is required

The next chapter will review the legislation underpinning the criminalisation of bribery and corruption.

544 Gower, *Review of Investor Protection – A Discussion Document* (n 220) 55–56.
545 Mansell (n 393).
546 Karen Harrison and Nicholas Ryder, *The Law Relating to Financial Crime in the United Kingdom* (Routledge 2017) 108.

3 The United Kingdom

Bribery and corruption

Introduction

This chapter examines the second element of the UK response to economic crime, namely bribery and corruption. It considers the background to the creation of the current institutional framework of the special prosecutor and the financial regulator. This examination illustrates how the endeavours of governments[1] to adapt to changing financial markets and economic conditions, had the unforeseen consequences of providing increased opportunity for 'white collar crime' and, according to Wright, leading to London being regarded as the 'financial crime capital' and the UK being condemned for its weak processes and controls.[2]

International conventions

Internationally, the Bribery Act 2010[3] supports the Organisation for Economic Co-operation and Development (OECD) Convention on Combating Bribery of Foreign Public Officials and the UN Convention against Corruption (UNCAC) 2003.[4] In addition, the EU, Council of Europe and International Chamber of Commerce (ICC) have a variety of conventions and rules.[5]

1 Conservative government 1979–97; Labour government 1979–2010; Conservative-Liberal Democrat coalition government 2010–15; Conservative government 2015 onwards.

2 Rosalind Wright, 'Keynote address to the 17th International Cambridge Symposium on Economic Crime' (2000) 9(4) JFC 304–307.

3 The expedient of using the Anti-terrorism, Crime and Security Act 2001 to combat bribery and corruption was intended to be temporary until introduction of comprehensive corruption legislation. The Bribery Act fulfilled that obligation. Monty Raphael, *Blackstone's Guide to the Bribery Act 2010* (OUP 2010) 116.

4 OECD, 'Convention on Combating Bribery of Foreign Public Officials in International Business Transactions' (OECD Convention), and the United Nations Convention against Corruption 2003 (UN Convention or UNCAC).

5 The Council of Europe is '[a]n international organisation [based] in Strasbourg which comprises 47 countries of Europe. It was set up to promote democracy and protect human rights and the rule of law in Europe.' Member states include the Russian Federation and most former Soviet Eastern European countries. 'The EU currently has 28 members that have delegated some of their sovereignty so that decisions on

The OECD Convention, adopted by 41 countries, including the UK,[6] 'establishes legally binding standards to criminalise bribery of foreign public officials in international business transactions'.[7] The OECD Convention is the only international anti-corruption instrument focused on the 'supply side' of the bribery transaction: the person making the bribe rather than the recipient.[8] The OECD feel that their convention is working, a point illustrated by almost 800 sanctions being imposed.[9] Enforcement action is taken by countries themselves, rather than the OECD acting as a 'global policeman'. Raphael stated that the use of the Anti-Terrorism Crime and Security Act 2001,[10] had the twin effects of extending the 'jurisdiction of [UK] domestic courts to acts of bribery committed abroad by UK nationals',[11] and 'ensured that the common law offence of bribery extended to persons holding public office outside the UK'.[12] Transparency International cite

specific matters of joint interest can be made democratically at European level. No country has ever joined the EU without first belonging to the Council of Europe.' Council of Europe, 'Do not get confused' www.coe.int/en/web/about-us/do-not-get-confused Accessed 28 September 2016. United Nations Office on Drugs and Crime (UNODC), 'United Nations Convention against Corruption' www.unodc.org/unodc/en/treaties/CAC/index.html Accessed 28 September 2016; International Chamber of Commerce, 'ICC Rules of Conduct and Recommendations on Combating Extortion and Bribery [in International Business Transactions]' https://iccwbo.org/publication/icc-rules-of-conduct-and-recommendations-to-combat-extortion-and-bribery-2005-edition/. Council of Europe, '20 Guiding Principles for the Fight Against Corruption' 1997. Adopted by the UK in 1999. www.coe.int/t/dghl/monitoring/greco/documents/Resolution(97)24_EN.pdf. Criminal Law Convention – adopted by the UK in 1999 and ratified 2003. http://conventions.coe.int/Treaty/Commun/QueVoulezVous.asp?NT=173&CM=1&DF=&CL=ENG. Council of Europe, 'Civil Law Convention on Corruption', adopted by the UK in 2000 but not ratified as at September 2016. http://conventions.coe.int/Treaty/Commun/QueVoulezVous.asp?NT=173&CM=1&DF=&CL=ENG Accessed 28 September 2016.

6 The UK signed in 1997. OECD, 'OECD Convention on Combating Bribery of Foreign Public Officials in International Business Transactions' (OECD Convention) www.oecd.org/daf/anti-bribery/oecdantibriberyconvention.htm Accessed 12 September 2016.

7 OECD, 'Convention' (n 6).

8 OECD, 'Convention' (n 6). 'The OECD Anti-Bribery Convention establishes legally binding standards to criminalise bribery of foreign public officials in international business transactions and provides for a host of related measures that make this effective. It is the first and only international anti-corruption instrument focused on the "supply side" of the bribery transaction. The 34 OECD member countries and seven non-member countries – Argentina, Brazil, Bulgaria, Colombia, Latvia, Russia, and South Africa – have adopted this Convention.' OECD, 'Convention' (n 6).

9 '361 individuals and 126 entities have been sanctioned under criminal proceedings for foreign bribery in 17 parties between the time the Convention entered into force in 1999 and the end of 2014. At least 110 individuals and 200 entities in 8 countries have been sanctioned for other offences relating to foreign bribery such as money laundering or accounting.' OECD, 'Fighting the crime of foreign bribery' www.oecd.org/daf/anti-bribery/Fighting-the-crime-of-foreign-bribery.pdf Accessed 12 September 2016.

10 Raphael, *Blackstone's Guide* (n 3) 20. Anti-terrorism, Crime and Security Act 2001.

11 '[O]r bodies incorporated under UK law.' Raphael, *Blackstone's Guide* (n 3) 20.

12 Raphael, *Blackstone's Guide* (n 3) 20.

the UK as one of only four countries actively enforcing bribery laws.[13] UNCAC[14] is 'the world's comprehensive platform for fighting corruption, promoting integrity and fostering good governance'.[15] It is the first legally binding, international anti-corruption instrument and provides a unique opportunity to mount a global response to corruption. UNCAC assists countries, particularly those with 'vulnerable, developing or transitional economies',[16] to develop and use solid anti-corruption measures applicable to all spheres of society. Compliance with UNCAC is reviewed on a regular basis through peer review, with all 21 countries reviewed in 2014 being found to have gaps in their compliance with the convention.[17]

EU measures to counter corruption have had mixed success. In 2008, the EU joined UNCAC. However, in terms of legal instruments,

> the EU took some important steps at an early stage in defining active and passive corruption and in requiring member states to ensure a system of effective, proportionate and dissuasive criminal penalties for certain corruption offences (…) These were reflected in the Protocols to the Convention on the Protection of European Communities Financial Interests, the Convention on the Fight against Corruption Involving Officials of the European Communities or Officials of Member States of the EU and the Council Framework Decision on Combating Corruption in the Private Sector.[18]

The implementation across the EU is 'unevenly transposed' and there are 'considerable differences among national criminal laws as well as in the level of enforcement'.[19]

Prosecutions for bribery have been few in number[20] but it would be stretching credulity to believe that foreign bribery does not take

13 Transparency International, 'Exporting Corruption 2015' www.transparency.org/whatwedo/publication/exporting_corruption_progress_report_2015_assessing_enforcement_of_the_oecd Accessed 4 December 2016.

14 Administered by the UNODC.

15 United Nations Office on Drugs and Crime: Annual Report 2009. 'Integrity and good governance: At the top of the agenda' www.unodc.org/documents/about-unodc/AR09_LORES.pdf Accessed 12 September 2016.

16 United Nations Office on Drugs and Crime: Annual Report 2009 (n 15).

17 United Nations Office on Drugs and Crime: Annual Report 2014 72 www.unodc.org/documents/AnnualReport2014/Annual_Report_2014_WEB.pdf Accessed 12 September 2016.

18 Raluca Stefanuc, 'Corruption, or how to tame the shrew with the European Union stick: the new anti-corruption initiative of the European Commission' (2011) 12 ERA Forum 427, 429–430 (footnotes omitted).

19 Stefanuc (n 18) 427, 432.

20 'Between the period 1993 and 2003, on average, 21 people were prosecuted each year under the Prevention of Corruption Acts, whereas by comparison 23,000 people were prosecuted each year for fraud between 1997 and 2001. There was, therefore, a significant difference between those prosecuted for public sector corruption and those prosecuted for private sector fraud.' Saleem Sheikh, 'The Bribery Act 2010: Commercial organisations beware!' (2011) 22(1) ICCLR 2.

place.[21] By way of comparison, statistics from 2014 illustrated that since 1999 the US has obtained 90 convictions, together with 54 Deferred Prosecution Agreements, whereas the UK brought eight and Australia none.[22] There could be a number of reasons for this: such cases may not have been discovered or may not have been reported, which is not unusual in the field of financial crime. A further possibility is that if matters have been reported, prosecutors' focus may either lie elsewhere, or has been subject to political influence not to take cases to trial; alternatively, the laws that the prosecutors are able to deploy are inadequate. Here, Wilson notes 'the fact that the old law was in a slightly jaded state can scarcely be a complete explanation for the dearth of successful prosecutions'.[23] As Wells remarks, 'it is hard to think that laws that are rarely invoked are functional'.[24] However, whatever the reasons for such a small number of UK cases, post-2010 legislation is not to blame. Following the Anti-terrorism, Crime and Security Act, the UK only achieved its first conviction of bribing a foreign public official in 2008.[25] In that case, Tobiasen was convicted under the Prevention of Corruption Act 1906 of bribing a Ugandan government official.[26]

A further contribution to the arena of bribery and corruption is from the International Organization for Standardization, 'an independent, non-governmental international organization with a membership of 163 national standards bodies'.[27] This Geneva-based organisation published 'the first international anti-bribery

21 See Transparency International, 'Bribe Payers Index 2011' for an analysis of companies' perceived willingness to pay bribes. Australia is the sixth least likely, the UK eighth and US ninth. www.transparency.org/bpi2011 Accessed 20 March 2017.

22 OECD, 'Annual Report of the OECD Working Group on Bribery 2014: Comparative table of enforcement data collected from 40 parties to the Anti-Bribery Convention Decisions on foreign bribery cases from 1999 to December 2013' www.oecd.org/daf/anti-bribery/WGB-AB-AnnRep-2014-EN.pdf Accessed 12 September 2016.

23 James Wilson, 'Time to Act' (2010) 160 NLJ 1572.

24 Celia Wells, 'Bribery: corporate liability under the draft Bill 2009' (2009) 7 Crim LR 479.

25 *Financial Times*, 'Guilty plea to bribery sets legal landmark' 23 August 2008 www.ft.com/cms/s/0/ff993ec6-70ad-11dd-b514-0000779fd18c.html#axzz2HOoOoVvn Accessed 18 October 2016.

26 Commonwealth heads of government met in Uganda where a government official (Tumukunde) was responsible for security measures and procured training and equipment from a UK firm (CBRN) worth £500,000. Tumukunde demanded extra payments for 'local taxes' from CBRN's director, Tobiasen, who made payments totalling £83,000. Tobiasen was convicted under the Prevention of Corruption Act 1906 s 1 and sentenced to five months' imprisonment (suspended), and Tumukunde (intercepted at Heathrow airport) was convicted for money laundering and sentenced to 12 months' imprisonment. *Financial Times*, 'Guilty plea to bribery sets legal landmark' 23 August 2008 www.ft.com/cms/s/0/ff993ec6-70ad-11dd-b514-0000779fd18c.html#axzz2HOoOoVvn Accessed 18 October 2016. The Commonwealth, 'CHOGM Kampala 2007' http://thecommonwealth.org/history-of-the-commonwealth/19th-chogm Accessed 8 January 2017.

27 International Organization for Standardization, 'About ISO' www.iso.org/iso/home/about.htm Accessed 18 October 2016.

management system standard designed to help organizations combat bribery risk in their own operations and throughout their global value chains'.[28] This standard offers the opportunity for organisations to have their systems and procedures validated by an external body. It is not a panacea to allegations of bribery but could be persuasive evidence of adequate procedures to prevent bribery and may offer comfort in relation to preparedness of third parties.

Bribery and corruption legislation

The Bribery Act 2010 overhauls the UK's patchwork of archaic corruption laws,[29] and is regarded as setting the 'gold standard' in bribery legislation.[30] The Bribery Act 'provides the UK with some of the most draconian and far-reaching anti-corruption legislation in the world',[31] with the potential for the UK to set the standard in fighting international bribery and corruption.[32]

The UK was late in joining international efforts to criminalise overseas bribery. Prior to the Bribery Act, the UK prosecuted the crime of bribery under common law[33] and a variety of disparate provisions dating back to the nineteenth century, commencing with the Public Bodies Corrupt Practices Act 1889.[34] That Act dealt with bribery of public officials, whereas the Prevention of Corruption Act 1906 and Prevention of Corruption Act 1916 extended the concept into the private sector (based on the Principal/Agent concept)[35] and the presumption of

28 International Organization for Standardization, 'ISO 37001:2016' www.iso.org/iso/home/store/catalogue_tc/catalogue_detail.htm?csnumber=65034 Accessed 18 October 2016.

29 John Benstead, 'Biting the Bullet' (2010) 160 NLJ 1291.

30 Transparency International, 'How effective is the UK Bribery Act?' www.transparency.org.uk/how-effective-is-the-uk-bribery-act/ Accessed 20 March 2017.

31 David Aaronberg and Nicola Higgins, 'The Bribery Act 2010: all bark and no bite ...?' (2010) Arch Rev 5, 6–9.

32 Transparency International, 'How effective is the UK Bribery Act?' (n 30). Note: the 'Act extends to England and Wales, Scotland and Northern Ireland'. Bribery Act 2010, s 18.

33 'Bribery at common law has evolved over time, and opinions differ as to whether it is to be regarded as a general offence (applying to a range of different offices or functions) or whether the common law is comprised of a number of offences of bribery (distinguished by the office or function to which a particular offence applies).' The Law Commission, 'Legislating the Criminal Code: Corruption' www.gov.uk/government/publications/legislating-the-criminal-code-corruption Accessed 6 December 2016.

34 Public Bodies Corrupt Practices Act 1889. Preamble: 'An Act for the more effectual Prevention and Punishment of Bribery and Corruption of and by Members, Officers, or Servants of Corporations, Councils, Boards, Commissions, or other Public Bodies.' s 1. Corruption in office a misdemeanour. (1) Every person who shall by himself or by or in conjunction with any other person, corruptly solicit or receive, or agree to receive, for himself, or for any other person (...) (2) Every person who shall by himself or by or in conjunction with any other person corruptly give, promise, or offer any gift, loan, fee, reward, or advantage whatsoever to any person (...)

35 Prevention of Corruption Act 1906 s 1. 'Punishment of corrupt transactions with agents. (1) If any agent corruptly accepts or obtains, or agrees to accept or attempts to

corruption relating to any payments to government officials.[36] The UK law on bribery was left untouched until the Committee on Standards in Public Life recommended that the government clarify the law.[37] This was followed by the Law Commission proposals, 'Legislating the Criminal Code: Corruption'.[38] The Anti-terrorism, Crime and Security Act brought in provisions to strengthen the law on international corruption, putting beyond doubt that the law of bribery applies to acts involving officials of foreign public bodies, government ministers, members of Parliament and judges, and to 'agents' of foreign 'principals'. This gave courts jurisdiction over bribery committed by UK nationals and UK incorporated bodies overseas.[39] The Criminal Justice and Immigration Act 2008 extended SFO powers to compel production of documents in foreign bribery cases.[40] The Bribery Act took effect from 2011 but was not retrospective, the general principle of criminal law being that earlier actions should be prosecuted under the old law.[41] Thus, the existing laws remain operative. The consequence of this is that cases continued to be brought under the old legislation because the events on which they were predicated took place before July 2011. Thus, it is not surprising that it took some time before cases appeared under the Bribery Act, enabling its provisions to be tested in court.

This part of the chapter critically assesses the offences created by the Bribery Act:[42] 'offences of bribing another person'; 'being bribed'; 'bribing a foreign public official'; and 'failure of commercial organisations to prevent bribery'.[43] The first two offences, which consolidate existing law, are general bribery offences.[44]

Offering a bribe consists of providing an advantage to a person in return for that person performing a 'relevant function or activity' improperly. This includes making payments such as facility fees, referral fees and commissions. There is an

obtain, from any person, for himself or for any other person, (…) in relation to his principal's affairs or business.'

36 Prevention of Corruption Act 1906, s 3. The Prevention of Corruption Act 1916, increased penalties (s 1) and introduced the presumption of corruption for public officials such that the defence had to prove the contrary. s 2. 'Steps taken to implement and enforce the OECD Convention.' OECD, 'Convention' (n 6).

37 Committee on Standards in Public Life, First Report, 'Standards in Public Life' (Nolan Committee) (HMSO 1995) 43. www.gov.uk/government/uploads/system/uploads/attachment_data/file/336919/1stInquiryReport.pdf Accessed 18 October 2016.

38 The Law Commission, 'Legislating the Criminal Code: Corruption' (n 33). Draft Corruption Bill 2003 www.publications.parliament.uk/pa/jt200203/jtselect/jtcorr/157/157.pdf Accessed 18 October 2016. Bribery: Reform of the Prevention of Corruption Acts and SFO powers in cases of bribery of foreign officials. Home Office December 2005. Law Commission (Law Comm No 313) 2008.

39 Anti-terrorism, Crime and Security Act 2001, s 108.

40 Criminal Justice and Immigration Act 2008, s 59.

41 Raphael (n 3) 11.

42 The Bribery Act 2010 (Commencement) Order 2011, effective from 1 July 2011.

43 Bribery Act 2010, s 6.

44 'Offences of bribing another person'; and 'Offences relating to being bribed'. Bribery Act 2010 s 1 and s 2. Bribery Act 2010 'explanatory notes'.

'expectation' test,[45] which relates the improper performance to the yardstick of UK standards of good faith or impartiality that a reasonable person in the UK may expect. This means that if the intention is to bribe then it will be an offence in the UK irrespective of whether such a payment might be culturally acceptable in another country. The only exception is if it is permissible by *written* law.[46] This goes some way to acknowledge national differences, but it is a narrow exception requiring 'normal business practice' being permitted by written law. This is in contrast to the US where the Foreign Corrupt Practices Act (FCPA) allows 'facilitation payments' or 'grease payments',[47] and payments to foreign political parties or officials 'to expedite or secure the performance of a routine government action'.[48] The UK government stated:

> We recognise that many UK businesses still struggle with petty corruption in some markets, but the answer is to face the challenge head-on, rather than carve out exemptions that draw artificial distinctions, are difficult to enforce, and have the potential to be abused. Providing exemptions for facilitation payments, as the US does, is not a universally accepted practice, and not something that we consider acceptable.[49]

The new offences are: bribing a foreign public official, where the only requirement is an intention to influence a foreign official in their official capacity;[50] and failure of commercial organisations to prevent bribery,[51] which targets situations where a person connected or 'associated' with a commercial organisation is involved.[52] The term 'associated person' is very wide and encompasses employees, agents and third parties, including other intermediaries, suppliers or joint venture partners. It is noteworthy that lack of control over the associated person is not a defence; the precise relationship is irrelevant.[53] This offence is one of strict liability and has only one defence – namely that the organisation had in place 'adequate procedures' to prevent bribery.[54]

Whereas US legislation permits payments to secure the performance of overseas ministerial and routine government action (issuance of permits, visas, unloading cargo or releasing goods from customs)[55] or hospitality-associated expenditure such as travel and accommodation costs relating to the promotion and explanation of a product, the Bribery Act criminalises such actions. The Ministry of Justice and

45 Bribery Act 2010, s 5.
46 Bribery Act 2010, s 5 (emphasis added).
47 Transparency International, 'Countering Small Bribes' www.transparency.org.uk/publications/countering-small-bribes/ Accessed 20 March 2017.
48 Aaronberg and Higgins (n 31) 5, 6–9. Foreign Corrupt Practices Act 1977.
49 Clare Ward, HC Deb 3 March 2010 vol 506 col 981.
50 Bribery Act 2010, s 6.
51 Bribery Act 2010, s 7.
52 Bribery Act 2010, s 7.
53 Bribery Act 2010, s 8.
54 Bribery Act 2010, s 7.
55 15 U.S.C. §§ 78dd-1(b).

the SFO have indicated that they will treat each case on its merits and the Bribery Act vests total discretion in the hands of the SFO, as prosecutors, to decide whether or not to pursue such payments as illegal bribes. Vesting prosecutorial discretion in the hands of the SFO is congruent with an objective to have one single economic crime agency and avoids issues of different bodies making contradictory decisions, which would be the case if the FCA used its regulatory powers to fine breaches of bribery procedures rather than allow the specific prosecutors to institute criminal proceedings.

It is for the commercial organisation to demonstrate that it has in place adequate procedures in order to provide a defence; the consequences of failing to do so risks unlimited fines and imprisonment up to ten years. One particular challenge for a commercial organisation is to ascertain whether or not its foreign counterparty is a government or public body because in other countries key sectors of the economy are not privatised, leading to a risk of inadvertently dealing with foreign public officials. Because of the broad scope and disquiet over the strict liability nature of the offence, the government consulted widely before providing guidance.[56]

It is important to examine the four offences that the Bribery Act created, to put into context apprehensions and misapprehensions, particularly of commercial organisations, in enforcing the Act. The first offence is 'offences of bribing another person'. A person is guilty of an offence if he promises or gives a financial or other advantage to another person either with the intention that there should be improper performance of a function or activity, or knowing that acceptance would constitute the improper performance – that improper performance being rewarded by the 'advantage'.[57] It does not matter whether the advantage is offered, promised or given directly between the parties or through an intermediary. Similarly, it does not matter whether the person receiving the offer is the same person due to perform the activity.[58] This makes plain that the intention to bribe is paramount, not the mechanism, and the provision removes the possibility of those involved distancing themselves by adopting circuitous means to ensure there is no evidence of their involvement.

The counterpart of the first offence is 'offences relating to being bribed'. A person is guilty of an offence if he requests, agrees to receive or accepts an advantage with the intention that he should perform a relevant function or activity improperly either by himself or by another person, or as a reward for such performance.[59] The mere request, agreement or acceptance constitutes the improper performance and it does not matter whether the advantage is received directly or through a third party, nor whether the benefit is to those same parties or another/

56 Ministry of Justice, 'Guidance about commercial organisations preventing bribery (section 9 of the Bribery Act 2010)' http://webarchive.nationalarchives.gov.uk/20101013220527/http://www.justice.gov.uk/consultations/briberyactconsultation.htm Accessed 18 October 2016.

57 Bribery Act 2010, s 1.

58 Bribery Act 2010, s 1(4) (5).

59 Bribery Act 2010, s 2.

others.[60] This includes cases where the improper performance has either been done or is yet to be done by the person or someone acting under his instruction or acquiescence. It does not matter whether the person performing the function or activity knows that it is improper. Improper performance occurs 'in breach of a relevant expectation'[61] which is of 'good faith or impartiality' arising from a 'position of trust'.[62] The implication of this is that the recipient of a bribe cannot hide behind a third party. The third bribery offence is that of 'bribing a foreign public official'.[63] A person who bribes a foreign public official is guilty of an offence if he intends to influence the official in performance of his capacity as a public official with the intention of obtaining or retaining business or a business advantage.[64] However, there is relief if such payments are permitted by the *written* law of that country. Mere custom or tolerance will not suffice.[65] This is not a new offence.

Some bribes are excused as merely 'facilitation payments' but, nevertheless, are still bribes.[66] This offence has the effect of penalising those who actively intend bribery as well as those who regard it as an accepted norm to facilitate or 'oil the wheels of local bureaucracy' by 'greasing' the palm of some public official to expedite performance, such as entry visas, permits, licences or, say, loading, unloading and release of perishable goods from the docks or provision of a telephone or electricity service.[67] These payments are small bribes or backhanders made to secure or advance the performance of a routine or necessary action to which the payer has a legal or other entitlement and are believed to be widespread in some areas and considered necessary.[68] In effect, 'small bribe takers thrive on inefficiency and bureaucratic obstacles'.[69] The distinction between a bribe and a facilitation payment is illusory. In reality, there is no distinction, for 'if companies pay these small bribes willingly, they are nevertheless bribes. If companies pay

60 Bribery Act 2010, ss 2(4)(5)(6).
61 Raphael (n 3) 39.
62 Raphael (n 3) 40.
63 Introduced by Anti-Terrorism Crime and Security Act 2001, s 108(1).
64 Bribery Act 2010, s 6.
65 Bribery Act 2010, s 6(3)(b).
66 Ward (n 49).
67 Tom Stocker, 'Overseas corruption – a toughening global regime: be aware. Be prepared' (2009) 8 IELR 288–292.
68 'Given the widespread practice of making facilitation payments in certain countries, such as Africa, some operators have questioned whether it is appropriate to criminalise them. Indeed, the Australia-Africa Mining Industry Group has recently suggested that anti-bribery laws in this context are counter-productive. They argue that many African governments are not in a position to pay officials the salaries they deserve and facilitation payments are therefore seen as a necessary supplement in such countries.' John Lurie, Nicholas Burkill and Jocelyn Knoll, 'Bribery and corruption in the construction industry: Challenges for international construction and engineering projects' (2013) Const LJ 26.
69 Trace International, 'The high cost of small bribes' 7 www.traceinternational.org/Uploads/PublicationFiles/TheHighCostofSmallBribes2015.pdf Accessed 6 December 2016.

these bribes because they believe they have no choice, they are extortionate'.[70] However, to add to the confusion, some payments of a small, customary nature are commonly made by the private sector, such as 'tipping'.[71]

The fourth offence is 'failure of commercial organisations to prevent bribery'. A relevant commercial organisation is guilty of an offence if a person associated with the organisation bribes another intending to obtain or retain business or a business advantage for the organisation.[72] It is a defence for a relevant commercial organisation to prove that it had in place adequate procedures designed to prevent persons associated with the commercial organisation bribing another person.[73] The Bribery Act seeks to end the practice of paying bribes through intermediaries while the commercial organisation claims not to be aware that bribery was taking place. The Act makes clear that it does not matter whether the 'advantage' is offered, given, requested, or received directly or through an intermediary. It is this new offence that caused concern and generated considerable debate because of its strict liability, wide scope and severe consequences. The strict (or absolute)[74] liability of the offence removes the opportunity for those not directly involved in making the bribe to avoid liability. This is because normally 'criminal liability generally rests upon proof of two things – *actus reus* and *mens rea*'[75] (that is, the 'guilty act' and the 'guilty mind'), and the traditional maxim is: 'the act is not guilty unless the mind is also guilty.'[76] Thus, as Lord Goddard CJ explained:

> It is of the utmost importance for the protection of the liberty of the subject that a court should always bear in mind that, unless a statute, clearly or by necessary implication, rules out *mens rea* as a constituent part of a crime, the court should not find a man guilty of an offence against the criminal law unless he has a guilty mind.[77]

The impact for a commercial organisation is that it is liable for the offence of bribery if an 'associate' of the organisation commits bribery without its knowledge, and it is clear that, no matter the circumstances, the commercial organisation cannot deny responsibility. Whatever the organisation did or did not know, it is guilty of the act. Notwithstanding the anxiety over Bribery Act s 7, for which the adequate procedures defence is discussed below, by mid-2016, only three such

70 Trace International (n 69) 4.
71 '"Tipping" of waiters and cab drivers is an example widespread across the world. Such a practice is not regarded as criminal bribery, so long as the tips are small and associated essentially with a display of gratitude rather than an attempt to secure better service than other customers.' Jeremy Horder, 'Bribery as a form of criminal wrongdoing' (2011) 127 LQR 37–54.
72 Bribery Act 2010, s 7.
73 Bribery Act 2010, s 7.
74 Michael T Molan, *Sourcebook on Criminal Law*, 2nd edn (Cavendish Publishing 2001) 177.
75 Molan (n 74) 93.
76 '*[A]ctus non facit reum nisi mens sit rea.*' Molan (n 74) 93.
77 *Brend v Wood* (1946) 175 LT 306, in Molan (n 74) 178.

cases had come to court, two of which were in connection with Deferred Prosecution Agreements.[78] However, the SFO has announced investigations into bribery at Rolls-Royce, Airbus, Unaoil and Alstom, which may provide further examples.[79]

Adequate procedures defence

The Bribery Act, having put in place a crime of 'failure of commercial organisations to prevent bribery', also provides a full defence to prosecution if a person associated with it bribes another person.[80] This is welcome and recognises that, whatever procedures it puts in place, there is a risk of failure. However, the commercial organisation has to demonstrate that it had in place *adequate procedures* designed to prevent persons associated with the commercial organisation from bribing another person. This builds on the requirements of the MLR2007[81] of customer due diligence and training, and SARs.[82] The expression 'adequate procedures' generated much debate. The MoJ published guidance to commercial organisations.[83] The SFO underlines that this is not an offence of strict liability because of the availability of the defence of 'adequate procedures'. Thus, 'if there are adequate procedures, then no offence has been committed. This is a complete defence and not just mitigation'.[84]

The MoJ guidance is formulated around six principles of general application which it regards as not being either prescriptive or 'one size fits all'. There is a health warning that questions of adequacy of procedures would have to be

78 *SFO v Standard Bank, SFO v XYZ, SFO v Sweett Group. SFO v XYZ Limited.* Southwark Crown Court U20150856.

79 Serious Fraud Office, 'News' www.sfo.gov.uk/news/ Accessed 18 October 2016.

80 Bribery Act 2010, s 7.

81 Money Laundering Regulations 2007, SI 2007/2157.

82 Money Laundering Regulations 2007, s 5, 21; Proceeds of Crime Act 2002, s 330. 'Where an organisation in the regulated sector (e.g. a bank, accountancy firm or legal firm) suspects that they may commit a money laundering offence, they are obliged to submit a Suspicious Activity Report (SAR) to the National Crime Agency (NCA), seeking consent to proceed. The SARs consent regime has the practical effect of preventing an activity from going ahead for an initial notice period of 7 days, and where appropriate, for a period of 31 days known as the "moratorium period". The moratorium period allows law enforcement agencies to gather evidence to determine whether further action, such as restraint of the funds, should take place.' The Criminal Finances Bill was introduced into Parliament in October 2016. It contains proposals to extend the moratorium period to six months. Home Office, 'Factsheet – Part 1, Chapter 2' www.gov.uk/government/uploads/system/uploads/attachment_data/file/564471/CF_Bill_-_Factsheet_4_-_SARs_moratorium_and_Request_Information_Power.pdf Accessed 30 November 2016.

83 Bribery Act 2010, s 9.

84 Serious Fraud Office, 'Richard Alderman: The Bribery Act 2010 – The SFO's approach and international compliance' 9 February 2011 http://webarchive.nationalarchives.gov.uk/20120408054128/http://www.sfo.gov.uk/about-us/our-views/director's-speeches/speeches-2011/the-bribery-act-2010—the-sfo's-approach-and-international-compliance.aspx Accessed 6 December 2016.

determined by the courts but that departure from the procedures would not give rise to a presumption of inadequacy.[85] Commercial organisations are invited to take a 'risk-based' approach and it is accepted that 'no bribery prevention regime will be capable of preventing bribery at all times', and thus invites self-reporting to SFO.

The first principle was that the procedures put in place should be proportionate to the risks faced by the organisation;[86] second, that in order to embed anti-bribery and corruption behaviours, top management (that is the board of directors or owners) must be able to demonstrate commitment to preventing bribery;[87] third, that a commercial organisation has to assess the risks of bribery for its business, which is familiar territory because it is standard practice for money laundering;[88] fourth, that the organisation will undertake due diligence[89] on all parties to its relationships;[90] fifth, the organisation will communicate and embed its bribery prevention policies throughout the organisation, including training (similar to MLRs);[91] and last, the sixth principle is that procedures should be subject to monitoring and review, which means that the policy has to be active rather than relying on, say, an external verification that standards are in place.[92] Thus, merely obtaining a lawyer's certificate of compliance is not a defence.[93]

As part of a risk-management strategy and ensuring adequate procedures is the need for a whistleblowing policy, as an important safeguard,[94] where existing legislation is the Public Interest Disclosure Act 1998.[95] This is outside the scope of this book, but the City regulators[96] require certain firms to have effective whistleblowing procedures, and to make senior management accountable as a 'Whistleblowing Champion'.[97] This was in response to suggestions from the

85 Ministry of Justice, 'The Bribery Act: Guidance' (n 56) 6.
86 For a detailed explanation, see: Ministry of Justice, 'The Bribery Act: Guidance' (n 56) 21.
87 For a detailed explanation, see: Financial Services Authority, *Handbook* SYSC 3.2.6 http://fsahandbook.info/FSA/html/handbook/SYSC/3/2#DES92 Accessed 26 September 2016.
88 For detailed explanation, see: Financial Conduct Authority, 'The risk-based approach to anti-money laundering (AML)' www.fca.org.uk/firms/financial-crime/money-laundering-terrorist-financing Accessed 20 March 2017. Ministry of Justice, 'The Bribery Act: Guidance' (n 56) 25.
89 For detailed explanation, see: Money Laundering Regulations 2007, s 5.
90 Ministry of Justice, 'The Bribery Act: Guidance' (n 56) 27.
91 Ministry of Justice, 'The Bribery Act: Guidance' (n 56) 29.
92 Ministry of Justice, 'The Bribery Act: Guidance' (n 56) 31.
93 TheBriberyAct.com, 'Richard Alderman: A lawyers certificate of Adequate Procedures compliance. How much would you pay?' http://thebriberyact.com/2011/08/02/a-lawyers-certificate-of-adequate-procedures-compliance-how-much-would-you-pay/ Accessed 6 September 2016.
94 Reuters, 'Tesco whistleblower's warnings were initially ignored – report' http://uk.reuters.com/article/2014/09/28/uk-tesco-accounts-investigation-idUKKCN0HN0JL20140928 Accessed 29 September 2016.
95 Public Interest Disclosure Act 1998.
96 Bank of England, Financial Conduct Authority and Prudential Regulation Authority.
97 Financial Conduct Authority, 'Financial Incentives for Whistleblowers. Note by the Financial Conduct Authority and the Prudential Regulation Authority for the Treasury

Parliamentary Commission on Banking Standards and involved researching US practice,[98] but concluding that financial incentives to report would not be adopted.[99] The US, as discussed in Chapter 4, does provide significant financial incentives, as does the CMA.[100]

Finally, the costs of implementing an anti-bribery regime for a commercial organisation are significant,[101] notwithstanding government emphasis that its guidance was on implementation in a workable way and that 'combating the risks of bribery is largely about common sense, not burdensome procedures'.[102] Not only do commercial organisations have costs, but so does the SFO, which forecast costs of enforcing estimated at £2m per annum;[103] however, this cost will have to be met from the SFO's existing and already shrinking 'core' budget.[104] The clear inference is that the SFO will have insufficient resources to take active steps to enforce the Act, as suggested in the past by the need for 'blockbuster' funding to pursue its objectives.

Select Committee' www.fca.org.uk/static/documents/financial-incentives-for-whistleblowers.pdf. Financial Conduct Authority, 'Whistleblowing' www.fca.org.uk/firms/whistleblowing Accessed 31 October 2016.

98 See Chapter 4.

99 Financial Conduct Authority, 'Financial Incentives for Whistleblowers' (n 97).

100 The CMA offers financial rewards of up to £100,000. Competition and Markets Authority, 'Rewards for information about Cartels' www.gov.uk/government/uploads/system/uploads/attachment_data/file/299411/Informant_rewards_policy.pdf Accessed 30 November 2016. Securities and Exchange Commission, 'SEC announces largest-ever whistleblower award' [$30m] www.sec.gov/News/PressRelease/Detail/PressRelease/1370543011290#.VCktK77HthY Accessed 6 July 2016.

101 'Anti-bribery compliance is getting expensive. Companies embroiled in enforcement actions routinely conclude that the fines are less expensive than the costs of the investigations and remediation. Companies not in the middle of ongoing investigations are urged to do more, hire more and pay more to keep it that way.' Alexandra Wrage, Trace International, 'Westlaw International Commentary Series' http://traceinternational.org/data/public/AW_Anti-BriberyResourcesthatCostWellNothingatAll_Westlaw_ThomsonReuters_01.2011-64899-1.pdf Accessed 6 July 2016.

102 Ministry of Justice, 'The Bribery Act: Guidance' (n 56) 2.

103 Lord McNally, HL Deb 24 January 2011 vol 724 WA90.

104 *The Telegraph*, 'SFO given just £2m to enforce Bribery Act' www.telegraph.co.uk/finance/newsbysector/banksandfinance/8290808/SFO-given-just-2m-to-enforce-Bribery-Act.html Accessed 6 December 2016. 'Serious Fraud Office investigates the most serious and complex cases of fraud, bribery and corruption. The quantity of such work is unpredictable. The SFO has a core budget which is supplemented as necessary by additional funding agreed with the Treasury. This includes "blockbuster" funding, which enables us to take on very big cases where the annual expenditure is expected to exceed an agreed percentage of our core budget. The current "blockbuster" funding arrangement was agreed in October 2012.' The SFO core budget showed actual reductions from £53.2m in 2008/09, to £29.6m in 2013/14. The core budget for 2016/17 is £35.7m. In 2013/14, additional blockbuster funding of £24m was made available, with £24.5m in 2014/15 and £28m in 2015/16. Serious Fraud Office, 'About Us' www.sfo.gov.uk/about-us/ Accessed 6 December 2016.

Penalties

Penalties under the Bribery Act are split between those for individuals and those for 'non-individuals'. The maximum penalty for individuals is an unlimited fine, imprisonment for up to ten years, or both.[105] An offence committed by a person other than an individual is punishable by an unlimited fine.[106] These penalties, which are congruent with those for fraud, nevertheless bear comparison with penalties in other jurisdictions, which will be discussed in Chapters 4 and 5, where it is clear that penalties are greater in the US. Whether the penalties are appropriate or not is an open question because by 2016 there had been just one SFO prosecution, which is not surprising given that the SFO consider that 'on average, it takes 19 months to investigate allegations and bring a case to charge'.[107]

Enforcement

It is the SFO's cases against BAE, Dougall and Innospec which have proven to be problematic. The most 'high-profile' case was BAE, a defence equipment supplier to the UK and US governments and, in this case, to Saudi Arabia, a key ally in the fight against international terrorism. BAE was accused of corruption in its dealing with Saudi Arabia and since BAE is a UK-based company, the SFO investigated. In addition to the 'high-octane' nature of the arms sales sector in general, the SFO's reputation was severely dented by the forced abandonment of its investigations into BAE Systems plc's sale of the Eurofighter jet aircraft to Saudi Arabia, the Al Yamamah contract. In the *Al Yamamah* case,[108] the SFO considered that bribery may have been involved in BAE being awarded highly lucrative contracts, and they commenced investigations. Saudi Arabia did not welcome this intervention and put pressure on the UK government for the investigation to cease, citing damage to future commercial interests as well as a fracturing of their relationship to counter the 'War on Terror'. Ultimately, the SFO discontinued the investigation – an action which was then subject to judicial review and which the House of Lords concluded was within its discretion.[109] The SFO's decision 'resulted in widespread anger and indignation throughout the global anti-corruption community'.[110]

105 Bribery Act 2010, s 11.
106 Raphael (n 3) 86.
107 Serious Fraud Office, 'Sweett Group PLC sentenced and ordered to pay £2.25 million after Bribery Act conviction' www.sfo.gov.uk/2016/02/19/sweett-group-plc-sentenced-and-ordered-to-pay-2-3-million-after-bribery-act-conviction/ Accessed 18 October 2016.
108 *R (on the application of Corner House Research and another) v Director of the Serious Fraud Office (BAE Systems plc, interested party)* [2008] All ER 927.
109 James Wilson, 'The day we sold the Rule of Law' Halsbury's Law Exchange www.halsburyslawexchange.co.uk/?s=the+day+we+sold+the+rule+of+law Accessed 24 November 2016.
110 Benstead (n 29) 1291.

This case encapsulates the issues facing prosecutors: namely that commercial interests may 'override' the strict rule of law. Although the *Al Yamamah* case predates the Bribery Act, it is unlikely that Act would have changed the outcome because the SFO continues to have discretion to act. In this case, the SFO took a 'balanced view' which naturally offends purists, offering such epithets as 'shameless capitulation of the rule of law', shameless 'selling-out of principles' and evidencing the 'murky nature' of the arms business.[111] Of course, this is an unusual case, but it highlights the 'real' issues faced in international commerce, when the SFO is superintended by the Attorney General, a government minister, who has to embrace political considerations.[112]

Enforcement of the Bribery Act is a key area and the paucity of prosecutions under previous legislation has already been noted.[113] The SFO has been criticised for its handling of cases, with adverse comments on timeliness and cost-effectiveness.[114] As a response and in an endeavour to emulate the successful outcomes achieved by US authorities, the SFO have sought to use other methods, which obviate the need for trials, such as Civil Recovery Orders (CROs).[115] The SFO may say that it is pure coincidence that since 2009, when de Grazia reported (see below), it has changed its approach to adopt different methods to achieve the aims of working on more cases a year and delivering outcomes faster at a reduced cost.[116] To do this, the SFO has introduced two different approaches: self-referral and 'plea bargaining', which has been formally introduced as Deferred Prosecution Agreements (DPAs), discussed below.

111 James Wilson, 'The day we sold the Rule of Law' (n 109).

112 John Cooper, 'The day we sold the Rule of Law' in Ian McDougall (ed), *Cases That Changed Our Lives* (LexisNexis 2010).

113 Sheikh (n 20).

114 HM Crown Prosecution Service Inspectorate, 'Report to the Attorney General on the inspection of the Serious Fraud Office' November 2012 www.justiceinspectorates.gov.uk/crown-prosecution-service/wp-content/uploads/sites/3/2014/04/SFO_Nov12_rpt.pdf Accessed 6 December 2016.

115 'The Serious Fraud Office has today deployed for the first time new powers made available to it as from April 2008. These powers include civil recovery under the Proceeds of Crime Act 2002, under which the SFO can recover property obtained by unlawful conduct. These provisions do not require a specific offence to be established against any particular company or individual, merely that the property sought is the proceeds of unlawful conduct.' Serious Fraud Office, 'Serious Fraud Office successfully obtains first ever Civil Recovery Order involving major plc' http://webarchive.nationalarchives.gov.uk/20110704124145/http://www.sfo.gov.uk/press-room/latest-press-releases/press-releases-2008/balfour-beatty-plc.aspx Accessed 6 December 2016. Companies Act 1965, s 221. 'Legislative Comment: The United Kingdom Bribery Bill' (2010) 26(2) Const L J 146–152. Serious Fraud Office, 'SFO obtains Civil Recovery Order against AMEC' http://webarchive.nationalarchives.gov.uk/20110704124145/http://www.sfo.gov.uk/press-room/latest-press-releases/press-releases-2009/sfo-obtains-civil-recovery-order-against-amec-plc.aspx Accessed 6 December 2016.

116 Serious Fraud Office, 'Annual Report 2009–10' 1 http://webarchive.nationalarchives.gov.uk/20120408054128/http://www.sfo.gov.uk/about-us/annual-reports–accounts/annual-reports/annual-report-2009-2010.aspx Accessed 6 December 2016.

Historically, one third of SFO's work was related to overseas corruption,[117] and to deal with this, the SFO[118] highlighted the benefits to be obtained from self-reporting. The attraction offered 'to the corporate will be the prospect (in appropriate cases) of a civil rather than a criminal outcome as well as the opportunity to manage, with us, the issues and any publicity proactively'.[119]

In 2011, the SFO reported M W Kellogg Limited's self-referral because of corruption by its US parent's joint venture company in Nigeria from which M W Kellogg Limited was due a dividend of £7m.[120] The parent company had been investigated and settled with the DoJ/SEC in 2009.[121] The SFO obtained a CRO for the dividend and costs under POCA, without a criminal prosecution.[122] In a clear invitation to others, the SFO commented that they:

> will continue to encourage companies to engage with us over issues of bribery and corruption in the expectation of being treated fairly. In cases such as this a prosecution is not appropriate. Our goal is to prevent bribery and corruption or remove any of the benefits generated by such activities. This case demonstrates the range of tools we are prepared to use.[123]

This philosophy is further demonstrated in relation to two publishers, Macmillan Publishers (Macmillan) and Oxford University Press (OUP). In Macmillan, an agent attempted to bribe officials in Sudan, which Macmillan reported to the SFO. OUP discovered tendering irregularities, investigated and self-reported. The similarities of the cases are that both involved the supply of educational material to African countries, funded by the World Bank.[124] Macmillan agreed to pay £11.3m

117 Serious Fraud Office, 'Annual report 2009–10' (n 116) 4.

118 Serious Fraud Office, 'Approach of the SFO to dealing with overseas corruption' www.sfo.gov.uk/2012/10/09/revised-policies/ Accessed 3 March 2017.

119 Serious Fraud Office, 'Approach of the SFO to dealing with overseas corruption' (n 118) 1.

120 Serious Fraud Office, 'M W Kellogg to pay £7m in SFO High Court action' 16 February 2011 http://webarchive.nationalarchives.gov.uk/20110606101921/http://www.sfo.gov.uk/press-room/latest-press-releases/press-releases-2011/mw-kellogg-ltd-to-pay-£7-million-in-sfo-high-court-action.aspx Accessed 3 March 2017.

121 Department of Justice, 'Kellogg Brown & Root LLC pleads guilty to foreign bribery charges and agrees to pay $402 million criminal fine' www.justice.gov/opa/pr/kellogg-brown-root-llc-pleads-guilty-foreign-bribery-charges-and-agrees-pay-402-million Accessed 8 November 2016.

122 Serious Fraud Office, 'M W Kellogg to pay £7m in SFO High Court action' (n 120).

123 Serious Fraud Office, 'M W Kellogg to pay £7m in SFO High Court action' (n 120).

124 World Bank, 'The International Bank for Reconstruction and Development (IBRD) aims to reduce poverty in middle-income and creditworthy poorer countries by promoting sustainable development through loans, guarantees, risk management products, and analytical and advisory services. Established in 1944 as the original institution of the World Bank Group, IBRD is structured like a cooperative that is owned and operated for the benefit of its 188 member countries.' http://web.worldbank.org/WBSITE/EXTERNAL/EXTABOUTUS/EXTIBRD/0,,menuPK:3046081~pagePK:64168427~piPK:64168435~theSitePK:3046012,00.html Accessed 8 January 2017.

to the SFO, representing the estimated earnings, which was taken under POCA, and were barred from tendering for the World Bank contracts for three years.

OUP reported concerns relating to its subsidiaries in Kenya and Tanzania. OUP reached agreement with the SFO to disgorge its gross profits on the contracts of £1.9m as a civil recovery under POCA, and volunteered to 'contribute £2m to not-for-profit organisations for teacher training and other educational purposes in sub-Saharan Africa'.[125] The SFO explained its reasoning for a CRO instead of prosecution as the difficulties a prosecution would face together with giving credit for the OUP self-referral. The SFO stated that it had 'previously been subject to criticism in relation to the transparency of the processes and proceedings in civil recovery matters. As a result the Consent Order and Claim (…) have been made public'.[126] Furthermore, the SFO would itself benefit from the recovery: 'the funds will be utilised in accordance with the Asset Recovery Incentivisation Scheme which, for cases of civil recovery, result in the SFO receiving up to 50% of the value [of] the monies remitted to the Home Office'.[127]

With the same objectives in mind of expeditiousness and cost-effectiveness, and in parallel with its policy to engage with corporate organisations through self-referral, the SFO endeavoured to respond to exhortations to adopt a more modern, or transatlantic, approach.[128] This entailed changing tack to negotiate outcomes with defendants in order to realise the advantages of cost savings and certainty, which has not been without difficulty. In two cases, the SFO plea discussions with defendants caused tensions with the judiciary. First, in *Innospec*,[129] the Court of Appeal criticised SFO for 'usurping' the judge's authority by agreeing punishment. Second, in *Dougall* [130] the judge rejected SFO claims for leniency.[131] Since these cases would appear to be part of a 'programme (…) instituted to encourage whistleblowing by city insiders, lawyers and accountants and to expand the SFO's role in public anti-fraud initiatives',[132] judicial antipathy is of clear concern. DPAs

125 Proceeds of Crime Act 2000, s 276. Serious Fraud Office, 'Oxford Publishing Ltd to pay almost £1.9 million as settlement after admitting unlawful conduct in its East African operations' 3 July 2012 www.sfo.gov.uk/2012/07/03/oxford-publishing-ltd-pay-almost-1-9-million-settlement-admitting-unlawful-conduct-east-african-operations/ Accessed 6 December 2016.

126 Serious Fraud Office, 'Oxford Publishing Ltd to pay almost £1.9 million' (n 125).

127 Serious Fraud Office, 'Oxford Publishing Ltd to pay almost £1.9 million' (n 125).

128 Jessica de Grazia, 'Review of the Serious Fraud Office. Final Report. June 2008' http://webarchive.nationalarchives.gov.uk/20080804145057/http://www.sfo.gov.uk/publications/pdfs/JdeGrazia_Final_Review_of_SFO.pdf Accessed 6 July 2016.

129 *R v Innospec*, 'Sentencing remarks of Lord Justice Thomas' 26 March 2010 http://hb.betterregulation.com/external/Regina%20v%20Innospec%20Limited%20-%2026%20March%202012.pdf Accessed 6 December 2016.

130 *R v Dougall* [2010] EWCA Crim 1048.

131 CMS Cameron McKenna, Law-Now, 'Further tensions emerge between judiciary and SFO in corruption sentencing' 16 April 2010 www.mondaq.com/x/98482/Corporate+Crime/Further+Tensions+Emerge+Between+Judiciary+and+SFO+in+Corruption+Sentencing Accessed 6 December 2016.

132 Fraud Advisory Panel, 'Roskill revisited: Is there a case for a unified prosecution office?' 23 March 2010, www.fraudadvisorypanel.org/wp-content/uploads/2015/

offer the opportunity for a commercial organisation to accept a financial penalty and terms and then be free from prosecution.[133]

Innospec was charged with conspiracy to corrupt employees of an Indonesian state-owned oil refinery.[134] A global settlement, to include Iraqi Oil-for-Food sanctions breaking charges brought by the DoJ, was agreed with a combination of guilty pleas resulting in fines in the US of $14.1m and the UK of $12.7m.[135] Court approval was thought to be a formality.[136] The courts, however, took an early opportunity to establish their primacy by appointing a senior judge to hear the case,[137] who said 'the SFO cannot enter into an agreement under the laws of England and Wales with an offender as to the penalty in respect of the offence charged'.[138] This affirmed the principle that sentencing is for the judiciary alone.[139] However, the judge recognised the exceptional nature of the case and approved the agreement because 'implicitly, that it would be too difficult to unpick the settlement'.[140] Thomas LJ said he would have imposed a higher fine, further criticising SFO for using civil remedies in serious bribery or corruption cases where criminal sanctions were appropriate.[141] Although this was before DPAs became available, it does demonstrate the difficulties faced when endeavouring to translate procedures from other jurisdictions with different traditions and culture. Here, the judge said 'there can be no doubt that corruption of foreign government officials or foreign government ministers is at the top end of serious corporate offending both in terms of culpability and harm. It is deliberate and intentional wrongdoing'.[142]

In *R v Dougall*, the SFO sought to agree a suspended 12-month prison sentence for Dougall for various reasons, including that he was 'the "first co-operating

04/Roskill-Revisited-Final-24-Mar10.pdf Accessed 6 December 2016. 'Convictions in 1994 in major cases as Wallace Smith, Roy Wharton (Castlegate) and four separate BCCI trials.' Jeffrey Bayes, 'The case against the Serious Fraud Office' (1994) 144 NLJ 1508.

133 Alec Samuels, 'Deferred Prosecution Agreements' (2012) 211 Co Law 2, 3.

134 *Innospec* (n 129). Serious Fraud Office, 'Four sentenced for role in Innospec corruption' www.sfo.gov.uk/2014/08/04/four-sentenced-role-innospec-corruption/ Accessed 6 December 2016. Serious Fraud Office, 'Innospec Judgment' www.sfo.gov.uk/2014/09/19/statement-innospec-judgement/ Accessed 6 December 2016.

135 Department of Justice, 'Innospec Inc. pleads guilty to FCPA charges and defrauding the United Nations; admits to violating the U.S. embargo against Cuba' www.justice.gov/opa/pr/innospec-inc-pleads-guilty-fcpa-charges-and-defrauding-united-nations-admits-violating-us Accessed 6 December 2016. Serious Fraud Office, 'Innospec Judgment' (n 134).

136 Presumably on the lines of a consent ('Tomlin') Order. *Dashwood v Dashwood* [1927] WN 276.

137 Thomas LJ, *Innospec* (n 129).

138 *Innospec* (n 129).

139 Eoin O'Shea, Nicola McLeod and Alex Beal, 'Regulatory: Back to the drawing board' (2010) 160 NLJ 759.

140 O'Shea, McLeod and Beal (n 139) 759.

141 O'Shea, McLeod and Beal (n 139) 759.

142 *Innospec* (n 129) para 30.

defendant" in a major SFO corruption investigation'.[143] Although doing so, the Court of Appeal yet again made clear that the power and responsibility of sentencing lies with the court, and the court alone.[144] This might create difficulties when the SFO wishes to conclude a DPA, since 'it should not seek to make recommendations on sentencing'.[145] Lord Judge CJ, used the opportunity to provide a reminder of the status of fraudsters, which are not some superior species of criminal.[146]

The Court of Appeal identified key features of fraud trials and difficulties posed which make a 'deal' with the criminal attractive, and endeavoured to balance DPA discussions with objectivity.[147]

Lord Judge warned that in fraud and corruption cases, the SFO should not believe that these are 'more respectable than other forms of crime',[148] or that these criminals 'should not be ordered to serve prison sentences because such sentences should be reserved for those they regard as common criminals'.[149]

The Court's stance left the SFO with a potential difficulty regarding BAE Systems.[150] In 2010, SFO and the DoJ agreed a 'global' settlement with BAE for £30m[151] and $400m, respectively.[152] BAE agreed to plead guilty to various 'relatively trivial' accounting offences,[153] and the SFO dropped considerably more serious bribery charges regarding BAE's 'dealings in a number of countries, as well as at least one individual',[154] and explained it was 'very pleased with the global

143 O'Shea, McLeod and Beal (n 139) 759.
144 *R v Dougall* [2010] EWCA Crim 1048 [25] Lord Judge CJ.
145 CMS Cameron McKenna, 'Court of Appeal overturns prison sentence in corruption case' www.cms-lawnow.com/ealerts/2010/05/court-of-appeal-overturns-prison-sentence-in-corruption-case?cc_lang=en Accessed 26 November 2016.
146 'For all the respectable and reputable fronts that many fraudsters and corrupt businessmen may present, they are criminals. What is sometimes described as white collar crime or commercial crime taking the form of fraud and corruption in particular is crime. And it is not victimless: sometimes identified individuals are victims, and at others, unnamed, unknown individuals in the entire community are victims, and sometimes the community itself is the victim.' *R v Dougall.*
147 The Judge sympathised with the task: 'So often however the criminal activities are buried under mountains of paper and myriads of figures so that the process of investigation, and ultimately any trial, requires huge resources and painstaking and sometimes protracted study, examination and analysis. All that is immensely frustrating.' *R v Dougall.* Serious Fraud Office, 'Guidelines on plea discussions' www.cps.gov.uk/publications/directors_guidance/director_s_guidance_to_accompany_the_attorney_general_s_guidelines_on_plea_discussions_in_cases_of_serious_or_complex_fraud.html Accessed 20 March 2017.
148 Lord Judge (n 144).
149 Lord Judge (n 144).
150 *The Times*, 'BAE must wait as judge puts £30m bribery plea deal at risk' www.thetimes.co.uk/tto/business/industries/engineering/article2687733.ece Accessed 18 October 2016.
151 O'Shea, McLeod and Beal (n 139) 759.
152 Department of Justice, 'BAE Systems PLC pleads guilty and ordered to pay $400 million criminal fine' 1 March 2010 www.justice.gov/opa/pr/2010/March/10-crm-209.html Accessed 18 October 2016.
153 Under the Companies Act 1985. David Corker, 'Time for a serious (SFO) rethink' (2010) 160 NLJ 783, 784.
154 O'Shea, McLeod and Beal (n 139) 759.

outcome achieved collaboratively with the DoJ. This was a first and it brought a pragmatic end to a long-running and wide-ranging investigation'.[155] Whilst undoubtedly pragmatic, bearing in mind multilateral investigations and prosecutors with their differing approaches, the Court's surprise attack on the SFO is a 'reminder that in criminal proceedings, the stick is mightier than the carrot and the court is the ultimate arbiter'.[156]

Bribery Act prosecutions

The Bribery Act took effect from July 2011 and was not retrospective. The first three cases did not fall within SFO parameters. Munir Patel[157] had the dubious distinction of being the first person to be convicted, in November 2011; the second was Mawia Mushtaq,[158] and the third Yang Li.[159] Patel was a Magistrates' Court clerk who pleaded guilty to being bribed to manipulate the court traffic offence database so that penalty points would not be recorded.[160] Although guilty of one charge of accepting £500, the prosecution believed there were another 53 occasions.[161] He was initially sentenced to six years' imprisonment (later reduced on Appeal to four years) for the Bribery Act s 2 offence and Misconduct in a Public Office.[162] In the second case, Mawia Mushtaq failed a driving test for a private-hire taxi licence, having failed several times before. He tried to bribe the licensing officer with between £200–£300. He was convicted of 'Bribing another person'[163] and sentenced to two months' imprisonment, suspended for 12 months, and a two-month curfew order.[164] In the third case, Yang Li was sentenced to 12 months' imprisonment for possession of an imitation firearm, and

155 Serious Fraud Office, 'BAE Systems plc' http://webarchive.nationalarchives.gov.uk/20110606101921/http://www.sfo.gov.uk/press-room/latest-press-releases/press-releases-2010/bae-systems-plc.aspx Accessed 6 December 2016.

156 O'Shea, McLeod and Beal (n 139) 759.

157 *R v Munir Patel* [2012] EWCA Crim 3075 [2013] 1 Cr App R (S) 48.

158 Monty Raphael, *Bribery: Law and Practice* (2016 OUP) 143.

159 BBC, 'University of Bath student jailed over tutor bribe bid' 23 April 2013 www.bbc.co.uk/news/uk-england-somerset-22269573 Accessed 18 October 2016.

160 Eoin O'Shea, 'Opinion: First conviction proves Bribery Act has sharp teeth', *The Lawyer* 28 November 2011 www.thelawyer.com/opinion-first-conviction-proves-bribery-act-has-sharp-teeth/1010398.article Accessed 18 October 2016.

161 *R v Munir Patel* [2012] EWCA Crim 3075, [2013] 1 Cr App R (S) 48. CMS Cameron McKenna, 'Second prosecution under the Bribery Act' www.lexology.com/library/detail.aspx?g=bfa16a29-7409-48e3-8d16-831532f58c74 Accessed 18 October 2016.

162 'Misconduct in public office is an offence at common law triable only on indictment. It carries a maximum sentence of life imprisonment. It is an offence confined to those who are public office holders and is committed when the office holder acts (or fails to act) in a way that constitutes a breach of the duties of that office.' Crown Prosecution Service, www.cps.gov.uk/legal/l_to_o/misconduct_in_public_office/#a016 Accessed 18 October 2016.

163 Bribery Act 2010, s 1.

164 CMS Cameron McKenna, 'Second prosecution under the Bribery Act' (n 161).

attempting to bribe a university professor with £5,000 to pass his Master's degree.[165] In the first case, Patel, a public officer, hence the seriousness of the sentence, sought and received a bribe, whereas in the second and third cases a bribe was attempted but not made. However, important as these cases are because they were the first under the Bribery Act, nevertheless they are minor crimes in relation to SFO parameters,[166] which is still prosecuting pre-Bribery Act cases under earlier legislation.[167] Thus, the theory is that the Bribery Act contains provisions which should enable the bribery and corruption aspects of economic crime to be prosecuted and convictions obtained.

Prosecutions under the Bribery Act have been relatively small in number[168] and, initially, by the Crown Prosecution Service for minor offences rather than the major instances of bribery projected when the legislation was enacted. The SFO had to wait until December 2014 for its first prosecution, of four former employees of Sustainable AgroEnergy plc for a £23m fraud, conspiracy to commit fraud and 'making and accepting a financial advantage'.[169] Three employees were convicted of the sale and promotion of investment products based on 'green biofuel' Jatropha tree plantations in Cambodia.[170]

165 BBC, 'University of Bath student jailed over tutor bribe bid' 23 April 2013 www.bbc.co.uk/news/uk-england-somerset-22269573 Accessed 18 October 2016.

166 'Since I took up post in April 2012, we have sharpened the strategic focus of the SFO on the casework for which the Roskill model was designed and intended. This is the topmost tier of serious and complex fraud and bribery. Consequently: (i) We are undertaking fewer but much larger and more complex investigations. Examples include LIBOR, Rolls-Royce, Barclays/Qatar, ENRC, Alstom, G4S Serco' (David Green). Serious Fraud Office, 'Annual Report and Accounts 2013–2014' www.sfo.gov.uk/download/annual-report-2013-2014/?wpdmdl=2199 Accessed 6 December 2016.

167 For example in July 2016, the SFO announced a prosecution of F H Birtling Limited under the Prevention of Corruption Act 1906. Serious Fraud Office, 'F.H. Bertling Ltd and seven individuals charged with bribery' www.sfo.gov.uk/2016/07/13/f-h-bertling-ltd-seven-individuals-charged-bribery/ Accessed 31 October 2016.

168 'The SFO has charged five individuals with Bribery Act offences; three in 2013/14 and two in 2015/16. The SFO has charged two companies with Bribery Act offences, both in 2015/16.' Serious Fraud Office, FOI2016-060 Bribery Act Offences [Freedom of Information Act request] www.sfo.gov.uk/publications/ Accessed 24 August 2016.

169 'Four men connected to Sustainable AgroEnergy plc have today been charged with offences of conspiracy to commit fraud by false representation and conspiracy to furnish false information, contrary to section 1 of the Criminal Law Act 1977, in connection with the investigation by the Serious Fraud Office into the promotion and selling of "bio fuel" investment products to UK investors. The value of the alleged fraud is approximately £23m and the offences are said to have taken place between April 2011 and February 2012 (…) [Three men] have also been charged with offences of making and accepting a financial advantage contrary to section 1 (1) and 2 (1) of the Bribery Act 2010.' Serious Fraud Office, 'Four charged in "bio fuel" investigation' www.sfo.gov.uk/cases/sustainable-agroenergy-plc-sustainable-wealth-investments-uk-ltd/ Accessed 6 December 2016.

170 Serious Fraud Office, 'Sustainable AgroEnergy Plc and Sustainable Wealth Investments UK Ltd' www.sfo.gov.uk/cases/sustainable-agroenergy-plc-sustainable-wealth-investments-uk-ltd/ Accessed 24 August 2016.

The judge described the fraud as a 'thickening quagmire of dishonesty (…) there were more than 250 victims of relatively modest means some of whom had lost all of their life savings and their homes', with bribery as an aggravating feature.[171] The Bribery Act convictions were for the general offences of either bribing another person or being bribed.[172]

Bribery Act s 6 concerns bribery of foreign public officials. However, the SFO's first conviction of bribing foreign public officials in 2014 was under the previous legislation, the Prevention of Corruption Act 1906. In Smith and Ouzman Limited, a UK printing company specialising in security documents such as ballot papers and examination certificates, the company and two employees were convicted of bribing public officials in Kenya and Mauritania totalling £395,000.[173] The company was ordered to pay fines and confiscation of £2.2m, with the two directors receiving custodial sentences of 18 months and three years respectively.[174]

The elements of the Bribery Act that attracted particular attention were s 7, the failure of a commercial organisation to prevent bribery, for which there is a full defence in s 7(2) of a commercial organisation having in place adequate procedures designed to prevent persons associated with the commercial organisation from undertaking such conduct.[175]

The first opportunity that the court had to consider the failure of a commercial organisation to prevent bribery was in *Serious Fraud Office v Standard Bank PLC*,[176] discussed below in relation to DPAs. The offence of failure of a commercial

171 'Gary West was sentenced to a total of 13 years' imprisonment. James Whale was sentenced to a total of 9 years' imprisonment. Stuart Stone was sentenced to a total of 6 years' imprisonment.' The fourth defendant was acquitted. Serious Fraud Office, 'Sustainable AgroEnergy Plc' (n 170).

172 Bribery Act 2010 s 1, s 2. Serious Fraud Office, 'City directors convicted in £23m "Green biofuel" trial' www.sfo.gov.uk/2014/12/05/city-directors-convicted-23m-green-biofuel-trial/ Accessed 26 August 2016.

173 Serious Fraud Office, 'Convicted printing company sentenced and ordered to pay £2.2 million' www.sfo.gov.uk/2016/01/08/convicted-printing-company-sentenced-and-ordered-to-pay-2-2-million/ Accessed 26 August 2016.

174 'The sum broken down included a fine of £1,316,799 as well as £881,158 to satisfy a confiscation order applied for by the SFO and £25,000 in costs. Two employees of the company were sentenced in February last year [2015] for their role in the corruption. Its chairman, Christopher John Smith, was sentenced to 18 months' imprisonment, suspended for two years, and was ordered to carry out 250 hours of unpaid work. Nicholas Charles Smith, the sales and marketing director of the company, was sentenced to three years' imprisonment. A confiscation order of £18,693 was today imposed on Nicholas Smith, payable within eight weeks. He was also ordered to pay costs of £75,000 within nine months. Christopher Smith was ordered to pay £4,500 in confiscation within seven days and costs of £75,000 within three months.' Serious Fraud Office, 'Convicted printing company sentenced and ordered to pay £2.2 million' www.sfo.gov.uk/2016/01/08/convicted-printing-company-sentenced-and-ordered-to-pay-2-2-million/ Accessed 26 August 2016.

175 Bribery Act 2010 s 7.

176 *Serious Fraud Office v Standard Bank PLC*, Preliminary Judgment U20150854 Southwark Crown Court 30 November 2015.

organisation to prevent bribery and the defence of having adequate procedures had not been tested in court prior to this case and, as such, represented a significant development in the field of anti-bribery and corruption. In this case, Stanbic was an associate of Standard Bank with different management. In order for Standard Bank to avail themselves of the 'adequate procedures' defence, they would have to demonstrate a clear policy.[177] However, the judgment found that the policy was unclear and was not re-enforced effectively through communication and training.[178] The failure to provide sufficient guidance on relevant obligations and procedures where two group companies were involved, led to a transaction with a government of a high-risk country with checks on a third party undertaken by a sister company where Standard Bank had no interest, oversight, control or involvement. Standard Bank did not undertake enhanced due diligence processes, did not identify the presence of politically exposed persons, nor the change in arrangements with the introduction of a third party charging a substantial fee.[179] The judgment concludes that an anti-corruption culture was not effectively demonstrated within Standard Bank as regards the transaction at issue.[180]

Shortly after Standard Bank, some six years after enactment of the Bribery Act, the SFO achieved its first conviction under the s 7 corporate offence of failing to prevent bribery. In *R v Sweett Group plc*,[181] the company pleaded guilty to making corrupt payments in Abu Dhabi for which it was ordered to pay fines and compensation amounting to £2.25m.[182] This is important because, although acknowledging the SFO's difficulties in facing a long lead time to bring a case to trial, the new key provision of making a commercial organisation responsible for failure to prevent bribery benefits from being ventilated in court.[183]

The reason this is important is that having adequate procedures offers a complete defence, but *Sweett* 'admitted that it did not have adequate procedures for the purpose of the defence in section 7(2) of the Bribery Act 2010 and so this issue was not tested before the court'.[184] However, if the SFO is able to evidence

177 *Serious Fraud Office v Standard Bank PLC* (n 176).
178 *Serious Fraud Office v Standard Bank PLC* (n 176).
179 *Serious Fraud Office v Standard Bank PLC* (n 176).
180 *Serious Fraud Office v Standard Bank PLC* (n 176).
181 *R v Sweett Group plc* (unreported).
182 'The company pleaded guilty in December 2015 to a charge of failing to prevent an act of bribery intended to secure and retain a contract with Al Ain Ahlia Insurance Company (AAAI), contrary to Section 7(1)(b) of the Bribery Act 2010.' 'The amount is broken down as £1.4m in fine, £851,152.23 in confiscation. Additionally, £95,031.97 in costs were awarded to the SFO.' Serious Fraud Office, 'Sweett Group PLC sentenced and ordered to pay £2.25 million after Bribery Act conviction' www.sfo.gov.uk/2016/02/19/sweett-group-plc-sentenced-and-ordered-to-pay-2-3-million-after-bribery-act-conviction/ Accessed 8 September 2016.
183 HHJ Beddoe. Serious Fraud Office, 'Sweett Group PLC sentenced and ordered to pay £2.25 million after Bribery Act conviction' (n 182).
184 CMS, 'Sweett Group plc: first conviction for Bribery Act corporate offence' www.cms-lawnow.com/ealerts/2016/02/sweett-group-plc-first-conviction-for-bribery-act-corporate-offence Accessed 18 October 2016.

cooperation to a court's satisfaction then this offers opportunities for the SFO to engage in DPAs, as demonstrated in *Serious Fraud Office v Standard Bank PLC*, discussed below. In *Sweett*, the SFO considered that the company had not cooperated with them and saw no reason to offer a DPA.[185]

Deferred Prosecution Agreements

A significant feature of the response to economic crime in the US is the availability of mechanisms to conclude agreements between prosecutors (the DoJ and SEC), and corporate entities, whereby in exchange for admission of guilt, payment of a fine and undertakings regarding remediatory action, the corporate entity and employees escape prosecution.[186] As an example of the financial penalties imposed, *The Times* reports that:

> Since 2010 JP Morgan has paid penalties totalling $28.7 billion for various failings relating to such matters as the misrepresentation to investors of bundled bad home loans as high-quality securities and the mis-selling of mortgage bonds to pension funds and other investors.[187]

This figure includes 'a non-tax deductible penalty of $1.7bn' relating to the Madoff fraud.[188] The settlement includes an agreement to cooperate with the authorities and not to commit any federal crimes but, as is typical of such settlements, no individuals were to be prosecuted.[189]

The coalition government decided to provide its prosecutors with a similar facility to that used extensively in the US, because 'tackling and combating financial and economic crime, which encompass an array of offences such as theft, fraud and bribery, is a key commitment within the Coalition agreement'.[190] The government pointed to the only two remedies available to prosecutors: those of 'criminal prosecution or, where this is not possible or appropriate, pursuing a civil recovery order against the person or organisation concerned'.[191] The MoJ recognised the disadvantages of these remedies where lengthy investigations are

185 Serious Fraud Office, 'Deferred Prosecution Agreements – the perspective from England and Wales' www.sfo.gov.uk/2016/09/14/deferred-prosecution-agreements-perspective-england-wales/ Accessed 6 December 2016.

186 See Chapter 4.

187 *The Times*, 'JP Morgan: paying the price of Madoff?' 23 January 2014 www.thetimes.co.uk/tto/law/article3983127.ece Accessed 18 October 2016.

188 Department of Justice, 'J P Morgan Chase Deferred Prosecution Agreement' www.justice.gov/usao/nys/pressconference/jpmcdpa/visual.pdf Accessed 18 October 2016.

189 Department of Justice, 'J P Morgan Chase Deferred Prosecution Agreement' (n 188).

190 See: www.cabinetoffice.gov.uk/sites/default/files/resources/coalition_programme_for_government.pdf. Ministry of Justice, 'Crime and Courts Bill: Fact Sheet: Deferred Prosecution Agreements' www.gov.uk/government/uploads/system/uploads/attachment_data/file/184857/fs-cj-deferred-prosecution.pdf Accessed 18 October 2016.

191 Ministry of Justice, 'Crime and Courts Bill: Fact Sheet' (n 190).

involved, 'and in the case of a criminal prosecution there is a strong likelihood of protracted court proceedings with no guarantee of a successful conviction'.[192] The outcome of a successful prosecution would be a financial sanction and, as outlined above, a financial penalty is a key ingredient of a DPA. The second remedy available to the SFO of CROs, 'even when successful, are solely a mechanism to recover the proceeds of "unlawful conduct" and do not enable sanctions for wrongdoing or compensation of victims'.[193]

Shortly after his appointment, SFO Director David Green outlined his vision and stated that 'I am keen on maximising the set of tools available to SFO as an investigation and prosecuting agency, and DPAs represent a new and imaginative tool to deal with serious economic crime committed by commercial organisations'.[194] Green considered that '[four] very important principles need to be observed': first, that 'sentencing in this jurisdiction is for the judge not the prosecution', and second, 'corporates cannot be seen to be allowed some special kid glove treatment; after (...) individuals will be prosecuted where that is the appropriate course of action'; last, 'admissions as to conduct must be realistic, factual and not fanciful'.[195]

Some 18 months later, DPAs became available to the SFO by virtue of the Crime and Courts Act 2013.[196] A DPA, which is a discretionary tool,[197] is subject to court approval.[198] The prosecutors are either the DPP or the director of the SFO, with the Act making it clear that powers to enter into a DPA must be exercised personally by the designated prosecutor.[199] The Act specifies the 'persons who may enter into a DPA with a prosecutor', which are in three categories: 'P may be a body corporate, a partnership or an unincorporated association, but may not be an individual.'[200] This latter provision differs from the US, so that in the UK 'DPAs will not be available for individuals, whether for individual crimes or for action undertaken on behalf of an organisation'.[201]

192 Ministry of Justice, 'Crime and Courts Bill: Fact Sheet' (n 190).
193 Ministry of Justice, 'Crime and Courts Bill: Fact Sheet' (n 190).
194 Serious Fraud Office, 'Speech by David Green – 10th Annual Corporate Accountability Conference held at PricewaterhouseCoopers on 14 June 2012' www.sfo.gov.uk/2012/06/14/10th-annual-corporate-accountability-conference-held-pricewaterhousecoopers/ Accessed 6 December 2016.
195 Serious Fraud Office, 'Speech by David Green' (n 194).
196 Crime and Courts Act 2013, s 45, Schedule 17, 24 February 2014. Ministry of Justice, 'A Guide to the Criminal Procedure (Amendment No. 2) Rules 2013 (S.I. 2013/3183)' www.justice.gov.uk/courts/procedure-rules/criminal/docs/2016/guide-to-the-criminal-procedure-amendment-no-2-rules-2016.pdf Accessed 18 October 2016.
197 Serious Fraud Office, 'Crime and Courts Act 2013: Deferred Prosecution Agreement Code of Practice' 1 www.sfo.gov.uk/publications/guidance-policy-and-protocols/deferred-prosecution-agreements/ Accessed 6 December 2016.
198 Crime and Courts Act 2013, s 45 Schedule 17.2.
199 Crime and Courts Act 2013, s 45 Schedule 17.3.
200 Crime and Courts Act 2013, s 45 Schedule 17.4.
201 Polly Dyer, 'Time to agree terms?' (2013) 163 NLJ 11, 12.

A DPA is likely to be available to companies that 'self-report suspected criminal misconduct to SFO'.[202] In such circumstances, the SFO would launch a formal criminal investigation to test the evidence and scale of offending.[203] The SFO's position is that:

> The available evidence may well pass the evidential test. But if the company has taken appropriate disciplinary action against those responsible, made appropriate amendments to its compliance regime, compensated victims, and genuinely and proactively cooperated with the SFO investigation, it is hard to see how it would be in the public interest to prosecute the company, as opposed to individuals.[204]

The SFO warn that 'if the corporate chooses to bury the misconduct rather than self-report, the risks attendant on discovery are truly unquantifiable'.[205] The first DPA was long awaited, being achieved almost two years after the provision became available, and it is subject to judicial supervision.[206] The expectation is that 'as experience is built up by all parties, this will generate consistency and therefore predictability around the likelihood of achieving a DPA'.[207]

The expectation was that 'the most likely candidate for the first DPA would be the type of case that would attract the lowest level of fine on a plea of guilty if proceedings were to take place'.[208] The clear issue for the SFO is that although it might well wish to avail itself of the new facility, given the history of judicial opprobrium, it would not wish to risk an adverse outcome, and the attendant publicity, of its first DPA presentation to court.

Serious Fraud Office v Standard Bank PLC [209] is a landmark case because it is not only the first case where the SFO has looked to prosecute a commercial organisation for failure to prevent bribery under the Bribery Act,[210] but also the first occasion when it has sought to enter a DPA. This case involved Standard Bank PLC, a UK bank and a subsidiary of Standard Bank Group Ltd, a South

202 Serious Fraud Office, 'Ethical business conduct: An enforcement perspective' www.sfo.gov.uk/2014/03/06/ethical-business-conduct-enforcement-perspective/ Accessed 24 November 2016.

203 Serious Fraud Office, 'Ethical business conduct: An enforcement perspective' (n 202).

204 Serious Fraud Office, 'Ethical business conduct: An enforcement perspective' (n 202).

205 Serious Fraud Office, 'Ethical business conduct: An enforcement perspective' (n 202).

206 Serious Fraud Office, 'Ethical business conduct: An enforcement perspective' (n 202). *Serious Fraud Office v Standard Bank PLC* (n 176).

207 Serious Fraud Office, 'Ethical business conduct: An enforcement perspective' (n 202).

208 *The Times*, 'Doing deals to avoid prosecution: which company will be first?' 27 February 2014 www.thetimes.co.uk/tto/law/article4017176.ece Accessed 18 October 2016.

209 *Serious Fraud Office v Standard Bank PLC* (n 176).

210 Bribery Act 2010 s 7.

African public company.[211] The Group was also the ultimate parent of Stanbic Bank Tanzania Ltd (Stanbic), a Tanzanian company. The government of Tanzania wished to raise funds and Stanbic, which was not licensed to undertake this type of transaction, engaged Standard Bank, which was licensed. At the outset of the transaction, in February 2012, Standard Bank/Stanbic quoted a fee of 1.4% of gross proceeds raised; later Stanbic increased the proposed fee to 2.4%, because 1% would be paid to a local Tanzanian partner, Enterprise Growth Market Advisors Limited (EGMA). One of EGMA's three directors and shareholders was the commissioner of the Tanzania Revenue Authority and, as such, a serving member of the Tanzania government. A second director was formerly chief executive of Tanzanian Capital Markets and Securities Authority. The outcome was that a DPA between the parties was held by the court to be in the interests of justice,[212] the terms and supporting documents were published so that the entirety of the process was open to public scrutiny,[213] and the Respondent, Standard Bank, had to make immediate payments totalling $32.6m (and a further $4.2m to US authorities[214]). Furthermore, Standard Bank has given undertakings to the SFO relating to its corporate compliance programme in the DPA.[215] A particular benefit to Standard Bank is that this matter, which commenced in 2012, with the transaction taking place in March 2013, reporting to SFO in April 2013 and the investigation report in July 2014, did not enter the public domain until 30 November 2015.

211 Now called ICBC Standard Bank plc. 'On 1 February 2015, the Industrial and Commercial Bank of China Limited [ICBC] acquired a 60% controlling interest in SB from Standard Bank Group Limited [SBG]. SBG retains a 40% interest in SB. ICBC did not own shares in SB at the time of the events described in this Statement of Facts and ICBC had no involvement in these facts in any way.' *Serious Fraud Office v Standard Bank PLC*, Statement of Facts 1–2 www.sfo.gov.uk/media/289866/20151127%20-%20sfo%20v%20icbc%20sb%20plc%20-%20statement%20of%20facts.pdf Accessed 3 December 2016.

212 *Serious Fraud Office v Standard Bank PLC* (n 176) 2.

213 *Serious Fraud Office v Standard Bank PLC* (n 176) 3.

214 Another feature of this case is the involvement of the US authorities. The $600m Sovereign Debt securities was marketed as a private placement in the US pursuant to Securities and Exchange Commission Regulations. By offering the Tanzanian sovereign bonds, Standard Bank had a duty to disclose to investors material facts that it knew or should have known concerning the transaction. It did not disclose the involvement of EGMA and the fee EGMA was to receive. As a result of the conduct in failing to disclose the material facts, Standard Bank committed violations of Sections 17(a)(2) of the Securities Act 1933. 'The SEC's order requires Standard to cease and desist from committing or causing any violations and any future violations of Section 17(a)(2) of the Securities Act of 1933 that prohibits obtaining money by any materially untrue statement or omission, and to pay a $4.2 million civil penalty.' US Securities and Exchange Commission, 'Standard Bank to Pay $4.2 Million to Settle SEC Charges' www.sec.gov/litigation/admin/2015/33-9981.pdf Accessed 4 December 2015.

215 Serious Fraud Office, 'Deferred Prosecution Agreement between Serious Fraud Office and Standard Bank PLC' www.sfo.gov.uk/media/289870/20151127%20-%20deferred%20prosecution%20agreement%20-%20sfo%20v%20icbc%20sb%20plc.pdf Accessed 4 December 2016.

Thus, by self-reporting and working with the SFO, Standard Bank was able to ensure the matter remained confidential, rather than being subject to publicity because of an announcement by SFO that it had accepted a case for formal investigation.[216]

The first DPA provided a comparatively straightforward application of the DPA principles and process, whereas the second case, *Serious Fraud Office v XYZ Limited*, [217] raised more complicated issues. The judge commented on 'the problems generated when a modestly resourced small to medium sized enterprise (SME) is demonstrably guilty of serious breaches of the criminal law'.[218] The court had to grapple with raising a penalty, which would make XYZ insolvent, and mitigating the penalty to allow the company to continue to trade. However, on the other hand, nothing must be done to encourage the pursuit of criminal behaviour through a corporate vehicle which can be abandoned as insolvent if necessary.[219] In this case, the role of the parent company was a key factor.

The judgment is considerably redacted and refers to the SME as XYZ and its parent as ABC, because of pending criminal proceedings, where two individuals have been charged.[220] Once the judge decided that it would not be in the public interest to force XYZ into the DPA, provisions were such that XYZ and ABC would disgorge gross profits and, thus, it provides an example of the value of self-reporting and cooperation with the SFO.[221] This was the first DPA with criminal charges against individuals.

The first two DPA cases have given the court the opportunity to adopt tailored rather than prescriptive approaches. An example is that Standard Bank paid a penalty based on the revenues earned under the tainted contract, whereas in XYZ the penalty was based on gross profits, a much lower amount. The court has placed great emphasis on self-reporting, an early guilty plea and a flexible approach to additional mitigation, stating 'a discount of 50% could be appropriate not least to encourage others how to conduct themselves when confronting criminality'.[222]

In the third DPA, Rolls-Royce had to pay £671m, including $170m to the US and $25m to Brazil, for '12 counts of conspiracy to corrupt, false accounting and failure to prevent bribery'.[223] A key element of this DPA was the length of

216 For a detailed analysis of *Serious Fraud Office v Standard Bank PLC*, see Axel Palmer and Nicholas Ryder, 'Is justice deferred, justice denied? Not necessarily' (2016) Financial Regulation International 19(2) March 2016 6.

217 *Serious Fraud Office v XYZ* (n 78).

218 *Serious Fraud Office v XYZ* (n 78) (Leveson P) 3.

219 *Serious Fraud Office v XYZ* (n 78) (Leveson P) 3.

220 *Serious Fraud Office v XYZ* (n 78) (Leveson P) 5.

221 Note: the terms of the DPA were: disgorgement of profits £6.2m; a financial penalty £353,000; continued cooperation with SFO; in the unusual circumstances of the case, the SFO did not seek payment of its costs.*Serious Fraud Office v XYZ* (n 78) (Leveson P) 37, 68.

222 *Serious Fraud Office v XYZ* (n 78) (Leveson P) 57.

223 Serious Fraud Office, 'SFO completes £497.25m Deferred Prosecution Agreement with Rolls-Royce PLC' www.sfo.gov.uk/2017/01/17/sfo-completes-497-25m-deferred-prosecution-agreement-rolls-royce-plc/ Accessed 20 March 2017.

conduct, which spanned three decades, relating to the sale of aero engines, energy systems and related services. 'The conduct covered by the UK DPA took place across seven jurisdictions: Indonesia, Thailand, India, Russia, Nigeria, China and Malaysia.'[224]

This raised a question for the judge as to 'whether it is necessary to inflict the undeniably adverse consequences on Rolls-Royce that would flow from prosecution because of the gravity of its offending even though it may now be considered a dramatically changed organisation'.[225] Leveson concluded that Rolls-Royce:

> will have to suffer the undeniably adverse publicity that will flow from the facts of its business practices which will be exposed by the DPA so that the way in which it has done business will be obvious. Any public procurement exercise will be conducted in the light of its history and it will doubtless only win contracts on the merits of its products. That, of course, is as it should be. Neither will the conduct of Rolls-Royce escape sanction: it could only ever be fined and the DPA has to be approached on the basis that it must be broadly comparable to the fine that a court would have imposed on conviction following a guilty plea.

DPAs are a developing area of fraud disposal with the first three exhibiting different features, indicating that the court's involvement is not necessarily disadvantageous *pace* the US.[226]

Regulatory bodies

Serious Fraud Office

It is logical that the SFO be given the lead role in enforcing the Bribery Act because it was already the lead agency for prosecution of corruption, both domestically and overseas.[227] The SFO was established to counter fraud and has had a chequered life, being dogged by controversy because of adverse publicity arising out of its prosecution, or not, of some high-profile cases.[228] This resulted in the Attorney General commissioning an external review by de Grazia.[229]

224 Serious Fraud Office, 'Rolls-Royce' (n 223).
225 Serious Fraud Office, 'Rolls-Royce' (n 223) (Leveson P).
226 Discussed in Chapter 4.
227 Although some prosecutions are undertaken by the Crown Prosecution Service, the main agency is the SFO.
228 *Bishopsgate Investment Management Ltd v Maxwell* [1993] Ch. 1; *R v Saunders* [1996] Crim LR 420; *Re Levitt* [1992] Ch. 457; *Re Arrows Ltd* (No. 4) [1994] 3 All ER 814. Some 66 charges of theft totalling £34m from Polly Peck International, which collapsed in 1990 with a deficiency of £1.3bn *R v Asil Nadir*. Serious Fraud Office, 'Annual Report 2004–2005' http://webarchive.nationalarchives.gov.uk/20080804145057/http://www.sfo.gov.uk/publications/annual_2005.asp Accessed 6 July 2016.
229 De Grazia (n 128).

De Grazia described the SFO as a 'demoralised and underperforming agency' with 'inadequate management and leadership', expending more resources whilst achieving far fewer convictions than US counterparts.[230] She highlighted that the SFO had a conviction rate of 61% compared with the Manhattan District Attorney's Office (DANY) of 92% for comparable periods.[231] De Grazia's view was that there were no fundamental differences in role between the SFO and New York agencies, but the US had 200 years' more experience.[232] De Grazia evidences that in a five-year period, the SFO employed more lawyers (56), and spent over £4m on external counsel,[233] than the DANY, which had 19 lawyers and did not contract out to the external Bar. De Grazia concluded that 'a criminal justice system that produces this little cannot be said to be effective in deterring, detecting or punishing criminals who commit serious crime'.[234] Essentially, the SFO was considered to be a costly and under-performing organisation.

Tellingly, de Grazia's key recommendations were not new for they had remarkable similarities with Roskill,[235] calling for: improvement in personnel and judges; use of police powers; team ownership of cases, from cradle to grave; and bringing advocacy 'in-house'. De Grazia's new point was the use of 'plea bargains'. In the US, because of the high probability of conviction on indictment, most cases are dealt with by the defendant 'pleading guilty at an early stage of the process in exchange for a reduced sentence'. This conserves resources for cases that merit a full trial.[236]

Following the review, the SFO promoted a new model of compliance by corporate entities with the criminal law, 'based in no small part on the US model of plea bargaining'.[237] The SFO's publication of *Approach of the Serious Fraud Office to Dealing with Overseas Corruption*, alongside the *Attorney General's Guidelines*, made plain their willingness to negotiate on penalties to encourage self-reporting and cooperation with SFO investigators,[238] the alternative being severe

230 *The Sunday Times*, 'She came, she saw, she scythed through SFO' 1 February 2009 www.thesundaytimes.co.uk/sto/business/article147170.ece Accessed 6 July 2016.

231 A comparison is made between the SFO and CPS, which has conviction rates approaching DANY. De Grazia (n 128).

232 Department of Justice, 'US Attorney's Office for Southern District New York established 1789' www.justice.gov/usao-sdny/office-history Accessed 6 July 2016. Mail Fraud Statute, Act of 8 June 1872, ch. 335, § 301, 17 Stat 283, 323, 18 U.S.C. § 1341. Peter J. Henning, 'Maybe it should be called federal fraud: The changing nature of the mail fraud statute' 36 BCL Rev (1995) 435–477.

233 £19.08m in 2013–14. *The Times*, 'Lawyers land fraud agency with £19m bill' 14 July 2014 www.thetimes.co.uk/tto/law/article4146834.ece Accessed 6 July 2016.

234 De Grazia (n 128) 10.

235 *Fraud Trials Committee Report* (HMSO 1986) (hereinafter Roskill).

236 De Grazia (n 128) 10.

237 O'Shea, McLeod and Beal (n 139) 759.

238 The SFO is the reporting point for overseas corruption. There are no other requirements to report fraud to the SFO. *Attorney General's Guidelines on Plea Discussions in Cases of Serious or Complex Fraud*. Attorney General, 'Guidelines' http://webarchive.nationalarchives.gov.uk/20120816224015/http://www.attorneygeneral.gov.uk/Publications/Documents/AG%27s%20Guidelines%20on%20Plea%20Discussions%20in

penalties.[239] This guidance incentivised companies that self-reported their complicity in corruption, 'with the emphasis being on the carrot and not the stick'.[240] The attraction for a commercial organisation in self-reporting bribery to SFO is the prospect of a civil rather than criminal penalty which, apart from providing the opportunity to manage publicity, ensures that the provisions of EU Public Sector Procurement Directive 2004,[241] which prescribes exclusion from participation, do not apply, thus allowing continued participation in publicly funded projects.

This policy 'made a number of big assumptions novel to UK prosecutors but common to (…) [DoJ] practice'.[242] To encourage self-reporting, lenient penalties would amount to civil fines and where prosecution is necessary, then the SFO and defendant company would determine the overall sanction.[243] In the US, such agreements are widely used and 'a policy of judicial acquiescence or self-restraint prevails'.[244]

The SFO is the lead agency for prosecution of cases of bribery and corruption[245] where the Bribery Act redefines the UK approach to bribery and corruption for which, historically, there have been few cases taken to trial.[246] This continued to be the case after the de Grazia review. However, in anticipating the future course of enforcement of the Bribery Act, it is instructive to consider how the SFO performed in a number of higher-profile cases where it was employing the existing legal remedies.[247] In *Mabey & Johnson*, a plea bargain resulted in a fine of £6.6m for paying €1m bribes through middlemen, together with two executives receiving custodial sentences.[248] This was the first conviction in the UK of a company for overseas

%20Cases%20of%20Serious%20or%20Complex%20Fraud.pdf Accessed 6 December 2016.

239 O'Shea, McLeod and Beal (n 139) 759.

240 Corker (n 153) 7420.

241 Directive 2004/17/EC http://eur-lex.europa.eu/LexUriServ/LexUriServ.do?uri=OJ:L:2004:134:0001:0113:EN:PDF Accessed 8 December 2016.

242 Corker (n 153) 7420.

243 Corker (n 153) 7420.

244 Corker (n 153) 7420.

245 Although there is overlap with the FCA and City of London Police.

246 Aaronberg and Higgins (n 31) 5, 6–9. Some 40 cases between 2001–05.

247 The SFO has instituted proceedings in a number of cases, under existing law: the Prevention of Corruption Act 1906. Serious Fraud Office, 'Alstom Network UK Ltd & Alstom Power Ltd' www.sfo.gov.uk/cases/alstom-network-uk-ltd-alstom-power-ltd/ Accessed 6 December 2016. Serious Fraud Office, 'Smith and Ouzman Limited' www.sfo.gov.uk/cases/smith-ouzman-ltd/ Accessed 6 December 2016.

248 'Two former directors and a sales manager of engineering firm Mabey & Johnson Ltd have been sentenced today for providing kickbacks to the Iraqi government of Saddam Hussein. Charles Forsyth, David Mabey and Richard Gledhill inflated the contract price for the supply of steel bridges and disguised illegal payments that were channelled through Jordanian banks.' The fine included compensation to Ghana, Jamaica and Iraq, confiscation and legal costs. Serious Fraud Office, 'Mabey & Johnson Ltd: Former executives jailed for helping finance Saddam Hussein's government' http://webarchive.nationalarchives.gov.uk/20110606101921/http://www.sfo.gov.uk/press-room/latest-press-releases/press-releases-2011/mabey–johnson-ltd-former-ex

corruption[249] and for breaking Iraq sanctions.[250] Balfour Beatty paid £2.25m to the SFO, being the first CRO, relating to 'payment irregularities' on an Egyptian contract;[251] and AMEC also agreed a £4.9m CRO relating to a South Korean contract for a Companies Act failure to keep accounting records.[252] These cases evidence a change in prosecution with a first prosecution for overseas corruption, first CRO and first conviction under the Companies Act with CRO.

Risk management and reporting bribery and corruption

The Bribery Act extends responsibility for bribery beyond the individuals intimately involved, to include the 'controlling minds' and those organisations involved or on whose behalf bribery took place or was contemplated. This can include individuals and organisations that are many steps distant from the organisation itself. Any failure risks the organisation being subject to a fine in addition to any action against the individuals. The wide scope of the Act significantly increases the commercial organisation's risk management issues. Thus, with there being corporate responsibility for failing to prevent bribery, with criminal consequences, it is vital for the organisation to put in place procedures and be alert so that, if necessary, it can report itself to the SFO.[253]

The ambit of the law is any commercial organisation with a business presence in the UK. This would bring into consideration any part of that organisation, even if the controlling body was overseas and the alleged bribery was also offshore. This should encourage businesses to review their existing anti-bribery policies and procedures and ensure their 'associates' are similarly compliant. Those organisations that are already subject to the US Foreign Corrupt Practices Act will have existing

ecutives-jailed-for-helping-finance-saddam-hussein's-government.aspx Accessed 6 December 2016.

249 The Prevention of Corruption Act 1906, s 1, after amendment by the Anti-terrorism, Crime and Security Act 2001.

250 'First UK company convicted for overseas corruption'. Company Lawyer, 'Case Comment' (2010) 31(1) Comp Law 16.

251 'The Serious Fraud Office has today deployed for the first time new powers made available to it as from April 2008. These powers include civil recovery under the Proceeds of Crime Act 2002, under which the SFO can recover property obtained by unlawful conduct. These provisions do not require a specific offence to be established against any particular company or individual, merely that the property sought is the proceeds of unlawful conduct.' Serious Fraud Office, 'Serious Fraud Office successfully obtains first ever Civil Recovery Order involving major plc' http://webarchive.nationalarchives.gov.uk/20110704124145/http://www.sfo.gov.uk/press-room/latest-press-releases/press-releases-2008/balfour-beatty-plc.aspx Accessed 6 December 2016.

252 Companies Act 1965, s 221. 'Legislative Comment: The United Kingdom Bribery Bill' (2010) 26(2) Const L J 146–152. Serious Fraud Office, 'SFO obtains Civil Recovery Order against AMEC plc' http://webarchive.nationalarchives.gov.uk/20110606101921/http://www.sfo.gov.uk/press-room/latest-press-releases/press-releases-2009/sfo-obtains-civil-recovery-order-against-amec-plc.aspx Accessed 6 December 2016.

253 As with *Standard Bank v XYZ*.

policies and procedures, but the Bribery Act is more extreme with its 'zero tolerance' stance. Internationally, the OECD Guidelines for Multinational Enterprises[254] and OECD Business Approaches to Combating Corrupt Practices[255] provide guidance, as do the US Federal Sentencing Guidelines.[256]

In the UK, the SFO is designated the national reporting point for 'all allegations of bribery of foreign public officials by British nationals or companies incorporated in the UK – even if the matter occurred overseas'.[257] However, the obligation to report is not well established because there is no statutory obligation to report bribery, corruption or fraud, unlike money laundering where reporting is required by the Proceeds of Crime Act 2002,[258] or terrorism financing where disclosure is required under the Terrorism Act 2000.[259] By contrast, the other significant actor in the UK, the FCA, which is responsible for regulating financial services, *imposes* obligations, whereby regulated firms have to tell the regulator promptly about anything relating to the firm of which the FCA would reasonably expect prompt notice.[260] The consequence is that the SFO, which takes the lead in bribery matters, lacks statutory backing to compel reporting, whereas the FCA in the sector it regulates does require bribery to be reported.[261] The relationship between the SFO and the regulator lies at the heart of UK efforts to control economic crime, and there is a need for this to be addressed so that one agency is responsible for dealing with cases of bribery, corruption and fraud, the reporting of which should be made a statutory obligation in all cases, and removing the overlap and gaps between agencies which would enable economic crime to be confronted by one body.

254 OECD, 'Guidelines for Multinational Enterprises' www.oecd.org/document/28/0,3343,en_2649_34889_2397532_1_1_1_1,00.html Accessed 18 October 2016.

255 OECD, 'Business approaches to combating bribery' www.oecd.org/corporate/mne/WP-2003_2.pdf Accessed 6 December 2016.

256 'Remedying harm from criminal conduct, and effective compliance and ethics program' in *US Federal Sentencing Guidelines* (2016) www.ussc.gov/guidelines/2016-guidelines-manual Accessed 6 December 2016.

257 Serious Fraud Office, 'Enforcing the UK Bribery Act – the UK Serious Fraud Office's perspective' www.sfo.gov.uk/2014/11/17/stuart-alford-qc-enforcing-uk-bribery-act-uk-serious-fraud-offices-perspective/ Accessed 6 December 2016.

258 Proceeds of Crime Act 2002 (Part 7). The Criminal Finances Bill was introduced into Parliament in October 2016. It contains proposals to enhance government ability to investigate the proceeds of crime (Part 1 Chapter 1). 'The Bill will introduces [sic] Unexplained Wealth Orders, where individuals whose assets are disproportionate to their known income will need [to] explain the origin of their wealth. Disclosure Orders will be extended to money laundering investigations and will provide an effective, efficient and flexible means of obtaining information.' Home Office, 'Factsheet – The Criminal Finances Bill' www.gov.uk/government/uploads/system/uploads/attachment_data/file/564464/CF_Bill_-_Factsheet_1_-_The_Bill.pdf Accessed 4 December 2016.

259 Terrorism Act 2000, ss 15–19. Anti-terrorism, Crime and Security Act 2001, Part 3.

260 Financial Conduct Authority, *Handbook*, SYSC 6.3 Financial crime www.handbook.fca.org.uk/handbook/SYSC/6/3.html Accessed 18 October 2016.

261 Financial Conduct Authority, *Handbook*, SYSC 6.3 (n 260).

Such a lack of a single decision maker was subject to parliamentary opprobrium in relation to LIBOR.[262]

The SFO 'Approach to Dealing with Overseas Corruption'[263] provides guidance and industry-specific codes of practice which give, for example, advice that 'a negotiated settlement rather than a criminal prosecution' would give protection against mandatory EU procurement disbarring.[264] Corporate hospitality is also covered, the government having recognised that the provision of corporate hospitality is part of business life and it has not been prescriptive in establishing parameters, preferring that the issue is left to prosecutorial discretion and common sense,[265] an uncertain state until tested at trial, though there is government comfort: 'rest assured – no one wants to stop firms getting to know their clients by taking them to events like Wimbledon or the Grand Prix.'[266] This guidance recognises that corporate hospitality and promotional expenditure are an everyday part of business life, with general recognition by both giver and receiver that this is part of relationship building. Nevertheless, it is 'clear that hospitality and promotional or similar business expenditure can be employed as bribes'.[267] This means that commercial organisations have to put in place clear procedures with the emphasis on expenditure being 'reasonable and proportionate',[268] and give direction to their employees to ensure that, at best, their motives are not misinterpreted.[269]

The risks managed by a commercial organisation are increased by the extra-territorial application of the Bribery Act because the UK has joined other countries in extending its jurisdiction over bribery beyond its borders in support of the global effort to reduce economic crime.[270] The Bribery Act creates an offence that

262 House of Commons Treasury Committee, 'Fixing LIBOR: Some preliminary findings Second Report of Session 2012–13 Volume I' www.publications.parliament.uk/pa/cm201213/cmselect/cmtreasy/481/481ii.pdf Accessed 18 October 2016.

263 Serious Fraud Office, 'Approach of the SFO' www.skadden.com/eimages/Approach_of_the_Serious_Fraud_Office_to_Dealing_with_Overseas_Corruption.pdf Accessed 6 December 2016.

264 EU Public Services Procurement Directive Council Directive 2004/18/EC: [2004] OJ L134/114. Implemented in UK by The Public Contracts Regulations 2006, which provides revised rules for the procurement of supplies, works and services by public authorities. The Utilities Contracts Regulations 2006 implement the revised Utilities Directive (2004/17/EC) which provides, in a similar way, revised rules for procurement in the utilities sector. Office of Government Commerce, HM Treasury, http://webarchive.nationalarchives.gov.uk/20130129110402/http://www.hm-treasury.gov.uk/d/competitive_dialogue_procedure.pdf Accessed 6 December 2016.

265 Serious Fraud Office, 'Bribery Act guidance' www.sfo.gov.uk/publications/guidance-policy-and-protocols/bribery-act-guidance/ Accessed 6 December 2016.

266 Ministry of Justice, 'The Bribery Act: Guidance' (n 56) 2.

267 Ministry of Justice, 'The Bribery Act: Guidance' (n 56) 12.

268 Ministry of Justice, 'The Bribery Act: Guidance' (n 56) 12.

269 As at September 2014, there had not been any prosecutions under Bribery Act 2010. For a discussion on hospitality see: Peter Alldridge, 'The law relating to free lunches' (2002) 23(9) Co L 264, 270.

270 All 40 signatories to the OECD Anti-bribery Convention have enacted anti-foreign bribery provisions. However, they desire 'adoption of the Convention by other major

is committed if 'any act or omission which forms part of the offence takes place (...) in the UK';[271] or, if not in the UK, then it would be an offence if 'done or made in the UK'[272] and the person had a close connection with the UK. A person is a 'British Citizen, British resident or body incorporated in the UK'[273] or is an 'associated person'. An associated person is 'a person who performs services for and on behalf of a relevant commercial organisation'.[274] The capacity in which those services are performed does not matter and, thus, the person can be an employee, agent or subsidiary.[275] The reach of s 7 jurisdiction to prosecute is unclear since the MoJ guidance states that mere admission of a company's securities to the UK Listing Authority's Official List and trading on the LSE does not necessarily qualify a company as carrying on a business in the UK, which does appear perverse and has not yet been tested in court;[276] however, the regulator,[277] acting against market abuse, has fined executives of a Turkish company (Genel Enerji) for insider dealing relating to the company's UK Listing.[278] Although the government's 'common sense' approach was intended to assuage international business fears, the courts would have to rule on jurisdictional disputes which, if the regulator can and does take action, would leave the SFO in the position of it, too, having jurisdiction. Two civil cases demonstrate that a business presence of nine days[279] or a mere office[280] were sufficient to establish jurisdiction. The nature of association is more closely defined in the FCPA.[281]

There is no clear definition of 'performing services' but the presumption is that an employee is performing services whilst the act stipulates that the relationship 'is to be determined by reference to all the relevant circumstances'.[282] However, as a 'strict liability' offence, the commercial undertaking can still be liable even if the activity was unknown by anyone. This is a significant change from the previous position, which stated that 'senior' management had to be involved.[283]

exporters, in particular by the four remaining G20 states China, India, Indonesia and Saudi Arabia.' OECD, 'Making sure that bribes don't pay' www.oecd.org/daf/anti-bribery/makingsurethatbribesdontpay.htm Accessed 18 October 2016.

271 Bribery Act 2010, s 12(1).
272 Bribery Act 2010, s 12(2).
273 Bribery Act 2010, s 12(4).
274 Bribery Act 2010, s 8(1).
275 Bribery Act 2011, s 8.
276 Ministry of Justice, 'The Bribery Act: Guidance' (n 56) 36.
277 Jennifer Craven, 'Reading between the guidelines' (2011) 161 NLJ 540.
278 Financial Services Authority, 'Three Turkish oil company executives fined £1.16m for market abuse' 16 February 2011 www.fsa.gov.uk/pages/Library/Communication/PR/2010/028.shtml Accessed 18 October 2016.
279 *Dunlop Pneumatic Tyre Company Ltd v Actien-Gesellschaft fur Motor und Motorfahzeugbau Vorm. Cudell & Co* [1902] 1 KB 342
280 *South India Shipping Corporation Ltd v Export-import Bank of Korea* [1985] 2 All ER 219.
281 Discussed in Chapter 4.
282 Bribery Act 2010, s 8.
283 *Tesco Supermarkets Ltd v Nattrass* [1972] AC153 HL.

The intention of this 'broad reach' is that multinational companies (and others) cannot avoid responsibility for bribery and corruption by saying that it happened elsewhere and they knew nothing about it. However, the Act's provisions go further than the FCPA and, thus, may 'catch out' US corporations. An example might be of a US incorporated corporation, which does business in the UK, employing a Korean agent which pays a bribe in China. If it fails to show that it had 'adequate procedures', it could be criminally liable.[284]

Other regulatory agencies

Although the SFO has the 'lead agency' role, other authorities are involved in policing the area, which can give rise to issues of overlapping responsibilities, leading to confusion over reporting and liability to differing sanctions.[285] Whereas the FSA had four equal objectives, one being 'the reduction of financial crime',[286] the FCA has 'a single overarching strategic objective to ensure that markets function well'.[287] Financial crime includes fraud or dishonesty, which the FCA interpret to include bribery and corruption.[288] The FCA has another objective, which is impacted by allegations of bribery and corruption: that of maintaining market integrity[289] on the basis that 'because bribery and corruption distort natural competition' this could 'affect the UK's reputation, making it a less attractive place for firms to conduct insurance or other business'.[290] The FCA is careful to clarify that it 'does not enforce or give guidance on the Bribery Act';[291] nevertheless, it does regulate bribery and

284 Nigel J Binnersley, 'UK Bribery Act 2010' www.blankrome.com/SiteFiles/Intl-Lit-3-2011.pdf15 Accessed 18 October 2016.

285 'The SFO is a specialist prosecuting authority tackling the top level of serious or complex fraud, bribery and corruption. We are part of the UK criminal justice system covering England, Wales and Northern Ireland, but not Scotland, the Isle of Man or the Channel Islands.' Serious Fraud Office, 'What we do' www.sfo.gov.uk/about-us/ Accessed 18 October 2016.

286 Financial Services and Markets Act 2000, s 6.

287 Financial Conduct Authority, 'Ensuring markets work well for consumers and for firms – FCA publishes guidance on its approach to objectives' www.fca.org.uk/news/press-releases/ensuring-markets-work-well-consumers-and-firms-–-fca-publishes-guidance-its Accessed 24 November 2016.

288 Financial Conduct Authority, 'Financial crime: A guide for firms Part 1: A firm's guide to preventing financial crime April 2015' 55 www.handbook.fca.org.uk/handbook/document/FC1_FCA_20150427.pdf Accessed 18 October 2016.

289 Financial Conduct Authority, 'The FCA's approach to advancing its objectives 2015' 33 www.fca.org.uk/publication/corporate/fca-approach-advancing-objectives-2015.pdf Accessed 18 October 2016.

290 Financial Services Authority, 'Anti-bribery and corruption in commercial insurance broking. Reducing the risk of illicit payments or inducements to third parties' 6. Accessed 18 October 2016.

291 Financial Conduct Authority, 'Financial crime: a guide for firms Part 1' (n 288).

corruption.[292] The FCA confirms that enforcement action is in the realm of the SFO and guidance on the 'adequate procedures' defence to the Bribery Act s 7 offence of 'failure to prevent bribery' is within the MoJ's purview.[293]

The regulator ventilated its concerns about the propensity of insurance companies to make illicit payments or inducements in order to obtain or retain business.[294] In two significant cases, the FSA fined major insurance companies for failings in their anti-bribery and anti–corruption systems and controls. For example, in 2009, AON was fined £5.25m for failing to 'properly assess the risks involved in its dealings with overseas firms and individuals (...) and failed to implement effective controls to mitigate those risks'.[295] Furthermore, Willis was fined £6.895m in 2011 for similar issues and failure to record 'an adequate commercial rationale' for the payments to high-risk jurisdictions such as Egypt and Russia.[296] In both cases, as a result of both firms' 'weak control environment', suspicious payments were made amounting to approximately $7m and £27m, respectively.[297] It is clear from these cases that the regulator enjoys the flexibility of using discretion over sanctions, which is not the norm for the SFO. Moreover, the regulator's credible deterrence strategy provides the opportunity to levy a fine in an 'out-of-court' process and gain publicity for its decisions,[298] whereas the SFO has to prosecute, with potential adverse publicity if unsuccessful.

Another agency is the NCA International Corruption Unit,[299] whose role is to investigate foreign bribery by UK business and nationals. It operates jointly with

292 'Corruption and bribery are criminal offences under current UK legislation and the Bribery Act 2010, which came into force on 1 July 2011. Authorised firms have additional, regulatory, obligations to put in place and maintain policies and processes to prevent corruption and bribery and to conduct their business with integrity. These are set out in SYSC 3.2.6R/SYSC 6.1.1R and Principle 1 of our Principles for Businesses (PRIN 2.1.1R).' Financial Conduct Authority, 'Financial crime: A guide for firms Part 1' (n 291).

293 Financial Conduct Authority, 'Financial crime: a guide for firms Part 1' (n 288).

294 Financial Services Authority, 'Letter 22 November 2007' www.fsa.gov.uk/pubs/ceo/ttp_letter.pdf Accessed 6 December 2016.

295 Financial Services Authority, 'FSA fines Aon Limited £5.25m for failings in its anti-bribery and corruption systems and controls' 8 January 2009 www.fsa.gov.uk/pages/Library/Communication/PR/2009/004.shtml Accessed 18 October 2016.

296 Financial Services Authority, 'FSA fines Willis Limited £6.895 million for anti-bribery and corruption systems and controls failings' 21 July 2011 www.fsa.gov.uk/pages/Library/Communication/PR/2011/066.shtml Accessed 18 October 2016.

297 Both firms cooperated with the FSA and were each given a 30% discount to the fine 'under the FSA's settlement discount scheme'. Financial Services Authority, 'FSA fines Aon Limited' (n 295). Financial Services Authority, 'FSA fines Willis Limited' (n 296).

298 Sara Teasdale, 'FSA to FCA: recent trends in UK financial conduct regulation' (2011) 26 JIBLR 583, 585. See Chapter 2 re the FCA, 'our policy of credible deterrence, pursuing enforcement cases to punish wrongdoing': Gary Wilson and Sarah Wilson, 'The FSA "credible deterrence", and criminal enforcement – a "haphazard pursuit"?' (2014) JFC 4.

299 In 2015, the remit of the Metropolitan Police, Proceeds of Corruption Unit and the COLP, Overseas Anti-Corruption Unit transferred to the new NCA unit, named the International Corruption Unit, to create a new central bribery and corruption unit

the SFO on some cases, which demonstrates an overlap. The COLP have charged a London solicitor and two Dutch businessmen with 'conspiracy to corrupt, conspiring to money launder and fraudulent trading in relation to alleged contract manipulation in a UN project to supply HIV and malaria drugs to [the Congo] one of the world's poorest countries'.[300] However worthy the Unit's endeavours, the presence of another agency represents further confusion for the SFO.

Conclusion

The theme of overlap between the SFO and the City Regulator continues in the arena of bribery and corruption but the SFO has the benefit of relatively new legislation, in the form of the Bribery Act and DPAs, which are bearing fruit. These measures provide the rationale for extending their scope into other areas of finance.

The Bribery Act offence of 'failure of a commercial organisation to prevent bribery' serves as a template for other legislation, such as the proposed new corporate offence of failure to prevent the criminal facilitation of tax evasion.[301] In 2016, the government announced that it would launch a consultation on plans to extend the 'failure to prevent' legislation to 'failure to prevent economic crime'. The consultation was opened in January 2017 for 'criminal offences designed to punish and prevent economic crimes such as fraud, false accounting and money laundering when committed on behalf or in the name of companies'. The government expected to respond in 2017.[302]

The SFO's 'enthusiastic support' for an offence of 'failing to prevent economic crime' is based upon the current law depending upon the 'identification principle' (*mens rea*, see above), which, '[i]n a world of increasingly complex corporate structures (…) can hobble the prosecutor in those cases where it is right to prosecute the company'.[303] The SFO advance that the 'principle is illogical in that at present it is the only route to liability for all major economic crime offences (fraud, false accounting, money laundering) except bribery and (soon) tax evasion'.[304] The current principle is unfair, because it is 'easier to identify the controlling mind

within the NCA by bringing together the resources from the Department for International Development-funded units. City of London Police, 'International Corruption Unit' www.cityoflondon.police.uk/advice-and-support/fraud-and-economic-crime/oacu/Pages/default.aspx Accessed 18 October 2016.

300 *Financial Times*, 'Briton charged with Congo corruption' 17 July 2009 www.ft.com/cms/s/0/90dfea6e-5ad3-11de-8c14-00144feabdc0.html?nclick_check=1#axzz1W9K4KVZK Accessed 18 October 2016.

301 The Criminal Finances Bill was introduced into Parliament in October 2016. Home Office, 'Factsheet – Part 3 – Corporate failure to prevent tax evasion' www.gov.uk/government/uploads/system/uploads/attachment_data/file/564480/CF_Bill_-_Factsheet_9_-_Tax_evasion_offence.pdf Accessed 30 November 2016.

302 Ministry of Justice, 'Corporate liability for economic crime: call for evidence' https://consult.justice.gov.uk/digital-communications/corporate-liability-for-economic-crime/ Accessed 16 January 2017.

303 Serious Fraud Office, Cambridge Symposium 2016 www.sfo.gov.uk/2016/09/05/cambridge-symposium-2016/ Accessed 6 December 2016.

304 Serious Fraud Office, Cambridge Symposium 2016 (n 303).

in a small company than a larger corporation'.[305] Furthermore, the SFO point to the principle acting as an unhelpful incentive to senior executives who on one hand can 'preach compliance' with Bribery Act provisions while distancing themselves from knowledge of operations.[306] An example is with Tom Hayes in the SFO's first successful LIBOR prosecution, where his employer was not held to account in the UK but was prosecuted in the US where vicarious liability applies.[307]

305 Serious Fraud Office, Cambridge Symposium 2016 (n 303).
306 Serious Fraud Office, Cambridge Symposium 2016 (n 303).
307 Serious Fraud Office, Cambridge Symposium 2016 (n 303).

4 The United States of America

Introduction

This chapter critically reviews and contrasts the US and UK approaches to economic crime. The US is chosen as a comparator country to study because it has a dominant position as the largest single country in terms of international trade.[1] It is logical to suggest that the largest trading nation would suffer economic crime and illogical to ignore its methods of dealing with these issues. The nature of international trade is that within a framework of international conventions countries should have their own economic crime legislation but being aware of jurisdictional arbitrage, whereby adherence to one country's laws might be more advantageous than another's.

This chapter considers the US approach to fraud, bribery and corruption, comparing its statutes with the UK and its regulatory bodies to ascertain whether the US model can offer a template for the UK. The key US statute to combat economic crime internationally is the Foreign Corrupt Practices Act 1977 (FCPA), which has a major difference from the UK in that it allows modest hospitality expenditure and small facilitation payments.[2] Additionally it permits payments to foreign political officials 'to expedite or secure the performance of a routine government action'.[3] The difference of approach is important because the US Department of Justice (DoJ) frequently prosecutes international companies alongside, or leading, the SFO.

The US takes breaches of the FCPA seriously, with threats of prosecutions leading to financial sanctions amounting to 'eye-watering' proportions when compared with the UK.[4] Many organisations conducting business internationally

1 Some 9.1% of global exports and 13.8% of global imports (UK accounted for 2.8% and 3.7% and China 13.8% and 10.1%, respectively). World Trade Organization, 'Table A6, Leading exporters and importers in world merchandise trade, 2015' www.wto.org/english/res_e/statis_e/wts2016_e/wts16_chap9_e.htm Accessed 12 December 2016.

2 Department of Justice and Securities and Exchange Commission, 'FCPA. A resource guide to the U.S. Foreign Corrupt Practices Act' 15 www.sec.gov/spotlight/fcpa/fcpa-resource-guide.pdf Accessed 14 November 2016.

3 David Aaronberg and Nicola Higgins, 'The Bribery Act 2010: All bark and no bite ...?' (2010) Arch Rev 5, 6–9.

4 Department of Justice, 'Alcatel-Lucent S.A. and three subsidiaries agree to pay $92 million to resolve Foreign Corrupt Practices Act investigation coordinated enforcement actions by Department of Justice and SEC result in penalties of more than $137

are already familiar with the FCPA because, although it is US domestic legislation, it applies to non-US companies such as those listed on the US stock exchanges or other capital markets or which use US telecommunications or banking systems. An example of the extra-territorial application of the FCPA is related to Alcatel-Lucent, a French company, which agreed to settle claims by the DoJ and SEC by paying $137m because they had bribed foreign government officials in Costa Rica, Honduras, Malaysia and Taiwan in order to secure a number of telecommunications contracts.[5] The DoJ's comments put this into perspective: 'foreign bribery weakens economic development, erodes confidence in the marketplace and distorts competition.'[6] The DoJ agreed a three-year deferral of prosecution during which Alcatel had to institute an enhanced corporate compliance programme and employ an independent compliance monitor to oversee the company's implementation and maintenance of that programme, and to submit yearly reports to the DoJ. Alcatel resolved to cease using sales and marketing agents worldwide because court documents showed that Alcatel's business model was 'prone to corruption'.[7] Consultants were used as conduits for bribery payments to foreign officials and business executives of private customers.[8] One Alcatel executive was imprisoned for conspiring to violate the FCPA, making corrupt payments, and laundering the bribe payments through a third party.[9]

In another case, Siemens agreed to pay $1.6bn in fines, penalties and disgorgement of profits to US and German authorities.[10] These headlines support the view that the US has taken the lead in anti-corruption endeavours with the FCPA in the vanguard of compliance and ethical conduct of international businesses.[11] The international

million' www.justice.gov/opa/pr/alcatel-lucent-sa-and-three-subsidiaries-agree-pay-92-million-resolve-foreign-corrupt Accessed 14 November 2016.

5 Department of Justice, 'Alcatel-Lucent S.A.' (n 4).

6 Department of Justice, 'Mythili Raman, Principal Deputy Assistant Attorney General DoJ. Press release' 27 December 2010 www.justice.gov/opa/pr/2010/December/10-crm-1481.html Accessed 8 December 2016.

7 DoJ, Raman, 'Press Release' (n 6).

8 DoJ, Raman, 'Press Release' (n 6).

9 'Christian Sapsizian, a French citizen and Alcatel CIT executive [was] charged in March 2007 with conspiring to violate the FCPA, making corrupt payments in violation of the FCPA, and laundering the bribe payments through a third-party. Sapsizian was arrested in Miami in late 2006 and pleaded guilty on June 6, 2007, to FCPA violations. He was sentenced on Sept. 23, 2008, in the U.S. District Court for the Southern District of Florida to 30 months in prison.' DoJ, Raman, 'Press Release' (n 6).

10 Department of Justice, 'Former Chief Financial Officer of Siemens Argentina pleads guilty to role in multimillion dollar foreign bribery scheme' www.justice.gov/opa/pr/former-chief-financial-officer-siemens-argentina-pleads-guilty-role-multimillion-dollar Accessed 6 December 2016.

11 Gerard McDermott, 'US/UK Comparison' (2010) 160 NLJ 1673. In 2014, China also became more active. See, for example, GlaxoSmithKline, where the SFO has opened an investigation. Serious Fraud Office, 'GlaxoSmithKline plc investigation' www.sfo.gov.uk/press-room/latest-press-releases/press-releases-2014/glaxosmithkline-plc-investigation.aspx. 'GSK could yet face further action from US and UK authorities which have the power to punish the company for overseas corruption.

nature of trade and the differing standards applied by countries militated in favour of a global framework to standardise approaches to bribery and corruption.

International conventions

In the economic crime arena, 'globalization has forced like-minded western capitalists to interact with their counterparts in lower-income countries, where interpretations of trust, reciprocity, honesty and social engagement may differ'.[12] As a consequence, demand grew for some international standards to be created to which all countries should adhere in order to create a 'level playing field'. According to Eicher, in the US by the mid-1970s, 'more than 400 [companies] openly admitted paying foreign government officials, politicians and political parties'.[13] In response to 'public discontent' as to why 'American companies [were] engaging in unethical practices and encouraging corruption in other countries',[14] the US Congress created the FCPA, which 'was ground-breaking for its time, as it was the first international anti-bribery statute of its type and scope in the world',[15] or, to be accurate, domestic statute with international scope.

One unintended consequence of the reach of the FCPA was that Congress later considered that 'American businesses have operated at a disadvantage relative to foreign competitors who have continued to pay bribes without fear of a penalty'.[16] Furthermore, other countries were criticised for making such payments 'tax deductible',[17] which would indicate that such payments were treated as a legitimate business expense.[18] The expectation of the US government was that other countries would follow the US in enacting similar legislation. However, as Griffin describes, 'foreign governments objected on a number of grounds'.[19] First, that

Investigations are under way in both countries.'*Financial Times*, 'GSK to pay £297m fine for Chinese bribes' www.ft.com/cms/s/0/dea9811e-3fd5-11e4-936b-00144feabdc0.html#axzz3Eo0GXH00 Accessed 8 December 2016.

12 Sharon Eicher, 'Introduction: What Corruption is and Why it Matters' in Sharon Eicher (ed), *Corruption in International Business: The Challenge of Cultural and Legal Diversity* (Ashgate 2009), 1.

13 Sharon Eicher, 'Risk management – playing by the rules' in Sharon Eicher (ed), *Corruption in International Business: The Challenge of Cultural and Legal Diversity* (Ashgate 2009), 116.

14 Eicher, 'Risk management – playing by the rules' (n 13).

15 Heidi L Hansberry, 'In spite of its good intentions, the Dodd-Frank Act has created an FCPA monster' (2012) 102 JCRLC 195.

16 Department of Justice, 'Proposed legislative history. International Anti-Bribery Act of 1998' www.justice.gov/criminal/fraud/fcpa/docs/leghistory.pdf Accessed 8 December 2016.

17 Department of Justice, 'Proposed legislative history' (n 16).

18 A newspaper report indicates that Russia takes a similar view. *The Telegraph*, 'Russian officials told bribes are not tax deductible' 4 September 2012 www.telegraph.co.uk/finance/financial-crime/9519292/Russian-officials-told-bribes-are-not-tax-deductible.html Accessed 8 December 2016.

19 Joseph P Griffin, 'New initiatives on bribery of foreign officials' (1994) 5(10) ICCLR 341.

'the extra-territorial application of national law is inconsistent with international law',[20] although that might have been because it was the US that was endeavouring to apply its national law extra-territorially. Second, that '"bribery" and "corruption" are difficult to define and even more difficult to police'.[21] Third, the suggestion that bribery is a 'public good' because 'the economic effects of bribery in developing countries often "trickle down" to disadvantaged members of the society'.[22] Fourth, that 'the focus should be on officials that solicit bribes'.[23]

The FCPA was not the only initiative in 1977. The International Chamber of Commerce (ICC) 'produced its first Report on Extortion and Bribery in International Business Transactions'.[24] The ICC objective was to end bribery and extortion by creating 'the Rules of Conduct to Combat Extortion and Bribery',[25] which would be voluntarily adopted 'by enterprises'.[26] The ICC recommendation 'that the United Nations (UN) adopt an international convention to prohibit corruption', can be seen in light of the FCPA as further supporting the international effort. However, as the ICC reports, 'UN efforts to reach such an agreement fell through in the 1980s'.[27] Griffin concluded that 'unfortunately, in the absence of an international treaty, there is no co-ordinating mechanism to ensure that the various initiatives do not result in inconsistent or burdensome legislation by numerous nations'.[28] It was not until 2000, that the UN General Assembly recognised 'that an effective international legal instrument against corruption (…) was desirable',[29] resulting in the UN Convention against Corruption (UNCAC),[30] to which 181 states are parties.[31]

US 'efforts to spread its gospel',[32] culminated in the creation of the OECD Convention on Combating Bribery of Foreign Public Officials in International Business Transactions, in 1997.[33] Furthermore, 'the Council of Europe and the

20 Griffin (n 19) 341.
21 Griffin (n 19) 341.
22 Griffin (n 19) 341.
23 Griffin (n 19) 341.
24 International Chamber of Commerce, 'Combating Extortion and Bribery: ICC Rules of Conduct and Recommendations (2005 Revision)' www.unglobalcompact.org/docs/issues_doc/7.7/2005_ICC_Anti-Corruption_Rules_FINAL.pdf Accessed 8 December 2016.
25 International Chamber of Commerce (n 24).
26 International Chamber of Commerce (n 24).
27 International Chamber of Commerce (n 24).
28 Griffin (n 19) 341.
29 'United Nations Convention against Corruption: Background of the United Nations Convention against Corruption' www.unodc.org/unodc/en/treaties/CAC/index.html Accessed 8 December 2016.
30 'United Nations Convention Against Corruption' www.unodc.org/documents/treaties/UNCAC/Publications/Convention/08-50026_E.pdf Accessed 8 December 2016.
31 United Nations Office on Drugs and Crime, 'United Nations Convention against Corruption Signature and Ratification Status as of 12 December 2016' www.unodc.org/unodc/en/treaties/CAC/signatories.html Accessed 8 December 2016.
32 Hansberry (n 15) 195.
33 US ratified in 1998 and took effect from 1999. Organisation for Economic Co-operation and Development (OECD), 'OECD Convention on Combating Bribery of Foreign Public Officials in International Business Transactions (1997)' www.oecd.

Organization of American States[34] each adopted recommendations that their member nations address the issue of bribery of foreign government officials'.[35] The Council of Europe adopted both civil and criminal Law Conventions in 1999 and the OAS adopted the Inter-American Convention against Corruption in 1996.[36] However, according to Carr:

> The scope of these conventions inevitably vary but all of them require contracting states to criminalize bribery from the supply side, although OECD Anti-Bribery Convention is restricted solely to bribery of foreign public officials in the context of international business transactions.[37]

The truism highlighted by Carr is that 'the success of any convention lies in it being ratified, implemented and enforced'.[38]

What is apparent is an issue commented upon by the ICC, which is that of coordination of conventions.[39] They highlight that 'from an international business standpoint the proliferation of anti-corruption instruments raises concerns about inconsistent rules, overlapping enforcement and lack of common definitions'.[40] The remedy that the ICC propose is that 'the OECD Convention should remain the principal instrument focusing on the supply side of international corruption'.[41] The regional conventions[42] 'should give priority to issues on which progress can be made by cooperation among their participating parties',[43] which would leave UNCAC to deal with issues that need worldwide cooperation.[44] Since all these bodies have their own monitoring programmes, the ICC propose that monitoring and assessment should be coordinated in order to remove duplication.[45]

org/corruption/oecdantibriberyconvention.htm. www.oecd.org/daf/anti-bribery/antibriberyconventionratification.pdf Accessed 6 December 2016.

34 Hereinafter OAS.

35 Griffin (n 19) 341.

36 The US signed in 1996 and ratified in 2000. Council of Europe Criminal Law Convention 1999. Organization of American States, Inter-American Convention against Corruption 1996 www.oas.org/juridico/english/fightcur.html Accessed 8 December 2016. 'The Inter-American Convention against Corruption, adopted in March, 1996, in Caracas, Venezuela, is the first legal instrument in this field which recognizes the international reach of corruption and the need to promote and facilitate cooperation between states in order to fight against it.' www.oas.org/juridico/english/corr_bg.htm Accessed 8 December 2016.

37 Indira Carr, *Financial Fraud Law Report 4: The UK Bribery Act: Business Integrity and Whistleblowers* (Thompson Media 2012) 362.

38 Carr (n 37) 363.

39 International Chamber of Commerce (n 24).

40 International Chamber of Commerce (n 24).

41 International Chamber of Commerce (n 24).

42 OAS, Council of Europe, African Union.

43 International Chamber of Commerce (n 24).

44 International Chamber of Commerce (n 24).

45 International Chamber of Commerce (n 24).

However, progress does appear to have been made for, as Feldman observed,[46] US advocacy that European and OECD nations should 'ramp up enforcement of their anti-bribery laws on both a domestic and international basis' has borne fruit, citing with approval the UK Bribery Act.[47] The US interest in this is because 'the United States has, for better or worse, been viewed as the policeman for the world'[48] and 'remains by far the most vigorous enforcer of white collar offenses'.[49] The US view is that 'in nations lacking strong legal institutions, law enforcement efforts against white collar offenses such as bribery of foreign officials has traditionally been spotty at best, and sometimes non-existent'.[50] Congruent with their belief that the US has set the standard for bribery enforcement, Feldman considers that 'although there is a movement in the international community toward greater white collar criminal enforcement, it will likely be some time before other countries take enforcement to the level that currently exists in the United States'.[51] Thus, in the absence of internationally agreed and binding standards, the US appears to have taken on the self-appointed role of 'policeman'. At a time when 'western-based multinational companies are increasingly expanding into other regions and developing nations',[52] the challenges faced by companies are in extending the boundaries of commerce 'often in jurisdictions where there is a high susceptibility to corruption than is typical in the jurisdictions of more developed nations'.[53] Here, Feldman cites China,[54] where traders 'will often be dealing with state-owned enterprises' and, in a telling phrase, 'under the US Department of Justice's *typically expansive view of its jurisdiction* employees of state-owned enterprises may well be viewed as government officials, creating potential exposure

46 Warren Feldman, 'Staying in Compliance: Key Issues for White Collar Law Attorneys and their Multinational Clients' in *International White Collar Enforcement, 2013 edition. Leading Lawyers on Preventative Measures, Regulatory Compliance, and Litigation* (Thompson Reuters/Aspatore 2013).
47 Feldman (n 46).
48 Feldman (n 46).
49 Feldman (n 46).
50 Feldman (n 46).
51 Feldman (n 46).
52 Feldman (n 46).
53 Feldman (n 46).
54 There is evidence of China taking steps to penalise corruption, as with GSK; however, Transparency International's view is that: 'Transparency International also favours transparency and justice. We know all too well that corruption charges can be used as a political tool. We know very little indeed about most corruption cases in China, including that of GSK. We often do not know the charges, the evidence or the defence. Confessions might appear, but it is unclear under what circumstances they have been obtained. This also leaves a sour taste. There has been some admirable anti-corruption activity in China over recent months. Perhaps the real test of the government's intent is when it starts to prosecute Chinese companies for paying bribes in overseas markets such as Africa.' Transparency International, 'GlaxoSmithKline – a wake up call for the pharma sector' www.transparency.org.uk/glaxosmithkline-a-wake-up-call-for-the-pharma-sector/ Accessed 10 November 2016. BBC, 'GlaxoSmithKline fined $490m by China for bribery' www.bbc.co.uk/news/business-29274822 Accessed 14 November 2016.

under FCPA'.[55] The DoJ's 'typically expansionist view of its jurisdiction' can be seen in cases where it has endeavoured to extend the boundaries of its remit.[56]

This chapter will now review the US criminalisation and regulatory regime which counters economic crime commencing with fraud. However, unlike bribery and corruption, fraud unfortunately does not benefit from an international convention.[57]

Fraud

The US government has, since enacting the FCPA, given priority to combating economic crime, including the creation of the Financial Fraud Enforcement Task Force (FFETF) to strengthen efforts to combat financial crime arising from the 2008 financial crisis.[58] This followed an announcement in May 2009 that the DoJ 'has been given $330m to investigate any suspected instances of mortgage fraud and to pursue any potential prosecutions that arise from those investigations'.[59] The contrast with the UK could not be more marked, since the budgeted resources available to the SFO were progressively cut from £53m in 2008/09 to £29m in 2014/15 before additional monies had to be made available,[60] unlike its sister organisation the FCA, which gained a 15% increase in funding.[61] Leaving

55 Feldman (n 46) (emphasis added).

56 For example, in *SEC v Magyar Telecom PLC*: 'Certain electronic communications made in furtherance of the improper payments and the concealment of the payments, including drafts of the agreements with the government officials and the offer to the minority party official, and copies of certain of the contracts with the intermediary, were transmitted by Magyar Telekom employees and others through U.S. interstate commerce or stored on computer servers located in the United States.' Securities and Exchange Commission, www.sec.gov/litigation/complaints/2011/comp22213-co.pdf Accessed 8 December 2016.

57 Nicholas Ryder, *Financial Crime in the 21st Century* (Edward Elgar 2011) 97.

58 Department of Justice, 'Press Release' 17 November 2009 www.sec.gov/news/press/2009/2009-249.htm Accessed 8 December 2016.

59 The White House, 'Reforms for American Homeowners and Consumers: President Obama Signs the Helping Families Save their Homes Act and the Fraud Enforcement and Recovery Act' 20 May 2009 www.whitehouse.gov/the-press-office/reforms-american-homeowners-and-consumers-president-obama-signs-helping-families-sa Accessed 14 November 2016.

60 'The Serious Fraud Office investigates the most serious and complex cases of fraud, bribery and corruption. The quantity of such work is unpredictable. The SFO has a core budget which is supplemented as necessary by additional funding agreed with the Treasury. This includes "blockbuster" funding, which enables us to take on very big cases where the annual expenditure is expected to exceed an agreed percentage of our core budget. The current "blockbuster" funding arrangement was agreed in October 2012.' The SFO core budget showed actual reductions from £53.2m in 2008/09, to £29.6m in 2013/14. The core budget for 2016/17 is £35.7m. In 2013/14, additional blockbuster funding of £24m was made available, with £24.5m in 2014/15 and £28m in 2015/16. Serious Fraud Office, 'About Us' www.sfo.gov.uk/about-us/ Accessed 6 December 2016.

61 'FCA and PRA to cost 15% more than FSA' (2013) 34(7) Co Law 217.

aside the disparity in domestic budgets, there is a clear contrast between the US, which has allocated additional financial resources to combat economic crime, and the UK, which is intent upon driving down costs. At this stage, it is important to recognise that this does represent a change in US strategy which, under President Bush, had concentrated resources on the 'war on terror'.[62] Ceresney highlights that 'following the September 11th attacks, the FBI shifted more than 1,800 agents, nearly one third of all agents in criminal programs, including many of those trained in financial investigations, to counterterrorism and intelligence duties'.[63] As a consequence, there were insufficient resources to deal with fraud and non-terrorism investigations.[64] Eventually, in 2008, 'the FBI announced operation "Malicious Mortgage", a multi-agency take down of more than 400 defendants charged with mortgage fraud schemes nationwide'.[65] This presaged the creation of the FFETF.[66] The purpose in creating the FFETF was:

> the understanding that no matter the office or agency – federal, state, or local; law enforcement or regulatory – all of us within government share a common desire and have a core obligation to do everything that we can do to protect the American public from the often devastating effects of financial fraud, whether it be mortgage fraud or investment fraud, grant or procurement fraud, consumer fraud or fraud in lending. And we know that *we can accomplish so much more by working together than working in isolated, compartmentalised silos.* [67]

President Obama's aim in creating the FFETF is neatly encapsulated by stating that working together is better than in isolation, which is a key theme of this book when applied to the UK. However, in terms of prosecuting economic crime, while the UK has many agencies, as previously discussed, the US as a federal country,[68] is not streamlined either, hence the exhortation for agencies to work together:

62 'On 24 September 2001 President George Bush proclaimed that "we will starve terrorists of funding", thus instigating the "financial war on terrorism".' Ryder, *Financial Crime in the 21st Century* (n 57) 51.

63 Andrew J Ceresney, Gordon Eng and Sean R Nuttall, 'Regulatory investigations and the credit crisis: The search for villains' (2009) 46 Am Crim L Rev 225 (footnotes omitted).

64 Ceresney, Eng and Nuttall (n 63) 225 (footnotes omitted).

65 Ceresney, Eng and Nuttall (n 63) 225 (footnotes omitted).

66 For a further discussion on the Financial Fraud Enforcement Task Force, see: Axel Palmer, 'The financial crisis and its relationship with white collar crime in the United States of America: Time for the Feds to fight back?' in N Ryder and others (eds), *The Financial Crisis and White Collar Crime – Legislative and Policy Responses. A Critical Assessment* (Routledge 2017).

67 Michael J. Bresnick, Financial Fraud Enforcement Task Force Executive Director. Speech, 20 March 2013 www.justice.gov/iso/opa/doj/speeches/2013/opa-speech-130320.html Accessed 14 November 2016 (emphasis added).

68 'Of, relating to, or characterized by that form of government in which a number of states constitute a political unit while remaining more or less independent with regard

> In the US, the picture is complicated even more by the Federal and state infrastructure. Federal agencies such as the [FBI] have jurisdiction over a wide range of different types of fraud and corruption, such as public sector fraud and corruption, mass marketing fraud and identity fraud.[69]

The SEC, investment fraud; the Internal Revenue Service, tax fraud; the US Postal Inspectors, mail fraud; the US Secret Service, credit card fraud and currency fraud. This is on top of a state bureaucracy of law enforcement which is often as diverse and complex as at federal level.[70]

In the US, 'the prevention of fraud is an essential part of many criminal statutes and it shows no signs of abating'.[71] However, as Podgor notes, the proliferation of fraud statutes is found to be 'problematic in that there is no specific group of statutes designated in the federal code as fraud statutes and no consistent definition'.[72] Podgor's view is that 'the term "fraud" is a "concept" (...)'[73] and 'although fraud is not a crime in itself, fraud is an integral aspect of several criminal statutes'.[74] In the absence of a single fraud statute, 'there appears to be an acceptance of an "I know it when I see it" approach. Judge Holmes of the Fifth Circuit stated that "the law does not define fraud; it needs no definition; it is as old as falsehood and as versable as human ingenuity"'.[75] The US is not alone in not providing a definition. The more recent UK Fraud Act also fails to do so.[76] In light of the lack of definition, this chapter will not explore the various terms by which fraud is expressed.[77]

US fraud statutes are either generic, such as 'conspiracy', 'mail' or 'wire' frauds; or specific, such as 'bankruptcy' fraud, 'healthcare' fraud and 'bank' fraud. At the 'generic' end of the spectrum the 'focus of the [fraud] statute is almost exclusively on the fraud and not the object of the offense'.[78] Thus, 'the emphasis of the crime of mail fraud is the fraudulent conduct as opposed to the mailing'.[79] In a similar manner, 'a conspiracy to defraud does not require agreement to violate a specific statute'.[80] The statute 'Conspiracy to commit offense or to defraud the United

to their internal affairs.' 'federal, adj. and n.' *OED Online* (Oxford University Press, 12 December 2016).

69 M Button and J Gee, *Countering Fraud for Competitive Advantage* (Wiley 2013) 52.
70 Button and Gee, *Countering Fraud for Competitive Advantage* (n 69).
71 Ryder, *Financial Crime in the 21st Century* (n 57) 103.
72 Ellen S Podgor, 'Criminal Fraud' (1999) 48 Am U L Rev 729 (footnotes omitted) 729.
73 Podgor (n 72) 729.
74 Podgor (n 72) 729.
75 Podgor (n 72) 729 (footnotes omitted).
76 Fraud Act 2006 does not define 'fraud', merely stating that '[a] person is guilty of fraud if he is in breach of any of the sections listed'. Fraud Act 2006 s 1.
77 For example: fraud, fraudulent, fraudulently, defraud, misrepresentation, concealment, non-disclosure.
78 Podgor (n 72) 729.
79 Podgor (n 72) 729.
80 Podgor (n 72) 729.

States'[81] has been interpreted to be 'so elastic over the years that it can potentially encompass any conduct which a court views as "collusive and dishonest" if some federal rule or regulation was violated in the process'.[82] As such, it is easy to understand the sentiments of the often quoted Judge Learned Hand, who in 1925 described the conspiracy statute as 'that darling of the modern prosecutor's nursery'.[83] The recognition of wrongdoing is one matter; the prosecution of wrongdoing is another and is in the hands of the federal authorities.

Criminalisation

Mail fraud and wire fraud

The conspiracy statute dates back to 1867 and was followed in 1872 by the Mail Fraud Statute,[84] which has mutated over time from being 'merely one section within the postal act'[85] into a general 'nonspecific' fraud statute.[86] The origin of the US Mail Fraud Statute lies in a mid-nineteenth-century desire to protect the US Post Office and prohibit its use for the transmission of letters or circulars for lotteries.[87] Henning describes this statute as being 'treated as a harmless stepchild by Congress' but now it has universal application: 'Today, the mailing element seemingly provides federal prosecutors with carte blanche to prosecute virtually any activity to which the mail or a shipment by interstate carrier can be linked, no matter how tangential.'[88]

Indeed, Congress has chosen to expand the remit of the Mail Fraud Statute to include the use of private delivery services and, because it has refused to define the meaning of its purpose[89] the outcome is that the statute can be regarded as the Federal Fraud Statute.[90] Judge Rakoff, when he was Chief of Business Fraud Prosecutions in New York, waxed lyrical about the federal Mail Fraud Statute:

81 18 U.S.C. § 371 – Conspiracy to Defraud the United States.

82 Steven D Gordon, 'The liability of colleges and universities for fraud, waste, and abuse in federally funded grants and project' (1992) 75 EDUc L REP 13.

83 *United States of America, Appellee, v Fred Eubanks, Eugene Martinez, Leroy Jones, Henry D. Yanez, appellants.* United States Court of Appeals, Ninth Circuit – 591 F.2d 513, 2 February 1979. As Amended 12 March 1979 http://law.justia.com/cases/federal/appellate-courts/F2/591/513/369568/ Accessed 14 November 2016, citing *Harrison v United States*, 7 F.2d 259, 263 (2d Cir. 1925) (Judge Learned Hand).

84 18 U.S.C. § 1341.

85 Podgor (n 72) 729.

86 Ryder, *Financial Crime in the 21st Century* (n 57) 103.

87 Peter J. Henning, 'Maybe it should just be called federal fraud: The changing nature of the Mail Fraud Statute' (1995) 36 BCL Rev 435.

88 Henning (n 87) 435.

89 Henning (n 87) 435, 440

90 Henning (n 87) 435.

> To federal prosecutors of white collar crime, the mail fraud statute is our Stradivarius, our Colt 45, our Louisville Slugger, our Cuisinart – and our true love. We may flirt with RICO, show off with 10b-5, and call the conspiracy law 'darling', but we always come home to the virtues of 18 USC § 134, with its simplicity, adaptability and comfortable familiarity.[91]

The Mail Fraud Statute was enacted in the aftermath of the American Civil War,[92] when the federal government embarked upon reconstruction of the United States and, according to Rakoff, concluded that 'rudimentary criminal codes, conceived for rural societies could not cope (…) [with the need] to dispel widespread fraud'.[93] Thus, the present-day statute, although amended, is a 'legal fiction' because:

> it has led courts, (…) to describe the element of mailing as the 'gist', 'essence', 'gravamen', and 'substance' of the crime of mail fraud, even though it is obvious that the prime concern of those who commit mail fraud, those who legislate against it, those who prosecute it, and those who judge it, is the fraud and not the mailing.[94]

The attraction of the Mail Fraud Statute, 'together with its lineal descendent, the wire fraud statute',[95] is that it is used as a 'first line of defence' against the development of new types of fraud until specific legislation is enacted.[96] The Wire Fraud Statute,[97] enacted in 1952, is nearly identically worded to the Mail Fraud Statute, except that instead of mailing, 'it requires some interstate or international communications by means of a "wire" (such as telephone lines), radio or television'.[98] The advantage of this consistent approach is that it 'utilizes the same definition of fraud (…) [with the consequence that] cases interpreting the mail fraud provision are of equal precedential value where (…) the defendant is accused of wire fraud'.[99] In the UK, 'Conspiracy to defraud'[100] is the closest common law equivalent.

91 Jed S Rakoff, 'The Federal Mail Fraud Statute (Part I)' (1980) 18 Duq L Rev 771. RICO (Racketeer Influenced and Corrupt Organizations Act, 18 U.S.C. §§ 1961–1968 (1976)) 10b-5 (17 C.F.R. § 240.10b-5 (1979) (Rule 10b-5) (employment of manipulative and deceptive devices in connection with the purchase or sale of any security)). Judge Learned Hand (n 83).
92 'American Civil War n. (b) the war fought in the United States from 1861 to 1865 between the eleven seceding Southern states (the Confederacy) and the remaining (northern) states (the Union). n. and adj.' *OED Online* (Oxford University Press, 12 December 2016).
93 Rakoff (n 91) 771 (footnotes omitted).
94 Rakoff (n 91) 771.
95 Rakoff (n 91) 771.
96 Rakoff (n 91) 771.
97 18 U.S.C. § 1343.
98 Rakoff (n 91) 771.
99 Hoag (n 89) 509.
100 See Chapter 2.

The importance that the US authorities place on the mail and wire statutes (and for which there is no UK equivalent statute) is, according to Zelcer, shown by their expansion to cover 'mailings delivered by private interstate commercial carriers',[101] and modern 'modes of communication such as facsimile, telex, modem, and internet transmissions'.[102] The applications of these statutes include any 'scheme or artifice to deprive another of the intangible right of honest services'.[103] Zelcer notes that this means that '[c]ourts generally agree that the defendant has a duty to provide the victim with honest services',[104] which was redefined in 2010 as to 'criminalize only bribery and kickback schemes'.[105] These statutes 'provide federal courts with jurisdiction over a broad array of frauds',[106] such as consumer, stock, land, bank, insurance, commodity and election, in addition to blackmail, counterfeiting, bribery and money laundering.[107] The provisions of 18 USC enable mail and wire fraud to be a predicate act for the purposes of the Racketeer Influenced and Corrupt Organizations Act 1970,[108] which 'aims to eliminate organised crime',[109] 'by preventing the reintegration of their proceeds of crime into the US economy'.[110]

In the US, government agencies have sought opportunities to stretch existing laws.[111] In the PNP case,[112] which concerned 'stock parking' (an arrangement whereby an investor nominally sells his shareholding to another party with an understanding to re-purchase at a later stage, without loss), prosecutors were able to extend their securities and tax fraud charges to other charges. In this case, PNP having been charged with tax fraud, was also charged with 'mail fraud'. This was purely on the basis that it had used the US Postal Service as part of the fraud merely by putting the tax returns in the post and which would have been avoided by hand delivery.[113] The line of reasoning, according to Strader, was that:

101 Amy Zelcer, 'Mail and Wire Fraud' (2012) 49 Am Crim L Rev 985.
102 Zelcer (n 101) 985.
103 18 U.S.C. § 1346 (2006).
104 Zelcer (n 101) 985.
105 Zelcer (n 101) 985, citing *Skilling v United States* 130 S Ct 2896 (2010).
106 Zelcer (n 101) 985.
107 Zelcer (n 101) 985 (footnotes omitted).
108 18 U.S.C. §§ 1961–1968 (2006 & Supp. 2009). Ryder also notes the opportunity to use RICO to prosecute mortgage fraud arising from the 2008 financial crisis. N Ryder, *The Financial Crisis and White Collar Crime – The Perfect Storm* (Edward Elgar 2014) 20.
109 R Squire and S Ostlund, 'Racketeer influenced and corrupt organizations' (2012) 49 Am Crim L Rev 1211.
110 N Ryder, 'To confiscate or not to confiscate? A comparative analysis of the confiscation of the proceeds of crime legislation in the United States of America and the United Kingdom' (2013) 8 JBL 767–798.
111 For example: Mail Fraud Statute 1872, Wire Fraud Statute 1952, The Racketeer Influenced and Corrupt Organizations Statute. 18 U.S.C.§§ 1961–1964 (2006).
112 9 *United States v Regan*, 37 F.2d 823, 826–827 (2nd Cir. 1991).
113 J Kelly Strader, 'White collar crime and punishment: Reflections on Michael, Martha and Milberg Weiss' (2007) 15 Geo Mason L Rev 94.

> Because it charged mail fraud, the government could bring charges under the RICO statute,[114] with mail fraud as the principle predicate acts. And because RICO contains forfeiture provisions, the government could, and did, assume control over PNP's assets prior to trial.[115]

What PNP demonstrates is that the linking of seemingly disparate legislation by the use of mail or wire fraud acts allows access to other parts of the criminal code than was originally intended: an alternative, as in the UK, would be simple and straightforward fraud legislation.[116] In the US, the RICO Statute was the end product of a long process of legislative effort to develop new legal remedies to deal with an old problem: organised crime.[117] At first, this might seem a strange bedfellow when linked with fraud, bribery and corruption but, as Ryder describes, RICO has been utilised to tackle insider trading because of the shortcomings of the Securities Exchange Act 1934,[118] since under RICO, 'it was only necessary for prosecutors to illustrate that "a defendant committed securities fraud twice within any ten-year period. Prosecutors also favoured the stiff penalties imposed for a RICO conviction"'.[119] However, RICO is not without criticism because of its 'broad and ambiguous language' coupled with the judiciary 'repeatedly interpreting the statute in a liberal, far-reaching manner'.[120] Nevertheless, 'whatever its weaknesses, RICO gives the government an effective threat against sophisticated crime (…) At least for a while, for white-collar criminals as well as gangsters, RICO appears to be evening up the odds'.[121] Nevertheless, Strader reports that difficulties created by 'vagueness of many white collar statutes'[122] provide scope for prosecutors to overreach themselves 'in instances of ambiguous harm and unproven legal theories'.[123] The conclusion that 'more carefully crafted statutes would begin to solve this problem',[124] is based on the reasoning that:

> Apart from being incomprehensible, the RICO statute's potential application is nearly boundless, principally because of its inclusion of the mail and wire

114 The Racketeer Influenced and Corrupt Organizations Statute. 18 U.S.C.§§ 1961–1964 (2006). 18 USC Chapter 96 – Racketeer Influenced and Corrupt Organizations www.law.cornell.edu/uscode/text/18/part-I/chapter-96 Accessed 14 November 2016.
115 Strader (n 113) 61.
116 Such as Fraud Act 2006.
117 G R Blakey and B Gettings, 'Racketeer Influenced and Corrupt Organizations (RICO): Basic concepts – criminal and civil remedies' (1980) 53 Temp LQ 1048.
118 Ryder, *Financial Crime in the 21st Century* (n 57) 152.
119 Ryder, *Financial Crime in the 21st Century* (n 57) 152 (footnotes omitted).
120 Coppola and N DeMarco, 'Civil RICO: How ambiguity allowed the Racketeer Influenced and Corrupt Organizations Act to expand beyond its intended purpose' (2012) 38 New Eng J on Crim & Civ Confinement 241.
121 Blakey and Gettings (n 117) 1048.
122 Strader (n 113) 96.
123 Strader (n 113) 96.
124 Strader (n 113) 96.

> fraud statutes as predicate acts. These statutes can be used just about anytime anyone puts anything in the mail, makes an interstate phone call, or sends an email in suspicious circumstances.[125]

Notwithstanding the use of existing statutes, other events such as the 'credit crunch' and the earlier corporate accounting scandals caused US legislators to expand the range of legislation by enacting the Dodd-Frank and Sarbanes-Oxley Acts.[126]

Dodd-Frank Wall Street Reform and Consumer Protection Act

The 2008 financial crisis, as Ceresney comments, 'will be known as the modern financial system's *annus horribilis*'.[127] A natural consequence of a crisis is that 'citizens are asking angrily how this happened and who is to blame'.[128] This then invites the enquiry that 'amidst this wreckage, as legislators consider proposals for sweeping regulatory reforms, prosecutors and regulatory agencies have begun the arduous and time-consuming process of determining whether any criminal wrongdoing led to the credit crisis'.[129] The outcome of this 'soul searching' was:

> The Dodd-Frank Wall Street Reform and Consumer Protection Act[130] (…) [which] set out to reshape the US regulatory system in a number of areas including but not limited to consumer protection, trading restrictions, credit ratings, regulation of financial products, corporate governance and disclosure, and transparency.[131]

The introduction to Dodd-Frank makes clear the legislation's intentions: 'to promote the financial stability of the United States by improving accountability and transparency in the financial system, to end "too big to fail", to protect the American taxpayer by ending bailouts, to protect consumers from abusive financial services practices, and for other purposes.'[132]

One particular aspect of Dodd-Frank, 'the Volcker Rule, prohibits a bank from engaging in proprietary trading, and from acquiring or retaining an ownership

125 Strader (n 113) 94.
126 The Dodd-Frank Wall Street Reform and Consumer Protection Act 2010 (Pub L 111–203, H.R. 4173), Sarbanes-Oxley Act 2002 (Pub L 107–204, 116 Stat 745, enacted 30 July 2002).
127 Ceresney, Eng and Nuttall (n 63) 225.
128 Ceresney, Eng and Nuttall (n 63) 225.
129 Ceresney, Eng and Nuttall (n 63) 225.
130 12 USC § 5322, which amends the Securities Exchange Act 1934. Hereinafter Dodd-Frank.
131 US Securities and Exchange Commission, 'The Laws that Govern the Securities Industry' www.sec.gov/about/laws.shtml#df2010 Accessed 14 November 2016.
132 The Dodd-Frank Wall Street Reform and Consumer Protection Act, 'Preamble' www.gpo.gov/fdsys/pkg/BILLS-111hr4173enr/pdf/BILLS-111hr4173enr.pdf Accessed 14 November 2016.

interest in a hedge fund or private equity fund'.[133] The intent of the Volcker Rule was to endeavour to replicate '[t]he US Banking Act of 1933, called the Glass-Steagall Act after its sponsors, [which] separated investment banking from retail banking by limiting the range and volume of securities-related transactions that the commercial entities could perform'.[134] This rule, though, does not merely affect US entities but also applies to foreign banks and entities that have a branch or agency in the US and clearly demonstrates the reach of US legislation.[135] However, the future is uncertain because in February 2017, President Trump announced a review of Dodd-Frank.[136]

An additional outcome of the review of the 'financial crisis' was that the SEC recognised that more information on breaches of securities law was required and has caused it to promote the role of the 'whistleblower'.[137] Dodd-Frank encourages 'whistleblowers' to report suspected violations direct to the SEC 'Office of the Whistleblower', which will reward[138] 'such suppliers of information who are eligible to receive between 10 percent and 30 percent of any enforcement penalty in excess of $1 million that the agency ultimately recovers as a result of the report'.[139] Since the programme commenced in 2011, the SEC has received over

133 The Dodd-Frank Wall Street Reform and Consumer Protection Act 2010, s 619. 'The Volcker Rule is named after its main sponsor, Paul Volcker, a former Chairman of the Board of Governors of the Federal Reserve System and an economic adviser to the President of the USA, Barack Obama.' Graeme Baber, 'A critical examination of the legislative response in banking and financial regulation to issues related to misconduct in the context of the crisis of 2007–2009' (2013) 20(2) JFC 237.

134 Baber (n 133) 237.

135 William E Stern, 'Impact of the Volcker rule and related Dodd-Frank Act requirements on fund sponsors affiliated with non-US banking organisations' (2013) 4 JIBFL 229.

136 *The New York Times*, 'Trump moves to roll back Obama-era financial regulations' 3 February 2017 www.nytimes.com/2017/02/03/business/dealbook/trump-congress-financial-regulations.html?_r=0 Accessed 4 February 2017.

137 'Means any individual, or 2 or more individuals acting jointly, who provides information relating to a violation of this Act to the Commission, in a manner established by rule or regulation by the Commission.' Dodd-Frank Act 2010, s 748(7).

138 The SEC established the 'Office of the Whistleblower', stating that the 'new whistleblower program is a part of our effort to enhance the agency's capacity to detect and prevent fraud'. US Securities and Exchange Commission, 'Speech by SEC Chairman: Opening Statement at SEC Open Meeting: Item 2 – Whistleblower Program' 25 May 2011 www.sec.gov/news/speech/2011/spch052511mls-item2.htm Accessed 14 November 2016. 'In addition to providing qualifying whistleblowers with a bounty, the Dodd-Frank Act protects whistleblowers in two other respects. First, it allows whistleblowers to remain anonymous up to the point of receiving their financial awards. Second, the Dodd-Frank Act allows whistleblowers to redeem their bounties unless they are convicted of a crime related to the reported FCPA violations.' Hansberry (n 15) 195.

139 These percentages are typical when compared with other statutes with similar whistleblowing provisions, such as the Internal Revenue Service Whistleblower Act and False Claims Act. Carol M. Welu, 'A brave (but scary) new world: Why private equity is not exempt from US and UK anti-corruption laws' 2 February 2011 www.squirepattonboggs.com/~/media/files/insights/publications/2011/02/china-outbound/

14,000 'tips' and made awards exceeding $107m, the largest of which was $30m.[140]

However, Dodd-Frank was not the first attempt at encouraging 'informers to come forward with information about fraud against the [US] government in return for a share of the damages recovered'.[141] In 1863, pre-dating both conspiracy to defraud (1867) and Mail Fraud (1872), the False Claims Act empowered citizens to sue 'on behalf of the government for fraud against the government'[142] and share in the fruits of litigation: since 2009, the DoJ has recovered over $31.3bn in False Claims Act cases.[143] In 2016, the DoJ brought an all-time high of 702 whistleblower cases,[144] thus demonstrating the economic value of an incentivised whistleblower. Thus, the rewards from the SEC clearly 'make it all the more likely that employees who notice such wrongdoing will take steps to bring it to light'.[145] However, this may be at the expense of reporting through companies' internal corporate risk management or governance channels. Indeed, 'the SEC recently reported receiving one to two "high value" tips per day, up from about a dozen a year prior to enactment' of Dodd-Frank.[146] Furthermore, there is also the risk of 'repeat bad faith' claims as in a 2014 case where the SEC banned an individual who had knowingly made 196 award applications that were false, fictitious or fraudulent in pursuit of an award.[147]

In noting the effect of Dodd-Frank, it is clear that the US has a long history of providing incentives. This is not a feature of UK culture and 'legislation, including the UK Bribery Act, does not provide for these rewards'.[148] The UK regulators FCA/PRA introduced new rules in 2016 to require firms to have effective

files/squiresandersnewschinaoutboundenglishpdf/fileattachment/squiresandersnewschinaoutboundenglishpdf.pdf Accessed 6 December 2016. Hansberry (n 15) 195. R S Bennett, H H LoCicero and B M Hanner, 'From regulation to prosecution to cooperation: Trends in corporate white collar crime enforcement and the evolving role of the white collar criminal defense attorney' (2013) 68 The Business Lawyer 411.

140 For further details, see: Securities and Exchange Commission, '2016 Annual Report to Congress on the Dodd-Frank Whistleblower Program' www.sec.gov/whistleblower/reportspubs/annual-reports/owb-annual-report-2016.pdf Accessed 5 January 2017. Securities and Exchange Commission, 'SEC Whistleblower Program surpasses $100 million in awards' 30 August 2016 www.sec.gov/news/pressrelease/2016-173.html Accessed 2 January 2017.

141 Carr (n 37) 368.

142 Carr (n 37) 369.

143 Department of Justice, 'Justice Department recovers, $4.7bn in false claims cases in fiscal year 2016 [more than $31.1 billion since 2009]' www.justice.gov/opa/pr/justice-department-recovers-over-47-billion-false-claims-act-cases-fiscal-year-2016 Accessed 5 January 2017.

144 Department of Justice, 'Justice Department recovers, $4.7bn in false claims cases in fiscal year 2016' (n 143).

145 Bennett, LoCicero and Hanner (n 139) 411.

146 Hansberry (n 15) 195.

147 Securities and Exchange Commission, 'Final Order' www.whistleblower-defense.com/files/2014/06/Final-Order7.pdf Accessed 14 November 2016.

148 Chris Warren-Smith, 'Regulatory: The year ahead' (2011) 161 NLJ 358.

whistleblowing procedures, and to make senior management accountable for delivering these,[149] but concluded that financial incentives to report would not be adopted.[150] This area is outside the scope of this book but would warrant further research because of the risk of regulatory arbitrage where, for UK companies falling within the purview of the SEC, whistleblowers may be tempted to report wrongdoing in the US rather than either to the UK authorities or through internal procedures, where no rewards exist.[151]

Some eight years before Dodd-Frank, in the wake of 'a spate of financial/ accounting scandals',[152] the Sarbanes-Oxley Act 2002 was enacted 'to protect Investors by improving the accuracy and reliability of corporate disclosures made pursuant to the securities laws, and for other purposes'.[153] This was a 'Congressional response to revelations of several high profile accounting fraud cases including Enron, WorldCom, Tyco, (…) that resulted in mass destruction of investor value and loss of investor confidence in the integrity of the financial markets'.[154] Eventually, as Yeager notes, 'these cases led to criminal charges of company officials and the bankruptcy of Arthur Andersen LLP, at the time arguably the most prestigious independent auditing firm in the world', discussed later in this chapter.[155] Consequently, a key feature of Sarbanes-Oxley was provision for whistleblowers: first, anti-retaliation measures, 'which involves protecting whistleblowers from employer retaliation after they disclose wrongdoing';[156] second, reporting arrangements, which 'requires that corporations provide employees with a standardized channel to report organizational misconduct internally within the corporation'.[157] A further feature of Sarbanes-Oxley was increased sentences: 'the

149 Financial Conduct Authority, 'Financial Incentives for Whistleblowers. Note by the Financial Conduct Authority and the Prudential Regulation Authority for the Treasury Select Committee' www.fca.org.uk/static/documents/financial-incentives-for-whistle blowers.pdf. Financial Conduct Authority, 'FCA introduces new rules on whistle blowing' www.fca.org.uk/news/press-releases/fca-introduces-new-rules-whistleblowing Accessed 14 November 2016.

150 Financial Conduct Authority, 'Financial Incentives for Whistleblowers' (n 149).

151 Hansberry (n 15) 195.

152 Fred Yeager and others, 'US legislation designed to improve corporate governance: An exploration' (2010) 33(1) Co Law 25.

153 Sarbanes-Oxley Act of 2002, 'Preamble' www.sec.gov/about/laws/soa2002.pdf Accessed 14 November 2016.

154 Yeager (n 152) 25.

155 Yeager (n 152) 25.

156 Richard E Moberly, 'Sarbanes-Oxley's structural model to encourage corporate whistleblowers' (2006) BYU L Rev 1107. Kiren Dosanjh Zucker, 'Cautionary tale for corporate whistleblowers: Lessons from Federal Courts' decisions on Sarbanes-Oxley employee retaliation claims' (2011) 62(2) Labor Law Journal 81. The protection for an employee is not to be 'discharged, demoted, suspended, harassed or discriminated against in any other way'. G R Salem and L M Franze, 'The whistleblower provisions of the Sarbanes-Oxley Act of 2002' http://apps.americanbar.org/labor/oshl comm/mw/Papers/2003/salem.pdf Accessed 14 November 2016.

157 *Lockheed Martin Corp. v Administrative Review Board*, No 11–9524, 2013 U.S. App. LEXIS 11159 (10th Cir. 4 June 2013). Moberly (n 156) 1107. Salem and Franze (n 156).

maximum penalty for wire and mail fraud from five years to twenty years imprisonment.'[158] This can be compared with the UK Fraud Act maximum of ten years.[159]

Sentencing

The white collar offender with the longest prison sentence on record is Shalmon Weiss. Weiss, whose misdeeds resulted in the collapse of National Heritage Life Insurance, was sentenced to 845 years in prison.[160] More recently, Bernard Madoff was sentenced to 150 years' imprisonment[161] and 'Sir' Allen Stanford was sentenced to 110 years' imprisonment[162] for a $7bn Ponzi[163] scheme.[164] In the UK, the maximum sentence under the Fraud Act and Bribery Act is ten years' imprisonment and/or an unlimited fine.[165] Asil Nadir, who fled to Northern Cyprus in 1993 before his original trial, was sentenced in 2012 to ten years' imprisonment for fraud dating back to 1987.[166] At first glance, it would appear that the UK might be unduly lenient in its sentencing options when compared with the US. There appear to be two factors contributing to the US approach. First, according to Anello and Albert, Congress has exerted:

158 Ryder, *Financial Crime in the 21st Century* (n 57) 107 (footnotes omitted).
159 Fraud Act 2006, s 1(3)(6).
160 Brian K Payne, *White-collar Crime* (Sage 2013) 370.
161 Daniel V Dooley and Mark Radke, 'Does severe punishment deter financial crimes' (2010) 4 Charleston L Rev 619.
162 US Department of Justice, 'Stanford' www.justice.gov/criminal/vns/caseup/stanfordr.html Accessed 14 November 2016.
163 Securities and Exchange Commission, 'What is a Ponzi Scheme?' 'A Ponzi scheme is an investment fraud that involves the payment of purported returns to existing investors from funds contributed by new investors. Ponzi scheme organizers often solicit new investors by promising to invest funds in opportunities claimed to generate high returns with little or no risk. In many Ponzi schemes, the fraudsters focus on attracting new money to make promised payments to earlier-stage investors and to use for personal expenses, instead of engaging in any legitimate investment activity.' www.sec.gov/answers/ponzi.htm Accessed 11 January 2017.
164 *The Times*, 'Stanford's bank "made up the numbers for more than 20 years"' 4 February 2012 www.thetimes.co.uk/tto/business/industries/banking/article3309416.ece Accessed 14 November 2016. There are some more recent examples of Ponzi schemes but they are of a smaller scale than Madoff and Stanford. For example: Department of Justic, 'Trevor Cook Sentenced to 25 Years in Prison for Swindling 923 Investors out of $158 Million' www.justice.gov/usao/mn/downloads/082410.Cook%20sentenced.pdf Accessed 14 November 2016. 'Scott Rothstein, the name partner in a 70-plus person law firm in Ft. Lauderdale, engaged in a $1.2 billion investment fraud scheme. He is currently serving a 50-year prison sentence.' Department of Justice, 'Assistant Attorney General Lanny A. Breuer of the Criminal Division speaks at the Association of Certified Fraud Examiners Annual Conference San Diego ~ Tuesday, June 14, 2011' www.justice.gov/iso/opa/ag/speeches/2011/ag-speech-110614.html Accessed 14 November 2016.
165 Fraud Act 2006, s 1(3)(b). Bribery Act 2010, s 11.
166 Under Theft Act 1968. Serious Fraud Office, 23 August 2012 www.sfo.gov.uk/2012/08/23/asil-nadir-sentenced/ Accessed 14 November 2016.

> Pressure to increase the penalties associated with fraud offenses, [resulting in] changes to Sentencing Guidelines over the past decade [which] have transformed sentences in high-loss fraud cases from less than five years under the original guidelines to a sentence of life imprisonment.[167]

What lies behind this is the federal government's desire to 'prosecute perceived white collar wrongdoing, along with the ever-expanding legislative response to the country's various financial crises, which has resulted in hundreds of new criminal laws and the seemingly limitless application of existing criminal statutes'.[168] The consequence of this is what Anello and Albert refer to as 'over criminalization', whereby federal prosecutors have 'access to too many charging choices'.[169] The temptation identified is that 'prosecutors could easily fall prey to the temptation of "picking the man, and then searching the law books (…) to pin some offense on him"'.[170] The availability of a large number of laws upon which to charge gives prosecutors considerable discretion whether to charge or not.[171]

The second aspect is that 'prosecutors will pile on charges to gain leverage in plea negotiations'.[172] Reynolds identifies that: 'when facing a hundred felony charges, the prospect that a jury might go along with even one of them is enough to make a plea deal look attractive, something many prosecutors count on.'[173] An example of this, which Anello and Albert note, though with tragic consequences, is the case of:

> Aaron Swartz, the 26 year-old Internet activist who committed suicide after being named in a federal indictment containing 13 felony counts carrying a possible 50-year sentence for allegedly hacking into a computer database to download academic journals.[174]

Concurrent with this disquiet is the concern of the US government about the costs of the prison system.[175] The Attorney General said: 'too many people go to

167 R J Anello and R F Albert, 'Overcriminalization of non-violent conduct: Time for real reform' (2013) 249 NYLJ 106.

168 Anello and Albert (n 167) 106.

169 Anello and Albert (n 167) 106. The SEC's 'civil enforcement response has generated a superabundance of high profile, record breaking, headline grabbing, and media friendly financial sanctions'. Ryder, *The Financial Crisis and White Collar Crime* (n 108) 152, 163–174.

170 Glenn Harlan Reynolds, 'Ham sandwich nation: Due process when everything is a crime' 20 January 2013. University of Tennessee Legal Studies Research Paper No 206. Available at SSRN: http://ssrn.com/abstract=2203713 or http://dx.doi.org/10.2139/ssrn.2203713 Accessed 14 November 2016.

171 Anello and Albert (n 167) 106.

172 Anello and Albert (n 167) 106.

173 Reynolds (n 170).

174 Anello and Albert (n 167) 106 (footnote omitted).

175 Eric Holder, US Attorney General, 'Speech to 15th Annual National Action Network Convention' 4 April 2013 www.justice.gov/iso/opa/ag/speeches/2013/ag-speech-130404.html Accessed 8 December 2016.

too many prisons for far too long for no good law enforcement reason.'[176] Holder poses a fundamental question regarding the US criminal justice system which is that '[s]tatutes passed by legislatures that *mandate* sentences, irrespective of the unique facts of an individual case, too often bear no relation to the conduct at issue'.[177] Recognising that such sentences 'breed disrespect and are ultimately counterproductive,[178] Holder urged that 'we need to ensure that incarceration is used to punish, to rehabilitate, and to deter – and not simply to warehouse and forget'.[179]

A key element in the criminalisation of fraud in the US is that of corporate criminal liability, a concept which was absent in the UK until the Bribery Act.[180] It was:

> established in the [US] by the Supreme Court in 1909. In that year, the court held that any criminal act committed by a corporation's employee within the scope of employment and in part intended to benefit the corporation could be imputed to the corporation.[181]

The effect of this is that instead of prosecuting the corporate entity or individuals, the DoJ and SEC enter Deferred Prosecution Agreements (DPAs). This avenue was not, until 2014, available in the UK because 'corporate criminal in English law it depends on the identification principle. A corporation is only liable for criminal conduct if the controlling mind (ie the top personnel) of the company can be shown to have been complicit in the criminality'.[182] As the SFO director acknowledged, 'this is very hard to prove: rarely does the email chain go above a certain level'.[183]

176 Holder, 'Speech to 15th Annual National Action Network Convention' (n 175).
177 Holder, 'Speech to 15th Annual National Action Network Convention' (n 175) (emphasis added).
178 Holder, 'Speech to 15th Annual National Action Network Convention' (n 175).
179 Holder, 'Speech to 15th Annual National Action Network Convention' (n 175).
180 Bribery Act 2010, s 7. 'Creates the offence of a commercial organisation "failing to prevent" bribery by its employees, with a statutory "adequate procedures" defence. Extending this approach, a Corporate, or certain types of Corporate (such as banks and companies listed on stock exchange) could be liable for failing to prevent certain types of criminal offence by their employees subject to a statutory defence.' Serious Fraud Office, 'David Green Speech' 26 March 2013 www.sfo.gov.uk/2013/03/26/inaugural-fraud-lawyers-association/ Accessed 14 November 2016.
181 Cindy A Schipani, 'Falling off the corporate ladder: Prosecution for financial fraud in the United States' (2011) 32(11) Co Law 336.
182 Serious Fraud Office, 'David Green Speech' (n 180). Individual directors may be subject to proceedings under the Directors Disqualification Act 1986. David Milman, 'Directors, governance and managerial responsibility: new developments in UK law' (2013) 346 Co LN 1, 5. Directors Disqualification may also feature in DPA discussions. Serious Fraud Office, 'Attorney General's Guidelines on plea discussions in cases of serious or complex fraud' www.sfo.gov.uk/publications/guidance-policy-and-protocols/codes-and-protocols/ Accessed 14 November 2016.
183 Serious Fraud Office, 'David Green Speech' (n 180).

Regulatory bodies

In the US, the primary regulatory body for fraud is the DoJ, which is considered in greater detail later in relation to bribery.

Department of Justice

The DoJ has 'control over all criminal prosecutions and civil suits in which the United States had an interest'.[184] Created in 1870, after the Civil War, the DoJ is headed by the Attorney General and comprises 40 components, including the Criminal Division, Fraud Section,[185] which:

> plays a unique and essential role in the Department's fight against sophisticated economic crime. The Section is a front-line litigating unit that acts as a rapid response team, investigating and prosecuting complex white collar crime cases throughout the country.[186]

The role of the DoJ is 'protecting taxpayer dollars and consumers against financial fraud while ensuring competitive advantage'.[187] The then Attorney General stated that they:

> Have charged and had sentenced a number of defendants involved in securities fraud and related investment fraud, mortgage fraud and Ponzi schemes. These defendants include CEOs, owners, board members, presidents, general counsel and other executives of Wall Street firms, hedge funds and banks.[188]

Although the DoJ state that they 'do not hesitate to bring charges against *anyone* [and] between 2009 and 2013, (…) charged more white-collar defendants than during any previous five-year period going back to at least 1994',[189] nevertheless the headlines are given to the significance of the penalties it imposes in 'over 60 cases against financial institutions since 2009, resulting in recoveries totalling over $85billion'.[190] As a response to claims that the DoJ was more interested in

184 Department of Justice, '2014 Budget' www.justice.gov/jmd/2014summary/pdf/fy14-bud-sum.pdf#bs Accessed 14 November 2016.

185 Department of Justice, '2014 Budget' (n 184).

186 Department of Justice, 'Criminal Division Fraud Section' www.justice.gov/criminal/sectionsoffices/chart Accessed 14 November 2016.

187 Department of Justice, 'Accomplishments under the leadership of Attorney General Eric Holder' www.justice.gov/accomplishments Accessed 16 January 2017.

188 Examples include: Allen, sentenced to 210 years' imprisonment for orchestrating $7 billion investment fraud; Barclays Bank $160m LIBOR violations; Department of Justice, 'Accomplishments under the leadership of Attorney General Eric Holder' (n 187).

189 Department of Justice, 'Attorney General Holder remarks on financial fraud prosecutions at NYU School of Law' www.justice.gov/opa/speech/attorney-general-holder-remarks-financial-fraud-prosecutions-nyu-school-law Accessed 14 November 2016.

190 Department of Justice, 'Attorney General Holder remarks on financial fraud prosecutions' (n 189).

obtaining financial settlements, in 2015, the DoJ issued the 'Yates Memorandum', which emphasised that fighting corporate fraud and other misconduct is a priority because it is 'important that the [DoJ] fully leverage its resources to identify culpable individuals at all levels in corporate cases', recognising that holding individuals to account 'is an important part of protecting the public [purse] in the long term'.[191] The first year showed that the DoJ had held individuals accountable but the emphasis was on financial settlements rather than custodial sentences.[192] This was further emphasised in 2016 with a one-year pilot programme to encourage self-reporting,[193] the first example of which in HMT LLC, the DoJ declined to prosecute subject to disgorgement and other actions.[194] One area that is starting to bear fruit is the pursuit of financial institutions for mortgage fraud which contributed to the 2008 financial crisis. In January 2017, Deutsche Bank agreed to pay the DoJ $7.2bn in settlement, being the largest single residential mortgage-backed security penalty:

> The settlement requires Deutsche Bank to pay a $3.1 billion civil penalty under the Financial Institutions Reform, Recovery and Enforcement Act (FIRREA). Under the settlement, Deutsche Bank will also provide $4.1 billion in relief to underwater homeowners, distressed borrowers and affected communities.[195]

There was a similar settlement in January 2017 with Credit Suisse for £5.28bn, in addition to 2016 settlements by Goldman Sachs for $5bn, and Morgan Stanley for $2.6bn. However, in a similar action, Barclays have chosen not to settle.[196]

191 Department of Justice, 'Individual accountability for corporate wrongdoing' (Yates Memorandum) 9 September 2015 www.justice.gov/dag/file/769036/download Accessed 2 January 2017.

192 Department of Justice, 'Justice Department recovers, $4.7bn in false claims cases in fiscal year 2016' (n 143).

193 Department of Justice, 'Criminal Division launches new FCPA Pilot Program' www.justice.gov/opa/blog/criminal-division-launches-new-fcpa-pilot-program Accessed 13 January 2017.

194 Department of Justice, 'Letter to HMT LLC' www.justice.gov/criminal-fraud/file/899116/download Accessed 13 January 2017.

195 Department of Justice, 'Deutsche Bank agrees to pay $7.2 billion for misleading investors in its sale of residential mortgage-backed securities' www.justice.gov/opa/pr/deutsche-bank-agrees-pay-72-billion-misleading-investors-its-sale-residential-mortgage-backed Accessed 15 February 2017.

196 Department of Justice, 'Credit Suisse agrees to pay $5.28 billion in connection with its sale of residential mortgage-backed securities' www.justice.gov/opa/pr/credit-suisse-agrees-pay-528-billion-connection-its-sale-residential-mortgage-backed Accessed 15 February 2017. Department of Justice, 'Goldman Sachs agrees to pay more than $5 billion in connection with its sale of residential mortgage backed securities' www.justice.gov/opa/pr/goldman-sachs-agrees-pay-more-5-billion-connection-its-sale-residential-mortgage-backed Accessed 15 February 2017. Department of Justice, 'Morgan Stanley agrees to pay $2.6 billion penalty in connection with its sale of residential mortgage backed securities' www.justice.gov/opa/pr/morgan-stanley-agrees-pay-26-billion-penalty-connection-its-sale-residential-mortgage-backed Accessed 15 February 2017. Department of Justice, 'United States sues barclays bank to recover civil penalties for fraud in the sale of residential mortgage-backed securities' www.justice.gov/opa/pr/united-

The DoJ as primary regulator and prosecutor is supported by the investigative tools of the FBI,[197] another division of the DoJ. Thus, the Attorney General has line management responsibility for both investigation and prosecution, as does the UK's SFO but with a more limited remit. Neither the DoJ nor the SFO have control over financial intelligence through FinCEN and the NCA, respectively – the former being part of the US Treasury and the latter the UK Home Office.[198]

Bribery and corruption

Criminalisation

The 'Watergate'[199] scandal saw the resignation of President Richard Nixon and provided the stimulus for creating the FCPA.[200] The Watergate Special Prosecutor disclosed 'corrupt payments to foreign officials and overseas agents by [US] domestic companies'.[201] In a 'reaction to a flurry of scandals during the 1970s',[202] the SEC reported that it had 'discovered that many public companies were maintaining cash "slush funds" from which illegal [political] campaign contributions were being made in the [US] and illegal bribes were being paid to foreign officials'.[203] Incidents of international bribery were revealed as widespread 'by over 300 companies involving corrupt payments of hundreds of millions of dollars'.[204] According to Cavico and Bahaudin, the philosophy underlying the FCPA is:

> The statute reflects the public policy of the United States that the payment of bribes to foreign officials in order to secure business was unethical, contrary to the democratic values of the people of the United States, as well as harmful to good governance and the rule of law, contrary to the principles of fair competition, an impediment to economic progress, and thus inimical to society.[205]

states-sues-barclays-bank-recover-civil-penalties-fraud-sale-residential-mortgage Accessed 15 February 2017.

197 Ryder, *Financial Crime in the 21st Century* (n 57) 102.

198 Financial Crimes Enforcement Network (FinCEN), www.fincen.gov Accessed 14 November 2016.

199 'A relentless investigation pays off, and the most famous journalistic feat of its time brings down a president. Two metro reporters stumble upon what at first seems to be a routine crime story – a break-in at a well-known Washington office-hotel complex. But belying the initial simplicity of the crime, it is a scandal that mushrooms into one of the biggest news stories in the history of journalism and brings about the fall of a president.' John Giuffo, 'Watergate' (2001) 40(4) Columbia JR 74.

200 15 U.S.C.§§ 78dd-1, 78dd-2, 78dd-3, 78m, 78ff.

201 H Lowell Brown, 'The Foreign Corrupt Practices Act redux: The anti-bribery provisions of the Foreign Corrupt Practices Act' (1994) 12 Int'l Tax & Bus Law 260.

202 Steven R Salbu, 'Bribery in the global market: A critical analysis of the Foreign Corrupt Practices Act' (1997) 54 Wash & Lee L Rev 229.

203 Department of Justice, 'Proposed legislative history' (n 16).

204 Brown (n 201) 260.

205 F J Cavico and M G Bahaudin, 'Baksheesh or bribe: Payments to government officials and the Foreign Corrupt Practices Act' (2010) 2(1) JBSQ 83.

Prior to 1976, bribery of a foreign official was not illegal if it occurred outside US territory.[206] The FCPA 'has the noble goal of deterring corporations and individuals from engaging in corrupt dealings with foreign officials',[207] and 'Congress intended the FCPA to be expansive, prohibiting not only the successful payment of bribes, but also attempts not fully consummated or effective in achieving their desired ends'.[208]

The FCPA takes a two-pronged approach. First, to 'prohibit individuals and businesses from bribing foreign government officials in order to gain or retain business'.[209] Second, 'the FCPA contains accounting provisions applicable to public companies (…) [which] prohibit off-the-books accounting'.[210] These are two different prohibitions that fall within the purview of two different regulators: the DoJ and SEC. The FCPA 'focuses primarily on US entities and citizens',[211] together with 'US and foreign public companies listed on stock exchanges in the United States or which are required to file periodic reports with the SEC issuers'.[212] US jurisdiction is, thus, established over 'domestic concerns'[213] and 'issuers',[214] which includes 940 foreign companies.[215] However, the ambit of the FCPA extends further because it takes territorial jurisdiction over 'foreign persons and foreign non-issuer entities that (…) engage in *any* act in furtherance of a corrupt payment (…) while in the territory of the United States'.[216] The territory of the US is, though, extended outside the US because the statute includes the 'use of the mails or any means of interstate commerce'.[217]

206 Hansberry (n 15) 195.
207 Hansberry (n 15) 195.
208 Salbu (n 202) 229.
209 DoJ/SEC (n 2)
210 DoJ/SEC (n 2) 38.
211 Griffin (n 19) 341.
212 15 U.S.C. § 78dd-1 (Issuers). DoJ/SEC (n 2) 2.
213 'A domestic concern is any individual who is a citizen, national or resident of the United States, or any corporation, partnership, association, joint stock company, business trust, unincorporated organization, or sole proprietorship that is organized under the laws of the United States or its states, territories, possessions, or commonwealths or that has its principle place of business in the United States.' 15 U.S.C. § 78dd-2. DoJ/SEC (n 2) 11.
214 15 U.S.C. § 78dd-1 [Section 30A of the Securities Exchange Act of 1934] Prohibited foreign trade practices by issuers. 'In practice, this means that any company with a class of securities listed on a national stock exchange in the United States, or any company with a class of securities quoted in the over-the-counter market in the United States and required to file periodic reports with SEC, is an issuer. Foreign companies with American Depository Receipts that are listed on a US exchange are also issuers.' DoJ/SEC (n 2) 11.
215 15 U.S.C. § 78dd-3. DoJ/SEC (n 200) 11. Securities and Exchange Commission, 'Market Summary 31 December 2013' www.sec.gov/divisions/corpfin/internatl/foreignmarketsumm2013.pdf Accessed 14 November 2016.
216 DoJ/SEC (n 2) 11.
217 15 U.S.C. § 78dd-1 [Section 30A of the Securities Exchange Act of 1934] Prohibited foreign trade practices by issuers. (a) prohibition.

The use of 'mails' provides a link to the Mail Fraud Statute[218] and 'interstate commerce', which:

> Means trade, commerce, transportation, or communication among the several States, or between any foreign country and any State or between any State and any place or ship outside thereof, and such term includes the use of – (A) a telephone or other interstate means of communication, or (B) any other interstate instrumentality.[219]

In this way, the use of telephone, fax, and/or email or travelling across US state or international borders are included, as is the use of the US banking system to make 'wire transfers' to or from the US.

Anti-bribery provisions

The DoJ describes the overall objective of the FCPA in relation to bribery as the 'business purpose test', because 'the FCPA applies only to payments intended to induce or influence a foreign official to use his or her position "in order to assist (…) in obtaining or retaining business for, or with, or directing business to, any person"'.[220] The FCPA contains sections relating to the three areas prohibited (issuers, domestic concerns and foreign persons)[221] and prohibitions, albeit with tailored introductions, being the same:

> It shall be unlawful for any [issuer; domestic concern; person other than issuer] (…) or for any officer, director, employee or agent (…) to make use of the mails or any means or instrumentality of interstate commerce corruptly in furtherance of an offer, payment, promise to pay, or authorization of the payment of any money, or offer, gift, promise to give, or authorization of the giving of anything of value (…)[222]

Thus, the FCPA encompasses anyone acting on behalf of the issuer (or domestic concern/person other than the issuer), using a means of interstate or international commerce, and providing or offering to provide 'anything of value'. Next, the recipient is identified as 'any foreign official'.[223]

> The term 'foreign official' means any officer or employee of a foreign government or any department or agency, or instrumentality thereof, or of a public international organization, or any person acting in an official capacity

218 18 U.S.C. § 1341.
219 DoJ/SEC (n 2) 11.
220 DoJ/SEC (n 2) 12.
221 15 U.S.C. § 78dd-1, 15 U.S.C. § 78dd-2, 15 U.S.C. § 78dd-3.
222 15 U.S.C. § 78dd-1(a), 15 U.S.C. § 78dd-2(a), 15 U.S.C. § 78dd-3(a).
223 15 U.S.C. § 78dd-1(a)(1), 15 U.S.C. § 78dd-2(a)(1), 15 U.S.C. § 78dd-3(a)(1).

> for or on behalf of any such government or department, agency, or instrumentality or (…) public international organization.[224]

This definition includes 'any foreign political party or official thereof or any candidate for foreign political office',[225] or 'any person, while knowing that all or a portion of such money or thing of value will be given (…) to any foreign official'.[226] The DoJ provides some clarification that the FCPA prohibits payments to foreign officials, not foreign governments, but warns that steps should be taken 'that no monies are used for corrupt purposes, such as the personal benefit of individual foreign officials'.[227] For example, in *SEC v Willbros*, a defendant:

> Admitted that (…) he conspired with others to make a series of corrupt payments totalling more than $6 million to various Nigerian officials and officials from a Nigerian political party to assist Willbros in obtaining and retaining the Eastern Gas Gathering System Project, which was valued at approximately $387m.[228]

Additionally, the DoJ stated that not all foreign governments are organised in the same fashion as the US (and, for that matter, the UK), with clearly identified government departments or agencies.

> Many [foreign governments] operate through state-owned and state-controlled entities, particularly in such areas as aerospace and defense manufacturing, banking and finance, healthcare and life sciences, energy and extractive industries, telecommunications and transportation.[229]

The FCPA also recognises and prohibits the possibility of routing payments indirectly, through a third party or intermediary.[230] Although the DoJ understand the way in which foreign business is undertaken, they do warn that:

224 15 U.S.C. § 78dd-1(f)(1)(A), 15 U.S.C. § 78dd-2(h)(2)(A), 15 U.S.C. § 78dd-3(f)(2)(A). Public international organisations are entities such as: the United Nations, the International Monetary Fund, OECD and World Bank, but also bodies such as the Korean Peninsula Energy Development Organization and Pan American Health Organization. 22 U.S.C. 288 – Sec. 288. '"International organization" defined; Authority of President' www.law.cornell.edu/uscode/text/22/288 Accessed 14 November 2016.

225 15 U.S.C. § 78dd-1(a)(2), 15 U.S.C. § 78dd-2(a)(2), 15 U.S.C. § 78dd-3(a)(2).

226 15 U.S.C. § 78dd-1(a)(3), 15 U.S.C. § 78dd-2(a)(3), 15 U.S.C. § 78dd-3(a)(3).

227 DoJ/SEC (n 2) 20.

228 Department of Justice, 'Former Willbros International executives sentenced to prison for their roles in $6 million foreign bribery scheme' 28 January 2010 www.justice.gov/opa/pr/2010/January/10-crm-102.html. *Securities and Exchange Commission v Willbros Group, Inc., et al.*, Civil Action No. 4:08-CV-01494 U.S.D.C./Southern District of Texas (Houston Division). Accessed 14 November 2016.

229 DoJ/SEC (n 2) 20.

230 15 U.S.C. § 78dd-1(a)(3), 15 U.S.C. § 78dd-2(a)(3), 15 U.S.C. § 78dd-3(a)(3).

> Many companies doing business in a foreign country retain a local individual or company to help them conduct business. Although these foreign agents may provide entirely legitimate advice regarding local customs and procedures and may help facilitate business transactions, companies should be aware of the risks involved in engaging third-party agents or intermediaries.[231]

Through the language of the FCPA and the enforcement department's explanatory notes, it is clear that a strict regime is to be adopted towards bribery being 'to "any" officer or employee of a foreign government and to those acting on a foreign government's behalf'.[232] The DoJ state that 'the FCPA thus covers corrupt payments to low-ranking employees and high-level officials alike'.[233]

Violations of the FCPA mean that 'corporations and other business entities are subject to a fine of up to $2 million' for each violation, whereas, '[i]ndividuals, including officers, directors, stockholders, and agents of companies are subject to a fine of up to $100,000 and imprisonment for up to five years'.[234] Furthermore, 'fines imposed on individuals may not be paid by their employer or principal'.[235] What this range of penalties leads to, as is discussed later in this chapter, is negotiations with the prosecutor regarding the outcome of a prosecution.

Facilitating or expediting payments

Rather prosaically termed in the FCPA is '15 U.S.C. § 78dd-1(b), Exception for routine government action'.[236] This is not expressly an exception for the US government itself, but:

> Means only an action which is ordinarily and commonly performed by a foreign official in – (i) obtaining permits, licenses, or other official documents to qualify a person to do business in a foreign country; (ii) processing governmental papers such as visas and work orders; (iii) providing police protection, mail pick up and delivery, or scheduling inspections associated with contract performance or inspections related to transit of goods across country; (iv) providing phone service, power and water supply, loading and unloading cargo or protecting perishable products or commodities from deterioration; or (v) actions of a similar nature.[237]

This exception is in contrast to the UK Bribery Act, which does not permit 'facilitation or grease payments'.[238] Furthermore, the DoJ recognise that it is

231 DoJ/SEC (n 2) 20.
232 DoJ/SEC (n 2) 20.
233 DoJ/SEC (n 2) 20.
234 DoJ/SEC (n 2) 68.
235 DoJ/SEC (n 2) 20.
236 15 U.S.C. § 78dd-1(b).
237 15 U.S.C. § 78dd-1(f)(3)(A).
238 See Chapter 3. 'We recognise that many UK businesses still struggle with petty corruption in some markets, but the answer is to face the challenge head-on, rather than

against 'the OECD's Working Group on Bribery [which] recommends that all countries encourage companies to prohibit or discourage facilitating payments'.[239] This provision recognises that there is not complete agreement amongst countries for a strict requirement. There is a warning, though, that such payments must be properly recorded in the issuer's books and records, failing which they will breach the FCPA.[240] This is an interesting point of disparity between the US and UK, because the FCPA exceptions were cited in submissions to the UK Ministry of Justice when the Bribery Act was being drafted,[241] and it was criticised when not permitted.[242] Thus, in analysing a key difference between US and UK anti-bribery legislation it can be seen that the US exemption was considered by the UK in drafting its Bribery Act and not adopted.[243] Indeed, such a change would be difficult for the SFO to justify because it stated that the UK prohibition on facilitation payments was consistent with the UN Convention and OECD policy, concluding that the 'Government and SFO are committed to stamping out bribery and upholding the rule of law. The SFO stands ready to take effective action against the use of facilitation payments, regardless of where they are requested', though as of 2016 the SFO had yet to test this in court.[244]

In the US, there is also a debate,[245] but Jordan's view is that 'the facilitation payments exception has become a dinosaur remnant of a bygone era [the 1970s], (…) when corruption was prevalent and no international treaty existed to prohibit foreign bribery'.[246] While that may have been reasonable at the time, because the

carve out exemptions that draw artificial distinctions, are difficult to enforce, and have the potential to be abused. Providing exemptions for facilitation payments, as the US does, is not a universally accepted practice, and not something that we consider acceptable.' Clare Ward, HC Deb 3 March 2010 vol 506 col 981.

239 DoJ/SEC (n 2) 25.

240 DoJ/SEC (n 2) 20.

241 Ministry of Justice, 'Guidance about commercial organisations preventing bribery (section 9 of the Bribery Act 2010)' http://webarchive.nationalarchives.gov.uk/20101013220527/http://www.justice.gov.uk/consultations/briberyactconsultation.htm Accessed 14 November 2016.

242 RealBusiness, 'Re-write the Bribery Act and allow "Facilitation Payments" says MP' http://realbusiness.co.uk/article/21413-rewrite-the-bribery-act-and-allow-facilitation-payments-saysmp Accessed 14 November 2016.

243 RealBusiness (n 242).

244 Serious Fraud Office, 'Bribery Act guidance' www.sfo.gov.uk/publications/guidance-policy-and-protocols/bribery-act-guidance/ Accessed 14 November 2016.

245 Transparency International reporting that: 'both the US Chamber of Commerce, which represents thousands of businesses, and the American Petroleum Institute, have been working overtime to weaken the Dodd-Frank financial reform legislation and the FCPA. Dodd-Frank includes provisions to increase transparency in the financial system and ensure that companies published more information about how and where they do business. The FCPA targets bribery of foreign officials.' Transparency International, 'Stop watering down anti-corruption legislation' www.transparency.org/news/feature/stop_watering_down_anti_corruption_legislation Accessed 14 November 2016.

246 Jon Jordan, 'The OECD's call for an end to "corrosive" facilitation payments and the international focus on the facilitation payments exception under the Foreign Corrupt Practices Act' (2011) 13 U Pa J Bus L 881.

rest of the world had not proscribed foreign bribery, the US had 'pushed hard for an international anti-bribery regime so that it would no longer be isolated in the fight against foreign bribery that left its domestic companies at an unfair disadvantage'.[247] The consequence of leading international efforts to reform global bribery legislation is that 'these efforts have also backfired on the United States, as it now finds itself awkwardly criticized by the rest of the world for its own anti-bribery deficiencies inherent in the facilitation payments exception'.[248] Thus, as Jordan proposes, the US should abandon the facilitation payments carve out and, in doing so, 'join the rest of the world in condemning facilitation payments and fulfil its leadership role in the fight against foreign bribery'.[249]

Accounting provisions

The second prong of the FCPA is its accounting provisions,[250] which are 'designed to "strengthen the accuracy of the corporate books and records and the reliability of the audit process which constitute the foundations of our system of corporate disclosure"'.[251] Sorensen describes the US commercial landscape leading to enactment of the FCPA as:

> The practice of exporters and investors offering special inducements to host country officials is at least as old as Marco Polo. But in the [US] a post-Watergate climate of pitiless exposure for all suspect practices connected with government has intensified both the investigations of these payments and the oversimplified publicity given to them (…) As a result, the US corporate officials have engaged in the most painful rush to public 'voluntary' confession since China's Cultural Revolution.[252]

At this time, there were clear tensions between all payments being condemned and the recognition that 'not every foreign consultant or sales agent is corrupt or retained to perform some improper function',[253] 'but *properly recorded* payments, of an amount appropriate under the circumstances, to a qualified and responsible professional for his performance of legitimate and necessary services, may well be perfectly justifiable'.[254] The words 'properly recorded' are key, according to Diersen, because:

247 Jordan (n 246) 881.
248 Jordan (n 246) 881.
249 Jordan (n 246) 881.
250 15 U.S.C. § 78m [Section 13 of the Securities Exchange Act of 1934].
251 DoJ/SEC (n 2) 38.
252 Theodore C Sorensen, 'Improper payments abroad: Perspectives and proposals' (1976) 54 Foreign Aff 719.
253 Sorensen (n 252) 719.
254 Sorensen (n 252) 719 (emphasis added).

> The record-keeping provisions are used to prevent three types of improprieties: (1) a failure to record improper transactions; (2) the falsification of records to conceal improper transactions; and (3) the creation of records that are quantitatively correct, but fail to specify the qualitative aspects of a transaction which might reveal the true purpose of a payment.[255]

The Act applies to 'every issuer which has a class of securities registered (…) and every issuer who is required to file reports'.[256] This means:

> Any issuer whose securities trade on a national securities exchange in the United States, including foreign issuers with exchange-traded American Depository Receipts. They also apply to companies whose stock trades in the over-the-counter market in the United States and which file periodic reports with the commission, such as annual or quarterly report.[257]

Thus, this part of the Act defines who falls within the purview of the SEC, where 'unlike the FCPA's anti-bribery provisions, the accounting provisions do not apply to private companies'.[258] The SEC-regulated 'issuers' are, first, required to 'make and keep books, records, and accounts, which, in reasonable detail, accurately and fairly reflect the transactions and dispositions of assets of the issuer'.[259] The second element applicable to 'issuers' is to 'devise and maintain a system of internal accounting controls sufficient to provide reasonable assurances' that transactions are properly authorised and recorded.[260] Underlying these provisions is the knowledge that 'in the past, "corporate bribery has been concealed by the falsification of books and records"',[261] with the consequence that accounting records have been inaccurate and do not 'fairly reflect the transactions and dispositions of assets of the issuer'.[262] Furthermore, as the DoJ and SEC state, 'the payment of bribes often occurs in companies that have weak internal control environments'.[263] Although the Act requires a system of internal controls to be in place, it does not prescribe the form of those controls. Instead, it is the responsibility of the 'issuer' to create controls appropriate to the business risks that it faces:[264]

255 Kari Lynn Diersen, 'Foreign Corrupt Practices Act' (1999) 36 Am Crim L Rev 753.
256 15 U.S.C. § 78m (b)(2).
257 DoJ/SEC (n 2) 43.
258 DoJ/SEC (n 2) 43.
259 15 U.S.C. § 78m (b)(2)(A).
260 15 U.S.C. § 78m (b)(2)(B).
261 DoJ/SEC (n 2) 39.
262 15 U.S.C. § 78m (b)(2)(A).
263 DoJ/SEC (n 2) 43. An example is United Continental, 'where shareholders wound up footing the bill so a public official could get more convenient flights'. Securities and Exchange Commission, 'United settles charges in case of flight route to benefit public official' 2 December 2016 www.sec.gov/news/pressrelease/2016-253.html Accessed 13 January 2017.
264 This is a common and familiar approach for businesses, also for money laundering and terrorism financing. Financial Action Task Force, 'Risk based approach' www.fatf-gafi.org/documents/riskbasedapproach/ Accessed 14 November 2016.

> The SEC considers several factors in order to determine the adequacy of a system of internal controls, including: the (1) role of the board of directors; (2) communication of corporate procedures and policies; (3) assignment of authority and responsibility; (4) competence and integrity of personnel; (5) accountability for performance and compliance with policies and procedures; and (6) objectivity and effectiveness of the internal audit function.[265]

It is the role of the 'issuer' to devise its own controls, which 'must take into account the operational realities and risks attendant to the company's business',[266] such as 'businesses whose operations expose them to a high risk of corruption will necessarily devise and employ different internal controls than businesses that have a lesser exposure to corruption'.[267]

Both the 'books and records' and 'internal controls' provisions are qualified by employing a 'prudent man' standard.[268] 'The terms "reasonable assurances" and "reasonable detail" mean such level of detail and degree of assurance as would satisfy prudent officials in the conduct of their own affairs.'[269] The reason for this qualification being adopted was 'in light of the concern that a standard, if unqualified, might connote a degree of exactitude and precision which is unrealistic'.[270] The DoJ further note that when Congress adopted the definition, 'the concept of reasonableness of necessity contemplates the weighing of a number of relevant factors, including the costs of compliance'.[271] Thus, it is clear that the FCPA contemplates a degree of interpretation of actions.

Criminal liability arises when companies and individuals 'knowingly circumvent or knowingly fail to implement a system of internal accounting controls or knowingly falsify any book, record or account'.[272] This requirement of intent, a (1988) refinement of the FCPA,[273] 'is an attempt to reduce the potential for unlimited liability as a result of accounting violations'.[274] The expression 'knowing' also embraces not knowing, or 'wilful blindness, or conscious attempts not to know', such as 'deliberately avoiding knowledge or adopting a "head in the sand approach"'.[275]

265 Diersen (n 255) 753.
266 DoJ/SEC (n 2) 40.
267 DoJ/SEC (n 2) 40.
268 Diersen (n 255) 753.
269 15 U.S.C. § 78m (b)(7).
270 DoJ/SEC (n 2) 39.
271 DoJ/SEC (n 2) 68.
272 15 U.S.C. § 78m (b)(5).
273 'The 1988 Trade Act directed the Attorney General to provide guidance concerning the Department of Justice's enforcement policy with respect to the Foreign Corrupt Practices Act of 1977.' US Department of Commerce, 'International Trade Administration' www.trade.gov/goodgovernance/adobe/bem_appendices/appendix_f.pdf Accessed 14 November 2016.
274 Diersen (n 255) 753.
275 Diersen (n 255) 753.

The penalties for each violation of the FCPA accounting provisions are a fine of up to $25 million for corporations, with individuals subject to a fine of $5 million and 20 years' imprisonment.[276] 'Fines imposed on individuals may not be paid by their employer or principal',[277] which clearly can be seen as an incentive for individuals to reach an accommodation with the authorities whereby the corporation bears the burden.

There is a defence 'to ensure that mundane accounting deficiencies would not violate the Act',[278] such as 'technical or insignificant accounting errors'.[279] Furthermore, a parent issuer, owning less than 50% of a subsidiary, may use its 'good faith' as a defence if it 'encourages compliance with FCPA accounting controls',[280] on the basis 'that it is "unrealistic to expect a minority owner to exert a disproportionate degree of influence over the accounting practices of a subsidiary"'.[281]

'The FCPA was not heavily enforced during the first twenty years of its existence',[282] and it appeared to Hotchkiss that:

> For many years, international firms and executives treated the Foreign Corrupt Practices Act as the proverbial sleeping dog, best left alone. The FCPA was perceived as an overreaching and naïve attempt by the US government to impose unrealistic standards on global business conduct.[283]

However, more recently, enforcement activities by both the DoJ and the SEC have increased dramatically.[284] The DoJ report that the 'Department has expanded efforts to combat corruption at home and abroad'.[285] 'Since 2009, the Department's FCPA-related enforcement has secured more than $2 billion in fines and penalties and increased prosecutions of individuals who have bribed foreign officials',[286] and the SEC $1.2bn between 2010 and 2013.[287]

276 DoJ/SEC (n 2) 20.
277 DoJ/SEC (n 2) 68.
278 Diersen (n 255) 753.
279 Diersen (n 255) 753.
280 Diersen (n 255) 753.
281 Diersen (n 255) 753.
282 Hansberry (n 15) 195.
283 Carolyn Hotchkiss, 'The sleeping dog stirs: New signs of life in efforts to end corruption in international business' (1998) 17(1) Journal of Public Policy & Marketing 108.
284 Federal Bureau of Investigation, 'Mortgage fraud' www.fbi.gov/investigate/white-collar-crime/mortgage-fraud Accessed 6 December 2016. Securities and Exchange Commission, 'SEC enforcement actions: FCPA cases' www.sec.gov/spotlight/fcpa/fcpa-cases.shtml Accessed 8 December 2016.
285 Department of Justice, 'Accomplishments under the leadership of Attorney General Eric Holder' (n 187).
286 Department of Justice, 'Accomplishments under the leadership of Attorney General Eric Holder' (n 187).
287 FCPA Professor, 'SEC enforcement of the FCPA – Year in review' www.fcpaprofessor.com/sec-enforcement-of-the-fcpa-year-in-review-3 Accessed 14 November 2016.

Regulatory bodies

The DoJ and the SEC share responsibility for enforcement of the FCPA and have the facility either to work independently or together.[288]

Department of Justice

The DoJ Criminal Division, Fraud Section, is responsible for authorising all FCPA criminal actions[289] and 'develops, enforces, and supervises the application of all federal criminal laws except those specifically assigned to other divisions'.[290] Thus, the DoJ 'is solely responsible for criminal enforcement but may institute civil proceedings',[291] whereas the SEC can only institute civil proceedings, with any criminal prosecutions being referred to the DoJ.[292] The DoJ maintains an FCPA Unit and works with the FBI, whose 'International Corruption Unit has primary responsibility for international corruption and fraud investigations and coordinates the FBI's national FCPA enforcement program'.[293] The DoJ has instituted a new initiative, the Kleptocracy Asset Recovery Initiative, to 'target and recover the proceeds of foreign official corruption that have been laundered into or through the United States'.[294] Their first success in 2012 was a $3 million restraining order against 'the former governor of the oil-producing Delta State in Nigeria', followed by another order for $4 million.[295]

In considering criminal penalties to be imposed for violation of the FCPA, the DoJ also has the availability of 'the Alternative Fines Act',[296] which can double the fines provided for in the FCPA.[297] Furthermore, there is a procedure for

288 15 U.S.C.§§ 78dd-1, 78dd-2, 78dd-3, 78m, 78ff.

289 Department of Justice, 'Assistant Attorney General Lanny A. Breuer' (n 164).

290 The United States Department of Justice, 'About the division' www.justice.gov/criminal/about-criminal-division Accessed 14 November 2016.

291 Cavico and Bahaudin (n 205) 83.

292 DoJ/SEC (n 2) 39.

293 DoJ/SEC (n 2) 39.

294 'A ruling body or order of thieves.' 'kleptocracy, n.' *OED Online* (Oxford University Press) www.oed.com/view/Entry/103832?rskey=cNHhIB&result=2 Accessed 19 December 2016. 'Once fully implemented, this Initiative will allow the Department to recover assets on behalf of countries victimized by high-level corruption, building on the Justice Department's already robust enforcement of the Foreign Corrupt Practices Act. Through the Kleptocracy Initiative, the Department will ensure that corrupt leaders cannot seek safe haven in the United States for their stolen wealth. And, if we uncover such wealth, the Justice Department will forfeit and return this stolen money to its rightful owners – the people and governments from whom it was taken.' Department of Justice, 'Assistant Attorney General Lanny A. Breuer' (n 164).

295 Department of Justice, 'Assistant Attorney General Lanny A. Breuer' (n 164).

296 18 U.S.C. § 3571.

297 '[The alternative fines] provision is intended to enable federal courts to impose fines that will prevent convicted offenders from ***profiting from their wrongdoing***' (emphasis added), 19 July 2012. *US v Sanford Ltd et al.*www.gpo.gov/fdsys/pkg/USCOURTS-dcd-1_11-cr-00352/pdf/USCOURTS-dcd-1_11-cr-00352-3.pdf Accessed 14 November 2016. The DoJ reports violations of the FCPA where in the

calculating the magnitude of fines, contained in the 'US Sentencing Guidelines',[298] which 'provide a very detailed and predictable structure for calculating penalties for all federal crimes, including violations of the FCPA'.[299] These are two significant differences between the manner in which enforcement is undertaken in the US and UK, where there is no such degree of certainty for defendants when considering their options.

An important point of difference between the UK and US is the ability of the US to negotiate an outcome with the defendant,[300] a proposition which the UK SFO found attractive but which generated judicial antipathy[301] prior to 2014 when DPA were allowed (see Chapter 3). In the US, the:

> DoJ may agree to resolve criminal FCPA matters against companies either through declination or, in appropriate cases, a negotiated resolution resulting in a plea agreement, deferred prosecution agreement, or non-prosecution agreement.[302]

In a Plea Agreement, 'the defendant generally admits to the facts supporting the charges, admits guilt, and is convicted of the charged crimes when the plea agreement is presented to and accepted by a court'.[303] For example, the publicly available letter detailing terms between the DoJ and Siemens AG[304] shows a settlement where Siemens AG 'and three of its subsidiaries, pleaded guilty to FCPA-related violations. *The parent was not required to plead guilty to a bribery violation*, thereby likely avoiding mandatory debarment in Europe'.[305] In the US, a guilty plea does not result in automatic debarment from US government contracting because an independent debarment authority will consider the

settlement agreement, the Alternative Fines Act was considered. In *Alcatel-Lucent* the Alternative Fines Act was used to set the fines parameter of up to twice the base fine $48m and the total agreed was $92m. Department of Justice, 'United States of America vs. Alcatel-Lucent, S.A., f/kla "Alcatel, S.A.," Deferred Prosecution Agreement' www.justice.gov/criminal/fraud/fcpa/cases/alcatel-etal/02-22-11alcatel-dpa.pdf Accessed 14 November 2016.

298 US Sentencing Commission, '2010 Federal Sentencing Commission Guidelines' www.ussc.gov/Guidelines/2010_guidelines/index.cfm Accessed 14 November 2016.

299 DoJ/SEC (n 2) 68.

300 Under Federal Rules of Criminal Procedure. DoJ/SEC (n 2) 74.

301 'The SFO cannot enter into an agreement under the laws of England and Wales with an offender as to the penalty in respect of the offence charged.' E O'Shea, N McLeod and A Beal, 'Regulatory: Back to the drawing board' (2010) 160 NLJ 759. (Thomas LJ.)

302 DoJ/SEC (n 2) 74.

303 DoJ/SEC (n 2) 74.

304 *United States v Siemens Aktiengesellschaft* Court Docket Number: 08-CR-367-RJL Plea Agreement, 12 December 2008 www.justice.gov/criminal/fraud/fcpa/cases/siemens/12-15-08siemensakt-plea.pdf Accessed 14 November 2016.

305 R W Tarun and P P Tomczak, 'A Proposal for a United States Department of Justice Foreign Corrupt Practices Act leniency policy' (2010) 47 Am Crim L Rev 153 (emphasis added).

issues.[306] However, in the UK, the EU Public Sector Procurement Directive applies.[307]

A second alternative is a DPA, which operates as a 'Sword of Damocles'[308] in that the DoJ 'files a charging document with the court, but simultaneously requests that the prosecution be deferred'.[309] The deferral, or not proceeding with the prosecution, is on the basis that the defendant pleads guilty but in return for a fine or other penalties and agreement, as in the case of Daimler AG, to 'an independent compliance monitor for three years',[310] and the DoJ agrees to dismiss the charges upon expiry of the agreement.[311] The attraction of a DPA is certainty, in the knowledge that a breach of the agreement would result in a criminal conviction, whereas, 'a company's successful completion of a DPA is not treated as a criminal conviction'.[312]

A third alternative agreement is a 'Non-Prosecution Agreement' (NPA). An NPA is less formal and restrictive than a DPA and, although the facts are disclosed, a charging document is not lodged with the court but is left to lie in the prosecutor's file, to be activated if there is a breach of the NPA. This would include a tolling[313] agreement to stay any statute of limitations issues.

The use of an NPA is demonstrated in the 2013 agreement with Ralph Lauren Corporation (RLC), which had a subsidiary in Argentina.[314] The facts were that

306 DoJ/SEC (n 2) 70.

307 Note: In the UK, the EU Public Sector Procurement Directive applies. The effect of this is that a commercial organization is excluded from participation in public sector contracts if convicted of fraud, bribery and corruption under Article 45. This provides the incentive to 'self-report' to the SFO with the prospect of negotiating an outcome and incurring a civil rather than criminal penalty. EU Public Services Procurement Directive 2004/18/EC Art. 45. Implemented in the UK by the Public Contracts Regulations 2006, which provide revised rules for the procurement of supplies, works and services by public authorities. The Utilities Contracts Regulations 2006 implement the revised Utilities Directive (2004/17/EC), which provides, in a similar way, revised rules for procurement in the utilities sector. Office of Government Commerce, HM Treasury http://webarchive.nationalarchives.gov.uk/20130129110402/http://www.hm-treasury.gov.uk/d/competitive_dialogue_procedure.pdf Accessed 14 November 2016.

308 'Sword of Damocles n. (also Damocles' sword) used by simile of an imminent danger, which may at any moment descend upon one.' ('Damocles, a flatterer, having extolled the happiness of Dionysius tyrant of Syracuse, was placed by him at a banquet with a sword suspended over his head by a hair, to impress upon him the perilous nature of that happiness.') 'Damocles, n.' *OED Online* (Oxford University Press, 13 December 2016).

309 DoJ/SEC (n 2) 74.

310 Tarun and Tomczak (n 305) 153.

311 *United States v Daimler AG* Court Docket Number: 10-CR-063-RJL. Deferred Prosecution Agreement, 22 March 2010 www.justice.gov/criminal/fraud/fcpa/cases/daimler/03-24-10daimlerag-agree.pdf Accessed 14 November 2016.

312 DoJ/SEC (n 2) 70.

313 'A tolling agreement is an agreement to waive a right to claim that litigation should be dismissed due to the expiration of a statute of limitations.' US Legal.com, 'Definitions' http://definitions.uslegal.com/t/tolling-agreement/ Accessed 14 November 2016.

314 Department of Justice, 'Ralph Lauren Corporation resolves Foreign Corrupt Practices Act investigation and agrees to pay $882,000 monetary penalty' www.justice.gov/opa/pr/2013/April/13-crm-456.html Accessed 14 November 2016.

over a five-year period, a manager of the subsidiary paid bribes and gifts totalling $593,000 to customs officials in Argentina to[315] improperly obtain paperwork necessary for goods to clear customs and or avoid inspection, while payments were disguised and false invoices created. 'RLC did not have an anti-corruption program and did not provide any anti-corruption training or oversight with respect to its subsidiary in Argentina.'[316]

In parallel with the DoJ, the SEC also agreed an NPA, which was the first occasion both regulators completed agreements with the same company. The SEC's reasoning was that 'when they found a problem, [RLC] did the right thing by immediately reporting it (…) and providing exceptional assistance (…) we will confer substantial benefits on companies that respond appropriately to violations and cooperate fully'.[317] The DoJ agreement gave credit[318] for, and rewarded, self-reporting by not prosecuting and, instead, entering NPAs with substantial fines. RLC have closed the Argentina operation.[319] This case involves the fashion industry where, 'this investigation highlights the expanding reach of the FCPA across all industries and its global impact on operations in foreign jurisdictions'.[320]

The DoJ has available the various options described above, as alternatives to criminal action. It also has a 'track record' of enforcement which has such severe

315 Securities and Exchange Commission, Press Release 22 April 2013, 'SEC announces non-prosecution agreement with Ralph Lauren Corporation involving FCPA misconduct' www.sec.gov/news/press/2013/2013-65.htm Accessed 14 November 2016.

316 Department of Justice, 'Ralph Lauren Corporation resolves Foreign Corrupt Practices Act investigation and agrees to pay $882,000 monetary penalty' (n 314).

317 Securities and Exchange Commission, 'SEC announces non-prosecution agreement with Ralph Lauren' (n 315) (footnotes omitted).

318 The agreement gave credit for 'timely, voluntary, and complete disclosure of the conduct; (…) extensive, thorough, and real-time cooperation with the Department, including conducting an internal investigation, voluntarily making employees available for interviews, making voluntary document disclosures, conducting a world-wide risk assessment, and making multiple presentations to the Department on the status and findings of the internal investigation and the risk assessment; (…) early and extensive remedial efforts already undertaken – including conducting extensive FCPA training for employees world-wide, enhancing the Company's existing FCPA policy, implementing an enhanced gift policy as well as other enhanced compliance, control and anti-corruption policies and procedures, enhancing its due diligence protocol for third-party agents, terminating culpable employees and a third-party agent, instituting a whistleblower hotline, and hiring a designated corporate compliance attorney – and to be undertaken, including enhancements to its compliance program (…); and (…) agreement to provide annual, written reports (…)' Department of Justice, 'Non prosecution Agreement' 22 April 2013 www.justice.gov/criminal/fraud/fcpa/cases/ralph-lauren/Ralph-Lauren.-NPA-Executed.pdf Accessed 14 November 2016.

319 Securities and Exchange Commission, 'SEC announces non-prosecution agreement with Ralph Lauren' (n 315).

320 Arent Fox, 'World renowned fashion giant Ralph Lauren Corporation resolves Foreign Corrupt Practices Act investigation with DOJ and SEC for $1.6 million' www.arentfox.com/newsroom/alerts/world-renowned-fashion-giant-ralph-lauren-corporation-resolves-foreign-corrupt Accessed 8 December 2016.

consequences that they encourage a defendant to compromise rather than fight a case through the courts. The DoJ emphasise that 'fighting corruption is, and always will be, a core priority':[321]

> Since 2005, the Department has secured close to three dozen corporate guilty pleas in FCPA cases. And just since 2009, the department has entered into over 400 corporate resolutions, including nine of the top 10 biggest resolutions in terms of penalties, resulting in approximately $2.5 billion in monetary fines. And, perhaps most important, in that same period, we have successfully secured the convictions of over three dozen individuals for engaging in foreign bribery schemes.[322]

The ability of the DoJ to negotiate outcomes is graphically demonstrated by the differing experience of two of the world's major accounting firms: Arthur Andersen and KPMG, as Bennett describes.[323] In the fallout of the Enron scandal[324] the first criminal charge in that case was also the first time a major accounting firm had been charged with obstruction of justice.[325] There was a marked difference in the experience of Arthur Andersen, which eventually had its guilty verdict overturned through Appeals to the US Supreme Court and final withdrawal by the prosecution, and KPMG, which negotiated with the DoJ. KPMG was subject to:

> An aggressive 2002 investigation into (...) [its] accounting practices (...) KPMG diligently cooperated with requests from [the DoJ] during the investigation and was rewarded with a deferred prosecution agreement in exchange for an admission of guilt and an agreement to remediate the wrongdoing and establish a more robust internal compliance system.[326]

The outcome of these two cases is that whereas 'KPMG remains a successful business to this day',[327] 'it was already too late for Arthur Andersen. Shortly after the indictment, the firm effectively collapsed'.[328] Thus, although it achieved a victory against the DoJ, it proved pyrrhic because 'the company's right to a jury trial was illusory, and the effect of the indictment was irreparable. Nothing from

321 Department of Justice, 'Acting Assistant Attorney General Mythili Raman delivers keynote address at the Global Anti-Corruption Congress' 17 June 2013 www.justice.gov/criminal/pr/speeches/2013/crm-speech-130617.html Accessed 8 December 2016.
322 Raman, 'Keynote Address' (n 321).
323 Bennett, LoCicero and Hanner (n 139) 411.
324 Bennett, LoCicero and Hanner (n 139) 411.
325 Bennett, LoCicero and Hanner (n 139) 411.
326 Bennett, LoCicero and Hanner (n 139) 411.
327 Bennett, LoCicero and Hanner (n 139) 411.
328 Bennett, LoCicero and Hanner (n 139) 411.

the Supreme Court could bring Arthur Andersen back from the dead'.[329] These examples show the value to firms in identifying breaches of the FCPA and taking opportunities to negotiate a settlement with the DoJ. The use of DPAs offers similar benefits to the UK in terms of certainty for a firm, and for the SFO bringing breaches of the Fraud Act and Bribery Act to a conclusion without protracted court proceedings, in appropriate cases.

Securities and Exchange Commission

The SEC 'is the primary regulator and enforcer of the [US] federal securities laws',[330] with a mission 'to protect investors, maintain fair, orderly, and efficient markets, and facilitate capital formation'.[331] The SEC is governed by the Securities Act 1933, 'often referred to as the "truth in securities" law', which has two main objectives: first, to 'require that investors receive financial and other significant information concerning securities being offered for public sale'; and second, to 'prohibit deceit, misrepresentations, and other fraud in the sale of securities'.[332] It also has powers under the Securities Exchange Act 1934, Sarbanes-Oxley Act 2002, Dodd-Frank Act 2010, and Jumpstart Our Business Startups (JOBS) Act 2012.[333]

The SEC is responsible for civil enforcement over 'issuers and their officers, directors, employees, agents', and has a 'specialized FCPA Unit'.[334] The emphasis for the SEC is on civil enforcement because it 'has a wide variety of civil and administrative powers to address corporate fraud'.[335] The remedies available to it are financial penalties both in terms of fines and disgorgement of gains, together with preventing individuals from serving as directors or officers of public companies, and it may suspend trading in a company's stock.[336]

> After the passage of Sarbanes-Oxley Act, the SEC may now also order a temporary freeze over payments the company is going to pay to its executives, and order CEOs and CFOs to forfeit any bonuses, incentive compensation and profits from the sales of securities when a company restates its financial statement due to misconduct.[337]

329 Bennett, LoCicero and Hanner (n 139) 411.
330 Securities and Exchange Commission, 'A new model for SEC enforcement: Producing bold and unrelenting results' 18 November 2016 www.sec.gov/news/speech/chair-white-speech-new-york-university-111816.html Accessed 5 January 2017.
331 US Securities and Exchange Commission, 'The investor's advocate: How the SEC protects investors, maintains market integrity, and facilitates capital formation' www.sec.gov/about/whatwedo.shtml Accessed 14 November 2016.
332 Securities and Exchange Commission, 'The investor's advocate' (n 331).
333 Securities and Exchange Commission, 'The investor's advocate' (n 331).
334 DoJ/SEC (n 2) 5.
335 Schipani (n 181) 336.
336 Schipani (n 181) 336.
337 CEO – Chief Executive Officer; CFO – Chief Financial Officer. Schipani (n 181) 336.

The SEC is judged on 'performance metrics', including case resolution: 'a case is considered "successfully resolved" if it results in a favourable outcome for the SEC, including through litigation, a settlement, or the issuance of a default judgment.'[338] Although the SEC states that it is a 'law enforcement agency',[339] tellingly it confirms that '[i]n many cases, the Commission and the party charged decide to settle a matter without trial'.[340] In 2016, the SEC took 868 enforcement actions and imposed over $4bn in 'monetary relief',[341] with a strategy to be more aggressive in enforcement and 'seeking stronger penalties, which raised the opportunity cost of malfeasance'.[342] The message conveyed to the market was clear: no institution is too large to be held to account and no violation is too small to escape scrutiny.[343]

The SEC's enforcement regime employs a practice known as 'neither admit nor deny'.[344] This civil settlement regime allows a settlement where the defendant neither admits the charge nor, subsequent to a settlement, is able to deny the charge. In the past, as Neumann notes, defendants having agreed a settlement could then protest their innocence and a settlement was only undertaken to avoid costs of litigation.[345] The SEC see these arrangements as positive because it 'can get relief within the range of what we could reasonably expect to achieve after winning at trial. By settling, the agency is able to eliminate all litigation risk, resolve the case, return money to victims more quickly, and preserve our enforcement resources to redeploy to do other investigations – ordinarily, a significant win-win'.[346] This practice has been criticised for the willingness of the SEC to settle rather than prosecute wrongdoing,[347] but the SEC point to a change in their policy to require admissions in certain cases, of which there have been 30

338 Securities and Exchange Commission, 'Strategic Plan – Fiscal Years 2010–2015' (2011: 735 cases; $2.8bn) www.sec.gov/about/secstratplan1015f.pdf Accessed 14 November 2016.

339 Securities and Exchange Commission, 'The investor's advocate' (n 331).

340 Securities and Exchange Commission, 'The investor's advocate' (n 331).

341 Securities and Exchange Commission, 'SEC announces enforcement results for FY [to September] 2016' www.sec.gov/news/pressrelease/2016-212.html Accessed 2 January 2017.

342 Securities and Exchange Commission, 'Fiscal year 2013 Agency Financial Report' 17 www.sec.gov/about/secpar/secafr2013.pdf Accessed 16 January 2017.

343 Securities and Exchange Commission, 'Fiscal year 2013 Agency Financial Report' (n 342) 17.

344 Matthew G Neumann, 'Neither admit nor deny: recent changes to the Securities and Exchange Commission's longstanding settlement policy' (2015) 40 J Corp L 793, 797.

345 Matthew G Neumann (n 344).

346 Securities and Exchange Commission, Speech by Mary Jo White, 'Deploying the full enforcement arsenal' 26 September 2013 www.sec.gov/news/speech/spch092613mjw Accessed 2 January 2017.

347 See comments of Judge Rakoff in: *SEC v Bank of Am. Corp.*, 653 F. Supp. 2d 507, 507 (S.D.N.Y. 2009) and *U.S. Securities and Exchange Commission v Citigroup Global Markets Inc* 827 F. Supp. 2d 328 (S.D.N.Y. 2011). Edward Greene and Caroline Odorski, 'SEC enforcement in the financial sector: addressing post-crisis criticism' (2015) 16(1) Business Law International 6.

individuals and 47 entities since 2013.[348] The SEC state that more work needs to be done to strengthen white collar crime enforcement, though stating that they have brought charges against individuals, including senior executives, which have led to settlements. The SEC cites with approval the UK Senior Manager Regime[349] for its wider remit to hold senior executives accountable for actions of their employees.[350]

Conclusion

The US has been the instigator internationally of a strong response to economic crime. It was an early adopter of domestic legislation to criminalise overseas bribery and has led the way in enforcement, achieving significant outcomes in terms of prison sentences and fines. The US has also brought into the enforcement equation the use of agreements either not to prosecute, or to defer prosecution (with the expectation of eventually not prosecuting), with the defendant agreeing the valuable consideration of paying a significant fine but not suffering either corporate or individual criminal convictions.

The international adoption of conventions to combat economic crime eventually led to the UK enacting legislation to counter fraud, bribery and corruption, the latter statute being some 33 years after US legislation.[351] In the UK, the SFO as lead prosecutor has been seen as slower to act, less successful than its US counterparts, and suffering from near-terminal damage to its reputation. This has resulted in pressure to ape the US by concluding 'deals' with defendants rather than prosecution. However, at a time when the UK has been enabled to conclude DPAs, the SFO have emphasised that they are a prosecution agency and 'did not have a preference for risk-free civil penalties'.[352]

The US is also subject to internal criticism that its laws are too strict and, especially, that the post-credit crunch Dodd-Frank legislation is too onerous. There is also some evidence of judicial disquiet about their mere 'rubber-stamping' role in DPAs, questioning whether the ambitions of prosecutors are weighted towards income rather than convictions. This latter aspect is one which had started to be seen in the UK. In relation to sentencing, there is a clear disparity between the length of sentences available in the US and in the UK – the former's being

348 '[W]e announced in June 2013 that the SEC would begin to require admissions as a condition for settlement in certain types of cases, including cases with harm to large numbers of investors or significant risk of harm to the market, where the settling party engaged in egregious conduct or obstructed Commission investigations, or where admissions would significantly enhance the deterrent message of the action.' Securities and Exchange Commission, Speech by Mary Jo White 'Deploying the full enforcement arsenal' (n 346).

349 Securities and Exchange Commission, 'Mary Jo White, Speech: A new model for SEC enforcement: Producing bold and unrelenting results' (n 330).

350 Securities and Exchange Commission, Speech by Mary Jo White 'Deploying the full enforcement arsenal' (n 346).

351 Bribery Act 2010. Foreign Corrupt Practices Act 1977.

352 Serious Fraud Office, 'David Green Speech' (n 180).

criticised for being too long and the latter's for being too short. Whereas the US has sentencing guidelines that facilitate prison sentences in excess of 100 years, the penalties in the UK have a ten-year maximum. However, it is clear that the US guidelines would not translate to the UK because they are outwith the structure of sentencing in the UK.[353]

The UK has simple, modern legislation to criminalise fraud and bribery and corruption, in contrast with the US which has myriad statutes and a reliance upon old statutes as a fall-back. Thus, in terms of legislation, this book does not consider that the UK would benefit from adopting US-style statutes.

The US experience demonstrates that having a regime that enjoys the possibility of lengthy prison sentences, together with a high probability of success at trial, gives the prosecutor the option to negotiate an agreement with the defendant in appropriate circumstances: since the Crime and Courts Act 2013, the SFO has had DPAs in its armoury. However, the perception of the SFO is that its success record at trial is low, thus acting as a disincentive to defendants to plead guilty or recognise that they would be found guilty at trial, which would then encourage settlement. The conclusion is that the prosecution of economic crime is handled with more determination and success in the US, and that this is because the DoJ is properly resourced and organised as a cohesive unit. Thus, at this stage it is considered that the UK prosecution authority should be similarly organised. The next chapter will examine the manner in which Australia approaches the same issues.

353 A Ashworth, 'Sentencing for fraud and related offences' (2014) 8 Crim LR 553, 554. 'Longer prison sentences for frauds that target the vulnerable and fresh sanctions against money-laundering are recommended in new judges' guidelines issued by the Sentencing Council.' *The Guardian*, 'Jail fraudsters for longer, judges told' www.theguardian.com/law/2014/may/23/jail-fraudsters-longer-judges-sentencing-council Accessed 14 November 2016. Sentencing Council, 'Fraud, bribery and money laundering offences: Definitive guideline' www.sentencingcouncil.org.uk/publications/item/fraud-bribery-and-money-laundering-offences-definitive-guideline/ Accessed 2 January 2017.

5 Australia

This chapter critically reviews and contrasts the Australian[1] and UK approaches towards economic crime, and follows the previous chapter which contrasted the US and UK. This chapter examines the place of Australia in the international financial community and its participation in international endeavours to combat economic crime. The issues of fraud, bribery and corruption are considered in light of the Australian Constitution, which has a federal and state structure with fraud, in general, falling within an Australian state's purview and external bribery being a Commonwealth of Australia matter. The design and implementation of the Australian financial regulatory structure is also examined, since its 'twin peaks' model has been thought to have successfully withstood the stresses of the 2008 financial crisis.[2]

1 'Australia's formal name is the Commonwealth of Australia.' Under the Australian Constitution, the country is federal. 'Under a federal system, powers are divided between a central government and several regional governments. In Australia, power was divided between the then Commonwealth Government and the governments of the six colonies, which were renamed "states" by the Constitution. Specific areas of legislative power ("heads of power") were given to the then Commonwealth Government, including: taxation; defence; foreign affairs; postal and telecommunications services (…) The wording of the law has often created situations where both the Australian Government and the states claim the authority to make laws over the same matter.' See state and territory government for a discussion of the federal-state relationship and how these conflicts are resolved. http://australia.gov.au/about-australia/our-government/australias-federation#Thefederalsystem. 'There are six states in Australia: New South Wales (NSW), Queensland (Qld), South Australia (SA), Tasmania (Tas.), Victoria (Vic.) and Western Australia (WA). Each state has its own state Constitution, which divides the state's government into the same divisions of legislature, executive, and judiciary as the Australian Government. The six state parliaments are permitted to pass laws related to any matter that is not controlled by the Commonwealth under Section 51 of the Australian Constitution.' Australian Government, 'Our Government' http://australia.gov.au/about-australia/our-government, http://australia.gov.au/about-australia/our-government/state-and-territory-government Accessed 8 December 2016.

2 Alison Lui, 'Macro and micro prudential regulatory failures between banks in the United Kingdom and Australia 2004–2009' (2013) JFR&C 242, 243. 'Many factors contributed to the resilience of the Australian economy over this period. One was the decisive fiscal stimulus measures introduced by the federal government in 2008 and 2009 that have attracted wide praise from international agencies like the OECD and the IMF, as well as from expert commentators. Another was the rapid return to

Introduction

Australia is chosen for comparison because, as the OECD comment, it is 'a significant economy, exporter and international investor', which means that it has the propensity to be a target for economic crime.[3] It is also a member of 'The Commonwealth', 'a voluntary association of 53 member countries'.[4] Sometimes known as the British Commonwealth, its 'roots go back to the British Empire when some countries were ruled directly or indirectly by Britain'.[5] This includes Australia, whose common law heritage[6] and ties to the UK provide an historic association which makes drawing comparisons pertinent. In the OECD Working Group, Australia was the '11th largest economy and 14th largest exporter of goods and services' and its largest trading partner was China.[7] Importantly, 'Australia also plays a significant role in many countries in Polynesia and the South Pacific that have serious corruption risks'.[8] However, Australia is not immune to such risks itself, and the size of its economy and financial markets does make it 'very susceptible to illicit financial activities'[9] and 'Australia has been described as one of the easiest places to launder money'.[10] Since the onset of the most recent financial crisis, and unlike the US and UK, Australia is regarded as having more successfully withstood the effects than other leading industrial nations, which, thus, invites enquiry into the underlying reasons.[11] One reason advanced for this is that Australia adopted the twin peaks[12] model of

growth in the Chinese economy which stimulated the demand for Australian mineral exports, while the strong financial regulatory framework introduced in Australia in the early 1990s and reforms to the labour market that increased flexibility have cushioned it from external shocks like the GFC [global financial crisis]. A large budget surplus and relative low public debt also provided room for the government to expand its fiscal stance without compromising its longer-term fiscal sustainability.' Peter Saunders and Melissa Wong, 'The social impact of the global financial crisis in Australia' (2011) 46(3) Australian Journal of Social Issues 292.

3 Organisation for Economic Co-operation and Development (OECD), 'Phase 3 Report on implementing the OECD Anti-Bribery Convention in Australia' October 2012 www.oecd.org/daf/anti-bribery/Australiaphase3reportEN.pdf Accessed 8 December 2016.

4 The Commonwealth, 'About us' http://thecommonwealth.org/about-us Accessed 8 December 2016.

5 The Commonwealth, 'History' http://thecommonwealth.org/our-history Accessed 10 December 2016.

6 Australian Government, Department of Foreign Affairs and Trade, 'About us. Legal system' www.dfat.gov.au/facts/legal_system.html Accessed 8 December 2016.

7 OECD, 'Phase 3 Report' (n 3).

8 OECD, 'Phase 3 Report' (n 3).

9 Nicholas Ryder, *Money Laundering – An Endless Cycle?* (Routledge 2012) 6.

10 Ryder, *Money Laundering – An Endless Cycle?* (n 9) 6.

11 Michael Levi and Russell G Smith, 'Fraud vulnerabilities and the global financial crisis' in *Trends and Issues in Crime and Criminal Justice* (Australian Institute of Criminology No. 422 July 2011) www.aic.gov.au/publications/current%20series/tandi/421-440/tandi422.html Accessed 4 December 2016.

12 'The "twin peaks" idea and nomenclature are attributable to Michael Taylor, a former officer of the Bank of England (…) In 1995, Taylor wrote an article entitled: *"Twin*

financial regulation,[13] which as discussed by Taylor, 'is to structure regulation around two agencies, one responsible for the safety and soundness of all financial firms and the other for regulating their sales practices'.[14] Lui observes that 'Australian banks have withstood the financial crisis better than UK banks. Australia did not have any bank runs. Four of the nine AA-rated banks around the world are Australian banks, so the Australian regulation system worked well'.[15] The irony of Australia's adoption of the twin peaks structure is that this was first advocated by Taylor, a Bank of England alumnus, in 1995, but this structure was not then adopted by the UK.[16]

The success of Australia in weathering 'the global financial crisis far better than many other developed economies'[17] does not, however, imply that it is unaffected by economic crime. As Tomasic observes, the 'financial crisis has revealed massive financial frauds and misconduct that have long been a part of our markets but have been submerged by the euphoria that has dominated these markets'.[18] Notwithstanding Australia's economic success, neither it nor any other country is immune to economic crime but, against that background, its experience and response will form a key part of this research to establish whether its formula can be of benefit to the UK. For example, the Australian Institute of Criminology reports that '[s]erious fraud in Australia is both widespread and costly (…) it is believed to be one of the most under-reported offences (…) with fewer than 50 per cent of incidents being reported to police or other authorities'.[19] The

Peaks": a regulatory structure for the new century' (Centre for the Study of Financial Innovation 1995). Jeremy Cooper, Australian Securities and Investments Commission, Paper 'The integration of financial regulatory authorities – the Australian experience', 4–5 September 2006, 2 http://download.asic.gov.au/media/1339352/integration-financial-regulatory-authorities.pdf Accessed 4 January 2017.

13 Cooper (n 12) 2.

14 Michael W Taylor, 'The Road from "Twin Peaks" – And the Way Back' (2009) 16(1) Connecticut ILJ 61.

15 Lui (n 2) 242, 243.

16 Caner Bakir, 'The governance of financial regulatory reform: The Australian experience' (2009) 87(4) Public Administration 910. However, one of the first policy announcements by the UK Conservative-Liberal Democrat coalition government in 2010 was the adoption of a 'twin peaks' model for the UK. HM Treasury, 'Speech by the Chancellor of the Exchequer, Rt Hon George Osborne MP, at Mansion House' 16 June 2010 www.gov.uk/government/speeches/speech-by-the-chancellor-of-the-exchequer-rt-hon-george-osborne-mp-at-mansion-house Accessed 8 December 2016. Bank of England, 'Prudential Regulation Authority' www.bankofengland.co.uk/pra/Pages/default.aspx Accessed 8 December 2016.

17 International Monetary Fund, 'Economic health check. Mining boom bodes bright future for Australia' www.imf.org/external/pubs/ft/survey/so/2010/car102810a.htm Accessed 16 December 2016.

18 Roman Tomasic, 'The financial crisis and the haphazard pursuit of financial crime' (2011) 18(1) JFC 7.

19 Australian Institute of Criminology, www.aic.gov.au/crime_types/economic/fraud.html Accessed 8 December 2016.

Australian Criminal Intelligence Commission estimates serious organised crime to cost Australia A$36bn per annum.[20]

The acknowledgement by the Australian government of the shortfall in reporting, then, invites a critique of the government's response. In this regard, it is helpful to have an external assessment. As a result of Australia's obligations under the UNCAC 2003,[21] an external review reported:

> Australia has several agencies, including the Australian Commission for Law Enforcement Integrity (ACLEI), the Australian Crime Commission (ACC), the Commonwealth Ombudsman and the Australian Federal Police (AFP), which prevent and detect corruption. The Government's approach to corruption is based on the idea that no single body should be solely responsible for anti-corruption. All Government agencies must maintain plans for preventing and reporting corruption.[22]

It is significant that the UNCAC should highlight that no single body should be responsible for anti-corruption because, as this chapter illustrates, the Australian regulatory structure faces organisational challenges that are not present in the UK.

The Commonwealth of Australia (hereinafter 'the Commonwealth') has, under the Australian Constitution, established 'a federal system in which legislative, executive and judicial powers are shared or distributed between the Commonwealth and six states'.[23] The essence of this is that 'the Constitution does not confer on the Commonwealth Parliament the power to make laws on all subjects but list subjects about which it can make laws'.[24] Therefore, in order to understand the legislative landscape, it is important to note that each state has its own constitution but is subject to the Commonwealth Constitution, contained in the

20 Australian Criminal Intelligence Commission, 'About us' www.acic.gov.au/about-crime Accessed 6 February 2017.

21 UNCAC, 'United Nations Convention against Corruption' www.unodc.org/documents/treaties/UNCAC/Publications/Convention/08-50026_E.pdf Accessed 8 December 2016. UNCAC, UNCAC Implementation Review Group meeting on 18 June 2012, 'Executive summary' www.ag.gov.au/CrimeAndCorruption/AntiCorruption/Pages/Globalleadershipincombatingcorruption.aspx Accessed 8 December 2016.

22 UNCAC (n 21) (emphasis added).

23 'It also enables the Commonwealth Parliament to make laws in relation to territories. There are ten territories, of which three are self-governing.' Australian Government, Attorney General's Department, 'The Commonwealth's approach to anti-corruption' 9 http://transparency.org.au/wp-content/uploads/2012/07/Anti-Corruption-Discussion-Paper-FINAL-PDF-15-March-2012.pdf Accessed 4 January 2017.

24 'They include defence; external affairs; interstate and international trade; taxation; foreign, trading and financial corporations; marriage and divorce; immigration; bankruptcy; and interstate industrial conciliation and arbitration.' Commonwealth of Australia Constitution Act 1900, s 51 (Legislative powers of the Parliament) s 52 (Exclusive powers of the Parliament). Parliament of Australia, 'The Constitution of Australia' www.aph.gov.au/About_Parliament/Senate/Powers_practice_n_procedures/Constitution.aspx Accessed 4 January 2017.

Commonwealth of Australia Constitution Act 1900.[25] However, it has been noted that, 'except for a few matters, a state parliament can make laws on any subject of relevance to that state. Accordingly, state parliaments can pass laws on a wider range of subjects than the Commonwealth Parliament'.[26] This brings into focus that, as Tomasic discusses, 'corporate law and practice is largely the product of national legal systems drawing upon their particular traditions and development trajectories'.[27] Therefore, this might appear complicated with potential for difficulties. However, the Attorney General suggests not, since 'the Commonwealth Parliament has vested state and territory courts with extensive jurisdiction to hear matters arising under federal law'.[28] Thus, it is clear that the states and territories may avail themselves of federal law. However, in relation to matters of criminalising fraud, bribery and corruption it is instructive to note that 'the Commonwealth Parliament does not have specific power with regard to criminal law'[29] since 'most criminal activity is governed by the laws of the states. This is true for offences of corruption, including fraud and bribery'.[30] Therefore, it can be seen that the six states are able to enact different laws that criminalise fraud, bribery and corruption. As Tomasic observes, 'once a pattern of corporate law and regulation is formed, deviation from this pattern becomes difficult, although not impossible, as the constitutional framework of Australian corporations law illustrates'.[31]

At the federal level, 'Commonwealth criminal legislation is primarily restricted to criminal activity against Commonwealth interests, officers or property or is directed at crimes with an international element such as the bribery of foreign officials'.[32] This is in contrast to the UK Bribery Act 2010, which applies to England and Wales, Scotland and Northern Ireland.[33] However, it is interesting to note that the Fraud Act 2006 does not extend to Scotland.[34] Bribery of Foreign Public Officials is the subject of the OECD Convention on Combating Bribery of

25 Commonwealth of Australia Constitution Act 1900.
26 Australian Government, 'The Commonwealth's approach to anti-corruption' (n 23).
27 Roman Tomasic, 'Governance and the evaluation of corporate law and regulation in Australia' (2001) 1(3) Corporate Governance 24.
28 Australian Government, 'The Commonwealth's approach to anti-corruption' (n 23).
29 'However, the Commonwealth can enact criminal laws relying on other powers, for example those that are expressly provided for under the Constitution.' Australian Government, 'The Commonwealth's approach to anti-corruption' (n 23).
30 Australian Government, 'The Commonwealth's approach to anti-corruption' (n 23).
31 Tomasic, 'Governance and the evaluation of corporate law and regulation in Australia' (n 27) 24.
32 Australian Government, 'The Commonwealth's approach to anti-corruption' (n 23).
33 Bribery Act 2010, s 18.
34 Fraud Act 2006, s 15. 'In Scotland, criminal fraud is mainly dealt with under the common law and a number of statutory offences. The main fraud offences in Scotland are: Common law fraud, uttering, embezzlement and statutory frauds.' One of the main differences is a maximum sentence of life imprisonment in addition to or instead of an unlimited fine, whereas in the rest of the UK, the maximum is 10 years' imprisonment. Fraud Advisory Panel, 'Fraud Facts: Fraud in Scotland' 17 October 2013 www.fraudadvisorypanel.org/wp-content/uploads/2015/04/Fraud-Facts-17B-Fraud-in-Scotland-Revised-March14.pdf Accessed 4 January 2017.

Foreign Public Officials in International Business Transactions 1997 (OECD Convention),[35] which sets the international standards to which Australia subscribes.

International treaties and influence on domestic concerns

Australia has adopted a number of international conventions[36] in the arena of economic crime and these provide international benchmarks for the establishment of standards to counter economic crime and the monitoring of progress to implement such standards.[37] For example, in 1999, Australia ratified the OECD Convention and, concurrently, amended the Commonwealth Criminal Code Act 1995[38] to criminalise bribery of foreign public officials.[39] In 2008, the OECD Working Group on Bribery 'recognised Australia's significant efforts to implement the Recommendations made by the Working Group', which deemed 'that Australia has fully implemented 12 out of the 22 Recommendations made [earlier] (...), while 10 Recommendations have either been partially implemented or not implemented'.[40] This report demonstrates, first, that there is an international

35 'The OECD Anti-Bribery Convention establishes legally binding standards to criminalise bribery of foreign public officials in international business transactions and provides for a host of related measures that make this effective. It is the first and only international anti-corruption instrument focused on the "supply side" of the bribery transaction.' OECD, 'OECD Convention on Combating Bribery of Foreign Public Officials in International Business Transactions' (OECD Convention) www.oecd.org/daf/anti-bribery/oecdantibriberyconvention.htm Accessed 8 December 2016.

36 OECD Convention (n 35). UNCAC (n 21) www.oecd.org/site/adboecdanti-corruptioninitiative/ Accessed 8 December 2016. Asian Development Bank, 'OECD anti-corruption initiative for Asia Pacific' www.oecd.org/site/adboecdanti-corruptioninitiative/ Accessed 8 December 2016. Financial Action Task Force on Money Laundering, www.fatf-gafi.org/ Accessed 8 December 2016.

37 OECD, 'Australia: phase 2 follow-up report on the implementation of the phase 2 recommendations application of the convention on combating bribery of foreign public officials in international business transactions and the 1997 revised recommendation on combating bribery in international business transactions' www.oecd.org/daf/anti-bribery/anti-briberyconvention/41305864.pdf Accessed 8 December 2016.

38 'The *Criminal Code Amendment (Bribery of Foreign Officials) Act 1999* (Cth) commenced on 17 December 1999 and the Convention came into force in Australia on the same date. The Act inserted a new Division into the *Criminal Code Act 1995* (Cth) (Criminal Code) to criminalise the bribery of foreign public officials.' Parliament of Australia, 'Australia's implementation of the OECD Anti-Bribery Convention' www.aph.gov.au/About_Parliament/Parliamentary_Departments/Parliamentary_Library/pubs/BN/2011-2012/AntiBribery Accessed 8 December 2016.

39 'The OECD Anti-Bribery Convention establishes legally binding standards to criminalise bribery of foreign public officials in international business transactions and provides for a host of related measures that make this effective. It is the first and only international anti-corruption instrument focused on the "supply side" of the bribery transaction.' OECD Convention (n 35). From March 2016, there is a new offence of 'false dealing with accounting documents', which will enable prosecution of corporations for concealing bribery and corruption. Criminal Code Act 1995 Part 10.9.

40 OECD, 'Australia: phase 2 follow-up report' (n 37).

mechanism to review the implementation of the OECD standards and, second, that Australia is working towards implementation. However, a review by the OECD found that 'Australia's enforcement of its foreign bribery laws has been extremely low, with just a single case leading to prosecutions out of 28 referrals in 13 years (…) Australia must vigorously pursue foreign bribery allegations'.[41]

This is an important conclusion because 'a significant portion of Australia's international activities are exposed to risks of foreign bribery',[42] and the OECD note that '75% of the top 100 companies and 63% of the top 200 companies listed on the Australian Stock Exchange operate in a high risk sector, a high risk country, or both'.[43] The particular sector of vulnerability is mining and resources, both in Australia and overseas, especially Africa: 'Australian companies (…) have more projects in Africa than any other region of the world.'[44] The penetration of Australian companies into Africa is of particular concern because, as the OECD comment, 'African countries still face significant obstacles to economic development. Corruption and lack of transparency and accountability in business transactions remain high on the list of investment risks in Africa'.[45]

Australia subsequently committed itself to further action against bribery when it signed the UNCAC in 2003.[46] The UNCAC was incorporated into domestic legislation by the Anti-Money Laundering and Counter-Terrorism Financing Act 2006.[47] UNCAC 'requires States Parties to criminalise bribery of foreign public

41 OECD, 'Seriously concerned by lack of foreign bribery convictions, but encouraged by recent efforts by the Australian Federal Police' www.oecd.org/newsroom/oecdseriouslyconcernedbylackofforeignbriberyconvictionsbutencouragedbyrecenteffortsbytheaustralianfederalpolice.htm Accessed 8 December 2016.

42 OECD, 'Phase 3 Report' (n 3).

43 OECD, 'Phase 3 Report' (n 3) (footnotes omitted).

44 'A significant portion of Australia's international economic activities are exposed to risks of foreign bribery. A recent study found that 75% of the top 100 companies and 63% of the top 200 companies listed on the Australian Stock Exchange operate in a high risk sector, a high risk country, or both. Of particular note is Australia's large mining and resource sector. Australia is home to some of the largest multinational corporations in this area, though many small- and medium-sized enterprises (SMEs) are also active. Over 220 listed exploration and mining companies with a combined market capitalisation in excess of AUD 250 billion (EUR 208.7 billion) are active in Africa. Australian companies in this sector have more projects in Africa than any other region of the world. Projects have nearly tripled since 2005, and investment has increased from AUD 20 billion (EUR 16.7 billion) in 2009 to an expected AUD 50 billion (EUR 41.7 billion). The sector also contributes to almost half of Australia's exports.' OECD, 'Phase 3 Report' (n 3) 8.

45 OECD, 'Stocktaking of business integrity and anti-bribery legislation, policies and practices in twenty African countries – OECD-AFDB Joint Initiative to Support Business Integrity and Anti-Bribery Efforts in Africa' 18 www.oecd.org/daf/anti-bribery/Stocktaking%20of%20business%20integrity%20and%20Anti-bribery%20Legislation,%20Policies%20and%20Practices%20in%20Twenty%20African%20Countries.pdf Accessed 8 December 2016.

46 Signed on 9 December 2003, ratified 17 December 2005. UNCAC (n 21).

47 Anti-Money Laundering and Counter-Terrorism Financing Act 2006, s 212(4). In performing the AUSTRAC CEO's functions under this Act, the AUSTRAC CEO must have regard to: (a) any relevant FATF Recommendations.

officials in the course of international business'.[48] Interestingly, as will be discussed later in the chapter, 'the Legislative Guide for the Implementation of UNCAC does not differentiate between bribery and facilitation payments'.[49] This is significant in the discussions that are current in Australia regarding their retention of the 'facilitation payments defence' to bribery of foreign public officials.[50]

Although Australia took steps to legislate against bribery in terms of enforcement, the risks of bribery and corruption are heightened when combined with poor money laundering control.[51] This is unhelpful because Australia has also been a member of the Financial Action Task Force (FATF) since 1990.[52] It has been argued that 'the FATF was highly critical of the minimal level of compliance with its 40 Recommendations which resulted in "both embarrassments for the Australian government and with it international scrutiny on the Australian AML [anti-money laundering] system"'.[53] This criticism of Australia's enforcement record was especially significant because of Australia's profile in promoting these standards in the region[54] and because it had leadership of the G20[55] in 2014, where it admitted in opening the G20 Anti-Corruption Roundtable that 'in Australia we have recently seen serious allegations of widespread corruption within our trade unions, representing a threat to honest businesses and important projects'.[56]

Australia's geographic and global economic presence facilitated it taking a leading role in the Asia-Pacific region, where Jensen and Png report that it 'agreed to set up a Secretariat for the purpose of obtaining regional commitment and

48 Australian Government, Attorney General's Department, 'Assessing the "facilitation payments" defence to the Foreign Bribery offence and other measures', Public Consultation Paper 15 November 2011 www.crimeprevention.gov.au/Financialcrime/Documents/v2Public%20consultation%20paper%20-%20amendments%20to%20bribery%20offences%20-%20corrected%20version%2018%20November%202011.pdf Accessed 8 December 2016.

49 Australian Government, 'Assessing the "facilitation payments" defence' (n 48).

50 Australian Government, 'Assessing the "facilitation payments" defence' (n 48).

51 Ryder, *Money Laundering – An Endless Cycle?* (n 9) 6.

52 Financial Action Task Force, 'Australia' www.fatf-gafi.org/countries/a-c/australia/ Accessed 8 December 2016.

53 Ryder, *Money Laundering – An Endless Cycle?* (n 9) 6.

54 For a discussion of Australia's role in the Pacific, see: Peter Brown, 'Australian influence in the South Pacific' Australian Defence College 3 www.defence.gov.au/ADC/Publications/Commanders/2012/07_Brown%20SAP%20Final%20PDF.pdf Accessed 4 January 2017. Elsina Wainwright, 'Our failing neighbour Australia and the future of Solomon Islands' 16 www.aspi.org.au/publications/our-failing-neighbour-australia-and-the-future-of-solomon-islands/solomons.pdf Accessed 8 December 2016.

55 G20, 'About G20'. 'The Group of Twenty (G20) is the premier forum for its members' international economic cooperation and decision-making. Its membership comprises 19 countries plus the European Union. Each G20 president invites several guest countries each year.' www.g20australia.org/about_G20.html Accessed 4 January 2017.

56 Attorney General, 'Address at the opening of the G20 Anti-Corruption Roundtable' www.attorneygeneral.gov.au/Speeches/Pages/2014/First%20Quarter%202014/28February2014-AddressattheopeningoftheG20AntiCorruptionRoundtable.aspx Accessed 8 December 2016.

establishing a regional[57] FATF-style body with practical objectives'.[58] The objective for 'the Asia/Pacific Group on Money Laundering[59] is to ensure the adoption, implementation and enforcement of internationally accepted anti-money laundering and counter-terrorist financing standards'.[60] Thus, Australia's adherence to the FATF standards is important for the region because 'the general level of compliance of these Developing Member Countries on a strict reading of the compliance ratings is not high'.[61]

The FATF, although clearly originally skewed towards anti-money laundering as a result of the US-led 'war on drugs'[62] and counter-terrorist financing strategies since 2001,[63] does provide a structure to assess the steps taken by countries to combat economic crime. The FATF objectives are:

> to set standards and promote effective implementation of legal, regulatory and operational measures for combating money laundering, terrorist financing and other related threats to the integrity of the international financial system.[64]

Furthermore, the FATF undertakes periodic reviews of member countries to evaluate compliance with its recommendations.[65] Although detailed analysis of such reports is outside the scope of this chapter because money laundering is not

57 '[T]he so-called "FATF-styled regional bodies" which are tasked with promoting the implementation of the FATF Recommendations at the regional level.' Neil Jensen and Cheong-Ann Png, 'Implementation of the FATF 40 + 9 recommendations: A perspective from developing countries' (2011) 14(2) JMLC 110, 111.

58 FATF, 'Asia/Pacific Group on Money Laundering' www.fatf-gafi.org/pages/asiapacificgrouponmoneylaunderingapg.html Accessed 4 January 2017.

59 'This group now has 41 members and includes US.' APG Members: Afghanistan; Australia; Bangladesh; Bhutan, Kingdom of; Brunei Darussalam; Cambodia; Canada; China, People's Republic of; Cook Islands; Fiji; Hong Kong, China; India; Indonesia; Republic of Korea (South Korea); Japan; Laos, People's Democratic Republic; Macao, China; Malaysia; Maldives; The Marshall Islands; Mongolia; Myanmar; Nauru; Nepal; New Zealand; Niue; Pakistan; Palau; Papua New Guinea; The Philippines; Samoa; Singapore; Solomon Islands; Sri Lanka; Chinese Taipei; Thailand; Timor Leste; Tonga; United States of America; Vanuatu; Vietnam. FATF, 'Asia/Pacific Group' (n 58).

60 '[A]s set out in the FATF Forty Recommendations and FATF Eight Special Recommendations.' FATF, 'Asia/Pacific Group' (n 58).

61 Jensen and Png (n 57) 110, 113. 'Save for a handful of the more developed DMCs [developing member countries] that are able to devote more resources in absorbing the information from these materials, a challenge for many DMCs (similar experiences may be shared by other developing countries and less developed countries) is the limited resources they have for assimilating the requirements and related materials in the FATF Recommendations before formulating and implementing suitable reforms.' Jensen and Png (n 57) 110, 114.

62 Nicholas Ryder, *Financial Crime in the 21st Century* (Edward Elgar 2011) 11.

63 Ryder, *Financial Crime in the 21st Century* (n 62) 59.

64 FATF, 'What do we do?' www.fatf-gafi.org/pages/aboutus/whatwedo/ Accessed 8 December 2016.

65 FATF, 'Summary of the third mutual evaluation report anti-money laundering and combating the financing of terrorism. 14 October 2005' www.fatf-gafi.org/media/fa

its focus, it is instructive to note that the FATF 'Third Mutual Evaluation Report' was critical of Australia's level of compliance: 'the key issue in terms of effective implementation of the money laundering offence is the low number of money laundering prosecutions at Commonwealth level (…), indicating that the regime is not being effectively implemented.'[66] This lack of prosecutions is a theme that recurs in relation to Australian prosecution of bribery. However, the 'Australian government responded by introducing the Anti-Money Laundering and Counter-Terrorism Financing Act 2006'[67] (and Rules in 2007 and Regulations in 2008),[68] 'to improve compatibility with the 40 Recommendations of the FATF'.[69] Thus, Australia has put in place legislation to meet its international obligations.[70]

Fraud

In Australia, 'most criminal activity is governed by the laws of the states. This is true for offences of corruption, including fraud and bribery'.[71] Furthermore, Smith comments that:

> in Australia, fraud is not recognised as a separate legal category of crime (other than conspiracy to defraud). Instead, a variety of property offences may be used to prosecute conduct which involves fraud and deception such as crimes of theft and obtaining a financial advantage by deception.[72]

The Attorney General provides that 'Australia has a strong legislative regime criminalising corrupt behaviour'.[73] Furthermore, its 'corruption offences cover a broad range of crimes, including bribery, embezzlement, nepotism and extortion'.[74] This is given as a reason why such 'corruption offences are not contained in any single Act of Parliament and are found in Commonwealth, state and territory legislation'.[75] This makes the anti-fraud arena more complicated when compared with the UK, for the Attorney General provides a shopping list of Commonwealth legislation: the Criminal Code Act 1995, Proceeds of Crime Act 2002, Financial Management and Accountability Act 1997, Anti-Money

tf/documents/reports/mer/MER%20Australia%20ES.pdf Accessed 8 December 2016.

66 FATF, 'Summary of the third mutual evaluation report' (n 65) 4.

67 Ryder, *Money Laundering – An Endless Cycle?* (n 9) 105.

68 Anti-Money Laundering and Counter-Terrorism Financing Rules 2007. Anti-Money Laundering and Counter-Terrorism Regulations 2008.

69 Ryder, *Money Laundering – An Endless Cycle?* (n 9) 106.

70 This legislation is deployed by AUSTRAC – Australian Transaction Reports and Analysis Centre.

71 Australian Government, 'The Commonwealth's approach to anti-corruption' (n 23).

72 Russell G Smith, 'Fraud and financial abuse of older persons' (2000) 11 Current Issues in Crim Just 273.

73 Australian Government, 'The Commonwealth's approach to anti-corruption' (n 23).

74 Australian Government, 'The Commonwealth's approach to anti-corruption' (n 23).

75 Australian Government, 'The Commonwealth's approach to anti-corruption' (n 23).

Laundering and Counter-Terrorism Financing Act 2006, Commonwealth Authorities and Companies Act 1997.[76] These are then combined with state legislation to criminalise fraud, thus clearly demonstrating the fragmented landscape, and can be seen in light of antipathy towards changing the structure. However, Australia is not alone in having a regime of fragmented legislation. In the US, as Podgor notes, 'the scope of fraud is problematic in that there is no specific group of statutes designated in the federal code as fraud statutes and no consistent definition to create the boundaries of what is encompassed within the term'.[77] Thus, while there are similarities between Australia and the US, these represent complicating factors when compared with the UK. The criminalisation of fraud in Australia reflects such constraints.

Criminalisation

Criminalisation of fraud in Australia reflects the constraints of operating in a fragmented constitutional system in that there is not just one piece of legislation to cover the Commonwealth, states, and territories. Some states and territories have criminal codes while others do not,[78] where 'codification has been defined as "the setting out in one statute of all the law affecting a particular topic whether it is to be found in statutes or common law"'.[79] This is not part of the UK tradition. However, in 1991, the Commonwealth government started to prepare a criminal code for all Australian jurisdictions but when the Commonwealth Criminal Code was enacted in 1995,[80] to cover matters purely within its own purview (that is, not states or territories), the theft, fraud and bribery provisions were absent, until the Code was amended in 2000.[81] These offences, which only apply to

76 Australian Government, 'The Commonwealth's approach to anti-corruption' (n 23).
77 E Podgor, 'Criminal fraud' (1999) 48 Am U L Rev 729, 740.
78 Queensland, Criminal Code 1899; Western Australia, 1902; Tasmania, 1924; Northern Territories 1983. Andrew Hemming, 'When is a code a code?' (2010) 15 Deakin L Rev 65, 66.
79 Hemming (n 78) 65, 66 (footnotes omitted).
80 Criminal Code Act 1995.
81 Criminal Code Amendment (Theft, Fraud, Bribery and Related Offences) Act 2000 (Cth). Criminal Code Act 1995, 's 131.1 Theft: (1) A person is guilty of an offence if: (a) the person dishonestly appropriates property belonging to another with the intention of permanently depriving the other of the property. s 134.1 Obtaining property by deception: (1) A person is guilty of an offence if: (a) the person, by a deception, dishonestly obtains property belonging to another with the intention of permanently depriving the other of the property. s 141.1 Bribery of a Commonwealth public official. (1) A person is guilty of an offence if: (a) the person dishonestly: (i) provides a benefit to another person; or (ii) causes a benefit to be provided to another person; or (iii) offers to provide, or promises to provide, a benefit to another person; or (iv) causes an offer of the provision of a benefit, or a promise of the provision of a benefit, to be made to another person; and (b) the person does so with the intention of influencing a public official (who may be the other person) in the exercise of the official's duties as a public official; and (c) the public official is a Commonwealth public official; and (d) the duties are duties as a Commonwealth public official.'

Commonwealth entities, all carried the same maximum penalty of ten years' imprisonment.[82] The purpose, according to Johns, was to simplify and reduce the Commonwealth statutes,[83] 'replacing overly complex provisions with a modern and transparent scheme as part of a national initiative'.[84] However, this only affected matters within the Commonwealth bailiwick, since fraud is a matter dealt within individual state jurisdictions.

The interplay between the authorities in the constitutional framework means that 'fraudulent offences can be statute or common law based criminal offences in federal and state criminal jurisdictions'.[85] However, only two states in the Commonwealth, New South Wales (NSW) and South Australia, 'retain the common law approach to fraud regulation'.[86] In NSW, which is Australia's largest state economy and, thus, particularly relevant,[87] 'the common law is based on the offence of larceny'.[88] Thus, in terms of evaluating the legislative underpinning to countering fraud in Australia, the lack of federal or common state legislation is a disadvantage. However, it is instructive to note that in NSW there has been legislative change by the Crimes Amendment (Fraud, Identity and Forgery Offences) Act 2009. It has been suggested by Steel that this law 'represents a significant change to fraud offences (…) the Act continues to move away from offences based on common law larceny and interference with property rights toward general offences based on a statutory defined concept of dishonesty'.[89]

The reason this step is instructive is because it post-dates the UK Fraud Act. The UK approach was to repeal various Theft Acts and to introduce a statutory offence of fraud. In NSW, legislators have found themselves hamstrung by existing legislation because 'the [Crimes Amendment] Act repeals over 30 fraud offences in the Crimes Act 1900 and replaces those offences with one general fraud offence, and three ancillary offences'.[90] Whereas the UK Fraud Act represented a

82 Criminal Code Act 1995, s 131.1(1); s 134.1(1); and s 141.1(5) 'punishable on conviction by imprisonment for not more than 10 years, a fine not more than 10,000 penalty units, or both'.

83 Rowena Johns, *Sentencing in Fraud Cases* (Judicial Commission of NSW 2012) 12 (footnotes omitted).

84 Johns (n 83) 12 (footnotes omitted).

85 Parliament of New South Wales, 'Fraud and identity theft' 3 (footnotes omitted) www.parliament.nsw.gov.au/researchpapers/Documents/fraud-and-identity-theft/08-03.pdf Accessed 4 January 2017.

86 Parliament of New South Wales, 'Fraud and identity theft' (n 85) 3.

87 'New South Wales is Australia's largest state economy, with 31% of the nation's GDP [gross domestic product] [AUD 1.5bn]. The next largest state, Victoria, contributes 22%.' NSW Government, 'Economic and Business Environment' www.business.nsw.gov.au/invest-in-nsw/about-nsw/economic-and-business-climate/state-economies Accessed 8 December 2016.

88 Parliament of New South Wales, 'Fraud and identity theft' (n 85) 4.

89 Alex Steel, 'New fraud and identity-related crimes in New South Wales', Judicial Commission of New South Wales (2010) Judicial Officers Bulletin 22(3) 18 http://works.bepress.com/alex_steel/19 Accessed 8 December 2016.

90 Steel (n 89) 19.

new departure, the foundations for the new NSW offences are the historic offences, which means that 'the complexity of this section is due to its heritage as the definitional section in the Theft Act 1968 (UK) – on which the theft and fraud offences in the Criminal Code (Cth) are based'.[91] The NSW legislators did have an opportunity to follow the UK lead but, according to Steel, considered that 'representation and general dishonesty based offences (…) [were] criticised for being too broadly defined',[92] which was found attractive by the UK. The NSW fraud offences are based on the 'traditional requirement of dishonest deception',[93] which is found in the definition in *R v Ghosh*. [94] The motivation for change can be traced back to the 1990s when 'the Standing Committee of the [Australian] Attorneys-General established the Model Criminal Law Officers Committee (MCLOC)'.[95] An outcome of this was to highlight 'the importance of simplifying fraud and forgery offences and orienting them to the use of computers'.[96] Thus, according to Johns, the intention was that states would take steps to align their individual legislation with that of the Commonwealth.[97]

If the Commonwealth and states had aligned their legislation, then that might present a structure which could be used to compare with the UK. The 'national approach' is the code adopted by the Commonwealth in 2000, rather than identical state laws, and whilst there may be 'some correlation between the maximum penalties for fraud and forgery offences in NSW and the Commonwealth',[98] there are marked differences between some of the penalties for their respective identity fraud offences.[99] However, what the Commonwealth does have is a ten-year head start in terms of judicial precedent which can inform state prosecution and sentencing decisions.[100]

There are two further aspects in relation to the application of Commonwealth and state law. First, when both laws apply, an offender punished under state law is not then liable for punishment under a Commonwealth offence,

91 Steel (n 89) 19.
92 Steel (n 89) 19.
93 Steel (n 89) 19.
94 *R v Ghosh* [1982] EWCA Crim 2. 'The first question is whether a defendant's behaviour would be regarded as dishonest by the ordinary standards of reasonable and honest people. If answered positively, the second question is whether the defendant was aware that his conduct was dishonest and would be regarded as dishonest by reasonable and honest people.'
95 Model Criminal Code Officers Committee of the Standing Committee of Attorneys-General, 'Model Criminal Code, Chapter 3, Theft, Fraud, Bribery and Related Offences' December 1995 http://www.aphref.aph.gov.au_house_committee_laca_criminalcode_chap1.pdf Accessed 4 January 2017.
96 Johns (n 83) 2.
97 Johns (n 83) 2 (footnotes omitted).
98 Johns (n 83) 114.
99 Johns (n 83) 114.
100 Johns (n 83) 115.

and vice versa.[101] Second, there should be consistency in sentencing similar cases.[102]

There is a degree of similarity between the Commonwealth and NSW maximum penalties of ten years' imprisonment.[103] In the Commonwealth, 'Obtain property by deception', 'Obtain financial advantage by deception', and 'Conspiracy to defraud the Commonwealth';[104] and in NSW, 'Obtain property belonging to another by deception', 'Obtain financial advantage or cause financial disadvantage by deception'.[105] However, there are marked differences between some of the penalties for the Commonwealth and NSW identity offences,[106] where in NSW 'the maximum penalties of seven years for possess identification information and ten years for deal in identification information are double those of the Commonwealth, reducing the utility of sentencing comparisons'.[107]

The purpose in comparing Commonwealth and NSW fraud legislation is to demonstrate that the federal government and the leading financial markets state are not in complete alignment. However, there are also differences in the other states. In South Australia, 'the MCLOC model was regarded as "not complying with the drafting style of the South Australian statute book"'.[108] Furthermore, in Victoria, although following NSW and the Commonwealth, 'numerous other fraud offences have been retained'.[109] In Queensland, 'there is still an assortment of provisions' and a variety of sentences, none of which 'correspond to the NSW or Commonwealth maximum penalty of 10 years for general fraud or forgery'.[110] In Western Australia, 'the general fraud offence (…) has a 7 year maximum penalty which, uniquely, rises to 10 years if the victim is aged 60 or over'.[111]

This review of the Australian approach to criminalisation of fraud shows that although some progress has been made in aligning legislation in the states to the Commonwealth, this process is incomplete and differences remain. The example of changes in NSW illustrate that the UK Fraud Act developments were rejected.[112] At

101 'Where an offender is sentenced for conduct which might constitute an offence against both Commonwealth and State laws, and the Commonwealth statutory regime is less punitive, there is no requirement for the [NSW state] court to reduce the sentence for the State offence to bring a degree of conformity with the Commonwealth offence.' Johns (n 83) 114.
102 Johns (n 83) 115, citing *DPP (Cth) v De La Rosa* (2010) 79 NSWLR 1 [297] (Simpson J).
103 Unlike Bribery of a Foreign Public Official (s 70.2(4)) and Bribery of a Commonwealth Public Official (s 141.1(5)), the Criminal Code does not contain financial penalties for fraud offences. This is the same as the UK Fraud Act 2006.
104 Johns (n 83) 13.
105 Johns (n 83) 5.
106 Johns (n 83) 14.
107 Crimes Act 1900, s 192K, s 192K. Johns (n 83) 14.
108 Johns (n 83) 17.
109 Johns (n 83) 17.
110 Johns (n 83) 18.
111 Johns (n 83) 18.
112 Steel (n 89) 19.

a time when the Fraud Act is working well[113] and there does not appear to be a demand for change, the lack of a clear unified approach by the Commonwealth and all the states does not provide a basis for the UK to follow Australia.

Regulatory bodies

The Australian constitutional structure of 'a federal system in which legislative, executive and judicial powers are shared or distributed between the Commonwealth and six states',[114] also embodies 'the Government's approach to corruption [which] is based on the idea that *no single body* should be solely responsible for anti-corruption'.[115] Thus, at the Commonwealth level there are three key regulatory bodies that cover the fields of intelligence, investigation and prosecution. The Australian Transaction Reports and Analysis Centre (AUSTRAC), Commonwealth Director of Public Prosecutions (CDPP), and the AFP.

Australian Transaction Reports and Analysis Centre

A key element in the response to economic and organised crime is financial intelligence. Financial intelligence 'analyses millions of financial transaction reports each year (…) using sophisticated modelling and predictive analysis tools to identify money laundering, terrorism financing and other serious crime'.[116] This then 'assists the authorities to trace the trail of illicit money, to combat money laundering and other serious crimes'.[117] In Australia, this is the responsibility of AUSTRAC, which is a Commonwealth institution,[118] 'has a key role in protecting the Australian community and economy from the risks and threats of [AML/counter-terrorism financing – CTF] and as the interface between national security, law enforcement and revenue agencies and industry'.[119] AUSTRAC undertakes its role through 'two interdependent functions: the AML/CTF regulator and as Australia's specialist financial intelligence unit'.[120] This includes working 'with law enforcement and other agencies to protect the integrity of the Australian financial

113 Ministry of Justice, 'Post-legislative assessment of the Fraud Act 2006. Memorandum to the Justice Select Committee' (Cm 8372) 10. Accessed 4 January 2016.

114 'It also enables the Commonwealth Parliament to make laws in relation to territories. There are ten territories, of which three are self-governing.' Australian Government, 'The Commonwealth's approach to anti-corruption' (n 23).

115 UNCAC (n 21) (emphasis added).

116 Australian Transaction Reports and Analysis Centre, 'AUSTRAC: Australia's financial intelligence unit' www.austrac.gov.au/about-us/intelligence#monitoring Accessed 3 February 2017.

117 Australian Transaction Reports and Analysis Centre, 'AUSTRAC Overview' www.austrac.gov.au/files/overview_brchr.pdf Accessed 8 December 2016.

118 Financial Transaction Reports Act 1988.

119 Australian Transaction Reports and Analysis Centre, 'AUSTRAC Corporate Plan 2016–20' www.austrac.gov.au/sites/default/files/austrac-corporate-plan-16-20-WEB.pdf Accessed 3 February 2017.

120 Australian Government, 'AUSTRAC Annual Report 2012–13' 6 www.austrac.gov.au/austrac-annual-report-2012-13 Accessed 6 February 2017.

system and fight serious crimes such as drug trafficking, tax evasion, fraud and people smuggling'.[121] The numbers of transactions involved are significant, with 96m individual reports of financial transactions in 2015–16, totalling A$4.9tn.[122] In addition, in 2015–16 there were 78,000 suspicious matter reports.[123] AUSTRAC point to the use made of its intelligence by the Australian Tax Office, which 'contributed to the recovery of tax totalling nearly [A]$2.8bn over 10 years'.[124]

This report of the use made of AUSTRAC's intelligence appears to demonstrate improvements since Australia was earlier criticised for its weaknesses in anti-money laundering.[125] An outcome of this criticism was the AML/CTF Act 2006, which served to comply with the FATF 40 recommendations.[126] This is something that Ryder applauds because 'it is extremely rare for a country to formally provide the measures of the FATF with recognition in primary legislation'.[127] Recognising the importance of the Australian legislation, Ryder contrasts 'with both the US and UK, which have adopted a piecemeal approach towards implementing the international AML legislative measures'.[128] However, although money laundering per se is not the focus of this chapter, reporting instances or suspicions of economic crime is germane. Thus, in contrast to the strict money laundering reporting requirements of the US and UK, the Australian approach is to adopt a 'risk-based'[129] stance, 'away from prescriptive, compliance-based approaches',[130] but this does place the onus on the 'reporting entities' to properly assess their own risks.

AUSTRAC regulates entities ranging 'from major banks and casinos to single-operator businesses in the key sectors of financial services, gambling, bullion dealers, remittance service providers and cash dealers'.[131] The burden of establishing the parameters lies with the reporting entities[132] because they are:

121 AUSTRAC, 'AUSTRAC annual report shows financial intelligence is crucial to combating contemporary criminal threats' www.austrac.gov.au/media/media-releases/austrac-annual-report-shows-financial-intelligence-crucial-combating Accessed 4 January 2017.
122 Australian Transaction Reports and Analysis Centre, 'AUSTRAC Annual Report 2015–16' 75 www.austrac.gov.au/sites/default/files/austrac-ar-15-16-FINAL-WEB-2.pdf Accessed 4 January 2017.
123 Australian Transaction Reports and Analysis Centre, 'AUSTRAC Annual Report 2015–16' (n 122) 75.
124 Australian Transaction Reports and Analysis Centre, 'AUSTRAC Annual Report 2015–16' (n 122) 9.
125 Ryder, *Money Laundering – An Endless Cycle?* (n 9) 105.
126 Ryder, *Money Laundering – An Endless Cycle?* (n 9) 105.
127 Ryder, *Money Laundering – An Endless Cycle?* (n 9) 107.
128 Ryder, *Money Laundering – An Endless Cycle?* (n 9) 107.
129 Australian Transaction Reports and Analysis Centre, 'Other Publications' www.austrac.gov.au/risk_management.html Accessed 8 December 2016.
130 Stuart Ross and Michelle Hannan, 'Australia's new anti-money laundering strategy' (2008) 19 Current Issues Crim Just 135, 142.
131 Australian Transaction Reports and Analysis Centre, 'AUSTRAC Annual Report 2015–16' (n 122) 10.
132 'A reporting entity is an individual, company or other entity that provides a "designated service" as defined in section 6 of the AML/CTF Act. Reporting entities include banks, non-bank financial services, remittance (money transfer) services, bullion dealers and gambling businesses.' Australian Government, Australian Transaction

> best placed to identify and assess the risks its business faces according to the types of customers it serves and the products and services it provides to customers. The risk-based approach also acknowledges that entities are best placed to develop controls, procedures and allocate resources that are proportionate to those risks.[133]

The costs of compliance are significant,[134] but non-compliance can bring enforcement,[135] where 'AUSTRAC has a range of enforcement powers at its disposal,[136] including issuing notices compelling businesses to provide information to the agency, and directing businesses to undertake a risk assessment or external audit'.[137] In 2015–16 these amounted to 22 actions.[138]

Commonwealth Director of Public Prosecutions

The CDPP 'is an independent prosecuting service established by the Parliament of Australia to prosecute alleged offences against Commonwealth law'.[139] The CDPP's role is in relation to offences against the Commonwealth, such as 'terrorism, serious drug offences, money laundering, human trafficking and slavery, people smuggling, child exploitation, cybercrime, revenue and benefit fraud, corporate and commercial offending'.[140] The CDPP is not an investigative agency and has no powers or statutory function to carry out its own investigations.[141] This is in contrast to the US, where the DoJ and its agencies investigate and prosecute,[142] and in the UK, where the key attribute of the SFO is its powers to

Reports and Analysis Centre, 'AML/CTF Reporting Obligations' www.austrac.gov.au/amlctf_compliance_report.html Accessed 8 December 2016.

133 Australian Transaction Reports and Analysis Centre, 'Chapter 6 – AML/CTF programs' www.austrac.gov.au/chapter-6-amlctf-programs Accessed 3 February 2017.

134 Milind Sathye, 'Estimating the cost of compliance of AMLCTF for financial institutions in Australia' (2008) JFC 347.

135 Anti Money Laundering and Counter Terrorism Financing Act 2006, s 135. 'It is an offence to: (a) produce false or misleading information; or (b) produce a false or misleading document; or (c) forge a document for use in an applicable customer identification procedure; or (d) provide or receive a designated service using a false customer name or customer anonymity; or (e) structure a transaction to avoid a reporting obligation under this Act.'

136 'The maximum civil penalty for a body corporate is AUD $11 million and AUD $2.2 million for an individual. AUSTRAC is able to apply for a civil penalty order without the consent of the Commonwealth Director of Public prosecutions.' Anti-Money Laundering and Counter-Terrorism Financing Act 2006, s 173.

137 Australian Transaction Reports and Analysis Centre, 'Enforcement Action' www.austrac.gov.au/enforcement-action Accessed 3 February 2017.

138 Australian Transaction Reports and Analysis Centre, 'AUSTRAC Annual Report 2015–16' (n 122) 28.

139 Director of Public Prosecutions Act 1983.

140 Commonwealth Director of Public Prosecutions, 'Annual Report 2015–2016' 16 www.cdpp.gov.au/Publications/Annual-Reports/CDPP-Annual-Report-2012-2013.pdf Accessed 3 February 2017.

141 Commonwealth Director of Public Prosecutions (n 140) 16.

142 Ryder, *Financial Crime in the 21st Century* (n 62) 102.

investigate and prosecute. Accordingly, it is a Commonwealth resource and 'received briefs from 43 Commonwealth investigative agencies' in the last financial year, including the AFP and Australian Tax Office.[143] In relation to economic crime, the role of the AFP is significant.

Australian Federal Police

The AFP is the Commonwealth government's primary policy agency with a mission to: 'enforce Commonwealth criminal law, contribute to combating complex, transnational, serious and organised crime impacting Australia's national security and protect Commonwealth interests from criminal activity in Australia and overseas.'[144] This includes providing 'policing services to the Australian Capital Territory community and Australia's territories',[145] and has strategic priorities relating to 'counter terrorism, human trafficking and sexual servitude, cybercrime, peace operations, protection and other transnational crimes'.[146]

The AFP has a limited role in policing across Australia because of the structure of the Commonwealth, its states and territories. Consequently, it works in 'multi-agency, multidisciplinary crime teams'.[147] The AFP established a 'Fraud and Anti-Corruption business area',[148] as a 'response to serious and complex fraud against the Commonwealth such as corruption, foreign bribery and complex identity crime, including the manufacture and abuse of identity credentials'.[149] This area includes the Serious Crime Task Force, a multi-agency taskforce targeting serious financial crime, including leading the Australian government response to the 'Panama Papers' data leak.[150] This area also addresses the OECD review of Australia's response to foreign bribery allegations.[151] The AFP is 'under Ministerial

143 Commonwealth Director of Public Prosecutions, 'Annual Report 2015–2016' (n 140) iii.

144 Australian Federal Police Act 1979. Australian Federal Police, 'AFP Corporate Plan 2016–17 Purpose' www.afp.gov.au/corporate-plan-2016-17#purpose Accessed 4 February 2017.

145 Australian Federal Police, 'Annual Report 2015–16' 7 www.afp.gov.au/sites/default/files/PDF/Reports/afp-annual-report-2015-2016.pdf Accessed 4 February 2017.

146 Australian Federal Police, 'About Us' www.afp.gov.au/about-us Accessed 4 February 2017.

147 Australian Federal Police, 'Annual Report 2012–13' 67 www.afp.gov.au/sites/default/files/PDF/Reports/afp-annual-report-2012-2013.pdf Accessed 4 February 2017.

148 Australian Federal Police, 'Annual Report 2012–13' (n 147) 67.

149 Australian Federal Police, 'Annual Report 2012–13' (n 147) 67. Minister for Justice, 'AFP-hosted Fraud and Anti-Corruption Centre' www.ministerjustice.gov.au/Mediareleases/Pages/2014/ThirdQuarter/31July2014-AFPHostedFraudAndAntiCorruptionCentre.aspx Accessed 8 December 2016.

150 Australian Federal Police, 'Annual Report 2015–16' (n 145) 63.

151 'In June 2015 the OECD working group acknowledged the AFP's recent work to implement change and enhance the Commonwealth's response to prevent and detect complex Commonwealth fraud and corruption, particularly in regard to foreign

Direction to focus on Commonwealth offences, including foreign bribery'.[152]

Although the CDPP and AFP work together, they are separate institutions. Thus, the investigation and prosecution of serious economic crime is split, whereas in the UK, the SFO is a single investigator and prosecutor. Furthermore, the SFO can operate across the whole of the UK, unlike the AFP/CDPP which have a limited remit and have to operate through a variety of multi-agency, multi-disciplinary crime teams, which consequently 'sometimes overlap with those of the states and territories making a collaborative approach to combating serious and organised crime essential',[153] and creating a need for a coordinated response in the form of a framework.[154] The purpose of the framework is to ensure that 'law enforcement, intelligence policy and regulatory agencies are collaborating effectively with each other, state, territory and international counterparts'.[155] The clear need for this in Australia is understandable because of their constitutional structure where 'the Commonwealth does not have a head of power with respect to criminal law'.[156] Because the UK does not have such a constitutional structure, the mechanisms employed in Australia to achieve a cohesive approach do not provide a template for adoption in the UK.

Bribery and corruption

Criminalisation – bribery of foreign public officials

As a consequence of Australia's obligations under the OECD Convention, Australia's Criminal Code was amended to criminalise bribery of foreign public officials.[157] The Australian government set out its values as:

> Bribery of foreign public officials in the course of international trade is unacceptable. Although Australian business has high ethical standards, it is important that Australia maintains a good reputation by supporting the OECD in

bribery.' Australian Federal Police, 'Annual Report 2014–15' www.afp.gov.au/afp-annual-report-2014-15 Accessed 6 February 2017.

152 Paul Latimer, 'Anti-bribery laws – compliance issues in Australia' (2017) 24(1) JFC 4, 12.

153 Attorney General, 'National Organised Crime Response Plan 2015–18' 22 www.ag.gov.au/CrimeAndCorruption/OrganisedCrime/Documents/NationalOrganisedCrimeResponsePlan2015-18.pdf Accessed 6 February 2017.

154 Attorney General, 'National Organised Crime Response Plan 2015–18' (n 153) 20.

155 Attorney General, 'Commonwealth organised crime strategic framework' 5 www.ag.gov.au/CrimeAndCorruption/OrganisedCrime/Documents/OrganisedCrimeStrategicFrameworkOverview.pdf Accessed 6 February 2017.

156 Attorney General, 'Commonwealth organised crime strategic framework' (n 155) 6.

157 Criminal Code Amendment (Bribery of Foreign Public Officials) Act 1999. 'In amending the Code to criminalise foreign bribery, the Australian government acknowledged the OECD Convention as a key driver, and justified [the Act] both on moral grounds and as a means to reduce the harms that flow from corruption.' Cindy Davids and Grant Schubert, 'Criminalising foreign bribery: Is Australia's bark louder than its bite?' (2011) 35 Crim L J 98.

this initiative and therefore benefiting from the improvements it should bring to world trade. In particular, a reduction in the role played by bribery should result in more merit based commercial decisions. This will advantage Australia because as a rule its businesses are competitive.[158]

This is an important statement because it provides that Australia already had high ethical standards and it was being collegiate with other nations in wanting all countries to adopt such standards. The rationale was that this would benefit Australia because international trade based on pure commercial considerations should reward competitive businesses. However, the government stated that their reputation would depend upon active enforcement of the law, although by 2014, only four of the 41 signatories to the OECD Convention were considered active in enforcement (including the US and UK), with Australia having improved from 'exhibiting little or no enforcement'[159] to moderate, based on having instigated new investigations rather than convictions achieved.[160]

Before considering enforcement, it is appropriate to examine the legislation. The criminal code dealt with 'the integrity and security of the international community and foreign governments: Bribery of foreign public officials'.[161] S 70.2(1) provides that a person is guilty of an offence if:

a the person: (i) provides a benefit to another person; or (ii) causes a benefit to be provided to another person; or (iii) offers to provide, or promises to provide, a benefit to another person; or (iv) causes an offer of the provision of a benefit, or a promise of the provision of a benefit, to be made to another person; and
b the benefit is not legitimately due to the other person; and
c the first-named does so with the intention of influencing a foreign public official (who may be the other person) in the exercise of the official's duties as a foreign public official in order to: (i) obtain or retain business; or (ii) obtain or retain a business advantage that is not legitimately due to the recipient, or intended recipient, of the business advantage (who may be the first-mentioned person).[162]

These provisions are broadly the same as the Bribery Act.[163] There are two defences to claims of foreign bribery: lawful conduct and 'facilitation payments'.[164]

158 'Criminal Code Amendment (Bribery of Foreign Public Officials) Bill 1999 – C2004B00419. Explanatory Memorandum' www.comlaw.gov.au/Details/C2004B00419/Explanatory%20Memorandum/Text Accessed 4 January 2017.
159 Davids and Schubert (n 157) 98, 99 (footnotes omitted).
160 Transparency International, 'Exporting corruption: Progress Report 2014: Assessing enforcement of the OECD Convention on Combatting Foreign Bribery' 4 www.transparency.org/whatwedo/publication/exporting_corruption_progress_report_2014_assessing_enforcement_of_the_oecd Accessed 6 February 2017.
161 Criminal Code Act 1995. Chapter 4, Division 70.
162 Commonwealth Criminal Code Act 1995, Division 70.
163 Bribery Act 2010, s 6.
164 'They exist in addition to the generally applicable defences of duress, mistake of fact, sudden or extraordinary emergency, and self-defence contained in Div 10 of the [Criminal] Code.' Davids and Schubert (n 157) 98, 110 (footnotes omitted).

Lawful conduct defence

The lawful conduct exemption[165] applies for activities that are lawful in the foreign public official's country, subject to 'a written law in force in that place' or 'a written law in force in the foreign country or in the part of the country, as the case may be'.[166] This, too, replicates the Bribery Act.[167] This defence was in 'the findings of the Cole enquiry[168] into the Australian Wheat Board affair'.[169] In that case, payments were made to Iraqi government officials 'in violation of United Nations sanctions imposed under the Oil-for-Food program but it was doubted that this alone could make them unlawful *under Iraqi law*'.[170] By way of background, 'in 1990, following the invasion of Kuwait, the UN imposed sanctions on Iraq'.[171] However, these sanctions imposed hardship on the Iraqi people because its government did not have hard currency to purchase foodstuffs.[172] In response, the UN passed Security Council Resolution 986 allowing Iraq to sell oil in order to purchase 'humanitarian goods, including foodstuffs'.[173] An outcome of the Australian Wheat Board case was a change to the Criminal Code to clarify that 'the benefit offered must be required or permitted in the *written* law of the place or country'.[174]

165 Criminal Code Act 1995, s 70.3.
166 Commonwealth Criminal Code Act 1995, Division 70(3)(1).
167 Bribery Act 2010, s 5.
168 Terence Cole, 'Report of the inquiry into certain Australian companies in relation to the UN Oil-for-Food Programme', Attorney-General's Department (Australia), 2006 http://apo.org.au/node/3765 Accessed 4 January 2017.
169 Davids and Schubert (n 157) 98, 110.
170 Davids and Schubert (n 157) 98, 110.
171 Cole (n 168) xiii.
172 Cole (n 168) xiii.
173 'Resolution 986: On 14 April 1995, acting under Chapter VII of the United Nations Charter, the Security Council adopted resolution 986, establishing the "oil-for-food" programme, providing Iraq with another opportunity to sell oil to finance the purchase of humanitarian goods, and various mandated United Nations activities concerning Iraq. The programme, as established by the Security Council, is intended to be a "temporary measure to provide for the humanitarian needs of the Iraqi people, until the fulfilment by Iraq of the relevant Security Council resolutions, including notably resolution 687 (1991) of 3 April 1991".' United Nations, Office of Iraq Programme, 'oil-for-food' www.un.org/Depts/oip/background/index.html Accessed 8 December 2016. 'By 1999 AWB was selling to Iraq about 10 per cent of Australia's annual wheat exports. It was a large and profitable market.' Cole (n 168) xiii.
174 International Trade Integrity Act 2007. 'An Act to implement the Australian Government's response to recommendations made by the Inquiry into Certain Australian Companies in relation to the United Nations Oil-for-Food Programme, and for other purposes.' Davids and Schubert (n 157) 98, 110 (emphasis added). ABC News, 'ASIC fails to prove former AWB executives knew about Iraq sanctions breach' www.abc.net.au/news/2016-12-15/asic-wheat-board-executives-sanctions-iraq-breach/8122276 Accessed 17 March 2017.

Facilitation payments defence

The second defence is that payments were 'facilitation payments'.[175] This is a contentious issue for Australia because the government is considering whether to remove the defence for facilitation payments by repealing section 70.4 of the Criminal Code.[176] The Criminal Code states that a person is not guilty of an offence if the value of the benefit was of a minor nature, the person's conduct was for the sole or dominant purpose of expediting or securing the performance of a routine government action, and that the conduct was recorded.[177]

The 'facilitation payments' defence is not available under the UK Bribery Act, but it is available under the US Foreign Corrupt Practices Act 1977.[178] However, the OECD report a 'general confusion about the facilitation payment defence (…) The evaluation team noted a lack of understanding of what constitutes a "facilitation payment" under Australian law'.[179] This leads to misunderstandings such as 'facilitation payments appear to be frequently equated with *any* bribes of small value'.[180] The OECD reminder is that what is 'often overlooked is the requirement that such payments must be made *to secure routine government action of a minor nature* that does not result in the obtaining of a business advantage'.[181] Furthermore, because such payments are lawful they benefit from tax deductibility.[182] However, instead of pressing for abolition of facilitation payments, the OECD recognised the difficulties inherent in endeavouring to eliminate such payments by exhorting that Australia:

> continues to raise awareness of the distinction between facilitation payments and bribes, and encourage companies to prohibit or discourage the use of small facilitation payments in internal company controls, ethics and compliance programmes or measures, recognizing that such payments must in all cases be accurately accounted for in such companies' books and financial records.[183]

Thus, although the OECD may not approve the use of facilitation payments, they recognise the reality that some countries, as in Australia and the US, allow such payments within their anti-bribery laws. However, although the Australian

175 Criminal Code Act 1995, s 70.4.
176 Australian Government, 'Assessing the "facilitation payments" defence' (n 48).
177 Criminal Code Act 1995, Division 70(4).
178 15 U.S.C. § 78dd-1(b).
179 OECD, 'Phase 3 Report' (n 3).
180 OECD, 'Phase 3 Report' (n 3) (emphasis added).
181 OECD, 'Phase 3 Report' (n 3) (emphasis added).
182 Income Tax Assessment Act 1997. Australian Government, 'Assessing the "facilitation payments" defence' (n 48).
183 In the follow-up report, OECD confirmed that Australia had taken steps to raise awareness. OECD, 'Australia: Follow-up to the Phase 3 Report & Recommendations April 2015 8' www.oecd.org/daf/anti-bribery/Australia-Phase-3-Follow-up-Report-ENG.pdf Accessed 6 February 2017.

government understood that there was an issue and conducted a public consultation in 2011, this lapsed and a further consultation was launched in 2015 and re-launched in 2016 to report in 2017.[184] The first consultation invitation[185] proffered reasons for and against removal of the 'facilitation payments defence', with key reasoning against being:

> Each of these arguments is based on an assumption that corruption and demands for bribes or facilitation payments are firmly entrenched in foreign jurisdictions. As the international business community continues to take steps against bribery and corruption, these arguments will become increasingly redundant.[186]

The Australian government cite 'commentaries to the Anti-Bribery Convention [which] considered facilitation payments to be separate to bribery on the grounds that "small facilitation payments" did not constitute an attempt "to obtain or retain business or other improper advantage"'.[187] Yet, in the following paragraph, the government points to Australia being a party to the UNCAC, the purpose of which is to 'criminalise bribery of foreign public officials in international business'.[188] This Convention, though, 'does not differentiate between bribery and facilitation payments',[189] thus adding weight to the view that the facilitation payments defence be reviewed. This is especially so because the UNCAC thank Australia 'for providing funding for the promotion' of UNCAC.[190]

The Australian government noted that 'Australian businesses operating overseas may be subject to UK, US and Australian foreign bribery laws'.[191] The Attorney General points to Australian law being 'modelled' on US law[192] but 'as the UK defines facilitation payments as illegal, Australian law represents an

184 Australian Government, Attorney General's Department, Crime Prevention, 'Bribery of Foreign Officials' www.crimeprevention.gov.au/Financialcrime/Pages/Briberyofforeignpublicofficials.aspx Accessed 8 December 2016. Parliament of Australia, 'Foreign Bribery' www.aph.gov.au/Parliamentary_Business/Committees/Senate/Economics/Foreignbribery45th Accessed 5 February 2017.

185 Australian Government, 'Assessing the "facilitation payments" defence' (n 48).

186 Ross Drinnan and Rachel Nicolson, 'Australia: Proposed reform to Australian foreign bribery legislation' (2012) 2 IELR 40.

187 Australian Government, 'Assessing the "facilitation payments" defence' (n 48).

188 Australian Government, 'Assessing the "facilitation payments" defence' (n 48).

189 Australian Government, 'Assessing the "facilitation payments" defence' (n 48) (footnote omitted).

190 Indeed, the UN specifically thank Australia (and other countries, including the UK and US) for 'their generosity in providing funding for the promotion of the United Nations Convention against Corruption'. Legislative guide for the implementation of the United Nations Convention against Corruption. United Nations Office of Drugs and Crime, 'Legislative guide for the implementation of the United Nations Convention against Corruption' www.unodc.org/pdf/corruption/CoC_LegislativeGuide.pdf Accessed 8 December 2016.

191 Australian Government, 'Assessing the "facilitation payments" defence' (n 48).

192 Australian Government, 'Assessing the "facilitation payments" defence' (n 48).

inconsistency'.[193] The clear implications are that Australia is moving closer to removing the 'facilitation payments defence', with the case against such action being summarised as:

> Each of these arguments has, at its source, the problem of corruption. These arguments predominantly arise in business environments where facilitation payments are common and will become [an] increasingly difficult argument to sustain. The Australian Government encourages Australian businesses to work actively to reduce corruption by resisting demands for facilitation payments and reporting them to authorities and works closely with foreign governments to improve governance and reduce corruption.[194]

Although a decision has not been made, the direction of travel is towards following the UK lead, rather than adhering to the US position. The impact of such a decision is difficult to assess because the existing law has not been tested since there have been no prosecutions under s 70 and, thus, the facilitation payments defence has yet to be considered by the courts.[195]

Enforcement: Securency *corruption case*

The 'bribery of foreign officials' provisions of the Criminal Code have yet to be tested in the courts, notwithstanding those provisions having been in place since 1999. However, in 2011, a case emerged with such potential: *Securency International Pty Ltd (Securency)* is a multi-faceted case, involving allegations of bribery and corruption in Nepal, Indonesia, Malaysia, Nigeria, Vietnam and the UK,[196] by Securency, 'a joint venture between Australia's central bank, the Reserve Bank of Australia and UK based Innovia Films',[197] with by 2016 'former executives on bail and in purgatory' awaiting the start of their trials.[198]

The importance of Australia's first bribery of foreign public officials case cannot be overstated because of adverse comments from the FATF[199] and the OECD[200] regarding its history of enforcement. There will be considerable attention on the

193 Australian Government, 'Assessing the "facilitation payments" defence' (n 48).
194 Australian Government, 'Assessing the "facilitation payments" defence' (n 48).
195 Drinnan and Nicolson (n 186) 40.
196 Trace International, 'Trace Compendium – Securency' www.traceinternational.org/TraceCompendium/Detail/162?class=casename_searchresult&type=1 Accessed 4 January 2017. Reserve Bank of Australia, 'Statement concerning Securency International Pty Ltd and Note Printing Australia Ltd' www.rba.gov.au/media-releases/2011/mr-11-14.html Accessed 4 January 2017.
197 Trace International, 'Trace Compendium – Securency' (n 196).
198 *The Border Mail*, 'UK leaves Australia for dead on Securency corruption prosecution' www.bordermail.com.au/story/3907034/uk-leaves-australia-for-dead-on-securency-corruption-prosecution/?cs=9 Accessed 12 February 2017.
199 FATF, 'Summary of the third mutual evaluation report' (n 65) 4.
200 Davids and Schubert (n 157) 98, 110.

eventual Securency trial but, in the meantime, there has been some peripheral activity.[201]

In 2012, Ellery, Securency's CFO, pleaded guilty to one charge of false accounting.[202] He received a six-month suspended prison sentence.[203] The prosecution was predicated upon a charge of false accounting under Victoria state legislation, rather than the Commonwealth Criminal Code of bribery of foreign public officials.

In the UK, the SFO charged a director of a connected company with conspiracy to corrupt, but he was acquitted at trial.[204]

In 2016, Chapman, Securency's Africa office manager, was convicted in an SFO case of four charges of bribery in Nigeria, having been extradited from Brazil. He was sentenced to 30 months' imprisonment.[205]

One objective of a comparative analysis of the practice in Australia relating to prosecution of bribery of foreign public officials cannot be satisfied because the only case in the last 17 years (Securency) is still a work in progress. As a consequence, there is no experience in Australia of prosecution of bribery of foreign public officials upon which to base comment. However, even within the constraints of the Securency case still being before the courts, bribery issues have been considered by the Australian Parliament, which concludes:

> The N[ote]P[rinting] A[ustralia]/Securency case raises the critical importance of integrity standards and due diligence. These need to be matched with clear processes in relation to reporting suspected misconduct and corruption as well as effective protection of whistleblowers. The case demonstrates how, in a situation in which established policies and procedures were not adhered to or subject to effective oversight (for reasons including the poor relationship between the respective company boards and management), an opaque culture of secrecy and collective amnesia (when asked to explain practices) came to characterise both companies.[206]

201 *The Guardian*, 'Australian court's gagging order condemned as "abuse of legal process"' www.theguardian.com/world/interactive/2014/jul/30/redacted-supreme-court-victoria-gagging-order Accessed 8 December 2016.
202 '[C]ontrary to s83(1)(a) of the Crimes Act 1958 (Vic)'. *R v Ellery* [2012] VSC 349.
203 *Ellery* (n 202).
204 *Financial Times*, 'Businessman cleared of Vietnam bribery' 6 December 2012 www.ft.com/content/77e60e7c-3fb7-11e2-b2ce-00144feabdc0 Accessed 6 February 2017.
205 Serious Fraud Office, 'Former Securency manager sentenced for corruption' www.sfo.gov.uk/2016/05/12/former-securency-manager-sentenced-corruption/ Accessed 1 February 2017.
206 Parliament of Australia, Joint Committee on the Australian Commission for Law Enforcement Integrity, 'Note Printing Australia and Securency – a case study on risk management and integrity practices' www.aph.gov.au/Parliamentary_Business/Committees/Joint/Australian_Commission_for_Law_Enforcement_Integrity/Completed_inquiries/2010-13/integrity_inter_op/report/c02 Accessed 8 December 2016.

It is clear that the Australian Parliament will wish to ensure that lessons are learned from the case once it is concluded and, especially, in terms of protecting any whistleblower.[207]

Sentencing

The maximum penalties for individuals in breach of s 70 are ten years' imprisonment and/or a A$1.7m fine. The penalty for companies is of the greater of: A$17m fine; three times the value of the benefit attributed to the conduct (if it can be determined); or 10% of the annual turnover.[208] This compares with in the UK ten years' imprisonment and/or an unlimited fine; and in the US $2m for corporates and five years, and $100,000 for each FCPA violation. However, in Australia, these provisions have yet to be deployed. One feature of the UK and US approaches to dealing with bribery and corruption is that of using DPAs. These do not feature in Australia, although the Attorney General launched a public consultation, which closed in 2016, and on which a government response is awaited.[209]

Regulatory bodies

Australian Prudential Regulation Authority

Australia became the first country in the world to adopt the twin peaks model of regulation, in 1998. This approach is 'to structure regulation around two agencies, one responsible for the safety and soundness of all financial firms and the other for

207 Parliament of Australia, Joint Committee on the Australian Commission for Law Enforcement Integrity (n 206). There have been calls for a Parliamentary Inquiry. Jo-Anne Gilbert and J C Sharman, 'Turning a blind eye to bribery: Explaining failures to comply with the international anti-corruption regime' (2016) 64(1) Political Studies 74, 83.

208 'Penalty for individual: (4) An offence against subsection (1) committed by an individual is punishable on conviction by imprisonment for not more than 10 years, a fine not more than 10,000 penalty units, or both. Penalty for body corporate: (5) An offence against subsection (1) committed by a body corporate is punishable on conviction by a fine not more than the greatest of the following: (a) 100,000 penalty units; [Penalty unit = A$180 – Effective from 31 July 2015, the *Crimes Legislation Amendment Penalty Unit Act 2015*]; (b) if the court can determine the value of the benefit that the body corporate, and any body corporate related to the body corporate, have obtained directly or indirectly and that is reasonably attributable to the conduct constituting the offence – 3 times the value of that benefit; (c) if the court cannot determine the value of that benefit – 10% of the annual turnover of the body corporate during the period (the *turnover period*) of 12 months ending at the end of the month in which the conduct constituting the offence occurred.' Criminal Code Act 1995, s 70 4(2)(4); s 70.2(2)(5); Crimes Act 1914 s 4AA.

209 Australian Government, Attorney General's Department, 'Deferred prosecution agreements – public consultation' www.ag.gov.au/Consultations/Pages/Deferred-prosecution-agreements-public-consultation.aspx Accessed 5 February 2017.

regulating their sales practices'.[210] The Commonwealth created 'two new regulators – prudential (Australian Prudential Regulation Authority, APRA) and disclosure (Australian Securities and Investment Commission, ASIC)'.[211] This simplified the system because the 'existing 10 regulators operating at federal, state and territory levels were abolished and the Reserve Bank of Australia (RBA) lost its bank regulation powers'.[212] The RBA's role is focused on 'monetary policy, stability of the financial system and the safety and efficiency of the payments system'. The Australian Competition and Consumer Commission 'is responsible for competition policy'.[213] However, it is the APRA[214] and ASIC that are the twin peaks: 'APRA is responsible for prudential supervision of individual financial institutions and for promoting financial system stability in Australia'.[215] This includes 'Australia's authorised deposit-taking institutions, life and general insurance and reinsurance companies, friendly societies and superannuation funds'.[216] The supervisory role of the APRA is focused on managing the risks of the institutions it supervises by establishing and enforcing 'prudential standards and practices designed to ensure that (…) financial promises made by the institutions it supervises are met within a stable, efficient and competitive financial system'.[217] The role of the APRA as one of the twin peaks is important but its activities are not central to this chapter, unlike its 'twin', ASIC.

Australian Securities and Investment Commission

The second 'twin' in the Australian twin peaks system is ASIC, 'Australia's corporate, markets and financial services regulator'.[218] It is an independent Commonwealth government body, established under the Corporations Act 2001.[219]

210 Taylor (n 14) 61.
211 Bakir (n 16) 910.
212 Bakir (n 16) 910.
213 Australian Prudential Regulation Authority, 'Protecting Australia's depositors, insurance policyholders and superannuation fund members' www.apra.gov.au/AboutAPRA/Publications/Pages/APRA-Brochure.aspx#What-is-APRA-s-role? Accessed 4 January 2017.
214 'Established in 1998, APRA is a Commonwealth statutory authority established under the *Australian Prudential Regulation Authority Act 1998*. APRA's high-level powers for the prudential supervision of institutions derive from this Act and from specific industry legislation: the *Banking Act 1959*; the *Insurance Act 1973*; the *Life Insurance Act 1995*; and the *Superannuation Industry (Supervision) Act 1993*.' Australian Prudential Regulation Authority, 'Protecting Australia's depositors' (n 213).
215 Australian Prudential Regulation Authority, 'Protecting Australia's depositors' (n 213).
216 Australian Prudential Regulation Authority, 'Protecting Australia's depositors' (n 213).
217 Australian Prudential Regulation Authority, 'Protecting Australia's depositors' (n 213).
218 Australian Securities and Investments Commission, 'About ASIC' http://asic.gov.au/about-asic/what-we-do/our-role/ Accessed 6 February 2017.
219 Australian Securities and Investments Commission, 'About ASIC' (n 218).

ASIC's mission is to 'contribute to Australia's economic reputation and wellbeing by ensuring that Australia's financial markets are fair and transparent, supported by confident and informed investors and consumers'.[220]

ASIC has a wide remit to 'regulate Australian companies, financial markets, financial services organisations and professionals who deal and advise in investments, superannuation, insurance, deposit taking and credit'.[221] ASIC is organised into three regulatory areas: as 'consumer credit regulator', 'financial services regulator', and 'markets regulator'.[222]

Relatively shortly after the establishment of the twin peaks institutions of APRA and ASIC, came a 'defining moment in APRA's history [that of] the US$3.75bn corporate collapse of Australian insurance group HIH in March 2001'.[223] A Royal Commission investigated and reported 'that there were difficulties in the relationship, which arose principally because APRA and ASIC had overlapping and clearly undelineated roles in relation to financial services providers'.[224] This is seen as one of the risk areas for twin peaks and serves to underline the need for proper exchange of information to ensure that regulation does not fall between two stools. The difficulty is explained by Carmichael, APRA's then chairman:

> The difficulty for a prudential regulator is that it is much easier for the community to identify when you are doing a poor job than it is for them to identify when you are doing a good job. Unlike a conduct regulator [ASIC], which can at least count 'heads on pikes', there is no ready metric for APRA's performance.[225]

ASIC has a wide range of responsibilities in relation to 2m companies and over 6,000 deposit takers, credit providers, insurers, investment banks and hedge fund managers; and it regulates 52 authorised financial markets.[226] ASIC notes that it is 'a regulator with many hats'[227] and, certainly, it has a significant number of matters within its purview. Accordingly, the adoption of a risk-based approach, as an alternative to principles-based, is unsurprising, as Cooper explains:

> This means that ASIC focuses on areas that it assesses as being of the *greatest risk*, such as misconduct and non-compliance that affect consumers' decisions, threaten the reputation of our markets or undermine Australia's international

220 Australian Securities and Investments Commission, 'About ASIC' (n 218).
221 Australian Securities and Investments Commission, 'About ASIC' (n 218).
222 Australian Securities and Investments Commission, 'About ASIC' (n 218).
223 Cooper (n 12) 5.
224 The HIH Royal Commission, www.hih.com.au/Group-HIHRoyalCommision.html Accessed 4 January 2017.
225 APRA, 'APRA speaks on Palmer' (The report of John Palmer was commissioned by APRA [in 2001] to investigate its role into the collapse of HIH and tendered as evidence to the HIH Royal Commission.) www.apra.gov.au/MediaReleases/Pages/02_52.aspx Accessed 4 January 2017.
226 Australian Securities and Investments Commission, 'About ASIC' (n 218).
227 Cooper (n 12) 7.

> reputation as a safe, well-regulated place to do business. It then decides what available regulatory tools best deal with those risks.[228]

ASIC operates under the Australian Securities and Investments Commission Act 2001 (ASIC Act), and administers the Corporations Act 2001.[229] ASIC has:

> wide ranging powers and can counter financial misconduct by: investigating matters; prosecuting in a criminal court, applying for a civil penalty order; bringing a civil action; disqualifying people from managing corporations or dealing in financial services; and accepting and enforcing undertaking.[230]

Penalties for non-compliance with the ASIC Act range from five penalty units (total A$900) at one end of the spectrum, to 100 penalty units (A$18,000 and/or two years' imprisonment) at the other.[231]

Notwithstanding the availability of powers of prosecution and regulation, the determination of the Australian government to take action is the subject of media speculation and parliamentary comment.[232] As already discussed in relation to Securency, the Commonwealth has yet to achieve its first prosecution for bribery of foreign public officials. Although ASIC fairly state that bribery is not within their purview,[233] it 'has declined to investigate Securency and NPA directors for breaches of directors' duties, despite a significant amount of evidence being sent to it by AFP',[234] the point being made that 'unlike the US and UK, Australia does have a public regulator that is empowered to prosecute individuals for breaches of directors['] duties'.[235] The conclusion is that 'one of ASIC's key problems is it is overstretched and understaffed, and, as a result Australia "gets what it pays for" from the regulator'.[236] Resource constraint is

228 Cooper (n 12) 8.

229 Australian Securities and Investments Commission Act 2001. Corporations Act 2001, s 5B.

230 George Gilligan, 'Financial crime in Australia' (2007) 27(1) Economic Affairs 10, 12.

231 Australian Securities and Investments Commission Act 2001, s 63.

232 *The Canberra Times*, 'Show the world we're fighting corruption' 3 October 2013 www.canberratimes.com.au/federal-politics/political-opinion/show-the-world-were-fighting-corruption-20131002-2ussl.html Accessed 8 December 2016.

233 'Bribery of foreign officials falls under the *Criminal Code Act 1995* and is a law mainly enforced by the AFP, not ASIC. This means it is the AFP that is responsible for investigating foreign bribery and corruption, and taking criminal action through the courts.' Australian Securities and Investments Commission, 'Setting the record straight: ASIC, bribery and enforcement action. A speech by Greg Medcraft, Chairman, Australian Securities and Investments Commission' http://asic.gov.au/about-asic/media-centre/speeches/setting-the-record-straight-asic-bribery-and-enforcement-action/ Accessed 4 January 2017.

234 *The Canberra Times*, 'Show the world we're fighting corruption' (n 232).

235 *The Canberra Times*, 'Show the world we're fighting corruption' (n 232).

236 *The Canberra Times*, 'Show the world we're fighting corruption' (n 232). 'ASIC has also been subject to the efficiency dividend applied to government departments and agencies. ASIC's funding over the forward estimates was also reduced as part of the

also an issue for the UK's SFO.[237] Nevertheless, Carmichael's analysis of 'heads on pikes' does strike a chord with media and parliamentarians, for although such a measure 'is not entirely reflective of our [ASIC's] ability to achieve this objective, it does at least provide one metric'.[238] In the year to June 2016, ASIC secured 22 convictions, 13 of which resulted in custodial sentences.[239] The most significant case (Hobbs),[240] prosecuted by the CDPP,[241] was a A$50m Ponzi scheme which achieved a 'penalty order of [A]$500,000 [which] is the largest awarded in ASIC's history'.[242] The judgment also included permanent prohibitions on managing corporations and disqualification from engaging in financial services.[243] These penalties can be seen in the light of the Madoff and Stanford penalties in the US of 150 and 100 years' imprisonment, respectively.[244]

most recent Budget. The amount of funding provided to ASIC and the funding model utilised to determine its funding clearly will have a significant impact on the agency's performance.' Parliament of Australia, 'The Senate: Economics References Committee' 3.3 http://www.aph.gov.au/Parliamentary_Business/Committees/Senate/Economics/ASIC/Final_Report/c23 Accessed 6 February 2017. 'ASIC had its funding cut by 12 per cent in this year's budget.' ABC News, 'Senate inquiry demands royal commission into Commonwealth Bank, ASIC' www.abc.net.au/news/2014-06-26/senate-inquiry-demands-royal-commission-into-asic-cba/5553102 Accessed 8 December 2016.

237 See Chapter 2.

238 Cooper (n 12) 8.

239 ASIC, 'Annual Report 2012–13' 32, 42 http://download.asic.gov.au/media/1311019/ASIC-Annual-Report-2012-13-complete.pdf Accessed 6 February 2017.

240 'David Hobbs was the "mastermind" of a large, unlicensed investment fund that targeted Australian investors and self-managed superannuation funds. The investment fund was facilitated by the set-up and operation of corporate structures and bank accounts in around 15 jurisdictions worldwide, including Anguilla, Australia, the British Virgin Islands, Hong Kong, New Zealand, the Turks and Caicos Islands, the United Kingdom, the United States and Vanuatu. More than $50 million was invested in the fund by more than 500 investors. In February 2013, Justice Ward in the Supreme Court (NSW) banned Mr Hobbs for life from working in the financial services industry and from managing companies in Australia, and imposed a record pecuniary penalty of $500,000. The matter is currently under appeal. Pivotal to achieving these outcomes was the evidence obtained with the assistance of around 15 regulators, including the US Commodity Futures Trading Commission, the New Zealand Financial Markets Authority and the Hong Kong Securities and Futures Commission.' ASIC, 'Senate inquiry into the performance of the Australian Securities and Investments Commission. Main submission by ASIC, October 2013' 124 http://download.asic.gov.au/media/1311361/ASIC-Main-submission-Senate-inquiry-October-2013.pdf Accessed 4 January 2017.

241 ASIC, '13–031MR Ponzi scheme "mastermind" handed record penalty' 17 February 2013 http://asic.gov.au/about-asic/media-centre/find-a-media-release/2013-releases/13-031mr-ponzi-scheme-mastermind-handed-record-penalty/ Accessed 4 January 2017.

242 ASIC, '13–031MR Ponzi scheme "mastermind"' (n 241).

243 ASIC, '13–031MR Ponzi scheme "mastermind"' (n 241).

244 Daniel V Dooley and Mark Radke, 'Does severe punishment deter financial crimes' (2010) 4 Charleston L Rev 619. US Department of Justice, 'Stanford' www.justice.gov/criminal/vns/caseup/stanfordr.html Accessed 8 December 2016.

In 2014 the Senate reported into the performance of ASIC,[245] 'following revelations in Fairfax Media that the regulator took 16 months to act on information from whistle-blowers about serious misconduct inside the Commonwealth Bank's financial planning unit [CFPL]'.[246] ASIC welcomed the inquiry into their performance[247] by outlining issues regarded by them 'as barriers to fulfilling [their] legislative responsibilities and obligations, and proposals for overcoming these barriers'.[248] ASIC also acknowledged that in 'the public discussion of the handling of the CFPL matter there has been a misapprehension that (…) ASIC was not active in relation to the matter'.[249] ASIC accept that 'all stakeholders would have been better served if (…) ASIC had been public about CFPL's agreement to undertake the [Continuous Improvement Compliance Program] in response' to previous negative review findings.[250] ASIC also accept that their communication with whistleblowers 'was not adequate',[251] and this has exposed areas of concern relating to whistleblowers, such as: 'expanding the definition' of a whistleblower; 'expanding the scope' of information protection; and, 'protecting information about a whistleblower'.[252]

In the face of a Parliamentary inquiry, ASIC has suggested a number of areas for enhancement, pointing out that its 'investigative powers were established in the Corporations Act and ASIC Act over a decade ago'.[253] ASIC then points out that 'financial services and markets have expanded rapidly and grown in complexity',[254] as has technology, but 'ASIC's investigative powers have not kept pace'.[255]

245 Parliament of Australia, 'The performance of the Australian Securities and Investments Commission' www.aph.gov.au/Parliamentary_Business/Committees/Senate/Economics/ASIC/Final_Report/index Accessed 6 February 2017.
246 *The Sydney Morning Herald*, 'Senate launches enquiry into ASIC' www.smh.com.au/business/senate-launches-inquiry-into-asic-20130620-2oksh.html#ixzz2l6sZzgpo Accessed 8 December 2016.
247 ASIC, 'Senate inquiry' (n 240) 7.
248 ASIC, 'Senate inquiry' (n 240) 7.
249 ASIC, '13–201MR ASIC submission to Senate inquiry' 5 http://asic.gov.au/about-asic/media-centre/find-a-media-release/2013-releases/13-201mr-asic-submission-to-senate-inquiry/ Accessed 4 January 2017.
250 ASIC, '13–201MR ASIC submission to Senate inquiry' (n 249) 16.
251 ASIC, '13–201MR ASIC submission to Senate inquiry' (n 249) 16.
252 ASIC, 'Senate inquiry' (n 240) 164.
253 ASIC, 'Senate inquiry' (n 240) 167.
254 ASIC, 'Senate inquiry' (n 240) 167.
255 'ASIC has access to search warrant powers under both the Commonwealth *Crimes Act 1914* (Crimes Act) and the ASIC Act. However, neither is entirely satisfactory: (a) the ASIC Act powers only authorise a limited range of search activities (e.g. entering premises and taking possession of "particular" books, which ASIC must attempt to name in applying for a warrant), posing significant practical difficulties for ASIC; and (b) by contrast, the Crimes Act authorises a far larger range of search activities (e.g. examining electronic equipment at the searched premises). However, the Crimes Act only authorises searches relating to suspected criminal offences, where the ASIC Act allows for searches relating to all of the provisions under ASIC's jurisdiction, including civil penalty provisions and administrative remedies.' ASIC, 'Senate inquiry' (n 240) 167.

Furthermore, ASIC points to inadequacies in what it calls its 'enforcement toolkit'.[256] It identifies as the key issue that 'the penalties available in corporations legislation have not been comprehensively reviewed for over a decade, and, in many cases, *do not meet community expectations*'.[257] ASIC make the point that the range of civil fines that they can make are markedly lower than those seen in the UK and US,[258] for example:

> JP Morgan was fined heavily for losses of over $6bn on the so-called 'London Whale trades' affair. The fines amounted to: £138m by the UK FCA; US $200m by the US SEC; US$200m by the US Federal Reserve; US$309m by the US Consumer Finance Protection Bureau; and US$300m by the US Office of the Comptroller of the Currency. In contrast, under the Corporations Act, the maximum civil penalty payable by a corporation for an offence is [A]$1m.[259]

Although Australia was less affected by the 2008 financial crisis than the UK, ASIC has accepted 'voluntary contributions' totalling A$3.6m from UBS, RBS and Paribas in relation to influencing benchmarks.[260] The deterrence effect of 'heads on pikes' relies on the enforcement penalties available, but 'shortcomings in the consistency or size of penalties'[261] can 'create gaps between community expectations of the appropriate regulatory response to a particular instance of misconduct and what ASIC can do in practice'.[262] They clearly adopt a cost/benefit analysis approach 'when considering whether to take civil penalty action',[263] one component of which is that 'if only a low civil penalty would be available, this might be one factor weighing against taking this kind of action'.[264] ASIC state that these issues 'can risk undermining confidence in the financial regulatory system',[265] which would appear to be precisely the case in Parliament undertaking a review. The Parliamentary report[266] presented ASIC with an opportunity to undertake its own review of its activities and suggest improvements,

256 ASIC, 'Senate inquiry' (n 240) 173.
257 ASIC, 'Senate inquiry' (n 240) 167 (emphasis added).
258 ASIC, 'Senate inquiry' (n 240) 170.
259 'Due to the "totality principle", multiple offences arising out of the same course of conduct will not usually give rise to a substantially greater penalty than a single offence. Accordingly, multiple offences cannot attract remotely comparable civil penalties in Australia, even assuming that the maximum penalty is applied.' ASIC, 'Senate inquiry' (n 240) 170.
260 Australian Securities and Investments Commission, 'Financial Benchmarks' www.asic.gov.au/media/3285136/rep440-published-8-july-2015.pdf Accessed 11 March 2017.
261 ASIC, 'Senate inquiry' (n 240) 169.
262 ASIC, 'Senate inquiry' (n 240) 169.
263 ASIC, 'Senate inquiry' (n 240) 170.
264 ASIC, 'Senate inquiry' (n 240) 170.
265 ASIC, 'Senate inquiry' (n 240) 169.
266 Parliament of Australia, 'The Senate: Economics References Committee' (n 236).

which is as well because the report found that 'ASIC has limited powers and resources but even so appears to miss or ignore clear and persistent early warning signs of corporate wrongdoing or troubling trends that pose a risk to consumers'.[267] Furthermore, 'it showed ASIC as a timid, hesitant regulator, too ready and willing to accept uncritically assurances of a large institution that there were no grounds for ASIC's concerns or intervention'.[268] The Parliamentary report compared Australian penalties with other jurisdictions: 'while ASIC's maximum criminal penalties are broadly consistent with those available in other countries, there are significantly higher prison terms in the US, and higher fines in some overseas countries for breaches of continuous disclosure obligations and unlicensed conduct.'[269] Moreover, 'there is a broader range of civil and administrative penalties in other countries, and the penalties are higher'.[270] This means, first, that Australia is found wanting in its penalties[271] and, second, that the UK has no need to look to Australia for an alternative model to adopt.

Since 2009, there have been 14 inquiries either about, or impacting upon, ASIC.[272] The Financial System Inquiry drew government response in 2015[273] and ASIC was then subject to a capability review. Two proposals have emerged from government: an increase in ASIC enforcement powers; and a change to 'an industry funding model for ASIC will ensure there is greater alignment between the costs of ASIC's regulatory activities and those industry participants who create the need for, and engage in, these activities'.[274] In October 2016, the government announced establishment of an 'ASIC Enforcement Review Taskforce'.[275] Thus, it is clear that there are concerns about ASIC's performance, but little by way of action.

The UK has already undergone a process of examining its regulatory structure and has adopted the twin peaks approach pioneered by Australia. A difference is that the UK FCA has a wider range of powers,[276] and certainly greater maxima in

267 Parliament of Australia, 'The Senate: Economics References Committee' (n 236).
268 Parliament of Australia, 'The Senate: Economics References Committee' (n 236).
269 Parliament of Australia, 'The Senate: Economics References Committee' (n 236) 23.7.
270 Parliament of Australia, 'The Senate: Economics References Committee' (n 236) 23.7.
271 Parliament of Australia, 'The Senate: Economics References Committee' (n 236) 41.
272 ABC News, 'Fact check: Can ASIC do the same job as a financial industry royal commission?' www.abc.net.au/news/2016-06-09/fact-check-asic-royal-commission-powers/7447682 Accessed 6 February 2017.
273 Australian Government, 'Fit for the future – A capability review of the Australian Securities and Investments Commission December 2015' www.treasury.gov.au/~/media/Treasury/Publications%20and%20Media/Publications/2016/Fit%20for%20the%20future/Downloads/PDF/ASIC-Capability-Review-Final-Report.ashx Accessed 6 February 2017.
274 ASIC, 'Annual Report 2015–16' 5 http://download.asic.gov.au/media/4058626/asic-annual-report-2015-2016-complete.pdf Accessed 6 February 2017.
275 Australian Government, Treasury, 'ASIC Enforcement Review Taskforce' http://kmo.ministers.treasury.gov.au Accessed 6 February 2017.
276 'In his evidence to the committee, Professor Justin O'Brien explained that the United States of America (US) has predominately taken a rules-based approach to financial

terms of financial penalties[277] than ASIC,[278] but even the UK lacks a single agency to deal with serious economic crime. The Commonwealth's position 'was that its multi-agency response is based "on the premise that *no single body* should be responsible", and that there is "no convincing case for the establishment of a *single over-arching* integrity commission".'[279] However, there is a recognition that 'many information sharing impediments faced by agencies are cultural rather than legislative'.[280] Thus, the prospects for a change of plan would appear to be limited, for 'once a pattern of corporate law and regulation is formed, deviation from this pattern becomes difficult, although not impossible'.[281]

Conclusion

The purpose in considering the regulatory responses to economic crime in Australia, a country which, according to Ryder, had more successfully weathered the storm of post-financial crisis economies than other nations,[282] was to establish whether it had methods and processes that might translate to the UK with benefit. The first aspect is in the nature of regulation itself: that Australia is considered to have managed its economy and institutions in a manner that has protected the country from the vicissitudes of the global market felt in the

regulation, while the United Kingdom (UK) has adopted a principles-based style. However, the choice between rules-based and principles-based regulation is generally not one at the expense of the other; for example, Professor Black noted that despite the UK's financial services regulations being designed using a principles-based approach, the rulebook of its regulator still comprises several thousand pages.' Parliament of Australia, 'The Senate: Economics References Committee' (n 236) 4.8.

277 Gary Wilson and Sarah Wilson, 'The FSA "credible deterrence" and criminal enforcement – a "haphazard pursuit"?' (2014) JFC 4.

278 'The penalties "are proportionately low given the seriousness and impact of civil penalty matters", and when compared with the penalties available in other jurisdictions such as the UK and US.' 'Recommendation 41. The committee recommends that the government commission an inquiry into the current criminal and civil penalties available across the legislation ASIC administers. The inquiry should consider: the consistency of criminal penalties, and whether some comparable offences currently attract inconsistent penalties; the range of civil penalty provisions available in the legislation ASIC administers and whether they are consistent with other civil penalties for corporations; and the level of civil penalty amounts, and whether the legislation should provide for the removal of any financial benefit.' Parliament of Australia, 'The Senate: Economics References Committee' (n 236) 23.5, 41.

279 Transparency International Australia, 'A ten-point integrity plan for the Australian government submission by Transparency International Australia on the proposed National Anti-Corruption Plan' May 2012 9 http://transparency.org.au/wp-content/uploads/2012/07/2012-TIA-NACP-Subv2-FINAL.pdf Accessed 4 January 2017 (footnotes omitted).

280 Attorney General, 'National organised crime response plan 2015–18' 17 www.ag.gov.au/CrimeAndCorruption/OrganisedCrime/Documents/NationalOrganisedCrimeResponsePlan2015-18.pdf Accessed 6 February 2017.

281 Tomasic, 'Governance and the evaluation of corporate law and regulation in Australia' (n 27) 24.

282 Levi and Smith (n 11).

UK and US.[283] The basis of this regulatory structure is the twin peaks model: as deployed in Australia, it combines the prudential regulator (APRA) with the 'corporate, markets and financial services regulator' ASIC.[284] It is ironic, therefore, that such a model should have a UK philosophical parentage by Taylor. As Ryder notes, the twin peaks model is being successfully applied to Canada.[285] This is another interesting feature: first, the UK, through the Financial Services Act 2012,[286] adopted the twin peaks structure but then, concurrent with passing that legislation, appointed the then Governor of the Bank of Canada to be Governor of the Bank of England,[287] in which role he chairs the Prudential Regulation Authority, one of the UK's 'twin peaks'.[288] Thus, it can be seen that the UK has adopted a regulatory regime and has had the benefit of Australia's 15 years' experience to inform its design.

The role of ASIC is to regulate consumer credit, financial services and markets.[289] It has a wide range of responsibilities and a significant number of entities to supervise.[290] However, ASIC's enforcement record has been subject to criticism, resulting in the establishment of various inquiries. In response, ASIC acknowledged that their investigatory powers had not kept pace with changes in technology,[291] and that the penalties available to them under corporations legislation were in need of review.[292] Thus, it would appear that ASIC has, prompted by Parliament, recognised the opportunities for improving its enforcement activities, highlighting in its 'London Whale' case study[293] the disparity between penalties available in the UK and US, and in Australia. Therefore, with ASIC casting covetous eyes on UK and US sanctions, it is they who will be considering the UK regulatory regime of the FCA, PRA and SFO, rather than offering a template for UK adoption.

The Australian Parliamentary inquiry[294] considered whether Australia and ASIC would benefit from establishment of an SFO.[295] The report reveals a range of views, including a former CDPP who said it would be a retrograde step,[296] and

283 Nicholas Ryder, *The Financial Crisis and White Collar Crime – The Perfect Storm* (Edward Elgar 2014) 196.
284 Australian Securities and Investments Commission, 'About ASIC' (n 218).
285 Ryder, *The Financial Crisis and White Collar Crime – The Perfect Storm* (n 283) 196.
286 Financial Services Act 2012.
287 From 1 July 2013. Bank of England, 'People. Mark Carney' www.bankofengland.co.uk/about/Pages/people/biographies/carney.aspx Accessed 8 December 2016.
288 Bank of England, 'People. Mark Carney' (n 287). 'The PRA works alongside the Financial Conduct Authority (FCA) creating a "twin peaks" regulatory structure in the UK.' Bank of England, 'Prudential Regulation Authority' www.bankofengland.co.uk/pra/Pages/default.aspx Accessed 8 December 2016.
289 Australian Securities and Investments Commission, 'About ASIC' (n 218).
290 ASIC, 'Annual Report 2012–13' (n 239).
291 ASIC, 'Senate inquiry' (n 240) 167.
292 ASIC, 'Senate inquiry' (n 240) 167.
293 ASIC, 'Senate inquiry' (n 240) 170.
294 Parliament of Australia, 'The Senate: Economics References Committee' (n 236).
295 Parliament of Australia, 'The Senate: Economics References Committee' (n 236) 23.26.
296 Parliament of Australia, 'The Senate: Economics References Committee' (n 236) 23.30.

ASIC that it would lead to fragmentation,[297] before concluding 'that there needs to be a shake-up of how complex fraud, bribery and corruption is addressed in Australia'.[298] Notwithstanding this, the report stated:

> the committee is of the view that the public interest would be better served if ASIC was more willing to litigate complex matters involving large entities. There appears to be either a disinclination to initiate court proceedings, or a penchant within ASIC for negotiating settlements and enforceable undertakings. The end result is that there is little evidence to suggest that large entities fear the threat of litigation brought by ASIC.[299]

This assessment highlights the preference for civil or regulatory penalties rather than criminal sanction as through the SFO, and the committee ended by urging the government to consider the issues and, meantime, ensure that existing agencies were properly resourced.[300]

Financial intelligence[301] is an important aspect of the response to economic and organised crime. In Australia, this is the responsibility of AUSTRAC, a Commonwealth institution. In the past, Australia was criticised for weaknesses in anti-money laundering and responded by enacting the AML/CTF Act[302] to comply with FATF requirements.[303] This is a single piece of legislation in contrast to the UK and US, which have adopted a piecemeal approach.[304] Although outside the scope of this chapter, the example of primary legislation for AML/CTF may provide an example for other countries to follow, or provide a template for future FATF recommendations.[305] However, in relation to economic crime, the intelligence gathering through risk-based reporting requirements does provide information for other agencies to use, as with the Australian Tax Office.[306] This fulfils a similar role to the NCA's SARs in the UK.

297 Parliament of Australia, 'The Senate: Economics References Committee' (n 236) 23.27.
298 Parliament of Australia, 'The Senate: Economics References Committee' (n 236) 23.33.
299 Parliament of Australia, 'The Senate: Economics References Committee' (n 236) 23.33.
300 'The committee urges the government to consider these issues further and, in the interim, to ensure that relevant enforcement agencies, the CDPP and the courts are adequately resourced to meet the community's expectations of law enforcement and to facilitate the swift delivery of justice.' Parliament of Australia, 'The Senate: Economics References Committee' (n 236) 23.34.
301 Australian Government, 'AUSTRAC annual report shows financial intelligence is crucial to combating contemporary criminal threats' (n 121).
302 Anti-Money Laundering and Counter-Terrorism Financing Act 2006.
303 Ryder, *Money Laundering – An Endless Cycle?* (n 9) 105.
304 Ryder, *Money Laundering – An Endless Cycle?* (n 9) 107.
305 Financial Action Task Force, 'International Standards on combating Money Laundering and the financing of terrorism – The FATF Recommendations' www.fatf-gafi.org/media/fatf/documents/recommendations/pdfs/FATF_Recommendations.pdf Accessed 8 December 2016.
306 Australian Transaction Reports and Analysis Centre, 'AUSTRAC Annual Report 2015–16' (n 122) 9.

Allied to AUSTRAC are the CDPP and AFP. The former 'investigates serious or complex crimes' against the Commonwealth,[307] while the latter 'is an independent prosecuting service (…) to prosecute alleged offences against Commonwealth law'.[308] These are two separate institutions, in contrast to the UK where the SFO is a single investigator and prosecutor. Furthermore, these are both Commonwealth institutions and 'can sometimes overlap with those of state and territory law enforcement, regulatory or criminal justice areas'.[309] As a consequence of the Australian constitutional structure of Commonwealth, states and territories, their institutions have to work in 'multidisciplinary crime teams'.[310] The UK does not have the same structural issues for an insight into the Australian approach to be of benefit.

The Australian approach to fraud is a reflection of its constitutional heritage with responsibility being divided between the Commonwealth and states. In its review of the theft, fraud, bribery and related offences landscape, the MCLOC opined that:

> The excesses of the 1980s have focussed a great deal of attention on the prosecution of fraud offences in Australia. Corruption in the public sector has also found focus in the Fitzgerald Report in Queensland and WA Inc in Western Australia. That focus finds the substantive law in such areas as theft, fraud, secret commissions and bribery fragmented and complex. The nine jurisdictions operate under nine sets of laws which adopt fundamentally different criteria.[311]

This demonstrates the extent of the task faced by Australian legislators to create a common standard which might then be described as the Australian fraud law. Since 1995, steps have been taken to move towards a 'uniform national approach',[312] but this is by no means complete and inconsistencies remain. Although the Commonwealth and states may adopt different terminology, they are becoming more aligned. The general direction of travel promoted by the 1995 Model Criminal Code report pre-dates the UK Fraud Act. It is clear from NSW 2009 legislation[313] that the UK legislation was given consideration, but the Fraud Act provisions were thought to be too broad and, therefore, were not adopted.[314] The UK's implementation of the Fraud Act, discussed in Chapter 2, is working well and meeting desired objectives. The patchy adoption of differing standards in

307 Australian Government, 'The Commonwealth's approach to anti-corruption' (n 23).
308 Director of Public Prosecutions Act 1983. Commonwealth Director of Public Prosecutions, www.cdpp.gov.au/ Accessed 8 December 2016.
309 Attorney General, 'Commonwealth organised crime strategic framework' (155) 6.
310 Australian Federal Police, 'Annual Report 2012–13' (n 147) 67.
311 Model Criminal Code Officers Committee (n 95).
312 Johns (n 83) 14.
313 Crimes Amendment (Fraud, Identity and Forgery Offences) Act 2009.
314 Steel (n 89) 19.

the Australian states leads to a conclusion that the UK would not benefit from taking the Australian approach.

In relation to bribery of foreign public officials, Australia has ratified both the OECD Convention in 1999 and UNCAC in 2005. These conventions, which both the UK and US have also ratified,[315] impose standards, but while the UK has enacted recent legislation[316] that is congruent with those conventions, the other two countries have not. In particular, the UK has made clear that a facilitation payment is a bribe and therefore illegal.[317] Thus, especially in view of the debate in Australia regarding following the UK lead, far from the UK potentially benefiting from the Australian experience, the reverse applies.

Therefore, fraud, bribery and corruption are handled differently in Australia, where the constitutional framework represents a complicating factor when considering whether any of its approaches to economic crime could be translated with benefit to the UK. However, notwithstanding the Constitution, it does have a different approach to prosecution which is not attractive.

Where Australia has a structure of benefit is in relation to financial regulation, where its twin peaks model of financial regulation is thought to have contributed to Australia successfully withstanding the stresses of the 2008 financial crisis.[318] The UK has since adopted such a structure. In considering the regulation and prosecution of economic crime, the Australian constitutional structure introduces some features that are not relevant to the UK and some complications – for example, regarding a variety of fraud legislation and the limited remit of some regulators and agencies, such as the CDPP and AFP. The prime corporate and markets regulator, ASIC, is under scrutiny for its enforcement record and itself acknowledges that its armoury needs enhancing, whereas the UK changed its regime in 2013.[319]

In relation to bribery of foreign public officials, the UK legislation, which is compliant with international standards, is more stringent than that of Australia, which has still to decide whether or not to remove the 'facilitation payments' defence to bribery. Thus, the conclusion reached by this chapter is that the one area where the UK could usefully look to Australia for insight was the twin peaks approach.[320]

315 US in 1998 and UK in 2002. OECD Convention (n 35).
316 Bribery Act 2010.
317 Serious Fraud Office, 'Enforcement of the United Kingdom's Bribery Act – Facilitation payments' www.sfo.gov.uk/publications/guidance-policy-and-protocols/bribery-act-guidance/ Accessed 4 January 2017.
318 Lui (n 2) 242, 243.
319 Financial Services Act 2012.
320 Bakir (n 16) 910.

6 Conclusions

Economic crime is a significant feature of the UK's economic landscape and as yet it is not a subject that readily engages with either the public or the authorities. As a consequence, and despite the then Conservative-Liberal Democrat coalition government's bold mission statements 'to hold those suspected of financial wrongdoing to account'[1] as part of their 'day of reckoning'[2] and 'serious about white collar crime'[3] agenda, it failed to achieve its objectives.[4] This book examines the history to creation of the UK's anti-economic crime institutions and accompanying legislation, providing a critique of their effectiveness and analyses of whether the regime established by the government is appropriate for the future and considers the contribution that could be made by reviewing the way two other countries face the issues.

The conclusion is that further change must take place: a new structure is required for the UK with the formation of a broad Economic Crime Agency (ECA) that incorporates the Serious Fraud Office (SFO) and Financial Conduct Authority (FCA).

This book takes as its starting point the change of UK government in 1979 and explains the significance of that political development which presaged a change in supervision of financial markets away from the metaphorical 'Governor's eyebrows' approach of informal control, to the establishment of a succession of formal City regulators. Coincident with designing a formal regulatory structure, government concerns over the management of fraud trials and the failure to secure convictions led ultimately to the creation of the SFO.

1 BBC, 'Cameron urges "day of reckoning"' 15 December 2008 http://news.bbc.co.uk/1/hi/7783350.stm Accessed 11 March 2017.
2 BBC, 'Cameron' (n 1).
3 HM Treasury, 'Speech at The Lord Mayor's Dinner for Bankers & Merchants of the City of London by The Chancellor of the Exchequer, The Rt Hon George Osborne MP, at Mansion House' 16 June 2010 http://webarchive.nationalarchives.gov.uk/20130129110402/http://www.hm-treasury.gov.uk/press_12_10.htm Accessed 11 March 2017.
4 '(…) our position as one of the world's leading global financial centres. (…) to create a single agency to take on the work of tackling serious economic crime that is currently dispersed across a number of Government departments and agencies.' HM Treasury, 'Speech at The Lord Mayor's Dinner' (n 3).

The range of regulatory and prosecutorial powers has been expanded, in particular with the Financial Services and Markets Act 2000 (FSMA), Fraud Act 2006 and Bribery Act 2010. Recent developments allow the SFO to reach court-supervised 'Deferred Prosecution Agreements' (DPAs),[5] in addition to allowing regulators to criminalise 'a decision causing a financial institution to fail'.[6] This latter provision is a consequence of the 2008 financial crisis, which severely affected the UK and revealed failings in the regulation and supervision of markets and institutions.

The response to failure in regulation and successful prosecutions assisted in the discussion of what it is that is encompassed in the expression 'economic crime' and the nature of the term 'white-collar crime', and whether the perception of differential treatment from other crimes is correct.

Examination of the UK financial services and markets landscape is not sufficient upon which to base any recommendations. Accordingly, this book has also embraced consideration of the way in which two other countries faced similar challenges by critically examining the regulatory responses to economic crime by the US and Australia. They were chosen for comparison because the former is the UK's most significant trading partner outside the EU,[7] and the latter is regarded as having more successfully withstood the effects of the financial crisis than other leading industrial nations.[8]

UK economic crime perspective

The coalition government came to power with a bold mission 'to create a single agency to take on the work of tackling serious economic crime that is currently dispersed across a number of Government departments and agencies'.[9]

The immediate change that the coalition set in motion was the adoption of a new economic regulatory model called 'twin peaks' because it considered that the previous financial regulatory, or 'tripartite', regime centred on the Financial Services Authority (FSA) as a 'super-regulator',[10] together with HM Treasury and the Bank of England, had failed to achieve its objectives, revealing 'gaps in the UK regulatory system'.[11] The FSA's performance was attributed to the weakness of its

5 Crime and Courts Act 2013, s 45, Schedule 17.
6 Financial Services (Banking Reform) Act 2013, s 36.
7 Note: The European Union was not selected for comparison, primarily because EU directives to establish a common regime across member states are absent, through lack of political will, as evidenced by complaints of patchy adoption of international corruption conventions.
8 Michael Levi and Russell G Smith, 'Fraud vulnerabilities and the global financial crisis' in *Trends and Issues in Crime and Criminal Justice* (Australian Institute of Criminology No. 422 July 2011) www.aic.gov.au/publications/current%20series/tandi/421-440/tandi422.html Accessed 11 March 2017.
9 HM Treasury, 'Speech at The Lord Mayor's Dinner' (n 3).
10 Eva Lomnicka, 'Reforming U.K. financial services regulation: The creation of a single regulator' (1999) (Sept) JBL 482.
11 The other 'twin peak' is the Prudential Regulation Authority. House of Commons Library, 'Financial Services Bill – Research paper 12/08' 12 researchbriefings.files.parliament.uk/documents/RP12-18/RP12-18.pdf Accessed 11 March 2017.

'light-touch' approach and, according to Tomasic, an 'overly close relationship with the City',[12] encouraged by political pressure to be 'business friendly' in competing with other financial centres, such as New York.[13] The government's response was to replace the tripartite model with the twin peaks model, where, first and pivotally,[14] the Bank of England was given responsibility for financial stability and for the prudential regulation of banking institutions. The second 'peak' was the creation of the FCA to take responsibility for protecting consumers and financial markets. The twin peaks model had previously been adopted in Australia and Canada, both of which are regarded as having withstood the financial crisis better than the UK and US.

The government's key concern was financial stability, which was a direct consequence of the way in which the financial crisis afflicted the UK. In the new structure, the Prudential Regulation Authority (PRA) was to be responsible for the prudential regulation and supervision of banks, building societies, credit unions, insurers and major investment firms,[15] with the statutory role of 'the promotion of the safety and soundness of PRA-authorised persons';[16] and 'specifically for insurers, to contribute to the securing of an appropriate degree of protection for policyholders'.[17] Concerns over the 'reckless' way in which some institutions imperilled their solvency without consideration of the risks to the country's financial system led to the PRA and FCA being given responsibility to prosecute a new criminal offence of 'relating to a decision causing a financial institution to fail'.[18] However, this would only apply to cases where a bank or financial institution had failed and entered insolvency. Thus, poor decision making at a bank or institution which did not result in insolvency would not be penalised. This is a significant deficiency and is not congruent with former Prime Minister Cameron's pre-coalition stance that 'those who break the law should face prosecution'.[19] Furthermore, the lack of criminal charges in the UK against any individual involved in the financial crisis casts doubt on the FCA's 'credible deterrence' strategy.[20] Thus, although the FCA has a range of administrative penalties and some criminal offences,[21] there is a gap for conduct that warrants a criminal

12 Roman Tomasic, 'The financial crisis and the haphazard pursuit of financial crime' (2011) 18(1) JFC 7, 8.
13 Tomasic, 'The financial crisis' (n 12) 7, 8.
14 HM Treasury, 'A new approach to financial regulation: The blueprint for reform' 3 June 2011 Cm 8083.
15 Prudential Regulation Authority, www.bankofengland.co.uk/PRA/Pages/default.aspx Accessed 11 March 2017.
16 Financial Services Act 2012, s 132.
17 Prudential Regulation Authority (n 15). Financial Services Act 2012, s 133.
18 Financial Services (Banking Reform) Act 2013, s 36.
19 Conservative Home, 'Cameron: We won't treat the richest any differently from the poorest' 15 December 2008 http://conservativehome.blogs.com/torydiary/2008/12/cameron-we-wont.html Accessed 11 March 2017.
20 Gary Wilson and Sarah Wilson, 'The FSA "credible deterrence" and criminal enforcement – a "haphazard pursuit"?' (2014) JFC 4.
21 Financial Services and Markets Act 2000 ss.19, 21, 24, 56(4), 85(3), 177, 398. Criminal Justice Act 1993 s 52. Financial Services Act 2012 ss 89, 90 & 91. Counter Terrorism Act 2008 Sch 7. Money Laundering Regulations 2007.

sanction in cases where there is no institutional failure or insolvency, and Fisher's proposal of a crime of 'reckless risk-taking'[22] provides an attractive solution.

The adoption of the twin peaks regulatory model represents a fulfilment of the coalition agreement, in contrast to the government's commitment to establish an ECA, where it has backtracked,[23] and which the following Conservative government from 2015 has not adopted. Instead of the SFO forming a key part of the overarching ECA, it had to fight for its continued existence because the Home Office established the National Crime Agency (NCA), an organisation responsible for activities ranging from border control to child exploitation and online protection but which includes an 'Economic Crime Command'.[24] This is a disappointment. Instead of the ECA being accountable to either the Attorney General, as a specialist prosecutor,[25] or HM Treasury, on a par with counter-terrorism financing, anti-money laundering or prudential regulation,[26] the NCA sits as a non-ministerial department within the Home Office.

The NCA has added another level of confusion because it has ambitions: 'it coordinates activity, shares intelligence and knowledge with partners, disrupting criminal activity, and seizing assets.'[27] Some of these activities are already undertaken by the SFO and FCA. Furthermore, the NCA has themes for its future work which include fraud,[28] bribery and corruption, market abuse, and insider dealing,[29] which are certainly key areas for the SFO and FCA.

Notwithstanding the claim of 'greater focus', the economic crime arena has become more rather than less diverse. Although the prospect of an ECA has receded, the two principal agencies have undoubtedly raised their profiles, but the SFO's future remains uncertain.[30] The profile of the FCA has been elevated because of its

22 Jonathan Fisher, 'Risk, Recklessness and Policing the Financial Markets' in N Ryder, U Turksen and S Hassler (eds), *Fighting Financial Crime in the Global Economic Crisis: Policy, Trends and Sanctions* (Routledge Cavendish 2014) 2.

23 BBC News, 'SFO saved by cabinet revolt' 28 May 2011 www.bbc.co.uk/news/13585972 Accessed 11 March 2017.

24 *Financial Times*, 'UK Economic Crime Agencies given fitness test' 12 March 2017 www.ft.com/content/cee98dde-05b0-11e7-aa5b-6bb07f5c8e12 Accessed 20 March 2017.

25 Who presently superintends SFO.

26 Which superintends the FCA, in addition to the Bank of England. However, even counter-terrorism financing suffers the same issues, as the Home Affairs Committee report: 'This is further compounded by the fact that in the UK, the responsibility for countering terrorism finance is spread across a number of departmental departments and agencies with no department in charge of overseeing the policy.' Home Affairs Committee, *Counter-terrorism* (HC 2013–14, 231) 50.

27 National Crime Agency, 'Economic Crime Command Director appointed to National Crime Agency' www.nationalcrimeagency.gov.uk/news/313-economic-crime-command-director-appointed-to-the-national-crime-agency Accessed 1 March 2017.

28 '[F]raud against the individual, the private and the third sectors; fraud against the public sector (these are high priority).' National Crime Agency, 'NCA Annual Plan 2014/15' 8 www.nationalcrimeagency.gov.uk/publications/176-nca-annual-plan-2014-15/file Accessed 1 March 2017.

29 National Crime Agency, 'NCA Annual Plan 2014/15' (n 28) 8.

30 *The Times*, 'Abolishing fraud agency "would cause chaos"' www.thetimes.co.uk/tto/news/politics/article4229101.ece Accessed 11 March 2017.

facility as a regulator to be able to impose financial penalties.[31] These penalties have been significant, mainly as a result of LIBOR failings, and in 2013 totalled £476m, £1.47bn in 2014 and £905m in 2015.[32]

The government's intention for the FCA was of 'delivering a regulatory regime under which the conduct of business of *all* retail financial services is regulated by a single body'.[33] The FCA has 'a single overarching strategic objective to ensure that markets function well'.[34] One of the FCA's operational objectives is integrity:[35] 'protecting and enhancing the integrity of the UK financial system',[36] and includes 'not being used for a purpose connected with financial crime'.[37] In pursuit of these objectives, the FCA has continued the policy of 'credible deterrence', for which 'the imposition of a financial penalty is central'.[38] This policy has certain fiscal attractions because significant monies are raised for the Exchequer.[39] However, 'many breaches of FSMA occur where firms lack adequate controls, supervision and organisation rather than where they display wilful misconduct'.[40] The 'credible deterrence' policy, whilst remunerative, has not answered questions such as that posed by Judge Rakoff in relation to the financial crisis of 'why have no high level executives been prosecuted?'[41] Thus, 'the failure of the government to bring to justice those responsible for such colossal fraud bespeaks weaknesses in our prosecutorial system that need to be addressed'.[42] Although Rakoff's perspective is in relation to the US, the same questions and reasoning equally apply to the UK.

The SFO is an organisation whose *raison d'être* is 'greater focus' on economic crime. It has a unique role because of its power both to investigate and prosecute crimes, unlike the police and Crown Prosecution Service, which have separate roles. The SFO has the recent benefit of the Bribery Act and DPAs, though

31 Financial Services and Markets Act 2000, s 206.
32 See Chapter 2.
33 HM Treasury, 'A new approach to financial regulation: Transferring consumer credit regulation to the Financial Conduct Authority' www.gov.uk/government/uploads/system/uploads/attachment_data/file/221913/consult_transferring_consumer_credit_regulation_to_fca.pdf Accessed 11 March 2017.
34 HM Treasury, 'A new approach to financial regulation' (n 33).
35 Financial Services Act 2012, s 1B(3).
36 Financial Services Act 2012, s 1D(1).
37 Financial Services Act 2012, s 1D(2)(b).
38 Peter Cartwright, 'Credible Deterrence and Consumer Protection through Imposition of Financial Penalties: Lessons for the Financial Conduct Authority' in N Ryder, U Turksen and S Hassler (eds), *Fighting Financial Crime in the Global Economic Crisis: Policy, Trends and Sanctions* (Routledge Cavendish 2014) 5.
39 Financial Conduct Authority, 'Financial services regulation and enforcement: recent developments and emerging issues' www.fca.org.uk/news/speeches/financial-services-regulation-enforcement Accessed 1 March 2017.
40 Cartwright (n 38) 6.
41 J S Rakoff, 'The financial crisis: Why have no high-level executives been prosecuted?' The New York Review of Books www.nybooks.com/articles/archives/2014/jan/09/financial-crisis-why-no-executive-prosecutions/ Accessed 24 November 2016.
42 Rakoff, 'The financial crisis' (n 41).

neither had an immediate impact for two reasons. First, because the prosecution of Bribery Act offences was for activities after July 2011[43] and there is a lengthy lead time for cases to reach trial. Second, because DPAs only became available from February 2014. However, the SFO has contributed to discussions on learning the lessons from the financial crisis and answering Rakoff's question: notwithstanding that it has only taken one case to trial under the Bribery Act s 7 (*Sweett*),[44] they have proposed an extension of the Bribery Act offence of 'failure to prevent bribery'.[45] Instead of having to prove that high-level executives were the 'controlling mind', the SFO proposed a corporate offence of 'failing to prevent economic crime',[46] which would make the firm liable for all such offences.

However, in terms of performance, the SFO has also been unable to shake off the past reputation of being maladroit because it seems that each success in investigation and prosecution is matched by examples of the SFO suffering from problems of its own making.

The facility to conclude DPAs has provided some positive headlines. The first two cases were relatively modest but in 2017, the SFO concluded a DPA with Rolls-Royce totalling £671m,[47] indicating that the SFO's DPA regime is gaining momentum.

Lessons from the US and Australia

United States

The US has a dominant position as the largest single country in terms of international trade[48] and its experience[49] of combating economic crime, consequently,

43 Prosecutions for events prior to July 2011 utilise: Public Bodies Corrupt Practices Act 1889, Prevention of Corruption Act 1906, Prevention of Corruption Act 1916, and Anti-terrorism, Crime and Security Act 2001.
44 *SFO v Sweett Group PLC* (Unreported).
45 Serious Fraud Office, 'Ethical business conduct: An enforcement perspective' www.sfo.gov.uk/2014/03/06/ethical-business-conduct-enforcement-perspective/ Accessed 11 March 2017.
46 Serious Fraud Office, 'Ethical business conduct' (n 45).
47 Serious Fraud Office, 'SFO confirms DPA in principle with Rolls-Royce PLC' www.sfo.gov.uk/2017/01/16/sfo-confirms-dpa-in-principle-with-rolls-royce-plc/ Accessed 20 March 2017.
48 Some 9.1% of global exports and 13.8% of global imports. World Trade Organization, 'Table A6, Leading exporters and importers in world merchandise trade, 2015' www.wto.org/english/res_e/statis_e/wts2016_e/wts16_chap9_e.htm Accessed 12 December 2016.
49 The DoJ state that between 2009 and 2013, they charged more white collar defendants than during any previous five-year period going back to at least 1994. Since 2009, over 60 cases against financial institutions have resulted in recoveries totalling over $85 billion. Department of Justice, 'Attorney General Holder remarks on financial fraud prosecutions at NYU School of Law' www.justice.gov/opa/speech/attorney-general-holder-remarks-financial-fraud-prosecutions-nyu-school-law Accessed 1 March 2017.

has to be relevant. This is demonstrated by the lead it took in contemporary measures against bribery and corruption by criminalising bribery and corruption internationally when it enacted the Foreign Corrupt Practices Act 1977 (FCPA).

The date of the FCPA is significant because it slightly pre-dates the 1979 base to significant structural changes in UK regulation and legislation. Thus, knowledge of US experience would have been available to UK governments to inform domestic decision making. Over the succeeding time period, the FCPA, as deployed by the Department of Justice (DoJ) and Securities and Exchange Commission (SEC), has become more prominent: considerable fines have been levied for FCPA breaches, together with an extensively interpreted extra-territorial jurisdiction. Furthermore, the US has been a driving force to encourage European and Organisation for Economic Co-operation and Development (OECD) nations to 'ramp up enforcement of their anti-bribery laws on both a domestic and international basis'.[50] The FCPA was a unique and original piece of legislation because it was the 'first international anti-bribery statute of its type and scope in the world',[51] or, to be more accurate, domestic statute with international scope. However, having introduced this legislation, the motivation for extension to other countries resulted, in Feldman's opinion, from the US being 'viewed as the policeman for the world'.[52] Congress later concluded that, because of the FCPA, 'American businesses have operated at a disadvantage relative to foreign competitors who have continued to pay bribes without fear of a penalty'.[53] Furthermore, other countries were criticised for making such payments tax deductible,[54] which would indicate that such payments were treated as a legitimate business expense.[55]

In looking to see what features of the US system to deal with fraud, bribery and corruption could be translated with benefit to the UK, this book has examined the US regulatory and legislative provisions and the institutions charged with their enforcement. Such research is in light of changes that have already taken place in the same areas in the UK of fraud, bribery and corruption.

50 Warren Feldman, 'Staying in Compliance: Key Issues for White Collar Law Attorneys and their Multinational Clients' in *International White Collar Enforcement, 2013 edition. Leading Lawyers on Preventative Measures, Regulatory Compliance, and Litigation* (Thompson Reuters/Aspatore 2013).

51 Heidi L Hansberry, 'In spite of its good intentions, the Dodd-Frank Act has created an FCPA monster' (2012) 102 JCRLC 195.

52 Feldman (n 50).

53 Department of Justice, 'Proposed legislative history. International Anti-Bribery Act of 1998' www.justice.gov/criminal/fraud/fcpa/docs/leghistory.pdf Accessed 11 March 2017.

54 Department of Justice, 'Proposed legislative history' (n 53).

55 Newspaper report indicates Russia takes a similar view. *The Telegraph*, 'Russian officials told bribes are not tax deductible' 4 September 2012 www.telegraph.co.uk/finance/financial-crime/9519292/Russian-officials-told-bribes-are-not-tax-deductible.html Accessed 11 March 2017.

Australia

Australia is chosen for comparison because it is 'a significant economy, exporter and international investor', which means that it has the propensity to be a target for economic crime.[56] In the OECD, Australia was the 12th largest economy and 14th largest exporter of goods and services, and its largest trading partner was China.[57] From a UK perspective, its connections with Australia 'go back to the British Empire when some countries were ruled directly or indirectly by Britain',[58] and it also has a common law tradition. Furthermore, since the onset of the most recent financial crisis, and unlike the US and UK, Australia is regarded as having withstood the effects more successfully than other leading industrial nations which, thus, invites enquiry into the underlying reasons.[59] One reason advanced for this is that Australia adopted the twin peaks[60] model of financial regulation[61] which 'structures regulation around two agencies, one responsible for the safety and soundness of all financial firms and the other for regulating their sales practices'.[62] Lui observes that 'Australian banks have withstood the financial crisis better than UK banks. Australia did not have any bank runs. Four of the nine AA-rated banks around the world are Australian banks, so the Australian regulation system worked well'.[63]

Nevertheless, the Australian Institute of Criminology is of the view that serious fraud in Australia is seen as both widespread and costly,[64] and 'one of the most under-reported offences in Australia, with fewer than 50 per cent of incidents being reported to police or other authorities'.[65] Furthermore, the United Nations Convention against Corruption (UNCAC),[66] reported that the Australian

56 Organisation for Economic Co-operation and Development (OECD), 'Phase 3 Report on implementing the OECD Anti-Bribery Convention in Australia' October 2012 www.oecd.org/daf/anti-bribery/Australiaphase3reportEN.pdf Accessed 1 March 2017.

57 World Bank, 'GDP ranking' http://data.worldbank.org/data-catalog/GDP-ranking-table Accessed 20 March 2017. OECD, 'Phase 3 Report' (n 56).

58 The Commonwealth, 'History' http://thecommonwealth.org/our-history Accessed 1 March 2017.

59 Levi and Smith (n 8).

60 'The "twin peaks" idea and nomenclature are attributable to Michael Taylor, a former officer of the Bank of England (…) In 1995, Taylor wrote an article entitled: *"Twin Peaks": a regulatory structure for the new century*' (Centre for the Study of Financial Innovation, London). Jeremy Cooper, Australian Securities and Investments Commission, 'The integration of financial regulatory authorities – the Australian experience', 4–5 September 2006 2 http://download.asic.gov.au/media/1339352/integration-financial-regulatory-authorities.pdf Accessed 11 March 2017.

61 Cooper (n 60) 2.

62 Michael W Taylor, 'The road from "Twin Peaks" – and the way back' (2009) 16(1) Connecticut ILJ 61.

63 Alison Lui, 'Macro and micro prudential regulatory failures between banks in the United Kingdom and Australia 2004–2009' (2013) 21(3) JFR&C 242, 243.

64 Australian Institute of Criminology, www.aic.gov.au/crime_types/economic/fraud.html Accessed 11 March 2017.

65 Australian Institute of Criminology (n 64).

66 UNCAC, www.unodc.org/documents/treaties/UNCAC/Publications/Convention/08-50026_E.pdf. UNCAC, 'UNCAC Implementation Review Group meeting on 18

'government's approach to corruption is based on the idea that *no single body* should be solely responsible for anti-corruption'.[67] This is interesting because it is a conclusion of this book that a multiplicity of UK anti-economic crime agencies is counter-productive.

Although Australia represents itself internationally as a single country, under the Commonwealth of Australia (Commonwealth) Constitution it is 'a federal system in which legislative, executive and judicial powers are shared or distributed between the Commonwealth and six states'.[68] The consequence of this structure for economic crime is that 'the Commonwealth Parliament does not have specific power with regard to criminal law'[69] as a result of which 'most criminal activity is governed by the [varying] laws of the states. This is true for offences of corruption, including fraud and bribery'.[70]

This chapter will draw conclusions on the issues of economic crime and regulation from the standpoints of the UK, the US and Australia to identify areas where UK practice can be improved or, alternatively, where the US and Australia might recognise advantages in a UK approach.

Fraud

United Kingdom

The UK has a number of agencies[71] that may either investigate or prosecute fraud but the only agency with a specific role for fraud is the SFO. The SFO was established[72] to tackle 'the topmost tier of serious and complex fraud and bribery',[73] in a clear contrast with financial regulators, which have been criticised for a 'light-touch' approach and an 'overly close relationship with the City'.[74] The SFO has a focused role: 'we are investigators and prosecutors of the topmost tier of

June 2012. Executive summary' www.ag.gov.au/CrimeAndCorruption/AntiCorruption/Pages/Globalleadershipincombatingcorruption.aspx Accessed 1 March 2017.

67 UNCAC (n 66) (emphasis added).

68 'It also enables the Commonwealth Parliament to make laws in relation to territories. There are ten territories, of which three are self-governing.' Australian Government, 'State and territory government' www.australia.gov.au/about-government/how-government-works/state-and-territory-government Accessed 11 March 2017.

69 'However, the Commonwealth can enact criminal laws relying on other powers, for example those that are expressly provided for under the Constitution.' Australian Government, 'The Commonwealth's approach to anti-corruption' http://transparency.org.au/wp-content/uploads/2012/07/Anti-Corruption-Discussion-Paper-FINAL-PDF-15-March-2012.pdf Accessed 4 January 2017 10.

70 Australian Government, Attorney General's Department, 'The Commonwealth's approach to anti-corruption' (n 69) 10.

71 Some 43 police forces, with the City of London Police as a specialist force; the SFO, the FCA, CMA, HMRC, and NCA.

72 Criminal Justice Act 1987, s 1(1).

73 Serious Fraud Office, 'Ethical business conduct' (n 45).

74 Tomasic, 'The financial crisis' (n 12) 7, 8.

serious and complex fraud, bribery and corruption. We are not a regulator, a deal-maker or a confessor.'[75]

In the economic crime arena, fraud was relatively neglected until the establishment of the SFO and then, following a significant gestation period, specific legislation: the Fraud Act. The Fraud Act 'has simplified the law by providing a new offence of fraud instead of a variety of ineffective deception offences under the Theft Acts'.[76]

Since 2014, the UK has been able to use DPAs, which have been extensively used in the US, a practice which provided a clear example to inform UK thinking and is evidence of the UK learning lessons from the manner in which another country is able to tackle economic crime. The view of the SFO is that 'DPAs provide an alternative response to *some* corporate criminality, a response which avoids that collateral damage [which would impact on innocent parties]. The route to a DPA should also be cheaper, quicker and more certain for all parties'.[77]

The SFO has recognised that even the Fraud Act might not be sufficient to counter the challenges faced in prosecuting the manipulation of LIBOR and have proposed an extension of the offence of 'failure to prevent bribery'[78] as their contribution to answering the Rakoff question. Instead of having to prove that high-level executives were the 'controlling mind', the SFO propose an offence of 'failing to prevent all acts of financial crime',[79] which would make the firm liable for all such offences by its staff. Not only would this have direct financial consequences but also carry with it the 'threat of debarment from tendering for public contracts of any kind across the whole of the EU, which is thought to be far more worrying for corporations than one-off fines, whatever the size'.[80]

LIBOR[81] involved allegations that bankers colluded to manipulate interest rates.[82] The City regulator fined Barclays £59.5m, followed by UBS £160m, RBS £87.5m, Lloyds £105m, Rabobank £105m and Deutsche £227m.[83] LIBOR is important because it is the 'benchmark reference rate fundamental to the operation of both UK and international financial markets, including markets in interest

75 Serious Fraud Office, 'Ethical business conduct: An enforcement perspective' (n 45).

76 David Ormerod, 'The Fraud Act 2006 – Criminalised lying?' (2007) Crim LR 193–219.

77 Serious Fraud Office, 'Ethical business conduct' (n 45). Explanation added.

78 Serious Fraud Office, 'Ethical business conduct' (n 45).

79 Serious Fraud Office, 'Ethical business conduct' (n 45).

80 *The Telegraph*, 'Firms face EU blacklist in bribery law change' www.telegraph.co.uk/finance/financial-crime/10613645/Firms-face-EU-blacklist-in-bribery-law-change.html Accessed 11 March 2017.

81 Financial Services Authority, 'Barclays fined £59.5 million for significant failings in relation to LIBOR and EURIBOR' www.fsa.gov.uk/library/communication/pr/2012/070.shtml Accessed 11 March 2017.

82 Attorney General's Office, 'Fighting economic crime in the modern world' www.gov.uk/government/speeches/fighting-economic-crime-in-the-modern-world Accessed 11 March 2017.

83 See Chapter 2.

rate derivatives contracts'.[84] Additionally, the SFO announced that it had agreed to investigate the alleged manipulation of LIBOR: 13 people were charged with fraud or conspiracy to defraud; five were convicted; six acquitted; and two are awaiting retrial. Some 11 people face similar charges relating to EURIBOR.[85] However, both the City regulator and SFO were criticised for earlier failing to initiate a criminal investigation.[86] The government described the LIBOR scandal as 'the most high profile current issue in the United Kingdom',[87] which serves to highlight the role of two different organisations where the regulator seemed satisfied to impose a financial penalty without addressing the issue of criminal sanctions. Clearly, with both FCA and SFO as part of an ECA, there could have been greater clarity of thinking and a cohesive approach.

The LIBOR scandal shone light on the financial system where the Bank of England is responsible for 'efficient and effective financial markets',[88] and 'for the stability of the system as a whole',[89] while the FCA has 'responsibility to oversee financial markets'.[90] This is clearly confusing but demonstrates that the anti-economic crime arena is multifaceted. Furthermore, other serious allegations have arisen of manipulation of the foreign exchange markets,[91] described by the FCA as 'every bit as bad as they have been with LIBOR'.[92] The SFO investigated but could not obtain sufficient evidence to prosecute, although the FCA fined five banks £1.1bn.[93] In this case, questions have arisen over the involvement of the Bank of England,[94] which responded that it would 'tighten

84 Financial Services Authority, 'Barclays Bank plc – Final Notice' 27 June 2012 www.fsa.gov.uk/static/pubs/final/barclays-jun12.pdf Accessed 1 March 2017.

85 Serious Fraud Office, 'LIBOR' www.sfo.gov.uk/cases/libor-landing/ Accessed 11 March 2017. Serious Fraud Office, 'Euribor' www.sfo.gov.uk/cases/euribor/ Accessed 11 March 2017.

86 House of Commons Treasury Committee, 'Fixing LIBOR: Some preliminary findings. Second Report of Session 2012–13 Volume I' www.publications.parliament.uk/pa/cm201213/cmselect/cmtreasy/481/481ii.pdf Accessed 11 March 2017.

87 Attorney General's Office, 'Fighting economic crime' (n 82).

88 Bank of England, 'News Release – Bank of England launches strategic plan' 18 March 2014 www.bankofengland.co.uk//publications/Pages/news/2014/058.aspx Accessed 1 March 2017.

89 *The Sunday Times*, 'FCA ignored warnings of false market' 6 April 2014 www.thesundaytimes.co.uk/sto/business/Finance/article1396697.ece Accessed 1 March 2017.

90 *The Sunday Times*, 'FCA ignored warnings of false market' 6 April 2014 (n 89).

91 *Financial Times*, 'Forex claims "as bad as Libor", says FCA' 4 February 2014 www.ft.com/cms/s/0/6d2f697a-8da8-11e3-bbe7-00144feab7de.html#axzz2wz74O2Ae Accessed 11 March 2017.

92 *Financial Times*, 'Forex claims "as bad as Libor", says FCA' 4 February 2014 (n 91).

93 Serious Fraud Office, 'SFO closes forex investigation' www.sfo.gov.uk/2016/03/15/sfo-closes-forex-investigation/ Accessed 9 March 2017. Financial Conduct Authority, 'FCA fines five banks £1.1 billion for FX failings and announces industry-wide remediation programme' www.fca.org.uk/news/fca-fines-five-banks-for-fx-failings Accessed 11 March 2017.

94 *Financial Times*, 'Bank of England suspends employee amid forex probe' 5 March 2014 www.ft.com/cms/s/260bfb68-a45e-11e3-b915-00144feab7de.html Accessed

its governance',[95] and 'establish an enquiry'.[96] Following the revelations about manipulation of LIBOR (there were similar issues in Australia),[97] and the foreign exchange markets, it was revealed that similar manipulation had taken place in the London Gold Market which, hitherto, had 'always managed to shroud itself in a carefully cultivated aura of glamorous mystery'.[98] The FCA has fined Barclays £26m,[99] and banned a trader for offences relating to the manipulation of the market for gold at a daily meeting known, ironically, as 'gold fixing'.[100]

Thus, the interplay between the regulators of the markets and potential for SFO investigations will be interesting to observe because it has the potential to reveal either gaps in regulation, or inertia caused by overlap between regulators. The need for primacy in regulation is underlined by the Bank of England's concern that its parallel regulator, the FCA, had caused a false market in shares when announcing an enquiry into zombie (insurance) funds in 2014.[101] If the tripartite regime was criticised for confusion over roles and responsibilities, it is important that the markets have one ultimate regulator and that should be the Bank of England because it is responsible for the stability of the system as a whole.

11 March 2017. Nicholas Ryder, 'The good, the bad and the ugly' (2014) 221 Crim Law 5.

95 BBC, 'Bank of England in shake-up after rate manipulation criticism' 11 March 2014 www.bbc.co.uk/news/business-26523995 Accessed March 2017.

96 *Financial Times*, 'Top barrister chosen to lead Bank of England forex enquiry' 12 March 2014 www.ft.com/cms/s/e2a5e2b6-aa03-11e3-8bd6-00144feab7de,html Accessed 11 March 2017.*The Telegraph*, 'Banks fined over £2bn after currency rigging investigation' www.telegraph.co.uk/finance/newsbysector/banksandfinance/11223764/Banks-fined-over-2bn-after-currency-rigging-investigation.html Accessed 1 March 2017.

97 Australian Securities and Investments Commission (ASIC), 'Financial benchmarks' www.asic.gov.au/media/3285136/rep440-published-8-july-2015.pdf Accessed 11 March 2017.

98 Hamish McRae and Frances Cairncross, *Capital City* (Eyre Methuen 1973) 190.

99 Financial Conduct Authority, 'Final Notice' www.fca.org.uk/static/documents/final-notices/barclays-bank-plc.pdf Accessed March 2017.

100 'The Gold Fixing is an important pricing mechanism which provides market users with the opportunity to buy and sell gold at a single quoted price.' Financial Conduct Authority, 'Barclays fined £26m for failings surrounding the London Gold Fixing and former Barclays trader banned and fined for inappropriate conduct' www.fca.org.uk/news/barclays-fined-26m-for-failings-surrounding-the-london-gold-fixing. Financial Services and Markets Act 2000, s 118(5). 'The FCA has fined Plunkett £95,600 and banned him from performing any function in relation to any regulated activity.' Financial Conduct Authority, 'Final Notice' www.fca.org.uk/static/documents/final-notices/daniel-james-plunkett.pdf Accessed 11 March 2017. There do not appear to be similar allegations in Australia and the US but the FBI have announced 'High-frequency trader indicted for manipulating commodities futures markets in first federal prosecution for spoofing': Federal Bureau of Investigation, www.fbi.gov/chicago/press-releases/2014/high-frequency-trader-indicted-for-manipulating-commodities-futures-markets-in-first-federal-prosecution-for-spoofing Accessed 11 March 2017.

101 *The Sunday Times*, 'FCA ignored warnings of false market' (n 89).

In the context of serious allegations about the markets and their supervision, the role of the SFO as an independent prosecutor is likely to be pivotal. There are other prosecutors but the SFO only tackles the 'top level of serious or complex fraud, bribery and corruption'.[102] However, the FCA prosecuted a £20m land banking fraud with charges being: 'conspiracy to defraud'; criminal offences relating to the carrying out of a regulated activity without authorisation; and money laundering.[103] This was a case described by the judge as 'complex and substantial',[104] and although marketed to the public, is evidence of conduct that would normally suggest serious fraud and, thus, be prosecuted by the SFO. To show the contrary approach, in the JJB case, which involved allegations of forgery[105] and making misleading statements to the stock market, the prosecution was undertaken by the SFO under the FSMA,[106] whereas since the conduct was related to the markets, the FCA would appear to have been more appropriate.

United States

The US has demonstrated its commitment to combating fraud by establishing the Financial Fraud Enforcement Task Force (FFETF), with '$330m to investigate any suspected instances of mortgage fraud and to pursue any potential prosecutions that arise from those investigations'.[107] This is in marked contrast to the UK's SFO, where the government planned to reduce its budget to £30m in 2014/15.[108] Thus, a key difference is the disparity in resources between the US and the UK. This is also a matter highlighted in examining the FCA's resources. Therefore, it can be seen that the SFO is not only disadvantaged in relation to its domestic regulatory counterpart but also to the US endeavour to prosecute fraud.

While the funding of the FFETF is important, there is an underlying reason which is to do with the US constitutional structure of federal and state law, and the number and variety of law enforcement and regulatory agencies, as is also seen in Australia.[109] The rationale of the FFETF was 'we know that we can accomplish

102 Serious Fraud Office, 'What we do' www.sfo.gov.uk/about-us/ Accessed 11 March 2017.

103 *Asset Land Investments v FCA* [2016] UKSC 17. Financial Services and Markets Act 2000, s 19; Proceeds of Crime Act 2002, s 329(1)(c). Financial Conduct Authority, 'FCA wins case in Supreme Court' www.fca.org.uk/news/press-releases/fca-wins-case-supreme-court Accessed 8 March 2017.

104 *Asset Land* (n 103).

105 Forgery and Counterfeiting Act 1981, s 3.

106 Financial Services and Markets Act 2000, s 397(1)(b). Serious Fraud Office, 'JJB Sports – D Jones and S Jones' www.sfo.gov.uk/cases/jjb-sports-sir-d-jones-s-jones/ Accessed 8 March 2017.

107 Nicholas Ryder and Clare Chambers, 'The Credit Crunch and Mortgage Fraud – Too Little Too Late? A Comparative Analysis of the Policies Adopted in the United States of America and the United Kingdom' in I Balogh and S Kis (eds), *Housing, Housing Costs and Mortgages: Trends, Impact and Prediction* (Nova Science Publishers 2010) 11.

108 See Chapter 2.

109 'In the USA, the picture is complicated even more by the Federal and state infrastructure. Federal agencies such as the Federal Bureau of Investigation (FBI) have

so much more by working together than working in isolated, compartmentalised silos'.[110] The UK may also have a variety of regulators and agencies but is not hampered by a federal constitution; this research does not propose a change to the UK's constitutional structure, but that does not mean that there are not aspects of the US response to fraud which should not be considered.

Legislation to criminalise fraud is another area for consideration. In the US, fraud statutes are either generic, such as 'conspiracy', 'mail' or 'wire' frauds; or specific, such as 'bankruptcy', 'healthcare' or 'bank' fraud. In the former category, Podgor notes that the 'focus of the statute is almost exclusively on the fraud and not the object of the offense'.[111] Thus, in the Mail Fraud Statute 'the mailing element seemingly provides federal prosecutors with carte blanche to prosecute virtually any activity to which the mail or a shipment by interstate carrier can be linked, no matter how tangential'.[112] The Wire Fraud Statute 'requires some interstate or international communications by means of a "wire" (such as telephone lines), radio or television'.[113] Together, these statutes amount to a federal fraud statute[114] and are also used as a predicate for other statutes.[115] In addition to being combined with conspiracy to defraud,[116] Gordon observes that it has been interpreted to be 'so elastic over the years that it can potentially encompass any conduct which a court views as "collusive and dishonest"'.[117]

The main differences between the US and the UK lie in their fraud statutes. However, whereas the US not only retains but builds upon its structure of a variety of fraud statutes, in the UK the Fraud Act has provided a clear statement that fraud is by 'false representation',[118] 'failing to disclose information',[119] and 'abuse of position'.[120] The conclusion of this research is that the UK has already

jurisdiction over a wide range of different types of fraud and corruption, such as public sector fraud and corruption, mass marketing fraud and identity fraud. However, there is also the Securities and Exchange Commission, which takes the lead on investment fraud; the Internal Revenue Service Criminal Investigation division, which deals with tax fraud; the United States Postal Inspectors, mail fraud; the United States Secret Service, credit card fraud/currency fraud; and many others with particular responsibilities. This is on top of a state bureaucracy of law enforcement which is often as diverse and complex as at Federal level.' Mark Button and Jim Gee, *Countering Fraud for Competitive Advantage* (Wiley 2013) 52.

110 Michael J. Bresnick, Financial Fraud Enforcement Task Force Executive Director, Speech, 20 March 2013 www.justice.gov/iso/opa/doj/speeches/2013/opa-speech-130320.html Accessed 11 March 2017.

111 Ellen S Podgor, 'Criminal fraud' (1999) 48 Am U L Rev 729.

112 Peter J Henning, 'Maybe it should just be called federal fraud: The changing nature of the mail fraud statute' (1995) 36 BCL Rev 435.

113 Jed S Rakoff, 'The Federal Mail Fraud Statute (Part I)' (1980) 18 Duq L Rev 771.

114 Henning (n 112) 435.

115 18 U.S.C. §§ 1961–1968 (2006 & Supp. 2009).

116 18 U.S.C. § 371 – Conspiracy to Defraud the United States.

117 Steven D Gordon, 'The liability of colleges and universities for fraud, waste, and abuse in federally funded grants and project' (1992) 75 EDUc L REP 13.

118 Fraud Act 2006, s 2.

119 Fraud Act 2006, s 3.

120 Fraud Act 2006, s 4.

modernised its legislation to produce a straightforward suite of criminal offences and would not benefit from a change to US-style legislation. By the same token the US is clearly wedded to its pattern of legislation and adopting a simplified UK-style fraud act would be difficult.[121]

While the US and UK use different mechanisms to criminalise fraud, another disparity is in sentencing. In the US, the economic crime offender with the longest prison sentence on record is Shalmon Weiss, sentenced in 2000 to 845 years in prison.[122] More widely known because of the financial crisis is Bernard Madoff, sentenced to 150 years' imprisonment,[123] and Allen Stanford to 110 years.[124] In contrast, in the UK, the maximum sentence under the Fraud Act and Bribery Act is ten years' imprisonment and/or an unlimited fine.[125] The UK has not seen frauds of this magnitude; however, in *R v James McCormick*, [126] McCormick was convicted and sentenced to ten years' imprisonment for selling fake explosives detectors to Iraq, the first maximum sentence. There is a clear disparity between headline sentences but, putting aside the appropriateness of UK sentencing, there is disquiet in the US about the length of sentences where pressure from Congress has 'transformed sentences in high-loss fraud cases from less than five years under the original guidelines to a sentence of life imprisonment'.[127] There is concern over 'over-criminalisation' whereby federal prosecutors have 'access to too many charging choices'[128] and that 'prosecutors will pile on charges to gain leverage in plea negotiations'.[129] The US Attorney General's view is that legislation with

121 Roman Tomasic, 'Governance and the evaluation of corporate law and regulation in Australia' (2001) 1(3) Corporate Governance 24.
122 Brian K Payne, *White-collar Crime* (Sage 2013) 370. Net loss to creditors. Federal Bureau of Investigation, 'Court of Appeals affirms Sholam Weiss' convictions on racketeering, fraud, and money laundering charges' www.fbi.gov/tampa/press-releases/2013/court-of-appeals-affirms-sholam-weiss-convictions-on-racketeering-fraud-and-money-laundering-charges Accessed 11 March 2017.
123 Daniel V Dooley and Mark Radke, 'Does severe punishment deter financial crimes' (2010) 4 Charleston L Rev 619. Net loss estimated to be $17.5bn. Reuters, 'UPDATE 1-Madoff, Stanford fraud victims dealt setbacks by U.S. top court' www.reuters.com/article/2014/06/30/usa-court-madoff-stanford-idUSL2N0PB0YE20140630 Accessed 11 March 2017.
124 'Allen Stanford sentenced to 110 years in prison for orchestrating $7 billion investment fraud scheme.' Department of Justice, www.justice.gov/opa/pr/2012/June/12-crm-756.html Accessed 11 March 2017.
125 Fraud Act 2006, s 1(3)(b). Bribery Act 2010, s 11. Asil Nadir was sentenced to ten years' imprisonment in 2012 but that was for offences under the earlier Theft Act 1968. Serious Fraud Office, 'Asil Nadir sentenced' www.sfo.gov.uk/2012/08/23/asil-nadir-sentenced/ Accessed 11 March 2017.
126 T20120228. Judiciary of England and Wales, 'Central Criminal Court, 2 May 2013, Sentencing remarks of His Honour Judge Hone QC' www.judiciary.gov.uk/wp-content/uploads/JCO/Documents/Judgments/r-v-mccormack-sentencing-remarks-20130502.pdf Accessed 11 March 2017.
127 Robert J Anello and Richard F Albert, 'Overcriminalization of non-violent conduct: Time for real reform' (2013) 249 NYLJ 106.
128 Anello and Albert (n 127) 106.
129 Anello and Albert (n 127) 106.

mandatory sentences that bear little relation to the conduct at issue[130] results in 'too many people go[ing] to too many prisons for far too long for no good law enforcement reason'.[131] The outcome of this is that such sentences 'breed disrespect and are ultimately counterproductive',[132] which means that there needs to be a change 'to ensure that incarceration is used to punish, to rehabilitate, and to deter – and not simply to warehouse and forget'.[133]

Thus, whilst there is some attraction in headlines given to long prison sentences in the US, as with the Australian 'heads on pikes',[134] in the UK, the Sentencing Guidelines Council has introduced guidelines that place 'victim impact at the centre of considerations of what sentence the offender should get. This may mean higher sentences for some offenders compared to the current guideline, particularly where the financial loss is relatively small but the impact on the victim is high'.[135] Furthermore, 'consecutive sentences may be appropriate for multiple offences where large sums are involved'.[136]

Having considered whether there are lessons that the UK could usefully learn from the US, from a pure fraud viewpoint, this research concludes that the UK Fraud Act, with its straightforward approach consolidating previous legislation, is more appropriate to the UK than the US style of myriad statutes. Sentencing is an area where the US differs from the UK by providing longer sentences where the 'Fraud Review' recommended a maximum of 14 years[137] instead of the current ten, but even without legislation this could be achieved by amending the Sentencing Guidelines. One aspect of US practice that has been adopted is that of DPAs, which are available for fraud offences.[138]

Australia

Fraud in Australia is criminalised by the individual states and territories under a variety of property offences such as 'theft and obtaining a financial advantage by deception',[139] together with 'conspiracy to defraud'.[140] At the Commonwealth

130 Eric Holder, US Attorney General, 'Speech to 15th Annual National Action Network Convention' 4 April 2013 www.justice.gov/iso/opa/ag/speeches/2013/ag-speech-130404.html Accessed 11 March 2017 (emphasis added).
131 Holder, 'Speech' (n 130).
132 Holder, 'Speech' (n 130).
133 Holder, 'Speech' (n 130).
134 Cooper (n 60) 6.
135 Sentencing Council, 'New sentencing guidelines bring increased focus to the impact of fraud on victims' www.sentencingcouncil.org.uk/news/item/new-sentencing-guidelines-bring-increased-focus-to-the-impact-of-fraud-on-victims/ Accessed 11 March 2017.
136 Sentencing Council, 'Fraud, bribery and money laundering offences. Definitive guideline' http://sentencingcouncil.judiciary.gov.uk/docs/Fraud_bribery_and_money_laundering_offences_-_Definitive_guideline.pdf Accessed 11 March 2017.
137 Attorney General's Office, *Fraud review – Final report* (London: Attorney General's Office 2006).
138 Fraud Act 2006 Part 2.
139 Russell G Smith, 'Fraud and financial abuse of older persons' (2000) 11 Current Issues in Crim Just 273.
140 Russell G Smith (n 139) 273.

level, law has been codified;[141] however, the Commonwealth Code 1995[142] only applies to matters within the Commonwealth purview and that does not extend to the individual states or territories. This book has considered the Australian constitutional structure but, as Tomasic notes, 'once a pattern of corporate law and regulation is formed, deviation from this pattern becomes difficult, although not impossible, as the constitutional framework of Australian corporations law illustrates'.[143] This provides a difficulty in considering whether the Australian endeavours to combat economic crime provide a template for the UK.

In New South Wales, the Crimes Act 1900 was amended in 2009 to introduce one general fraud offence and three ancillary offences, but the significance of the change, according to Steel, was that New South Wales did not follow the UK's Fraud Act, criticising it for being too broadly defined,[144] and instead because of its legislative heritage based its new law on the UK Theft Act 1968.[145] The other Australian states and territories have differing approaches from each other and the Commonwealth, which exhibit complicating factors leading to a conclusion that there are no attractions for the UK in adopting Australian fraud legislation.

Notwithstanding the complications occasioned by the suite of statutes to criminalise fraud, the second aspect of considering whether Australia provides an example that could be adopted by the UK is the manner in which the laws are deployed. In this respect, although the Commonwealth Director of Public Prosecutions (CDPP) and Australian Federal Police (AFP) work together, not only are they separate institutions, which means that investigation and prosecution of serious economic crime is split, unlike with the SFO, but also they have no national overarching remit. As a consequence the AFP/CDPP have to operate through a variety of multi-agency, multidisciplinary crime teams where 'Commonwealth responsibilities can sometimes overlap with those of state and territory law enforcement, regulatory or criminal justice areas'.[146] Whereas Australia has created a framework[147] to ensure that 'law enforcement, intelligence, policy and regulatory agencies are collaborating effectively with each other, with their State, Territory and international counterparts',[148] the SFO has no need to establish its jurisdiction. Thus, although it is understandable that the Commonwealth should have to establish such structures because of its constitutional arrangements, the UK does not have such a need and, accordingly, the mechanisms employed in Australia to achieve a cohesive approach do not provide a template for adoption in the UK.

141 Andrew Hemming, 'When is a code a code?' (2010) 15 Deakin L Rev 65, 66.
142 Criminal Code Act 1995.
143 Roman Tomasic, 'Governance' (n 121) 24.
144 Alex Steel, 'New fraud and identity-related crimes in New South Wales', Judicial Commission of New South Wales (2010) Judicial Officers Bulletin 22(3) 19. http://works.bepress.com/alex_steel/19 Accessed 11 March 2017.
145 Steel (n 144) 19.
146 Attorney General, 'Commonwealth organised crime strategic framework' 6 www.ag.gov.au/CrimeAndCorruption/OrganisedCrime/Documents/OrganisedCrimeStrategicFrameworkOverview.pdf Accessed 11 March 2017.
147 Attorney General, 'Commonwealth organised crime strategic framework' (n 146) 5.
148 Attorney General, 'Commonwealth organised crime strategic framework' (n 146) 5.

Bribery and corruption

United Kingdom

The SFO is the prime UK agency for investigation and prosecution of bribery and corruption. Since 2011, the SFO has been provided with two new legislative instruments to prosecute bribery and corruption: the Bribery Act and DPAs. Taken together, these measures represent considerable enhancement defining criminal behaviour and providing an alternative approach to a criminal trial.

Unlike the US, which legislated against foreign bribery in 1977, the UK waited until 2001.[149] Notwithstanding the temporary expedient of incorporating provisions in the Anti-Terrorism, Crime and Security Act 2001[150] to criminalise bribery outside the UK, which carried out in the UK would be corrupt, in order to satisfy the UK's international obligations to the OECD,[151] it was not until 2010 that the comprehensive Bribery Act was enacted[152] to overhaul the UK's patchwork of archaic corruption laws.[153] The Bribery Act is regarded as setting the 'gold standard' in combating bribery.[154] Aaronberg and Higgins are of the view that the Act 'provides the UK with some of the most draconian and far-reaching anti-corruption legislation in the world',[155] and has the potential to propel the UK to the forefront in fighting international bribery and corruption.[156]

The Bribery Act is notable for the introduction of a new corporate offence of 'failure of commercial organisations to prevent bribery', as well as the absence of a provision to permit 'facilitation payments'.

The corporate offence of 'failure of commercial organisations to prevent bribery'[157] targets employees or associated persons such as third parties, intermediaries, suppliers or joint venture partners.[158] Although a 'strict liability' offence, 'or perhaps more accurately, vicarious liability based on the actions of an associated person,[159] there is a defence if the commercial organisation can show

149 Public Bodies Corrupt Practices Act 1889, Prevention of Corruption Act 1906, and Prevention of Corruption Act 1916, Anti-Terrorism, Crime and Security Act 2001. Monty Raphael *Blackstone's Guide to the Bribery Act 2010* (OUP 2010) 116.

150 Raphael (n 149) 116. Anti-Terrorism, Crime and Security Act 2001, s 108, s 109.

151 OECD Working Group on Bribery, 'Annual Report 2008' 43 www.oecd.org/tax/crime/oecdworkinggrouponbribery-annualreport.htm Accessed March 2017.

152 Bribery Act 2010.

153 John Benstead, 'Biting the bullet' (2010) 160 NLJ 1291.

154 Transparency International, 'How effective is the UK Bribery Act?' www.transparency.org.uk/how-effective-is-the-uk-bribery-act/ Accessed 20 March 2017.

155 David Aaronberg and Nicola Higgins, 'The Bribery Act 2010: All bark and no bite ...?' (2010) Arch Rev 5, 6–9.

156 Transparency International, 'How effective is the UK Bribery Act?' (n 154). Note: the 'Act extends to England and Wales, Scotland and Northern Ireland.' Bribery Act 2010, s 18.

157 Bribery Act 2010, s 7.

158 Bribery Act 2010, s 8.

159 Raphael (n 149) 61.

that it had in place "adequate procedures" designed to prevent persons associated with the commercial organisation bribing another person'.[160]

The UK position regarding facilitation payments,[161] which aligns with the OECD, is not to permit such payments. The government faced the issue clearly and acknowledged the disparity with the US:

> We recognise that many UK businesses still struggle with petty corruption in some markets, but the answer is to face the challenge head-on, rather than carve out exemptions that draw artificial distinctions, are difficult to enforce, and have the potential to be abused. Providing exemptions for facilitation payments, as the US does, is not a universally accepted practice, and not something that we consider acceptable.[162]

Therefore, in terms of criminalising bribery and corruption, it is clear that the UK had taken cognisance of the US legislation in framing the Bribery Act and is stricter than the FCPA in not allowing facilitation payments, alongside creating a new corporate offence. Thus, unsurprisingly, the UK's bribery and corruption legislation is not in need of improvement.

Therefore, the UK has up-to-date legislation with which to tackle bribery and corruption, alongside a modern Fraud Act. Both these sectors now benefit from the facility for prosecutors to enter into DPAs.[163]

The Ministry of Justice saw the attraction of adopting the US model which recognised the 'potentially harmful effects that prosecuting a commercial organisation can have on investors, employees, pensioners, suppliers, customers and associated communities who were not involved in the organisation's criminal behaviour'.[164] The bankruptcy of Arthur Andersen,[165] caused the US to look for alternative sanctions, such as DPAs, that would not lead to the economic collapse of a firm. Further motivating factors are potential unequal treatment internationally in the event of conviction, and opportunity for jurisdictional arbitrage.

160 Bribery Act 2010, s 7(2).

161 Facilitation payments are 'unofficial payments made to public officials in order to secure or expedite the performance of a routine or necessary action. Sometimes referred to as "speed" or "grease" payments.' The Serious Fraud Office, 'Bribery Act 2010: Joint prosecution guidance of the Director of the Serious Fraud Office and the Director of Public Prosecutions' www.sfo.gov.uk/publications/guidance-policy-and-protocols/bribery-act-guidance/ Accessed 11 March 2017.

162 Claire Ward MP, HC Deb 3 March 2010 vol 506 col 981.

163 Crime and Courts Act 2013, s 45, Schedule 17.

164 Ministry of Justice, 'Consultation on a new enforcement tool to deal with economic crime committed by commercial organisations: Deferred Prosecution Agreements' 16 https://consult.justice.gov.uk/digital-communications/deferred-prosecution-agreements/supporting_documents/deferredprosecutionagreementsconsultation.pdf Accessed 26 November 2016.

165 Robert S Bennett, Hilary Holt LoCicero and Brooks M Hanner, 'From regulation to prosecution to cooperation: Trends in corporate white collar crime enforcement and the evolving role of the white collar criminal defense attorney' (2013) 68 The Business Lawyer 411.

In the US, a guilty plea does not result in automatic debarment from US government contracting because an independent debarment authority will consider the issues.[166] However, in the UK, the EU Public Sector Procurement Directive applies.[167] The effect of this is that a commercial organisation is excluded from participation in public sector contracts if convicted of fraud, bribery and corruption under Article 45, thus providing an incentive to 'self-refer' to the SFO with the prospect of negotiating an outcome and incurring a civil rather than a criminal penalty.[168] Nevertheless, the Rolls-Royce DPA indicates that the court will consider this aspect in a pragmatic manner.

The opportunity for jurisdictional arbitrage is an interesting area. Therefore, the historic disparity of enforcement mechanisms between UK and US prosecutors may mean that 'resolving a case in the US may also be attractive given the wider and more flexible range of enforcement tools, including (…) DPAs which do not result in a criminal conviction'.[169]

Whilst it is quite clear that the UK was informed by US experience in creating its own DPA regime, it did not replicate its model, instead creating a bespoke arrangement for the UK.[170] The main difference between the two models is the involvement of the courts where the US is criticised for its lack of judicial oversight,[171] which would not be congruent with the UK constitution and legal traditions.[172]

United States

The US was an early adopter of measures to combat bribery of foreign officials, through enactment of the FCPA.[173] The catalyst for the US was the 'Watergate' scandal,[174] which revealed 'that many public companies were maintaining cash "slush funds" from which illegal [political] campaign contributions were being made in the US and illegal bribes were being paid to foreign officials'.[175]

Prior to the FCPA, it was not illegal in the US to bribe foreign officials. Both the US and UK criminalise bribery and corruption both at home and abroad, though the FCPA has a wide interpretation of its territorial jurisdiction including

166 US Department of Justice and US Securities and Exchange Commission, 'FCPA. A resource guide to the U.S. Foreign Corrupt Practices Act' 70 www.sec.gov/spotlight/fcpa/fcpa-resource-guide.pdf Accessed 11 March 2017.
167 EU Public Services Procurement Directive 2004/18/EC Art. 45. Implemented in UK by The Public Contracts Regulations 2006.
168 Directive 2004/17/EC: [2004] OJ L134/1.
169 Ministry of Justice, Deferred Prosecution Agreements (n 164) 12.
170 Ministry of Justice, Deferred Prosecution Agreements (n 164) 19.
171 Ministry of Justice, Deferred Prosecution Agreements (n 164) 19.
172 Ministry of Justice, Deferred Prosecution Agreements (n 164) 19.
173 Public Bodies Corrupt Practices Act 1889, Prevention of Corruption Act 1906, and Prevention of Corruption Act 1916, Anti-Terrorism, Crime and Security Act 2001. Raphael (n 149) 116.
174 J Giuffo, 'Watergate' (2001) 40(4) Columbia JR 74.
175 Department of Justice, 'Proposed legislative history' (n 53).

'US and foreign public companies listed on stock exchanges in the US or which are required to file periodic reports with the SEC'.[176] However, the ambit of the FCPA extends further because it takes territorial jurisdiction over 'foreign persons and foreign non-issuer entities that (…) engage in *any* act in furtherance of a corrupt payment (…) while in the territory of the United States'.[177] The territory of the US is extended outside the US border because the statute includes the 'use of the mails or any means of interstate commerce'.[178] The use of 'mails' provides a link to Mail Fraud Statute[179] and 'interstate commerce' to the Wire Fraud Statute.[180] There is, though, a significant point of difference between the US and UK (and also OECD), and that is the 'exception for routine government action'.[181] These are intended to be small 'facilitation payments', 'to expedite or secure the performance of a routine government action', but are alternatively considered to be 'repetitive bribes which support a systemic culture of corruption and encourage the payment of low wages to public officials while continuing to foster low commercial ethical standards'.[182] The UK position is not to permit such payments.[183]

Therefore, in terms of criminalising bribery and corruption, it is clear that the UK has taken cognisance of the US legislation in framing the Bribery Act. Thus, unsurprisingly, the UK legislation is not in need of improvement but there is international pressure for the US to adopt the UK stance on facilitation payments.

Australia

The Australian Commonwealth government stated that 'bribery of foreign public officials in the course of international trade is unacceptable'.[184] Australia implemented the OECD Convention well ahead of the UK, but by 2011, only seven of the 37 signatories to the OECD Convention were considered active in enforcement (including the US and UK), whereas Australia was cited as 'one of the 20

176 15 U.S.C. § 78dd-1 (Issuers). US Department of Justice and US Securities and Exchange Commission, 'FCPA, resource guide' (n 166) 2.
177 US Department of Justice and US Securities and Exchange Commission, 'FCPA, resource guide' (n 166) 11.
178 15 U.S.C. § 78dd-1 [Section 30A of the Securities Exchange Act of 1934] Prohibited foreign trade practices by issuers. (a) prohibition.
179 18 U.S.C. § 1341.
180 US Department of Justice and US Securities and Exchange Commission, 'FCPA, resource guide' (n 166) 11.
181 15 U.S.C. § 78dd-1(b), 'Exception for routine government action'. US Department of Justice and US Securities and Exchange Commission, 'FCPA, resource guide' (n 166) 11.
182 Raphael (n 149) 112.
183 Serious Fraud Office, 'Facilitation payments' www.sfo.gov.uk/publications/guidance-policy-and-protocols/bribery-act-guidance/ Accessed 11 March 2017.
184 'Criminal Code Amendment (Bribery of Foreign Public Officials) Bill 1999 – C2004B00419. Explanatory Memorandum' www.comlaw.gov.au/Details/C2004B00419/Explanatory%20Memorandum/Text Accessed 11 March 2017.

countries that is judged as exhibiting "little or no enforcement"'.[185] Indeed, in *Securency*, the first such case had still not come to trial by early 2017.

This book has considered the Criminal Code provisions in light of the Bribery Act and there is one significant difference. Facilitation payments are permitted,[186] as they are in the US, but the OECD noted a lack of understanding about what constitutes a facilitation payment under the Criminal Code,[187] pointing out that 'facilitation payments appear to be frequently equated with *any* bribes of small value'.[188] Instead, although permitted, what is 'often overlooked is the requirement that such payments must be made *to secure routine government action of a minor nature* that does not result in the obtaining of a business advantage'.[189] Although the Australian government launched a consultation in 2011 on the elimination of facilitation payments, by the end of 2016 there had not been an outcome. In 2013, the government changed and, in 2014, Australia was president of the G20[190] and chaired the Anti-Corruption Roundtable,[191] which states ironically that the G20 should lead by example in combating foreign bribery.[192] Although Australia adopted the OECD Convention ahead of the UK, its bribery legislation remains less extensive than the Bribery Act and it has yet to take its first foreign bribery case to trial.

Regulatory enforcement

United Kingdom

The UK financial services regulator is the FCA. Following the financial crisis, the nature of UK regulation changed with the adoption of the twin peaks model, which ended the primacy of the financial services 'super-regulator'[193] and, instead,

185 Cindy Davids and Grant Schubert, 'Criminalising foreign bribery: Is Australia's bark louder than its bite?' (2011) 35 Crim L J 98, 99 (footnotes omitted).

186 Australia Attorney General, 'Divisions 70 and 141 of the Criminal Code Act 1995. Assessing the "facilitation payments" defence to the Foreign Bribery offence and other measures', Public Consultation Paper 15 November 2011 www.crimeprevention.gov.au/Financialcrime/Documents/v2Public%20consultation%20paper%20-%20amendments%20to%20bribery%20offences%20-%20corrected%20version%2018%20November%202011.pdf Accessed 11 March 2017.

187 OECD, 'Phase 3 Report' (n 56).

188 OECD, 'Phase 3 Report' (n 56) (emphasis added).

189 OECD, 'Phase 3 Report' (n 56) (emphasis added).

190 G20, 'History' www.g20.org/Content/EN/StatischeSeiten/G20/Texte/2016-12-01-g20-geschichte-der-gipfel_en.html Accessed 20 March 2017.

191 Attorney General for Australia, 'Address at the opening of the G20 Anti-Corruption Roundtable' www.attorneygeneral.gov.au/Speeches/Pages/2014/First%20Quarter%202014/28February2014-AddressattheopeningoftheG20AntiCorruptionRoundtable.aspx Accessed 11 March 2017.

192 Attorney General for Australia, 'Address at the opening of the G20 Anti-Corruption Roundtable' (n 191).

193 Lomnicka (n 10) 482.

launched a new model headed by the Bank of England.[194] The government's intention for the FCA was of 'delivering a regulatory regime under which the conduct of business of *all* retail financial services is regulated by a single body'.[195] The FCA has 'a single overarching strategic objective to ensure that markets function well',[196] unlike its predecessor, the FSA, which had four equal objectives, of which one was 'the reduction of financial crime'.[197] One of the FCA's operational objectives is integrity[198] – 'protecting and enhancing the integrity of the UK financial system'[199] – and includes 'not being used for a purpose connected with financial crime'.[200] In pursuit of these objectives, the FCA has continued the policy of 'credible deterrence', for which, according to Cartwright, 'the imposition of a financial penalty is central'.[201] Ryder considers that the challenge for the FCA is to demonstrate that it is not merely a rebranded FSA[202] which is more difficult because the 'credible deterrence' strategy has certain fiscal attractions since significant monies are raised for the Exchequer.[203] However, the 'credible deterrence' policy, whilst remunerative, has not answered the Rakoff question: 'why have no high level executives been prosecuted?'[204]

The scope of the FCA's activity was broadened in 2014 when it took over responsibility for regulating 50,000 consumer credit firms from the Office of Fair Trading.[205] While it was the government's intention that the FCA became the single body to regulate all financial services,[206] it is a major increase from regulating the existing 26,000 firms. The FCA stated that they are 'more committed than ever to showing firms and individuals that they must play by the rules; because if they do not, robust sanctions are a matter of course'.[207]

The FCA Business Plan[208] states that their 'enforcement powers[209] enable them, to deter firms and individuals from wrongdoing by making it clear that there are real and

194 The other 'twin peak' is the Prudential Regulation Authority. House of Commons Library (n 11).
195 HM Treasury, 'A new approach to financial regulation' (n 14).
196 HM Treasury, 'A new approach to financial regulation' (n 14).
197 Financial Services and Markets Act 2000, s 6.
198 Financial Services Act 2012, s 1B(3).
199 Financial Services Act 2012, s 1D(1).
200 Financial Services Act 2012, s 1D(2)(b).
201 Cartwright (n 38) 5.
202 Nicholas Ryder, *The Financial Crisis and White Collar Crime – the Perfect Storm* (Edward Elgar 2014) 18. Wilson and Wilson (n 20) 4, 5.
203 Financial Conduct Authority, 'Financial services regulation and enforcement' (n 39).
204 Rakoff, 'The Financial Crisis' (n 41).
205 Financial Conduct Authority, 'PS14/3: Final rules for consumer credit firms' www.fca.org.uk/news/ps14-3-final-rules-for-consumer-credit-firms Accessed 11 March 2017.
206 HM Treasury, 'A new approach to financial regulation' (n 14).
207 Financial Conduct Authority, 'Financial services regulation and enforcement' (n 39).
208 Financial Conduct Authority, 'Business Plan 2014/15' 13 www.fca.org.uk/news/about-us/business-plan-2014-15 Accessed 11 March 2017.
209 'We use a wide range of Enforcement powers – criminal, civil and regulatory – to protect consumers and to take action against firms or individuals that do not meet our

meaningful consequences for poor practice'.[210] The increase in the number of fines, according to Haines, appears to show that their strategy to prosecute a steady stream of cases to demonstrate that they 'mean business' is bearing fruit.[211] The total fines were at modest levels (£35m) until 2010, when they increased to £1.47bn in 2014 and decreased to £22m in 2016.[212] However, the main engine for the increase in fines is the LIBOR scandal,[213] which is noteworthy because the FCA was criticised by the Treasury Committee for not wishing to pursue criminal charges.[214]

The FCA is also involved in measures to combat bribery and corruption,[215] where criminal prosecutions fall within the purview of the SFO. The SFO derives its powers from the Bribery Act in which the FCA is not involved in enforcement.[216] However, the FCA uses its regulatory powers 'where authorised firms fail adequately to address corruption and bribery risk',[217] and the FCA does not require evidence of corrupt conduct in order to take regulatory action.[218] Naturally, the SFO as a prosecutor *does* require evidence of corrupt conduct in order to enforce under the Bribery Act, but if a commercial organisation can positively show it has adequate procedures to prevent bribery then it has a complete defence.[219] This is a confusing picture where a prosecutor needs evidence on which to base a prosecution, whereas a regulator can impose penalties in the absence of evidence. Clearly, such issues would benefit from a single agency being able to consider across its realm the appropriate regulatory or criminal course of action.

United States

In the US, the principal bodies for enforcement are the DoJ and SEC. The DoJ has 'control over all criminal prosecutions and civil suits in which the United States had an interest',[220] and has a criminal division to prosecute crime and the

standards.' Financial Conduct Authority, 'Enforcement' www.fca.org.uk/about/enforcement Accessed 11 March 2017.

210 Financial Conduct Authority, 'Business Plan 2014/15' (n 208) 13.

211 Jason D Haines, 'FSA determined to improve cleanliness of markets: Custodial sentences continue to be a real threat' (2008) 29(12) Co Law 370.

212 For detailed analysis of fines, see Chapter 2.

213 Attorney General's Office, 'Fighting economic crime' (n 82).

214 House of Commons Treasury Committee, 'Fixing LIBOR' (n 86).

215 Authorised firms have additional, regulatory, obligations to put in place and maintain policies and processes to prevent corruption and bribery and to conduct their business with integrity. These are set out in SYSC 3.2.6R/SYSC 6.1.1R and Principle 1 of the Principles for Businesses (PRIN 2.1.1R). Financial Conduct Authority, 'Bribery and Corruption' www.fca.org.uk/firms/financial-crime/bribery-corruption Accessed 11 March 2017.

216 Financial Conduct Authority, 'Bribery and Corruption' (n 215).

217 Financial Conduct Authority, 'Bribery and Corruption' (n 215).

218 Financial Conduct Authority, 'Bribery and Corruption' (n 215).

219 'Section 7: Failure of commercial organisations to prevent bribery.' Ministry of Justice, 'The Bribery Act 2010 – Guidance' www.justice.gov.uk/downloads/legislation/bribery-act-2010-guidance.pdf Accessed 11 March 2017.

220 Department of Justice, '2014 Budget' www.justice.gov/jmd/2014summary/pdf/fy14-bud-sum.pdf#bs Accessed 11 March 2017.

FBI to investigate, which means that it is responsible for fraud, bribery and corruption prosecutions. However, whilst the DoJ 'is solely responsible for criminal enforcement it may institute civil proceedings'.[221] The SEC, which shares responsibility for FCPA enforcement, can only institute civil proceedings, involving administrative and financial sanctions only, with any criminal prosecutions being referred to the DoJ.[222] In the UK, the SFO investigates and prosecutes fraud, bribery and corruption, whereas the FCA only has limited prosecution powers.[223] Both the SEC and FCA, as regulators, have the facility to impose financial penalties but the SFO as a prosecutor has only been able to prosecute, in contrast to the DoJ which can either prosecute or conclude 'plea bargains' with defendants instead of taking cases to trial. Such DPAs have been part of the DoJ's armoury since the 1990s,[224] and have been utilised on a frequent basis,[225] whereas attempts by the SFO to agree outcomes with defendants in the absence of a DPA have historically been subject to judicial opprobrium. The DoJ's reasoning was:

> the increased use of DPAs has meant far greater accountability for corporate wrongdoing. Whereas prosecutors often declined when their only choice was to indict or walk away, now companies know that avoiding the disaster scenario of an indictment does not mean an escape from accountability.[226]

This is clearly the issue that faced the SFO with the availability of DPAs. What is clear from the first three cases is the high level of court supervision, where the US courts complained about their role being merely to act as a 'rubber stamp'. Thus, the historic disparity in tools to combat economic crime has now been eliminated and whilst this is an example of the UK adopting a successful US procedure, there does not appear to be any further procedure or legislation employed by the DoJ/ SEC which the UK might beneficially duplicate.

221 Frank J Cavico and Mujtaba G Bahaudin, 'Baksheesh or bribe: Payments to government officials and the Foreign Corrupt Practices Act' (2010) 2(1) JBSQ 83.
222 US Department of Justice and US Securities and Exchange Commission, 'FCPA, resource guide' (n 166) 42.
223 Criminal Justice Act 1993, s 52.
224 Department of Justice, 'Assistant Attorney General Lanny A. Breuer speaks at IBC Legal's World Bribery & Corruption Compliance Forum. London ~ October 23, 2012' www.justice.gov/criminal/pr/speeches/2012/crm-speech-121023.html Accessed 11 March 2017.
225 'The 2011 Year-end update on corporate Deferred Prosecution Agreements and Non Prosecution Agreements', by the American law firm Gibson Dunn, illustrates the variety of offences in relation to which DPAs and NPAs are used. A notable category is FCPA violations, which accounted for 41% of the total agreements in 2011, compared with about 44 % in 2010, 24% in 2009, 37% in 2008, 26% in 2007, and 9% in 2006. 2013: 27 agreements – 12 NPAs and 15 DPAs. Gibson Dunn, '2013 Year end update on corporate Non-Prosecution Agreements (NPAs) and Deferred Prosecution Agreements (DPAs)' www.gibsondunn.com/publications/Documents/2013-Year-End-Update-Corporate-Non-Prosecution-Agreements-and-Deferred-Prosecution-Agreements.pdf Accessed 11 March 2017.
226 Department of Justice, 'Breuer' (n 224).

It is the level of enforcement that has marked out the DoJ/SEC and, even making allowances for its head start in having the FCPA and DPAs, the US has given a lead for the UK's SFO and FCA to emulate.

Australia

The Australian criminal enforcement landscape is, unsurprisingly because of the constitutional structure, more complicated than that in the UK. At Commonwealth level, intelligence, investigation and prosecution are split between three bodies: the Australian Transaction Reports and Analysis Centre (AUSTRAC), the CDPP and AFP.

AUSTRAC's role is 'to protect the integrity of Australia's financial system and (…) countering money laundering and the financing of terrorism',[227] and it receives a significant number of transaction reports: 96 million in 2015–16.[228] These reports cover a range of activities in combating 'serious crimes such as drug trafficking, tax evasion, fraud and people smuggling'.[229] In this area, Australia has reacted to criticism[230] of its anti-money laundering (AML) regime by incorporating the Financial Action Task Force's 40 recommendations into primary legislation,[231] in contrast to both the US and UK which have a piecemeal approach to AML legislation.[232]

In the key areas of economic crime, Australia's constitutional structure means that deployment of its legislation follows a different pattern from the UK. Fraud is prosecuted at state level (apart from fraud against the Commonwealth body itself), with legislation differing between states. These measures do not offer benefits to the UK compared with the Fraud Act. In relation to bribery, Australia has Commonwealth legislation to meet OECD obligations but had not by early 2017 achieved a prosecution, which lack of experience does not suggest any lessons to improve the Bribery Act.

However, Australia has particular experience of a different economic and regulatory structure which was seen to be of benefit, and the UK has adopted the twin peaks approach.

Conclusion and recommendations

The UK needs a cohesive and effective anti-economic crime policy and the government was right to propose an ECA as part of its white collar crime agenda,

227 Australian Government, Australian Transaction Reports and Analysis Centre, 'AUSTRAC Annual Report 2012–13' 6 www.austrac.gov.au/annual_report.html Accessed 11 March 2017.

228 See Chapter 5.

229 AUSTRAC, 'AUSTRAC annual report shows financial intelligence is crucial to combating contemporary criminal threats' www.austrac.gov.au/media/media-releases/austrac-annual-report-shows-financial-intelligence-crucial-combating Accessed 11 March 2017.

230 Nicholas Ryder, *Money Laundering – An Endless Cycle?* (Routledge 2012) 105.

231 Ryder, *Money Laundering – An Endless Cycle?* (n 230) 105.

232 Ryder, *Money Laundering – An Endless Cycle?* (n 230) 107.

where it said that its mission was to hold to account people suspected of financial wrongdoing,[233] on a day of reckoning,[234] which demonstrated that the government was serious about white collar crime.[235] Notwithstanding such lofty ambitions, the government was wrong to be diverted from that course. Whilst, a generation earlier, Roskill advanced a clear rationale for the SFO's creation, it can also be concluded that its limited role and remit owed more to political expediency and infighting than a firm belief in the finished article, with the consequence that it has failed to meet expectations. The government has successfully created the Competition and Markets Authority (CMA), which has overarching responsibility for its sector and subsidiary regulators. This is a template that should be employed for the economic crime arena by an ECA encompassing the SFO and FCA (and employing the resources of the City of London Police and regional police forces). The CMA is a credible agency in itself, whereas the current economic crime equivalent is merely a division of the NCA.

What a strong ECA offers is the prospect of an independent authority to bring the regulatory structure and enforcement regime of the FCA together with the investigation and prosecution powers of the SFO. Just as the CMA has the ability to take over actions by its constituent regulatory bodies, so an ECA should be able to deploy the powers of both the SFO and FCA to ensure that the correct sanction is advanced rather than each organisation being either hamstrung by its own powers or adopting civil remedies when particular conduct demands a criminal sanction. In this regard, while the availability of an 'offence relating to a decision causing a financial institution to fail',[236] or reckless banking, is of some benefit in relation to an insolvent financial institution, the gap between the tectonic plates of economic crime would be covered by the addition of a further criminal sanction for '[r]eckless risk-taking on the financial markers'.[237] This may be modern language but it harkens back to the conclusion of Roskill that:

> The public no longer believes that the legal system in England and Wales is capable of bringing the perpetrators of serious frauds expeditiously and effectively to book. The overwhelming weight of the evidence laid before us suggests that the public is right.[238]

Thus, the creation of an ECA, adopting the CMA template and encompassing the existing bodies of the SFO and FCA, would remove both areas of overlap and underlap and, within an overarching structure, ensure that existing and new legislative powers are available to match the imperatives of dynamic financial markets.

233 BBC, 'Cameron' (n 1).
234 BBC, 'Cameron' (n 1).
235 HM Treasury, 'Speech at The Lord Mayor's Dinner' (n 3).
236 Financial Services (Banking Reform) Act 2013, s 36.
237 Fisher (n 22) 2.
238 *Fraud Trials Committee Report* (HMSO 1986) (Roskill) 1.

Bibliography

Aaronberg, D, and N Higgins, 'The Bribery Act 2010: All bark and no bite …?' (2010) *Arch Rev* 5, 6–9.

ABC News, 'Senate inquiry demands royal commission into Commonwealth Bank, ASIC' www.abc.net.au/news/2014-06-26/senate-inquiry-demands-royal-commission-into-asic-cba/5553102 Accessed 8 December 2016.

ABC News, 'Fact check: Can ASIC do the same job as a financial industry royal commission?' www.abc.net.au/news/2016-06-09/fact-check-asic-royal-commission-powers/7447682 Accessed 6 February 2017.

ABC News, 'ASIC fails to prove former AWB executives knew about Iraq sanctions breach' www.abc.net.au/news/2016-12-15/asic-wheat-board-executives-sanctions-iraq-breach/8122276 Accessed 17 March 2017.

Action Fraud, 'About us' www.actionfraud.police.uk/about-us/who-we-are Accessed 24 November 2016.

Anderson Committee on Unit Trusts, 1936 Cmd 5239.

Anello, R J, and R F Albert, 'Overcriminalization of non-violent conduct: Time for real reform' (2013) 249 *NYLJ* 106.

APRA, 'APRA speaks on Palmer' (The report of John Palmer was commissioned by APRA [in 2001] to investigate its role into the collapse of HIH and tendered as evidence to the HIH Royal Commission) www.apra.gov.au/MediaReleases/Pages/02_52.aspx Accessed 4 January 2017.

Arent Fox, 'World renowned fashion giant Ralph Lauren Corporation resolves Foreign Corrupt Practices Act investigation with DOJ and SEC for $1.6 million' www.arentfox.com/newsroom/alerts/world-renowned-fashion-giant-ralph-lauren-corporation-resolves-foreign-corrupt Accessed 8 December 2016.

Ashworth, A, 'Sentencing for fraud and related offences' (2014) 8 *Crim LR* 553.

Asian Development Bank, 'OECD anti-corruption initiative for Asia Pacific' www.oecd.org/site/adboecdanti-corruptioninitiative/ Accessed 8 December 2016.

ASIC, 'Annual Report 2012–13' 32, 42 http://download.asic.gov.au/media/1311019/ASIC-Annual-Report-2012-13-complete.pdf Accessed 6 February 2017.

ASIC, '13–031MR Ponzi scheme "mastermind" handed record penalty' 17 February 2013 http://asic.gov.au/about-asic/media-centre/find-a-media-release/2013-releases/13-031mr-ponzi-scheme-mastermind-handed-record-penalty/ Accessed 4 January 2017.

ASIC, 'Senate inquiry into the performance of the Australian Securities and Investments Commission. Main submission by ASIC, October 2013' 124 http://download.asic.gov.

au/media/1311361/ASIC-Main-submission-Senate-inquiry-October-2013.pdf Accessed 4 January 2017.

ASIC, '13–201MR ASIC submission to Senate inquiry' 5 http://asic.gov.au/about-asic/media-centre/find-a-media-release/2013-releases/13-201mr-asic-submission-to-senate-inquiry/ Accessed 4 January 2017.

ASIC, 'Annual Report 2015–16' 5 http://download.asic.gov.au/media/4058626/asic-annual-report-2015-2016-complete.pdf Accessed 6 February 2017.

ASIC, 'Financial benchmarks' http://www.asic.gov.au/media/3285136/rep440-published-8-july-2015.pdf Accessed 11 March 2017.

Attorney General's Office, *Fraud Review – Final Report* (Attorney General's Office 2006) 130.

Australian Criminal Intelligence Commission, 'About us' www.acic.gov.au/about-crime Accessed 6 February 2017.

Australian Federal Police, 'Annual Report 2012–13' 67 www.afp.gov.au/sites/default/files/PDF/Reports/afp-annual-report-2012-2013.pdf Accessed 4 February 2017.

Australian Federal Police, 'Annual Report 2014–15' www.afp.gov.au/afp-annual-report-2014-15 Accessed 6 February 2017.

Australian Federal Police, 'Annual Report 2015–16' 7 www.afp.gov.au/sites/default/files/PDF/Reports/afp-annual-report-2015-2016.pdf Accessed 4 February 2017.

Australian Federal Police, 'About us' www.afp.gov.au/about-us Accessed 4 February 2017.

Australian Federal Police, 'AFP Corporate Plan 2016–17 purpose' www.afp.gov.au/corporate-plan-2016-17#purpose Accessed 4 February 2017.

Australian Government, 'Our government' http://australia.gov.au/about-australia/our-government/state-and-territory-government Accessed 8 December 2016.

Australian Government, 'AUSTRAC Annual Report 2012–13' 6 www.austrac.gov.au/austrac-annual-report-2012-13 Accessed 6 February 2017.

Australian Government, 'Fit for the future – A capability review of the Australian Securities and Investments Commission December 2015' www.treasury.gov.au/~/media/Treasury/Publications%20and%20Media/Publications/2016/Fit%20for%20the%20future/Downloads/PDF/ASIC-Capability-Review-Final-Report.ashx Accessed 6 February 2017.

Australian Government, Attorney General, 'National organised crime response plan 2015–18' 22 www.ag.gov.au/CrimeAndCorruption/OrganisedCrime/Documents/NationalOrganisedCrimeResponsePlan2015-18.pdf Accessed 6 February 2017.

Australian Government, Attorney General, 'Commonwealth organised crime strategic framework' 5 www.ag.gov.au/CrimeAndCorruption/OrganisedCrime/Documents/OrganisedCrimeStrategicFrameworkOverview.pdf Accessed 6 February 2017.

Australian Government, Attorney General, 'Address at the opening of the G20 Anti-Corruption Roundtable' www.attorneygeneral.gov.au/Speeches/Pages/2014/First%20Quarter%202014/28February2014-AddressattheopeningoftheG20AntiCorruptionRoundtable.aspx Accessed 8 December 2016.

Australian Government, Attorney General, 'National organised crime response plan 2015–18' 17 www.ag.gov.au/CrimeAndCorruption/OrganisedCrime/Documents/NationalOrganisedCrimeResponsePlan2015-18.pdf Accessed 6 February 2017.

Australian Government, Attorney General, 'Bribery of foreign officials' www.crimeprevention.gov.au/Financialcrime/Pages/Briberyofforeignpublicofficials.aspx Accessed 8 December 2016.

Australian Government, Attorney General's Department, 'The Commonwealth's approach to anti-corruption' 9 http://transparency.org.au/wp-content/uploads/2012/07/

Anti-Corruption-Discussion-Paper-FINAL-PDF-15-March-2012.pdf Accessed 4 January 2017.

Australian Government, Attorney General's Department, 'Assessing the "facilitation payments" defence to the foreign bribery offence and other measures', Public Consultation Paper 15 November 2011 www.crimeprevention.gov.au/Financialcrime/Documents/v2Public%20consultation%20paper%20-%20amendments%20to%20bribery%20offences%20-%20corrected%20version%2018%20November%202011.pdf Accessed 8 December 2016.

Australian Government, Attorney General's Department, 'Deferred prosecution agreements – public consultation' www.ag.gov.au/Consultations/Pages/Deferred-prosecution-agreements-public-consultation.aspx Accessed 5 February 2017.

Australian Government, Department of Foreign Affairs and Trade, 'About us. Legal system' www.dfat.gov.au/facts/legal_system.html Accessed 8 December 2016.

Australian Government, Treasury, 'ASIC Enforcement Review Taskforce' http://kmo.ministers.treasury.gov.au Accessed 6 February 2017.

Australian Institute of Criminology, www.aic.gov.au/crime_types/economic/fraud.html Accessed 8 December 2016.

Australian Prudential Regulation Authority, 'Protecting Australia's depositors, insurance policyholders and superannuation fund members' www.apra.gov.au/AboutAPRA/Publications/Pages/APRA-Brochure.aspx#What-is-APRA-s-role? Accessed 4 January 2017.

Australian Securities and Investments Commission, 'About ASIC' http://asic.gov.au/about-asic/what-we-do/our-role/ Accessed 6 February 2017.

Australian Securities and Investments Commission, 'Setting the record straight: ASIC, bribery and enforcement action. A speech by Greg Medcraft, Chairman, Australian Securities and Investments Commission' http://asic.gov.au/about-asic/media-centre/speeches/setting-the-record-straight-asic-bribery-and-enforcement-action/ Accessed 4 January 2017.

Australian Securities and Investments Commission, 'Senate inquiry into the performance of the Australian Securities and Investments Commission. Main submission by ASIC, October 2013' www.asic.gov.au/asic/asic.nsf/byHeadline/13-300MR%20ASIC%20lodges%20major%20Senate%20Inquiry%20submission?opendocument Accessed 18 October 2016.

Australian Transaction Reports and Analysis Centre, 'AUSTRAC annual report shows financial intelligence is crucial to combating contemporary criminal threats' www.austrac.gov.au/media/media-releases/austrac-annual-report-shows-financial-intelligence-crucial-combating Accessed 4 January 2017.

Australian Transaction Reports and Analysis Centre, 'AUSTRAC Annual Report 2015–16' 75 www.austrac.gov.au/sites/default/files/austrac-ar-15-16-FINAL-WEB-2.pdf Accessed 4 January 2017.

Australian Transaction Reports and Analysis Centre, 'Other publications' www.austrac.gov.au/risk_management.html Accessed 8 December 2016.

Australian Transaction Reports and Analysis Centre, 'AML/CTF reporting obligations' www.austrac.gov.au/amlctf_compliance_report.html Accessed 8 December 2016.

Australian Transaction Reports and Analysis Centre, 'Chapter 6 – AML/CTF programs' www.austrac.gov.au/chapter-6-amlctf-programs Accessed 3 February 2017.

Australian Transaction Reports and Analysis Centre, 'Enforcement action' www.austrac.gov.au/enforcement-action Accessed 3 February 2017.

Australian Transaction Reports and Analysis Centre, 'AUSTRAC: Australia's financial intelligence unit' www.austrac.gov.au/about-us/intelligence#monitoring Accessed 3 February 2017.

Australian Transaction Reports and Analysis Centre, 'Austrac overview' www.austrac.gov.au/files/overview_brchr.pdf Accessed 8 December 2016.

Australian Transaction Reports and Analysis Centre, 'AUSTRAC Corporate Plan 2016–20' www.austrac.gov.au/sites/default/files/austrac-corporate-plan-16-20-WEB.pdf Accessed 3 February 2017.

Avon and Somerset Constabulary, 'Disgraced Somerset businessman faces huge confiscation order' 15 June 2016 www.avonandsomerset.police.uk/newsroom/disgraced-somerset-businessman-faces-huge-confiscation-order/ Accessed 17 October 2016.

Baber, G, 'A critical examination of the legislative response in banking and financial regulation to issues related to misconduct in the context of the crisis of 2007–2009' (2013) 20(2) *JFC* 237.

Bakir, C, 'The governance of financial regulatory reform: The Australian experience' (2009) 87(4) *Public Administration* 910.

Baldwin, J, and M McConville, *Jury trials* (Clarendon 1979).

Bank of England, 'History of the Bank of England' www.bankofengland.co.uk/about/Pages/history/default.aspx Accessed 24 November 2016.

Bank of England, 'The secondary banking crisis and the Bank of England's support operations' www.bankofengland.co.uk/archive/Documents/historicpubs/qb/1978/qb78q2230239.pdf Accessed 17 October 2016.

Bank of England, 'Prudential Regulation Authority' www.bankofengland.co.uk/pra/Pages/default.aspx Accessed 8 December 2016.

Bank of England, 'News release – Bank of England launches strategic plan' 18 March 2014 www.bankofengland.co.uk//publications/Pages/news/2014/058.aspx Accessed 18 October 2016.

Bank of England, 'Speech given by Mark Carney' 18 March 2014 www.bankofengland.co.uk/publications/Documents/speeches/2014/speech715.pdf Accessed 18 October 2016.

Bank of England, 'News release – foreign exchange – the perfect storm' www.bankofengland.co.uk/publications/Pages/news/2014/044.aspx Accessed 24 November 2016.

Bank of England, 'Bank of England foreign exchange market investigation – a report by Lord Grabiner QC' www.bankofengland.co.uk/publications/Documents/news/2014/grabiner.pdf Accessed 18 October 2016.

Bank of England, 'Liquidity insurance' www.bankofengland.co.uk/markets/Pages/sterlingoperations/liquidityinsurance.aspx Accessed 24 November 2016.

Bank of England, 'People. Mark Carney' www.bankofengland.co.uk/about/Pages/people/biographies/carney.aspx Accessed 8 December 2016.

Bank of England, 'Prudential Regulation Authority' www.bankofengland.co.uk/pra/Pages/default.aspx Accessed 8 December 2016.

BBC, 'Fraud police chief warns of lack of officers' www.bbc.co.uk/news/uk-29507414 Accessed 10 October 2016.

BBC, 'UBS "rogue trader": Loss estimate raised to $2.3bn' 18 September 2011 www.bbc.co.uk/news/business-14965438 Accessed 24 November 2016.

BBC, 'GlaxoSmithKline fined $490m by China for bribery' www.bbc.co.uk/news/business-29274822 Accessed 14 November 2016.

Bennett, R S, H H LoCicero, and B M Hanner, 'From regulation to prosecution to cooperation: Trends in corporate white collar crime enforcement and the evolving role of the white collar criminal defense attorney' (2013) 68 *The Business Lawyer* 411.

Benstead, J, 'Biting the bullet' (2010) 160 *NLJ* 1291.

The Holy Bible, English Standard Version (HarperCollins 2007).

Blakey, G R, and B Gettings, 'Racketeer Influenced and Corrupt Organizations (RICO): Basic concepts – criminal and civil remedies' (1980) 53 *Temp LQ* 1012.

Blair, W, 'The reform of financial regulation in the UK' (1998) 13(2) *JIBL* 43, 45.

Bloomberg, 'FX traders surprised by scope of Bank of England probe' www.bloomberg.com/news/2014-09-09/fx-traders-said-to-be-surprised-by-scope-of-boe-probe.html Accessed 24 November 2016.

The Border Mail, 'UK leaves Australia for dead on Securency Corruption prosecution' www.bordermail.com.au/story/3907034/uk-leaves-australia-for-dead-on-securency-corruption-prosecution/?cs=9 Accessed 12 February 2017.

British Bankers' Association, 'Understanding BBA LIBOR – a briefing by the British Bankers' Association' www.bbalibor.com/news-releases/understanding-bba-libor Accessed 24 November 2016.

Brown, L H, 'The Foreign Corrupt Practices Act redux: The anti-bribery provisions of the Foreign Corrupt Practices Act' (1994) 12 *Int'l Tax & Bus Law* 260.

Brown, P, 'Australian influence in the South Pacific' Australian Defence College 3 www.defence.gov.au/ADC/Publications/Commanders/2012/07_Brown%20SAP%20Final%20PDF.pdf Accessed 4 January 2017.

Buchanan, G C, 'Funding the cost of litigation' (2014) 161 *SPEL* 8.

Buffett, W, 'Chairman's letter to shareholders', Berkshire Hathaway 2001 www.berkshirehathaway.com/letters/2001pdf.pdf Accessed 14 January 2017.

Bureau of Justice Statistics, US Department of Justice, *Dictionary of Criminal Justice Data Terminology* 215 www.ncjrs.gov/App/publications/abstract.aspx?ID=76939 Accessed 14 January 2017.

Butterworths, 'Suspicious Activities, Reporting and Data Protection' in *Butterworths Banking Law Handbook* http://lexisweb.co.uk/guides/sources/butterworths-banking-law-handbook?contentonly=true.

Button, M, and J Gee, *Countering Fraud for Competitive Advantage* (Wiley 2013).

Button, M, D Shepherd, and D Blackbourn, 'The fraud "justice systems": A scoping study on the civil, regulatory and private paths to "justice" for fraudsters main report' November 2016 www.port.ac.uk/media/contacts-and-departments/icjs/ccfs/Fraud-Justice-Systems-2016—Final-Report.pdf Accessed 29 November 2016.

Callaghan, V, and Z Ullah, 'The LIBOR scandal – the UK's legislative response' (2013) 28 (40) *JIBLR* 160.

The Canberra Times, 'Show the world we're fighting corruption' 3 October 2013 www.canberratimes.com.au/federal-politics/political-opinion/show-the-world-were-fighting-corruption-20131002-2ussl.html Accessed 8 December 2016.

Capie, F, *The Bank of England: 1950's – 1979* (CUP 2010).

Carr, I, 'Fighting corruption through the United Nations Convention on Corruption 2003: A global solution to a global problem?' (2005) 11(1) *Int TLR* 24–29.

Carr, I, *Financial Fraud Law Report 4: The UK Bribery Act: Business Integrity and Whistleblowers* (Thompson Media 2012).

Cartwright, P, 'Credible Deterrence and Consumer Protection through Imposition of Financial Penalties: Lessons for the Financial Conduct Authority' in N Ryder, U Turksen, and S Hassler (eds), *Fighting Financial Crime in the Global Economic Crisis: Policy, Trends and Sanctions* (Routledge Cavendish 2014).

Cavico, F J, and M G Bahaudin, 'Baksheesh or bribe: Payments to government officials and the Foreign Corrupt Practices Act' (2010) 2(1) *JBSQ* 83.

Ceresney, A J, G Eng, and S R Nuttall, 'Regulatory investigations and the credit crisis: The search for villains' (2009) 46 *Am Crim L Rev* 225.

Christopher, W, 'Trillion dollar bribery' (2011) 161 *NLJ* 25.

City of London Police, Economic Crime Department, 'Fraud Act 2006' www.cityoflondon.police.uk/CityPolice/Departments/ECD/Fraud/preventingfraud.htm Accessed 18 October 2016.

City of London Police, 'What is fraud and cybercrime?' www.actionfraud.police.uk/what-is-fraud Accessed 18 October 2016.

CMS Cameron McKenna, Law-Now, 'Further tensions emerge between judiciary and SFO in corruption sentencing' 16 April 2010 www.mondaq.com/x/98482/Corporate+Crime/Further+Tensions+Emerge+Between+Judiciary+and+SFO+in+Corruption+Sentencing Accessed 6 December 2016.

Cohen, P, and A Marriott, *International Corruption* (Sweet & Maxwell 2010).

Cole, T, 'Report of the inquiry into certain Australian companies in relation to the UN Oil-for-Food Programme', Attorney-General's Department (Australia) http://apo.org.au/node/3765 Accessed 4 January 2017.

Collins, J, 'Fraud by abuse of position and unlicensed gangmasters' (2016) 79(2) *MLR* 341.

Collins, P, 'Looking ahead to change' 18 October 2012, King's College http://webarchive.nationalarchives.gov.uk/20140402142426/http://www.oft.gov.uk/shared_oft/speeches/2012/0812.pdf Accessed 18 October 2016.

The Commonwealth, 'About us' http://thecommonwealth.org/about-us Accessed 8 December 2016.

The Commonwealth, 'History' http://thecommonwealth.org/our-history Accessed 10 December 2016.

The Commonwealth, 'CHOGM Kampala 2007' http://thecommonwealth.org/history-of-the-commonwealth/19th-chogm Accessed 8 January 2017.

Commonwealth Director of Public Prosecutions, 'Annual Report 2015–2016' 16 www.cdpp.gov.au/Publications/Annual-Reports/CDPP-Annual-Report-2012-2013.pdf Accessed 3 February 2017.

Commonwealth Director of Public Prosecutions, www.cdpp.gov.au/ Accessed 8 December 2016.

Company Lawyer, 'How many regulators?' (1996) 17(2) *Comp Law* 34.

Company Lawyer, 'FCA and PRA to cost 15% more than FSA' (2013) 34(7) *Comp Law* 217.

Competition and Markets Authority, 'What we do' www.gov.uk/government/organisations/competition-and-markets-authority Accessed 16 October 2016.

Competition and Markets Authority, 'Speech Redesigning regulatory architecture – the UK experience', Speech given by CMA Chairman David Currie to the Institute of International and European Affairs, Dublin 22 January 2014 www.gov.uk/government/speeches/redesigning-regulatory-architecture-the-uk-experience Accessed 17 January 2017.

Competition and Markets Authority, 'Cartel Offence Prosecution Guidance, consultation document September 2013' www.gov.uk/government/uploads/system/uploads/attachment_data/file/243709/5-cartel-offence-prosecution-guidance-consultation.pdf Accessed 24 November 2016.

Competition and Markets Authority, 'Supply of galvanised steel tanks for water storage: Criminal investigation' www.gov.uk/cma-cases/criminal-investigation-into-the-supply-of-galvanised-steel-tanks-for-water-storage Accessed 18 October 2016.

Competition and Markets Authority, 'Fridge supplier fined £2.2 million for restricting online discounts' www.gov.uk/government/news/fridge-supplier-fined-22-million-for-restricting-online-discounts Accessed 27 October 2016.

Competition and Markets Authority, 'CMA issues final decision in online cartel case' www.gov.uk/government/news/cma-issues-final-decision-in-online-cartel-case Accessed 27 October 2016.

Competition and Markets Authority, 'CMA issues bathroom fittings infringement decision and fine' www.gov.uk/government/news/cma-issues-bathroom-fittings-infringement-decision-and-fine Accessed 27 October 2016.

Competition and Markets Authority, 'Sarah Cardell speaks about the CMA's enforcement priorities and approach' www.gov.uk/government/speeches/sarah-cardell-speaks-about-the-cmas-enforcement-priorities-and-approach Accessed 27 October 2016.

Competition and Markets Authority, 'Director sentenced to 6 months for criminal cartel' www.gov.uk/government/news/director-sentenced-to-6-months-for-criminal-cartel Accessed 27 October 2016.

Competition and Markets Authority, 'Annual Report and Accounts 2015–16' www.gov.uk/government/publications/cma-annual-report-and-accounts-2015-to-2016 Accessed 27 October 2016.

Competition and Markets Authority, 'Rewards for information about cartels' www.gov.uk/government/uploads/system/uploads/attachment_data/file/299411/Informant_rewards_policy.pdf Accessed 30 November 2016.

Coolican, T, 'Time out for fraud' (2006) 156 *NLJ* 1460.

Cooper, J, 'The integration of financial regulatory authorities – the Australian experience', Australian Securities and Investments Commission 4–5 September 2006, 2 http://download.asic.gov.au/media/1339352/integration-financial-regulatory-authorities.pdf Accessed 4 January 2017.

Coppola, L, and N DeMarco, 'Civil RICO: How ambiguity allowed the Racketeer Influenced and Corrupt Organizations Act to expand beyond its intended purpose' (2012) 38 *New Eng J on Crim & Civ Confinement* 241.

Corker, D, 'Time for a serious (SFO) rethink' (2010) 160 *NLJ* 783, 784.

Council of Europe, 'Criminal Law Convention 1999; Organisation of American States Inter-American Convention against Corruption 1996' www.oas.org/juridico/english/fightcur.html Accessed 8 December 2016.

Croall, H, 'Who is the white-collar criminal?' (1989) 29 *Brit J Criminology* 164.

Crockett, A, *Money: Theory, Policy and Institutions* (Nelson 1973).

Crown Prosecution Service, 'Sentencing manual' www.cps.gov.uk/legal/s_to_u/sentencing_manual/index.html Accessed 6 July 2016.

Crown Prosecution Service, 'Specialist fraud division' www.cps.gov.uk/your_cps/our_organisation/sfd.html#a01 Accessed 18 October 2016.

Dale, R, 'Bank crises management: The case of the United Kingdom' (1995) 10(8) *JIBL* 326–333.

Davids, C, and G Schubert, 'Criminalising foreign bribery: Is Australia's bark louder than its bite?' (2011) 35 *Crim L J* 98.

Denning, A T, 'The independence and impartiality of the judges' (1954) 71 *S African L J* 345.

Department for Business, Energy and Industrial Strategy, 'Works with 47 agencies and public bodies' www.gov.uk/government/organisations#department-for-business-energy-and-industrial-strategy Accessed 24 August 2016.

Department for Business, Innovation and Skills, 'Competition Regime: Response to consultation on statement of strategic priorities for the CMA, 1 October 2013. Strategic steer for the Competition and Markets Authority 2014–2017' 10 www.gov.uk/government/uploads/system/uploads/attachment_data/file/245607/bis-13-1210-competi tion-regime-response-to-consultation-on-statement-of-strategic-priorities-for-the-cma.pdf Accessed 24 November 2016.

Department for Business, Innovation and Skills, 'New competition authority comes into existence' www.gov.uk/government/news/new-competition-authority-comes-into-existence Accessed 18 October 2016.

Department for Business, Innovation and Skills, 'Competition Minister Jo Swinson launches shadow Competition and Markets Authority (CMA)' 1 October 2013 www.gov.uk/government/speeches/competition-and-markets-authority-launch Accessed 18 October 2016.

Department of Justice, 'Alcoa World Alumina agrees to plead guilty to foreign bribery and pay $233 million in fines and forfeiture' 9 January 2014 www.justice.gov/usao/paw/news/2014/2014_january/2014_01_09_02.html Accessed 24 November 2016.

Department of Justice, 'Barclays Bank PLC admits misconduct related to submissions for the London Interbank Offered Rate and the Euro Interbank Offered Rate and agrees to pay $160 million penalty' www.justice.gov/opa/pr/2012/June/12-crm-815.html Accessed 24 November 2016.

Department of Justice, 'Justice Department recovers, $4.7bn in false claims cases in fiscal year 2016 [more than $31.1 billion since 2009]' www.justice.gov/opa/pr/justice-department-recovers-over-47-billion-false-claims-act-cases-fiscal-year-2016 Accessed 5 January 2017.

Department of Justice, 'Non prosecution agreement' 22 April 2013 www.justice.gov/criminal/fraud/fcpa/cases/ralph-lauren/Ralph-Lauren.-NPA-Executed.pdf Accessed 14 November 2016.

Department of Justice, 'Acting Assistant Attorney General Mythili Raman delivers keynote address at the Global Anti-Corruption Congress' 17 June 2013 www.justice.gov/criminal/pr/speeches/2013/crm-speech-130617.html Accessed 8 December 2016.

Department of Justice, 'About the division' www.justice.gov/criminal/about-criminal-division Accessed 14 November 2016.

Department of Justice, 'United States of America vs. Alcatel-Lucent, S.A., f/kIa "Alcatel, S.A.," Deferred Prosecution Agreement' www.justice.gov/criminal/fraud/fcpa/cases/alcatel-etal/02-22-11alcatel-dpa.pdf Accessed 14 November 2016.

Department of Justice, 'Stanford' www.justice.gov/criminal/vns/caseup/stanfordr.html Accessed 14 November 2016.

Department of Justice, 'Alcatel-Lucent S.A. and three subsidiaries agree to pay $92 million to resolve Foreign Corrupt Practices Act investigation coordinated enforcement actions by Department of Justice and SEC result in penalties of more than $137 million' www.justice.gov/opa/pr/alcatel-lucent-sa-and-three-subsidiaries-agree-pay-92-million-resolve-foreign-corrupt Accessed 14 November 2016.

Department of Justice, 'Mythili Raman, Principal Deputy Assistant Attorney General DoJ. Press release' 27 December 2010 www.justice.gov/opa/pr/2010/December/10-crm-1481.html Accessed 8 December 2016.

Department of Justice, 'Former Chief Financial Officer of Siemens Argentina pleads guilty to role in multimillion dollar foreign bribery scheme' www.justice.gov/opa/pr/former-chief-financial-officer-siemens-argentina-pleads-guilty-role-multimillion-dollar Accessed 6 December 2016.

Department of Justice, 'Press release' 17 November 2009 www.sec.gov/news/press/2009/2009-249.htm Accessed 8 December 2016.

Department of Justice, '2014 Budget' www.justice.gov/jmd/2014summary/pdf/fy14-bud-sum.pdf#bs Accessed 14 November 2016.

Department of Justice, 'Criminal Division Fraud Section' www.justice.gov/criminal/sectionsoffices/chart Accessed 14 November 2016.

Department of Justice, 'Accomplishments under the leadership of Attorney General Eric Holder' www.justice.gov/accomplishments Accessed 16 January 2017.

Department of Justice, 'Attorney General Holder remarks on financial fraud prosecutions at NYU School of Law' www.justice.gov/opa/speech/attorney-general-holder-remarks-financial-fraud-prosecutions-nyu-school-law Accessed 14 November 2016.

Department of Justice, 'Individual accountability for corporate wrongdoing' (Yates Memorandum) 9 September 2015 www.justice.gov/dag/file/769036/download Accessed 2 January 2017.

Department of Justice, 'Criminal Division launches new FCPA Pilot Program' www.justice.gov/opa/blog/criminal-division-launches-new-fcpa-pilot-program Accessed 13 January 2017.

Department of Justice, 'Letter to HMT LLC' www.justice.gov/criminal-fraud/file/899116/download Accessed 13 January 2017.

Department of Justice, 'Former Willbros International executives sentenced to prison for their roles in $6 million foreign bribery scheme' 28 January 2010 www.justice.gov/opa/pr/2010/January/10-crm-102.html.

Department of Justice, 'Trevor Cook sentenced' www.justice.gov/usao/mn/downloads/082410.Cook%20sentenced.pdf Accessed 14 November 2016.

Department of Justice, 'Assistant Attorney General Lanny A. Breuer of the Criminal Division speaks at the Association of Certified Fraud Examiners Annual Conference San Diego – Tuesday, June 14, 2011' www.justice.gov/iso/opa/ag/speeches/2011/ag-speech-110614.html Accessed 14 November 2016.

Department of Justice, 'Innospec Inc. pleads guilty to FCPA charges and defrauding the United Nations; admits to violating the U.S. embargo against Cuba' www.justice.gov/opa/pr/innospec-inc-pleads-guilty-fcpa-charges-and-defrauding-united-nations-admits-violating-us Accessed 6 December 2016.

Department of Justice, 'Proposed legislative history. International Anti-Bribery Act of 1998' www.justice.gov/criminal/fraud/fcpa/docs/leghistory.pdf Accessed 8 December 2016.

Department of Justice, 'Non prosecution agreement' 22 April 2013 www.justice.gov/criminal/fraud/fcpa/cases/ralph-lauren/Ralph-Lauren.-NPA-Executed.pdf Accessed 14 November 2016.

Department of Justice, 'Acting Assistant Attorney General Mythili Raman delivers keynote address at the Global Anti-Corruption Congress' 17 June 2013 www.justice.gov/criminal/pr/speeches/2013/crm-speech-130617.html Accessed 8 December 2016.

Department of Justice, 'About the division' www.justice.gov/criminal/about-criminal-division Accessed 14 November 2016.

Department of Justice, 'Ralph Lauren Corporation resolves Foreign Corrupt Practices Act investigation and agrees to pay $882,000 monetary penalty' www.justice.gov/opa/pr/2013/April/13-crm-456.html Accessed 14 November 2016.

Department of Justice, 'Eric Holder, US Attorney General, speech to 15th Annual National Action Network Convention' 4 April 2013 www.justice.gov/iso/opa/ag/speeches/2013/ag-speech-130404.html Accessed 8 December 2016.

Department of Justice, 'Deutsche Bank agrees to pay $7.2 billion for misleading investors in its sale of residential mortgage-backed securities' www.justice.gov/opa/pr/deutsche-bank-agrees-pay-72-billion-misleading-investors-its-sale-residential-mortgage-backed Accessed 15 February 2017.

Department of Justice, 'Credit Suisse agrees to pay $5.28 billion in connection with its sale of residential mortgage-backed securities' www.justice.gov/opa/pr/credit-suisse-agrees-pay-528-billion-connection-its-sale-residential-mortgage-backed Accessed 15 February 2017.

Department of Justice, 'Goldman Sachs agrees to pay more than $5 billion in connection with its sale of residential mortgage backed securities' www.justice.gov/opa/pr/goldman-sachs-agrees-pay-more-5-billion-connection-its-sale-residential-mortgage-backed Accessed 15 February 2017.

Department of Justice, 'Morgan Stanley agrees to pay $2.6 billion penalty in connection with its sale of residential mortgage backed securities' www.justice.gov/opa/pr/morgan-stanley-agrees-pay-26-billion-penalty-connection-its-sale-residential-mortgage-backed Accessed 15 February 2017.

Department of Justice, 'United States sues Barclays Bank to recover civil penalties for fraud in the sale of residential mortgage-backed securities' www.justice.gov/opa/pr/united-states-sues-barclays-bank-recover-civil-penalties-fraud-sale-residential-mortgage Accessed 15 February 2017.

Department of Justice and Securities and Exchange Commission, 'FCPA. A resource guide to the U.S. Foreign Corrupt Practices Act' 15 www.sec.gov/spotlight/fcpa/fcpa-resource-guide.pdf Accessed 14 November 2016.

Devlin Lord, 'Trial by jury for fraud' (1986) 6 *Oxford J Legal Stud* 313.

Dictionary of Accounting, s.v. 'Deregulation' www.credoreference.com.ezproxy.uwe.ac.uk/entry/acbaccount/deregulation Accessed 18 October 2016.

Diersen, K L, 'Foreign Corrupt Practices Act' (1999) 36 *Am Crim L Rev* 753.

Doig, A, *Fraud* (Willan 2006).

Doig, A, and M Levi, 'Inter-agency work and the UK public sector investigation of fraud, 1996–2006: Joined-up rhetoric and disjointed reality' (2009) 19(3) *Policing and Society* 199–215.

Dooley, D V, and M Radke, 'Does severe punishment deter financial crimes' (2010) 4 *Charleston L Rev* 619.

Drinnan, R, and R Nicolson, 'Australia: Proposed reform to Australian foreign bribery legislation' (2012) 2 *IELR* 40.

Dunne, N, 'Recasting competition concurrency under the Enterprise and Regulatory Reform Act 2013' (2014) 77(2) *MLR* 254.

Eckert, S, 'The US Regulatory Approach to Terrorist Financing' in T Biersteker, and S Eckert (eds), *Countering the Financing of Terrorism* (Routledge Cavendish 2008).

The Economist, 'The LIBOR scandal: The rotten heart of finance' 7 July 2012 www.economist.com/node/21558281 Accessed 24 November 2016.

Eicher, S, 'Introduction: What Corruption is and Why it Matters' in S Eicher (ed) *Corruption in International Business: The Challenge of Cultural and Legal Diversity* (Ashgate 2009).

Eicher, S, 'Risk Management – Playing by the Rules' in S Eicher (ed) *Corruption in International Business: The Challenge of Cultural and Legal Diversity* (Ashgate 2009).

European Commission, 'European Anti-Fraud Office' http://ec.europa.eu/anti-fraud/home_en Accessed 17 October 2016.

European Commission, 'Welcome to Fin-net' http://ec.europa.eu/internal_market/fin-net/index_en.htm Accessed 18 October 2016.

European Union, 'Commission steps up efforts to forge a comprehensive anti-corruption policy at EU level' 3 June 2011 http://europa.eu/rapid/pressReleasesAction.do?refer

ence=MEMO/11/376&format=HTML&aged=0&language=EN&guiLanguage=en Accessed 17 January 2017.

FATF, 'Asia/Pacific Group on Money Laundering' www.fatf-gafi.org/pages/asiapacificgrouponmoneylaunderingapg.html Accessed 4 January 2017.

FATF, 'What do we do?' www.fatf-gafi.org/pages/aboutus/whatwedo/ Accessed 8 December 2016.

FATF, 'Summary of the third mutual evaluation report anti-money laundering and combating the financing of terrorism' 14 October 2005 www.fatf-gafi.org/media/fatf/documents/reports/mer/MER%20Australia%20ES.pdf Accessed 8 December 2016.

FCPA Professor, 'SEC enforcement of the FCPA – Year in review' www.fcpaprofessor.com/sec-enforcement-of-the-fcpa-year-in-review-3 Accessed 14 November 2016.

Federal Bureau of Investigation, 'Mortgage fraud' www.fbi.gov/investigate/white-collar-crime/mortgage-fraud Accessed 6 December 2016.

Federal Bureau of Investigation, 'White collar crime' www.fbi.gov/about-us/investigate/white_collar/whitecollarcrime Accessed 14 January 2017.

Federal Bureau of Investigation, '2010 mortgage report' www.fbi.gov/stats-services/publications/mortgage-fraud-2010 Accessed 24 November 2016.

Federal Bureau of Investigation, 'Financial crimes report to the public. Fiscal years 2010–2011' www.fbi.gov/stats-services/publications/financial-crimes-report-2010-2011/financial-crimes-report-2010-2011#Mortgage Accessed 18 October 2016.

Feldman, W, 'Staying in Compliance: Key Issues for White Collar Law Attorneys and their Multinational Clients' in *International White Collar Enforcement: Leading Lawyers on Preventative Measures, Regulatory Compliance, and Litigation* (Thompson Reuters/Aspatore 2013).

Financial Action Task Force, 'Risk based approach' www.fatf-gafi.org/documents/riskbasedapproach/ Accessed 14 November 2016.

Financial Action Task Force, 'Australia' www.fatf-gafi.org/countries/a-c/australia/ Accessed 8 December 2016.

Financial Action Task Force, 'International standards on combating money laundering and the financing of terrorism – The FATF recommendations' www.fatf-gafi.org/media/fatf/documents/recommendations/pdfs/FATF_Recommendations.pdf Accessed 8 December 2016.

Financial Action Task Force on Money Laundering, www.fatf-gafi.org/ Accessed 8 December 2016.

Financial Conduct Authority, 'About us' www.fca.org.uk/about Accessed 14 January 2017.

Financial Conduct Authority, 'Principles of good regulation' www.fca.org.uk/about/principles-good-regulation Accessed 24 November 2016.

Financial Conduct Authority, '*Handbook. Supervision. Fraud, Errors and Other Irregularities*' (SUP 15.3.17) www.handbook.fca.org.uk/handbook/SUP/15/3.html?searchtext=suspected%20fraud&searchtype=boolean Accessed 24 November 2016.

Financial Conduct Authority, 'Politically exposed persons' www.handbook.fca.org.uk/handbook/document/FC1_FCA_20130401.pdf#search='politically%20exposed%20person Accessed 24 November 2016.

Financial Conduct Authority, 'ICAP Europe Limited fined £14 million for significant failings in relation to LIBOR' www.fca.org.uk/news/icap-europe-limited-fined Accessed 24 November 2016.

Financial Conduct Authority, 'The FCA fines Rabobank £105 million for serious LIBOR-related misconduct' www.fca.org.uk/news/the-fca-fines-rabobank-105-million-for-serious-libor-related-misconduct Accessed 24 November 2016.

Financial Conduct Authority, '2013 Fines' www.fca.org.uk/news/news-stories/2013-fines.

Financial Conduct Authority, '2014 Fines' www.fca.org.uk/news/news-stories/2014-finesFinancial Conduct Authority Accessed 18 October 2016.

Financial Conduct Authority, '2015 Fines' www.fca.org.uk/news/news-stories/2015-fines Accessed 18 October 2016.

Financial Conduct Authority, 'Our future mission' www.fca.org.uk/publication/corporate/our-future-mission.pdf Accessed 27 October 2016.

Financial Conduct Authority, 'Market abuse' www.fca.org.uk/firms/markets/market-abuse Accessed 18 October 2016.

Financial Conduct Authority, 'Financial services regulation and enforcement: Recent developments and emerging issues' 9 October 2013 www.fca.org.uk/news/speeches/financial-services-regulation-enforcement Accessed 18 October 2016.

Financial Conduct Authority, 'Business Plan 2014/15' www.fca.org.uk/news/about-us/business-plan-2014-15 Accessed 18 October 2016.

Financial Conduct Authority, 'Enforcement' www.fca.org.uk/about/enforcement Accessed 24 November 2016.

Financial Conduct Authority, 'Warning notice 14/1' www.fca.org.uk/static/documents/warning-notice-statements/warning-notice-statement-14-1individual.pdf Accessed 24 November 2016.

Financial Conduct Authority, 'Final notice' www.fca.org.uk/publication/final-notices/paul-white.pdf.

Financial Conduct Authority, 'FCA publishes Decision Notice for former UBS LIBOR trader' www.fca.org.uk/news/press-releases/fca-publishes-decision-notice-former-ubs-libor-trader Accessed 18 October 2016.

Financial Conduct Authority, 'FCA bans former Deutsche Bank trader, Michael Ross Curtler, following LIBOR fraud' www.fca.org.uk/news/press-releases/fca-bans-former-deutsche-bank-trader-michael-ross-curtler-following-libor-fraud Accessed 18 October 2016.

Financial Conduct Authority, 'FCA fines five banks £1.1 billion for FX failings and announces industry-wide remediation programme' www.fca.org.uk/news/press-releases/fca-fines-five-banks-£11-billion-fx-failings-and-announces-industry-wide Accessed 16 September 2016.

Financial Conduct Authority, 'Handbook: Decision Procedures and Penalties Manual' DEPP 6.1.2 www.fshandbook.info/FS/html/FCA/DEPP/6/1 Accessed 18 October 2016.

Financial Conduct Authority, 'Insider dealers sentenced in Operation Tabernula trial' www.fca.org.uk/news/press-releases/insider-dealers-sentenced-operation-tabernula-trial Accessed 18 October 2016.

Financial Conduct Authority, 'JPMorgan Chase Bank N.A. fined £137,610,000 for serious failings relating to its Chief Investment Office's "London Whale" trades' www.fca.org.uk/news/jpmorgan-chase-bank-na-fined Accessed 18 October 2016.

Financial Conduct Authority, 'FCA Final Notice 2014: Mark Stevenson' www.fca.org.uk/your-fca/documents/final-notices/2014/mark-stevenson Accessed 18 October 2016.

Financial Conduct Authority, 'Financial incentives for whistleblowers. Note by the Financial Conduct Authority and the Prudential Regulation Authority for the Treasury Select

Committee' www.fca.org.uk/static/documents/financial-incentives-for-whistleblowers.pdf.

Financial Conduct Authority, 'FCA introduces new rules on whistleblowing' www.fca.org.uk/news/press-releases/fca-introduces-new-rules-whistleblowing Accessed 14 November 2016.

Financial Conduct Authority, 'Fines Table' 2013 www.fca.org.uk/news/news-stories/2013-fines2013 Accessed 18 October 2016.

Financial Crimes Enforcement Network, US Department of the Treasury, 'Mandatory e-filing FAQs' www.fincen.gov/mandatory-e-filing-faqs Accessed 24 November 2016.

Financial Crimes Enforcement Network (FinCEN), www.fincen.gov Accessed 14 November 2016.

Financial Fraud Enforcement Task Force, 'Bresnick M J, speech, 20 March 2013' www.justice.gov/iso/opa/doj/speeches/2013/opa-speech-130320.html Accessed 14 November 2016.

Financial Services Authority, 'FSA Business Plan 2012/13' www.fsa.gov.uk/static/pubs/plan/bp2012-13.pdf Accessed 18 October 2016.

Financial Services Authority, 'Banks' management of high money-laundering risk situations' www.fca.org.uk/publication/corporate/fsa-aml-final-report.pdf Accessed 24 November 2016.

Financial Services Authority, 'FSA publishes results of money laundering investigation' 8 March 2001 www.fsa.gov.uk/Pages/Library/Communication/PR/2001/029.shtml Accessed 24 November 2016.

Financial Services Authority, 'A reminder to FSA regulated firms after recent events in the Middle-East' 18 February 2011 www.fsa.gov.uk/pages/About/What/financial_crime/events_middle-east.shtml Accessed 4 November 2016.

Financial Services Authority, 'A regulatory response to the global banking crisis March' (Turner Review) www.fsa.gov.uk/pubs/other/turner_review.pdf Accessed 14 January 2017.

Financial Services Authority, 'Barclays fined £59.5 million for significant failings in relation to LIBOR and EURIBOR' www.fsa.gov.uk/library/communication/pr/2012/070.shtml Accessed 14 January 2017.

Financial Services Authority, 'Barclays Bank plc – Final Notice' 27 June 2012 www.fsa.gov.uk/static/pubs/final/barclays-jun12.pdf Accessed 18 October 2016.

Financial Services Authority, 'UBS fined £160 million for significant failings in relation to LIBOR and EURIBOR' http://webarchive.nationalarchives.gov.uk/20130301170532/http://www.fsa.gov.uk/library/communication/pr/2012/116.shtml Accessed 18 October 2016.

Financial Services Authority, 'FSA Final Notice 2013: The Royal Bank of Scotland' www.fca.org.uk/your-fca/documents/final-notices/2013/fsa-final-notice-2013-the-royal-bank-of-scotland-plc Accessed 18 October 2016.

Financial Services Authority, *Handbook SYSC 6.3* http://fsahandbook.info/FSA/html/handbook/SYSC/6/3 Accessed 18 October 2016.

Financial Services Authority, 'Enforcement Annual Performance Account. 2012/13' http://fca.org.uk/static/documents/annual-report/fsa-enforcement-performance-account-2012-13.pdf Accessed 18 October 2016.

Financial Services Authority, 'Fines Table' 2002 http://webarchive.nationalarchives.gov.uk/20130301170532/http://www.fsa.gov.uk/about/press/facts/fines/2002 Accessed 18 October 2016.

Financial Services Authority, 'Fines Table' 2003 http://webarchive.nationalarchives.gov.uk/20130301170532/http://www.fsa.gov.uk/about/press/facts/fines/2003 Accessed 18 October 2016.
Financial Services Authority, 'Fines Table' 2004 http://webarchive.nationalarchives.gov.uk/20130301170532/http://www.fsa.gov.uk/about/press/facts/fines/2003 Accessed 18 October 2016.
Financial Services Authority, 'Fines Table' 2005 http://webarchive.nationalarchives.gov.uk/20130301170532/http://www.fsa.gov.uk/about/press/facts/fines/2003 Accessed 18 October 2016.
Financial Services Authority, 'Fines Table' 2006 http://webarchive.nationalarchives.gov.uk/20130301170532/http://www.fsa.gov.uk/about/press/facts/fines/2003 Accessed 18 October 2016.
Financial Services Authority, 'Fines Table' 2007 http://webarchive.nationalarchives.gov.uk/20130301170532/http://www.fsa.gov.uk/about/press/facts/fines/2003 Accessed 18 October 2016.
Financial Services Authority, 'Fines Table' 2008 http://webarchive.nationalarchives.gov.uk/20130301170532/http://www.fsa.gov.uk/about/press/facts/fines/2008 Accessed 18 October 2016.
Financial Services Authority, 'Fines Table' 2009 http://webarchive.nationalarchives.gov.uk/20130301170532/http://www.fsa.gov.uk/about/press/facts/fines/2009 Accessed 18 October 2016.
Financial Services Authority, 'Fines Table' 2010 http://webarchive.nationalarchives.gov.uk/20130301170532/http://www.fsa.gov.uk/about/press/facts/fines/2010 Accessed 18 October 2016.
Financial Services Authority, 'Fines Table' 2011 http://webarchive.nationalarchives.gov.uk/20130301170532/http://www.fsa.gov.uk/about/press/facts/fines/2010 Accessed 18 October 2016.
Financial Services Authority, 'Fines Table' 2012 http://webarchive.nationalarchives.gov.uk/20130301170532/http://www.fsa.gov.uk/about/press/facts/fines/2010 Accessed 18 October 2016.
Financial Services Authority, 'Solicitor and his father-in-law found guilty in FSA insider dealing case' www.fsa.gov.uk/library/communication/pr/2009/042.shtml Accessed 18 October 2016.
Financial Services Authority, 'Former corporate broker intern and father found guilty of insider dealing' www.fsa.gov.uk/library/communication/pr/2009/149.shtml Accessed 18 October 2016.
Financial Services Authority, 'Former Cazenove broker sentenced to 21 months in prison for insider dealing' 11 March 2010 www.fsa.gov.uk/library/communication/pr/2010/043.shtml Accessed 18 October 2016.
Financial Services Authority, 'Ex-hedge fund trader sentenced for insider dealing' www.fsa.gov.uk/library/communication/pr/2010/104.shtml Accessed 18 October 2016.
Financial Services Authority, 'Insider dealing: Financial Services Authority prosecutes Mr Neil Rollins' www.fsa.gov.uk/library/communication/pr/2009/002.shtml Accessed 18 October 2016.
Financial Services Authority, 'Investment banker, his wife and family friend plead guilty to insider dealing' www.fsa.gov.uk/library/communication/pr/2011/002.shtml Accessed 18 October 2016.
Financial Services Bill 2012, www.parliament.uk/briefing-papers/RP12-8 Accessed 18 October 2016.

Financial Times, 'GSK to pay £297m fine for Chinese bribes' 14 September 2014 www.ft.com/cms/s/0/dea9811e-3fd5-11e4-936b-00144feabdc0.html#axzz3Eo0GXH00 Accessed 8 December 2016.

Financial Times, 'Horsemeat report calls for "food fraud" unit' 4 September 2014 www.ft.com/cms/s/0/ecc37282-3409-11e4-8832-00144feabdc0.html#axzz3D6kg3eVz Accessed 17 January 2017.

Financial Times, 'SFO faced uphill struggle in Nadir case' 22 August 2012 www.ft.com/cms/s/0/9a0dfb06-e53d-11e1-8ac0-00144feab49a.html#axzz2ucpXDq2D Accessed 16 September 2016.

Financial Times, 'SFO admits Tchenguiz case errors' 22 February 2012 www.ft.com/cms/s/0/01068b74-5d68-11e1-889d-00144feabdc0.html Accessed 16 September 2016.

Financial Times, 8 April 2014 www.ft.com/cms/s/0/5f0e1f06-bf41-11e3-a4af-00144feabdc0.html#axzz2yUAjxFyc Accessed 24 November 2016.

Financial Times, 'Alcoa in $384m deal to settle Bahrain bribery charges' 10 January 2014 www.ft.com/cms/s/0/62b10d60-793e-11e3-91ac-00144feabdc0.html#axzz2ucpXDq2D Accessed 24 November 2016.

Financial Times, 'Forex claims "as bad as Libor", says FCA' 4 February 2014 www.ft.com/cms/s/0/6d2f697a-8da8-11e3-bbe7-00144feab7de.html#axzz2wz74O2Ae Accessed 18 October 2016.

Financial Times, 'Top barrister chosen to lead Bank of England Forex enquiry' 12 March 2014 www.ft.com/content/e2a5e2b6-aa03-11e3-8bd6-00144feab7de Accessed 14 January 2017.

Financial Times, 'Businessman cleared of Vietnam bribery' 6 December 2012 www.ft.com/content/77e60e7c-3fb7-11e2-b2ce-00144feabdc0 Accessed 6 February 2017.

Financial Times, 'UK Economic Crime Agencies given fitness test' 12 March 2017 www.ft.com/content/cee98dde-05b0-11e7-aa5b-6bb07f5c8e12 Accessed 20 March 2017.

Finnerty, N, 'Judges set for fraud crackdown' *The Lawyer* (10 June 2013) 8.

Fisher, J, *The Times* 11 March 2010 www.thetimes.co.uk/tto/law/article2464153.ece Accessed 18 October 2016.

Fisher, J, 'Risk, Recklessness and Policing the Financial Markets' in N Ryder, U Turksen, and S Hassler (eds), *Fighting Financial Crime in the Global Economic Crisis: Policy, Trends and Sanctions* (Routledge Cavendish 2014).

Fisher, J, and J Bewsey, *The Law of Investor Protection* (Sweet & Maxwell 1997).

Fraud Advisory Panel, 'The Fraud Review: Ten years on' www.fraudadvisorypanel.org/wp-content/uploads/2016/06/The-Fraud-Review-Ten-Years-On-WEB.pdf Accessed 8 September 2016.

Fraud Advisory Panel, 'Fraud facts: Fraud in Scotland' 17 October 2013 www.fraudadvisorypanel.org/wp-content/uploads/2015/04/Fraud-Facts-17B-Fraud-in-Scotland-Revised-March14.pdf Accessed 4 January 2017.

Fraud Advisory Panel, 'Roskill revisited: Is there a case for a unified prosecution office?' 23 March 2010 www.fraudadvisorypanel.org/wp-content/uploads/2015/04/Roskill-Revisited-Final-24-Mar10.pdf Accessed 6 December 2016.

Fraud Trials Committee Report (HMSO 1986).

G20, 'About G20' www.g20australia.org/about_G20.html Accessed 4 January 2017.

G20, 'History' www.g20.org/Content/EN/StatischeSeiten/G20/Texte/2016-12-01-g20-geschichte-der-gipfel_en.html Accessed 20 March 2017.

Galpin, R D, 'A Central Banker's View' in *The Banks and Risk Management* (The Chartered Institute of Bankers 1988).

George, B, 'Edwin Hardin Sutherland: Sociological Criminologist' (1951) 16(1) *American Sociological Review* 2–9.

Gilbert, J-A, and J C Sharman, 'Turning a blind eye to bribery: Explaining failures to comply with the international anti-corruption regime' (2016) 64(1) *Political Studies* 74.

Gilligan, G, 'Financial crime in Australia' (2007) 27(1) *Economic Affairs* 10.

Gilligan, G, 'Jérôme Kerviel the "rogue trader" of Société Générale: Bad luck, bad apple, bad tree or bad orchard?' (2011) 32(12) *Co Law* 355–362.

Gilligan, G P, 'The origins of UK financial services regulation' (1997) 18(6) *Comp Law* 167–176.

Giuffo, J, 'Watergate' (2001) 40(4) *Columbia JR* 74.

Gordon, S D, 'The liability of colleges and universities for fraud, waste, and abuse in federally funded grants and project' (1992) 75 *EDUc L REP* 13.

Gower, L C B, *Review of Investor Protection* (HMSO 1984).

Gower, L C B, '"Big bang" and City regulation' (1988) 51 *MLR* 21.

de Grazia, J, 'Review of the Serious Fraud Office. Final Report. June 2008' http://webarchive.nationalarchives.gov.uk/20080804145057/http://www.sfo.gov.uk/publications/pdfs/JdeGrazia_Final_Review_of_SFO.pdf Accessed 6 July 2016.

Green, E, *Debtors to their Profession* (Routledge 2012).

Greene, E, and C Odorski, 'SEC enforcement in the financial sector: Addressing post-crisis criticism' (2015) 16(1) *Business Law International* 6.

Griffin, J P, 'New initiatives on bribery of foreign officials' (1994) 5(10) *ICCLR* 341.

The Guardian, 'SFO focuses on role of Robert Tchenguiz' 11 March 2011 www.theguardian.com/business/2011/mar/11/tchenguiz-kaupthing-serious-fraud-office?INTCMP=SRCH&guni=Article:in%20body%20link Accessed 16 September 2016.

The Guardian, 'SFO raids offices in Luxembourg over failed Icelandic bank Kaupthing' 29 March 2011 www.guardian.co.uk/business/2011/mar/29/robert-tchenguiz-kaupthing Accessed 16 September 2016.

The Guardian, 'Ex-chief of Fraud Office apologises over £1m severance payments' 15 March 2013 www.theguardian.com/law/2013/mar/15/fraud-office-chief-apology Accessed 24 November 2016.

The Guardian, 'Allen Stanford loses bid for retrial' 23 March 2012 www.guardian.co.uk/world/2012/mar/23/allen-stanford-loses-twitter-bid-retrial Accessed 13 April 2012.

The Guardian, 'Jail fraudsters for longer, judges told' www.theguardian.com/law/2014/may/23/jail-fraudsters-longer-judges-sentencing-council Accessed 14 November 2016.

The Guardian, 'Failing student jailed for trying to bribe professor' www.guardian.co.uk/uk/2013/apr/23/student-jailed-bribe-professor Accessed 14 November 2016.

The Guardian, 'Australian court's gagging order condemned as "abuse of legal process"' www.theguardian.com/world/interactive/2014/jul/30/redacted-supreme-court-victoria-gagging-order Accessed 8 December 2016.

Haines, J D, 'FSA determined to improve cleanliness of markets: Custodial sentences continue to be a real threat' (2008) 29(12) *Comp Law* 370.

Hammond, P, Chancellor of the Exchequer, 8 November 2016 HCWS 247.

Hansberry, H L, 'In spite of its good intentions, the Dodd-Frank Act has created an FCPA monster' (2012) 102 *JCRLC* 195.

Harrison, K, and N Ryder, *The Law Relating to Financial Crime in the United Kingdom* (Routledge 2017) 108.

HC, 8 November 1983 vol 48 col 83–84W.

HC Deb, 14 January 1986 vol 89 cc925–934.

HC Deb, 13 February 1986 vol 91 cc1148–1185.

HC Deb, 3 March 2010 vol 506 col 981.

HC Deb, 2 July 2012 col 612.

HC Deb, 2 July 2012 col 616.

HC Deb, 11 September 2013 vol 567 col 707W.

HC Deb, 30 January 2014 col 39WS.

HC Deb, 30 January 2014 vol 574 col 39W.

HC Deb, 4 February 2014 vol 575 col 147W.

HC Deb, 7 February 2017 vol 621 col 50WH.

Hemming, A, 'When is a code a code?' (2010) 15 *Deakin L Rev* 65.

Henning, P J, 'Maybe it should just be called federal fraud: The changing nature of the Mail Fraud Statute' (1995) 36 *BCL Rev* 435.

The HIH Royal Commission, www.hih.com.au/Group-HIHRoyalCommision.html Accessed 4 January 2017.

HL, 8 November 1983 vol 444 col WA790.

HM Crown Prosecution Service Inspectorate, 'Review of the Fraud Prosecution Service' 2008, 5 www.justiceinspectorates.gov.uk/crown-prosecution-service/wp-content/uploads/sites/3/2014/04/FPS_2008_thm_rpt.pdf Accessed 4 December 2016.

HM Crown Prosecution Service Inspectorate, 'Report to the Attorney General on the inspection of the Serious Fraud Office' November 2012 www.justiceinspectorates.gov.uk/crown-prosecution-service/wp-content/uploads/sites/3/2014/04/SFO_Nov12_rpt.pdf Accessed 6 December 2016.

HM Government, 'Elliott Review into the Integrity and Assurance of Food Supply Networks – Final Report' www.gov.uk/government/uploads/system/uploads/attachment_data/file/350726/elliot-review-final-report-july2014.pdf Accessed 14 January 2017.

HM Inspectorate of Constabulary, 'Policing in austerity' 33 www.hmic.gov.uk/wp-content/uploads/policing-in-austerity-meeting-the-challenge.pdf Accessed 18 October 2016.

HM Revenue and Customs, 'Guidance. Money laundering supervision: guidance for money service businesses.' https://www.gov.uk/government/publications/anti-money-laundering-guidance-for-money-service-businesses Accessed 24 November 2016.

HM Treasury, 'A new approach to financial regulation: Building a stronger system' (Cm 8012).

HM Treasury, 'A new approach to financial regulation: Transferring consumer credit regulation to the Financial Conduct Authority' www.gov.uk/government/uploads/system/uploads/attachment_data/file/221913/consult_transferring_consumer_credit_regulation_to_fca.pdf Accessed 18 October 2016.

HM Treasury, 'What we do' www.gov.uk/government/organisations/hm-treasury/about Accessed 18 October 2016.

HM Treasury, 'Financial sanctions: Regime-specific lists and release' www.gov.uk/government/collections/financial-sanctions-regime-specific-consolidated-lists-and-releases Accessed 18 October 2016.

HM Treasury, 'Speech by the Chancellor of the Exchequer, Rt Hon George Osborne MP, at Mansion House' 16 June 2010 www.gov.uk/government/speeches/speech-by-the-chancellor-of-the-exchequer-rt-hon-george-osborne-mp-at-mansion-house Accessed 8 December 2016.

HM Treasury, Office of Government Commerce, 'Competitive dialogue in 2008' http://webarchive.nationalarchives.gov.uk/20130129110402/http://www.hm-treasury.gov.uk/d/competitive_dialogue_procedure.pdf Accessed 14 November 2016.

Hoag, A D, 'Defrauding the Wire Fraud Statute: United States v. LaMacchia' (1995) 8 *Harv JL & Tech* 511.

Home Office, 'Home Secretary's speech to the FCA's Financial Crime Conference' www.gov.uk/government/speeches/home-secretarys-speech-to-the-fcas-financial-crime-conference Accessed 1 December 2016.

Home Office, 'Factsheet – Part 1 Chapter 2 – Power to obtain further information and extend the SARs moratorium period' www.gov.uk/government/uploads/system/uploads/attachment_data/file/564471/CF_Bill_-_Factsheet_4_-_SARs_moratorium_and_Request_Information_Power.pdf Accessed 24 November 2016.

Home Office, 'Factsheet – Criminal Finances Bill' www.gov.uk/government/uploads/system/uploads/attachment_data/file/564464/CF_Bill_-_Factsheet_1_-_The_Bill.pdf Accessed 24 November 2016.

Home Office, 'Counting rules for recorded crime' http://webarchive.nationalarchives.gov.uk/20110314171826/http://rds.homeoffice.gov.uk/rds/pdfs10/countgeneral10.pdf Accessed 14 January 2017.

Home Office, 'What we do' www.gov.uk/government/organisations/home-office/about Accessed 24 November 2016.

Honess, T M, M Levi, and E A Charman, 'Juror competence in serious frauds since Roskill: A research based assessment' (2004) 11(1) *JFC* 17.

Horder, J, 'Bribery as a form of criminal wrongdoing' (2011) 127 *LQR* 37.

Hotchkiss, C, 'The sleeping dog stirs: New signs of life in efforts to end corruption in international business' (1998) 17(1) *Journal of Public Policy & Marketing* 108.

House of Commons Committee of Public Accounts, 'Serious Fraud Office – redundancy and severance arrangements. Tenth Report of Session 2013–14' www.publications.parliament.uk/pa/cm201314/cmselect/cmpubacc/360/360.pdf Accessed 24 November 2016.

House of Commons Justice Committee, 'Serious Fraud Office supplementary estimate 2013–14' www.publications.parliament.uk/pa/cm201314/cmselect/cmjust/1005/1005.pdf Accessed 24 November 2016.

House of Commons Treasury Committee, 'Fixing LIBOR: Some preliminary findings Second Report of Session 2012–13 Volume I' www.publications.parliament.uk/pa/cm201213/cmselect/cmtreasy/481/481.pdf Accessed 24 November 2016.

The Independent, 'SFO left shamefaced after US nails City fraudster' 9 January 2014 www.independent.co.uk/news/uk/crime/sfo-left-shamefaced-after-us-nails-city-fraudster-9050099.html Accessed 24 November 2016.

Interdepartmental Committee on Sharepushing (Bodkin Committee), 1937 Cmd 5539.

International Association of Anti-Corruption Authorities, 'European Anti-Fraud Office' www.iaaca.org/AntiCorruptionAuthorities/ByInternationalOrganizations/InterGovernmentalOrganization/201202/t20120215_805457.shtml Accessed 17 October 2016.

International Chamber of Commerce, 'Combating extortion and bribery: ICC rules of conduct and recommendations (2005 revision)' www.unglobalcompact.org/docs/issues_doc/7.7/2005_ICC_Anti-Corruption_Rules_FINAL.pdf Accessed 8 December 2016.

International Monetary Fund, 'Financial system abuse, financial crime and money laundering – background paper' 5 www.imf.org/external/np/ml/2001/eng/021201.pdf Accessed 3 November 2016.

International Monetary Fund, 'Economic health check. Mining boom bodes bright future for Australia' www.imf.org/external/pubs/ft/survey/so/2010/car102810a.htm Accessed 16 December 2016.

International Organization for Standardization, 'About ISO' www.iso.org/iso/home/about.htm Accessed 18 October 2016.

International Organization for Standardization, 'ISO 37001:2016' www.iso.org/iso/home/store/catalogue_tc/catalogue_detail.htm?csnumber=65034 Accessed 18 October 2016.

Irving, J, *The City at Work* (Andre Deutsch 1981).

Jensen, N, and C-A Png, 'Implementation of the FATF 40 + 9 recommendations: A perspective from developing countries' (2011) 14(2) *JMLC* 110.

Johns, R, *Sentencing in Fraud Cases* (Judicial Commission of NSW 2012) 12.

Jordan, J, 'The OECD's call for an end to "corrosive" facilitation payments and the international focus on the facilitation payments exception under the Foreign Corrupt Practices Act' (2011) 13 *U Pa J Bus L* 881.

Joshua, J, 'OFT's credibility is in tatters following the failed BA price-fixing trial' www.lawgazette.co.uk/analysis/ofts-credibility-is-in-tatters-following-the-failed-ba-price-fixing-trial/55531.article Accessed 24 November 2016.

Judiciary of England and Wales, 'Central Criminal Court 2 May 2013, sentencing remarks of His Honour Judge Hone QC' www.judiciary.gov.uk/wp-content/uploads/JCO/Documents/Judgments/r-v-mccormack-sentencing-remarks-20130502.pdf Accessed 17 October 2016.

Julian, R F, 'Judicial perspectives on the conduct of serious fraud trials' (Oct 2007) *Crim L R* 751, 768.

Kay, J A, and D J Thompson, 'Privatisation: A policy in search of a rationale' (1986) 96(3) *The Economic Journal* 18–32.

Keeton, G W, 'Reports of committees' (1938) 1 *MLR* 313.

Kirk, D N, and A J Woodcock, *Serious Fraud: Investigation and Trial*, 2nd edn (Butterworths 1997).

KPMG, 'Value of UK fraud breaks £1 billion barrier for the first time in five years' https://home.kpmg.com/uk/en/home/insights/2017/01/uk-fraud-value-reaches-1bn-first-time-five-years.html Accessed 25 January 2017.

Latimer, P, 'Anti-bribery laws – compliance issues in Australia' (2017) 24(1) *JFC* 4.

The Law Commission, *Fraud* (*Law Com* No 276, 2002).

The Law Commission, *Reforming Bribery* (Law Com No 313, 2008).

The Law Commission, 'Legislating the Criminal Code: Corruption' www.gov.uk/government/publications/legislating-the-criminal-code-corruption Accessed 6 December 2016.

Leong, A, 'Definitional analysis: The war on terror and organised crime' (2004) 8(1) *Journal of Money Laundering Control* 22.

Levi, M, 'Blaming the jury: Frauds on trial' (1983) 10 *JL & Soc'y* 257.

Levi, M, 'Fraud in the courts. Roskill in context' (1986) 26(4) *Br J Criminal* 394.

Levi, M, 'Reforming the criminal fraud trial: An overview of the Roskill proposals' (1986) 13 *JL & Soc'y* 117.

Levi, M, 'Fraud on trial: What is to be done?' (2000) 21(2) *Co Law* 54, 55.

Levi, M, 'The Roskill Fraud Commission revisited: An assessment' (2003) 11(1) *JFC* 38.

Levi, M, 'Suite revenge? The shaping of folk devils and moral panics about white-collar crimes' (2009) *Brit J Criminol* 48.

Levi, M, and R G Smith, 'Fraud Vulnerabilities and the Global Financial Crisis' in *Trends and Issues in Crime and Criminal Justice*, Australian Institute of Criminology No 422 July 2011 www.aic.gov.au/publications/current%20series/tandi/421-440/tandi 422.html Accessed 17 January 2017.

Lomnicka, E, 'The future of consumer credit regulation: A chance to rationalise sanctions for breaches of financial services regulatory regimes?' (2013) 34(1) *Co Law* 13.

Lui, A, 'Macro and micro prudential regulatory failures between banks in the United Kingdom and Australia 2004–2009' (2013) *JFR&C* 242.

Lurie, J, N Burkill, and J Knoll, 'Bribery and corruption in the construction industry: Challenges for international construction and engineering projects' (2013) *Const LJ* 26.

McDermott, G, 'US/UK comparison' (2010) 160 *NLJ* 1673.

MacNeil, I, 'The trajectory of regulatory reform in the UK in the wake of the financial crisis' (2010) 11 *EBOR* 483.

McRea, H, and F Cairncross, *Capital City. London as a Financial Centre* (Eyre Methuen 1974).

Milman, D, 'Directors, governance and managerial responsibility: New developments in UK law' (2013) 346 *Co LN* 1.

Minister for Justice, 'AFP-hosted Fraud and Anti-Corruption Centre' www.ministerjustice.gov.au/Mediareleases/Pages/2014/ThirdQuarter/31July2014-AFPHostedFraudAndAntiCorruptionCentre.aspx Accessed 8 December 2016.

Ministry of Justice, 'Corporate liability for economic crime: Call for evidence' https://consult.justice.gov.uk/digital-communications/corporate-liability-for-economic-crime/ Accessed 16 January 2017.

Ministry of Justice, 'Post-legislative assessment of the Fraud Act 2006. Memorandum to the Justice Select Committee (Cm 8372)' 10 Accessed 4 January 2016.

Ministry of Justice, 'Explanatory notes to the Fraud Act 2006' www.opsi.gov.uk/acts/acts2006/en/ukpgaen_20060035_en_1.htm Accessed 18 October 2016.

Ministry of Justice, 'Explanatory document to the Public Bodies (Merger of the Director of Public Prosecutions and the Director of Revenue and Customs Prosecutions) Order 2014' www.legislation.gov.uk/ukdsi/2014/9780111107041/pdfs/ukdsiem_9780111107041_en.pdf Accessed 18 October 2016.

Ministry of Justice, 'Guidance about commercial organisations preventing bribery (section 9 of the Bribery Act 2010)' http://webarchive.nationalarchives.gov.uk/20101013220527/http://www.justice.gov.uk/consultations/briberyactconsultation.htm Accessed 14 November 2016.

Moberly, R E, 'Sarbanes-Oxley's structural model to encourage corporate whistleblowers' (2006) *BYU L Rev* 1107.

Model Criminal Code Officers Committee of the Standing Committee of Attorneys-General, 'Theft, Fraud, Bribery and Related Offences' in *Model Criminal Code* (December 1995) www.aphref.aph.gov.au_house_committee_laca_criminalcode_chap1.pdf Accessed 4 January 2017.

The Money Laundering Regulations 2007, SI 2007/2157.

Munday, R, 'The Roskill report on fraud trials' (1986) 45 *CLJ* 177.

National Archives, 'Magna Carta 1215' www.nationalarchives.gov.uk/museum/item.asp?item_id=3 Accessed 14 January 2017.

National Crime Agency, 'Submitting a Suspicious Activity Report (SAR) within the regulated sector' www.nationalcrimeagency.gov.uk/publications/517-submitting-a-suspicious-activity-report-sar-within-the-regulated-sector/file Accessed 24 November 2016.

National Crime Agency, 'What we do' www.nationalcrimeagency.gov.uk/about-us/what-we-do Accessed 24 November 2016.

National Fraud Authority, '2009 Annual Report & Accounts' http://webarchive.nationalarchives.gov.uk/20120816224015/http://www.attorneygeneral.gov.uk/nfa/GuidetoInformation/Documents/NFSA%20Accounts%20to%2031%20March%2009.pdf Accessed 18 October 2016.

National Fraud Authority, 'Annual fraud indicator' March 2012 www.homeoffice.gov.uk/publications/agencies-public-bodies/nfa/annual-fraud-indicator/annual-fraud-indicator-2012?view=Binary Accessed 18 October 2016.

National Fraud Authority, 'National Fraud Intelligence Bureau' www.gov.uk/government/organisations/national-fraud-authority/about Accessed 20 March 2017.

Neumann, M G, 'Neither admit nor deny: Recent changes to the Securities and Exchange Commission's longstanding settlement policy' (2015) 40 *J Corp L* 793.

The New York Times, 'Trump moves to roll back Obama-era financial regulations' 3 February 2017 www.nytimes.com/2017/02/03/business/dealbook/trump-congress-financial-regulations.html?_r=0 Accessed 4 February 2017.

NSW Government, 'Economic and business environment' www.business.nsw.gov.au/invest-in-nsw/about-nsw/economic-and-business-climate/state-economies Accessed 8 December 2016.

The Office of Fair Trading, 'Accountability' http://webarchive.nationalarchives.gov.uk/20140402142426/http://www.oft.gov.uk/about-the-oft/oft-structure/accountability/ Accessed 18 October 2016.

The Office of Fair Trading, 'What we do' http://webarchive.nationalarchives.gov.uk/20140402142426/http://www.oft.gov.uk/about-the-oft/what/ Accessed 18 October 2016.

The Office of Fair Trading, 'Frequently asked questions' http://webarchive.nationalarchives.gov.uk/20140402142426/http://www.oft.gov.uk/about-the-oft/faqs/ Accessed 18 October 2016.

The Office of Fair Trading, 'OFT announces criminal charges in estate agent investigations' http://webarchive.nationalarchives.gov.uk/20140402142426/http://www.oft.gov.uk/news-and-updates/press/2012/80-12 Accessed 18 October 2016.

The Office of Fair Trading, 'Owner of mileage correction business jailed for car clocking' 22 November 2012 www.gov.uk/cma-cases/mileage-correction-services-provider-investigation-and-conviction Accessed 24 November 2016.

The Office of Fair Trading, 'Trading Standards impact' http://oft.gov.uk/shared_oft/about_oft/oft1085.pdf Accessed 7 January 2013.

The Office of Fair Trading, 'Irresponsible lending' http://oft.gov.uk/about-the-oft/legal-powers/legal/cca/irresponsible Accessed 7 January 2013.

The Office of Fair Trading, 'Anti-money laundering registration' www.oft.gov.uk/OFTwork/aml/guidance#named5 Accessed 7 January 2013.

The Office of Fair Trading, 'Memorandum of understanding between the Office of Fair Trading and the Director of the Serious Fraud Office' October 2003 www.gov.uk/government/uploads/system/uploads/attachment_data/file/307038/MoU_CMAandSFO.PDF Accessed 17 January 2017.

The Office of Fair Trading, 'What is a cartel?' www.gov.uk/government/uploads/system/uploads/attachment_data/file/284413/oft435.pdf Accessed 17 January 2017.

Organisation for Economic Co-operation and Development (OECD), 'Phase 3 Report on implementing the OECD Anti-Bribery Convention in Australia' October 2012 www.oecd.org/daf/anti-bribery/Australiaphase3reportEN.pdf Accessed 8 December 2016.

Organisation for Economic Co-operation and Development (OECD), 'Australia: Phase 2 follow-up report on the implementation of the phase 2 recommendations application of the convention on combating bribery of foreign public officials in international business transactions and the 1997 revised recommendation on combating bribery in international business transactions' www.oecd.org/daf/anti-bribery/anti-briberyconvention/41305864.pdf Accessed 8 December 2016.

Organisation for Economic Co-operation and Development (OECD), 'Business approaches to combating bribery' www.oecd.org/corporate/mne/WP-2003_2.pdf Accessed 6 December 2016.

Organisation for Economic Co-operation and Development (OECD), 'Seriously concerned by lack of foreign bribery convictions, but encouraged by recent efforts by the Australian Federal Police' www.oecd.org/newsroom/oecdseriouslyconcernedbylackofforeignbriberyconvictionsbutencouragedbyrecenteffortsbytheaustralianfederalpolice.htm Accessed 8 December 2016.

Organisation for Economic Co-operation and Development (OECD), 'Stocktaking of business integrity and anti-bribery legislation, policies and practices in twenty African countries – OECD-AFDB Joint Initiative to Support Business Integrity and Anti-Bribery Efforts in Africa' 18 www.oecd.org/daf/anti-bribery/Stocktaking%20of%20business%20integrity%20and%20Anti-bribery%20Legislation,%20Policies%20and%20Practices%20in%20Twenty%20African%20Countries.pdf Accessed 8 December 2016.

Organisation for Economic Co-operation and Development (OECD), 'Australia: Follow-up to the phase 3 report & recommendations April 2015 8' www.oecd.org/daf/anti-bribery/Australia-Phase-3-Follow-up-Report-ENG.pdf Accessed 6 February 2017.

Organisation for Economic Co-operation and Development (OECD), 'OECD Convention on Combating Bribery of Foreign Public Officials in International Business Transactions (1997)' www.oecd.org/corruption/oecdantibriberyconvention.htm www.oecd.org/daf/anti-bribery/antibriberyconventionratification.pdf Accessed 6 December 2016.

O'Shea, E, N McLeod, and A Beal, 'Regulatory: Back to the drawing board' (2010) 160 *NLJ* 759.

Organisation of American States, 'The Inter-American Convention against Corruption' www.oas.org/juridico/english/corr_bg.htm Accessed 8 December 2016.

Ormerod, D, 'The Fraud Act 2006 – Criminalised lying?' *Crim LR* (Mar 2007) 193–219.

Oxford English Dictionary Online (Oxford University Press, December 2016) Accessed 12 December 2016.

Page, F, 'Defining fraud: An argument in favour of a general offence of fraud' (1997) 4(4) *JFC* 288.

Palmer, A A, 'The Financial Crisis and its Relationship with White Collar Crime in the United States of America: Time for the Feds to Fight Back?' in N Ryder and others (eds), *The Financial Crisis and White Collar Crime – Legislative and Policy Responses. A Critical Assessment* (Routledge 2017).

Parliament of Australia, 'The Constitution of Australia' www.aph.gov.au/About_Parliament/Senate/Powers_practice_n_procedures/Constitution.aspx Accessed 4 January 2017.

Parliament of Australia, 'Australia's implementation of the OECD Anti-Bribery Convention' www.aph.gov.au/About_Parliament/Parliamentary_Departments/Parliamentary_Library/pubs/BN/2011-2012/AntiBribery Accessed 8 December 2016.

Parliament of Australia, 'Foreign bribery' www.aph.gov.au/Parliamentary_Business/Committees/Senate/Economics/Foreignbribery45th Accessed 5 February 2017.

Parliament of Australia, 'The Senate: Economics References Committee' 3.3 http://www.aph.gov.au/Parliamentary_Business/Committees/Senate/Economics/ASIC/Final_Report/c23 Accessed 6 February 2017.

Parliament of Australia, 'The performance of the Australian Securities and Investments Commission' www.aph.gov.au/Parliamentary_Business/Committees/Senate/Economics/ASIC/Final_Report/index Accessed 6 February 2017.

Parliament of Australia, 'Joint Committee on the Australian Commission for Law Enforcement Integrity. Note Printing Australia and Securency – a case study on risk management and integrity practices' www.aph.gov.au/Parliamentary_Business/Committees/Joint/Australian_Commission_for_Law_Enforcement_Integrity/Completed_inquiries/2010-13/integrity_inter_op/report/c02 Accessed 8 December 2016.

Parliament of New South Wales, 'Fraud and identity theft' 3 www.parliament.nsw.gov.au/researchpapers/Documents/fraud-and-identity-theft/08-03.pdf Accessed 4 January 2017.

Payne, B K, *White-collar Crime* (Sage 2013).

Peat, R, I Mason, and S Bazley, 'The FSA as a criminal prosecutor' (2010) *Co Law* 31(4) 119.

Pickworth, J, 'The Fraud Act 2006: A death knell for conspiracy to defraud – the "prosecutor's darling"?' *Euro News* (Aug 2009) 64, 1–4.

Podgor, E S, 'Criminal fraud' (1999) 48 *Am U L Rev* 729.

Practical Law, 'Insider dealing: FCA criminal prosecutions tracker' http://uk.practicallaw.com.ezproxy.uwe.ac.uk/5-502-2966?q=insider+dealing#a598239 Accessed 18 October 2016.

Rakoff, J S, 'The financial crisis: Why have no high-level executives been prosecuted?' *The New York Review of Books* www.nybooks.com/articles/archives/2014/jan/09/financial-crisis-why-no-executive-prosecutions/ Accessed 24 November 2016.

Rakoff, J S, 'The Federal Mail Fraud Statute (Part I)' (1980) 18 *Duq L Rev* 771.

Raphael, M, *Blackstone's Guide to the Bribery Act 2010* (OUP 2010).

Raphael, M, *Bribery: Law and Practice* (OUP 2016) 143.

Rawlings, P, 'Reform of bank regulation in the United Kingdom: The opening salvo' (2010) *JIBLR* 522.

RealBusiness, 'Re-write the Bribery Act and allow "facilitation payments" says MP' http://realbusiness.co.uk/article/21413-rewrite-the-bribery-act-and-allow-facilitation-payments-saysmp Accessed 14 November 2016.

Recker, C, 'The National Crime Agency: A Critical Analysis of its Potential Impact on the UK's Financial Crime Policy' in N Ryder and others (eds), *The Financial Crisis and White Collar Crime – Legislative and Policy Responses. A Critical Assessment* (Routledge 2017).

Report of the Committee to Review the Functioning of the Financial Institutions (Wilson Committee), Cmd 7937 (HMSO 1980).

Report of the Departmental Committee on Jury Service (1965) Cmnd 2627.

Reserve Bank of Australia, 'Statement concerning Securency International Pty Ltd and Note Printing Australia Ltd' www.rba.gov.au/media-releases/2011/mr-11-14.html Accessed 4 January 2017.

Reuters, 'Turkey releases Polly Peck fraudster Nadir after repatriation from Britain' http://uk.reuters.com/article/uk-turkey-britain-nadir-idUKKCN0XJ0G4 Accessed 24 November 2016.

Reuters, 'UK bribery trial collapses in blow to anti-fraud agency' 10 December 2013 www.reuters.com/article/2013/12/10/britain-bahrain-trial-idUSL6N0JP2FL20131210 Accessed 24 November 2016.

Reuters, 'UK fraud prosecutor seeks extra 19 million pounds for Libor, other cases' 30 January 2014 http://uk.reuters.com/article/2014/01/30/uk-sfo-budget-idUKBREA0T14O20140130 Accessed 4 November 2016.

Reuters, 'U.S. charges two ex-JPMorgan bankers over "London Whale" loss' 14 August 2013 http://uk.reuters.com/article/2013/08/14/us-jpm-whale-charges-idUSBRE97D0QU20130814 Accessed 18 October 2016.

Reynolds, G H, 'Ham sandwich nation: Due process when everything is a crime' University of Tennessee Legal Studies Research Paper No. 20620 January 2013 http://ssrn.com/abstract=2203713 or http://dx.doi.org/10.2139/ssrn.2203713 Accessed 14 November 2016.

Ritchie, R, *What Goes On in the City?* (Woodhead Faulkner 1986).

Robb, G, *White-Collar Crime in Modern England* (CUP 1992).

Robb, V, 'The Genesis of Regulation' in *Financial Stability Review – Autumn 1997* (Bank of England) 29 www.bankofengland.co.uk/archive/Documents/historicpubs/fsr/1997/fsrfull9710.pdf Accessed 18 October 2016.

Ross, S, and M Hannan, 'Australia's new anti-money laundering strategy' (2008) 19 *Current Issues Crim Just* 135.

Russo, G, 'Target criminal "upperworld"' *Baltimore Sun* 11 June 2002 http://articles.baltimoresun.com/2002-07-11/news/0207110056_1_ethos-tax-evasion-dapper Accessed 14 January 2017.

Ryder, N, 'The Financial Services Authority and money laundering. A game of cat and mouse' (2008) 67(3) *CLJ* 639.

Ryder, N, *Financial Crime in the 21st Century* (Edward Elgar 2011).

Ryder, N, *Money Laundering – An Endless Cycle?* (Routledge 2012).

Ryder, N, *The Financial Crisis and White Collar Crime – The Perfect Storm* (Edward Elgar 2014).

Ryder, N, 'White collar crime and the global financial crisis; How long will we have to wait for the day of reckoning?' (2013) 57 *Criminal Law News* 5, 11.

Ryder, N, 'To confiscate or not to confiscate? A comparative analysis of the confiscation of the proceeds of crime legislation in the United States of America and the United Kingdom' (2013) 8 *JBL* 767.

Salbu, S R, 'Bribery in the global market: A critical analysis of the Foreign Corrupt Practices Act' (1997) 54 *Wash & Lee L Rev* 229.

Salem, G R, and L M Franze, 'The whistleblower provisions of the Sarbanes-Oxley Act of 2002' http://apps.americanbar.org/labor/oshlcomm/mw/Papers/2003/salem.pdf Accessed 14 November 2016.

Sathye, M, 'Estimating the cost of compliance of AMLCTF for financial institutions in Australia' (2008) *JFC* 347.

Saunders, P, and M Wong, 'The social impact of the global financial crisis in Australia' (2011) 46(3) *Australian Journal of Social Issues* 292.

Schipani, C A, 'Falling off the corporate ladder: Prosecution for financial fraud in the United States' (2011) 32(11) *Co Law* 336.

Securities and Exchange Commission, 'A new model for SEC enforcement: Producing bold and unrelenting results' www.sec.gov/news/speech/chair-white-speech-new-york-university-111816.html Accessed 5 January 2017.

Securities and Exchange Commission, 'The investor's advocate: How the SEC protects investors, maintains market integrity, and facilitates capital formation' www.sec.gov/about/whatwedo.shtml Accessed 14 November 2016.

Securities and Exchange Commission, 'Strategic Plan – Fiscal Years 2010–2015' www.sec.gov/about/secstratplan1015f.pdf Accessed 14 November 2016.

Securities and Exchange Commission, 'SEC announces enforcement results for FY [to September] 2016' www.sec.gov/news/pressrelease/2016-212.html Accessed 2 January 2017.

Securities and Exchange Commission, 'Fiscal year 2013 Agency Financial Report' 17 www.sec.gov/about/secpar/secafr2013.pdf Accessed 16 January 2017.

Securities and Exchange Commission, 'Speech Mary Jo White: Deploying the full enforcement arsenal' 26 September 2013 www.sec.gov/News/Speech/Detail/ Speech/ 13705398412022016 Accessed 2 January 2017.

Securities and Exchange Commission, 'The laws that govern the securities industry' www.sec.gov/about/laws.shtml#df2010 Accessed 14 November 2016.

Securities and Exchange Commission, 'Speech by SEC chairman: Opening statement at SEC open meeting: Item 2 – whistleblower program' 25 May 2011 www.sec.gov/news/speech/2011/spch052511mls-item2.htm Accessed 14 November 2016.

Securities and Exchange Commission, '2016 Annual Report to Congress on the Dodd-Frank whistleblower program' www.sec.gov/whistleblower/reportspubs/annual-rep orts/owb-annual-report-2016.pdf Accessed 5 January 2017.

Securities and Exchange Commission, 'SEC whistleblower program surpasses $100 million in awards' 30 August 2016 www.sec.gov/news/pressrelease/2016-173.html Accessed 2 January 2017.

Securities and Exchange Commission, 'Final order' www.whistleblower-defense.com/files/2014/06/Final-Order7.pdf Accessed 14 November 2016.

Securities and Exchange Commission, 'Market summary 31 December 2013' www.sec.gov/divisions/corpfin/internatl/foreignmarketsumm2013.pdf Accessed 14 November 2016.

Securities and Exchange Commission, 'United settles charges in case of flight route to benefit public official' 2 December 2016 www.sec.gov/news/pressrelease/2016-253.html Accessed 13 January 2017.

Securities and Exchange Commission, 'SEC enforcement actions' www.sec.gov/spotlight/enf-actions-fc.shtml Accessed 8 December 2016.

Securities and Exchange Commission, 'Press release. SEC announces non-prosecution agreement with Ralph Lauren Corporation involving FCPA misconduct' 22 April 2013 www.sec.gov/news/press/2013/2013-65.htm Accessed 14 November 2016.

Securities and Exchange Commission, 'SEC v Magyar Telecomm and Deutsche Telecomm' www.sec.gov/litigation/complaints/2011/comp22213-co.pdf Accessed 8 December 2016.

Securities and Exchange Commission, 'What is a Ponzi scheme?' www.sec.gov/answers/ponzi.htm Accessed 11 January 2017.

Sentencing Council, 'Fraud, bribery and money laundering offences: Definitive guideline' www.sentencingcouncil.org.uk/publications/item/fraud-bribery-and-money-launder ing-offences-definitive-guideline/ Accessed 2 January 2017.

Serious Fraud Office, 'About us' www.sfo.gov.uk/about-us/ Accessed 6 December 2016.

Serious Fraud Office (Green, D), 'Cambridge Symposium 2014' www.sfo.gov.uk/2014/09/02/cambridge symposium-2014/ Accessed 18 October 2016.

Serious Fraud Office, 'Former Securency manager sentenced for corruption' www.sfo.gov.uk/2016/05/12/former-securency-manager-sentenced-corruption/ Accessed 1 February 2017.

Serious Fraud Office, 'Enforcement of the United Kingdom's Bribery Act – Facilitation payments' www.sfo.gov.uk/publications/guidance-policy-and-protocols/bribery-act-guidance/ Accessed 4 January 2017.

Serious Fraud Office, 'Guidelines on plea discussions' www.cps.gov.uk/publications/directors_guidance/director_s_guidance_to_accompany_the_attorney_general_s_guidelines_on_plea_discussions_in_cases_of_serious_or_complex_fraud.html Accessed 20 March 2017.

Serious Fraud Office, 'Alstom Network UK Ltd & Alstom Power Ltd' www.sfo.gov.uk/ca ses/alstom-network-uk-ltd-alstom-power-ltd/ Accessed 6 December 2016.

Serious Fraud Office, 'Smith and Ouzman Limited' www.sfo.gov.uk/cases/smith-ouzman-ltd/ Accessed 6 December 2016.

Serious Fraud Office, 'GlaxoSmithKline plc investigation' www.sfo.gov.uk/press-room/latest-press-releases/press-releases-2014/glaxosmithkline-plc-investigation.aspx.

Serious Fraud Office, 'Bribery Act guidance' www.sfo.gov.uk/publications/guidance-policy-and-protocols/bribery-act-guidance/ Accessed 14 November 2016.

Serious Fraud Office, 23 August 2012 www.sfo.gov.uk/2012/08/23/asil-nadir-sentenced/ Accessed 14 November 2016.

Serious Fraud Office, 'What is fraud?' http://webarchive.nationalarchives.gov.uk/20130704104410/http://www.sfo.gov.uk/fraud/what-is-fraud.aspx Accessed 18 October 2016.

Serious Fraud Office, 'What we do and who we work with' www.sfo.gov.uk/about-us/what-we-do-and-who-we-work-with.aspx.

Serious Fraud Office, 'Annual Report 2009–10' 1 http://webarchive.nationalarchives.gov.uk/20120408054128/http://www.sfo.gov.uk/about-us/annual-reports–accounts/annual-reports/annual-report-2009-2010.aspx Accessed 6 December 2016.

Serious Fraud Office, 'Ethical business conduct: An enforcement perspective' www.sfo.gov.uk/2014/03/06/ethical-business-conduct-enforcement-perspective/ Accessed 11 March 2017.

Serious Fraud Office, 'The Serious Fraud Office – More effective and costing less' 7 April 2011 www.sfo.gov.uk/press-room/latest-press- releases/press-releases-2011/serious-fraud-office-more-effective-and-costing-less.aspx Accessed 24 March 2014.

Serious Fraud Office, 'Asil Nadir found guilty' www.sfo.gov.uk/2012/08/22/asil-nadir-found-guilty/ Accessed 16 September 2016.

Serious Fraud Office, 'Kaupthing hf' www.sfo.gov.uk/cases/kaupthing-hf/ Accessed 16 September 2016.

Serious Fraud Office, 'Annual Report and Accounts 2011–2012' www.sfo.gov.uk/publications/corporate-information/annual-reports-accounts/ Accessed 24 November 2016.

Serious Fraud Office, 'Annual Report and Accounts 2012–2013' www.sfo.gov.uk/publications/corporate-information/annual-reports-accounts/ Accessed 24 November 2016.

Serious Fraud Office, 'Annual Report and Accounts 2013–2014' www.sfo.gov.uk/download/annual-report-2013-2014/?wpdmdl=2199 Accessed 6 December 2016.

Serious Fraud Office, 'Annual Report and Accounts 2015–16' www.sfo.gov.uk/publications/corporate-information/annual-reports-accounts/ Accessed 6 September 2016.

Serious Fraud Office, 'Speech by David Green – 10th Annual Corporate Accountability Conference held at PricewaterhouseCoopers on 14 June 2012' www.sfo.gov.uk/2012/06/14/10th-annual-corporate-accountability-conference-held-pricewaterhousecoopers/ Accessed 6 December 2016.

Serious Fraud Office, 'Deferred prosecution agreements – The perspective from England and Wales' www.sfo.gov.uk/2016/09/14/deferred-prosecution-agreements-perspective-england-wales/ Accessed 6 December 2016.

Serious Fraud Office, 'Statement on data loss incident' www.sfo.gov.uk/2013/08/08/statement-data-loss-incident/ Accessed 26 September 2016.

Serious Fraud Office, 'Richard Alderman, The Bribery Act 2010 – The SFO's approach and international compliance' 9 February 2011 http://webarchive.nationalarchives.gov.uk/20120408054128/http://www.sfo.gov.uk/about-us/our-views/director's-speeches/speeches-2011/the-bribery-act-2010—the-sfo's-approach-and-international-compliance.aspx Accessed 6 December 2017.

Serious Fraud Office, 'Victor Dahdaleh charged with bribery' www.sfo.gov.uk/press-room/press-release-archive/press-releases-2011/victor-dahdaleh-charged-with-bribery.aspx Accessed 13 January 2014.

Serious Fraud Office, 'Statement: R v Dahdaleh' www.sfo.gov.uk/2013/12/10/statement-r-v-dahdaleh-2/ Accessed 24 November 2016.

Serious Fraud Office, 'Four sentenced for role in Innospec corruption' www.sfo.gov.uk/2014/08/04/four-sentenced-role-innospec-corruption/ Accessed 6 December 2016.

Serious Fraud Office, 'Innospec judgment' www.sfo.gov.uk/2014/09/19/statement-innospec-judgement/ Accessed 6 December 2016.

Serious Fraud Office, 'LIBOR' www.sfo.gov.uk/cases/libor-landing/ Accessed 18 October 2016.

Serious Fraud Office, 'Cambridge Symposium 2016' www.sfo.gov.uk/2016/09/05/cambridge-symposium-2016/ Accessed 8 September 2016.

Serious Fraud Office, 'Crime and Courts Act 2013: Deferred Prosecution Agreement Code of Practice' 1 www.sfo.gov.uk/publications/guidance-policy-and-protocols/deferred-prosecution-agreements/ Accessed 6 December 2016.

Serious Fraud Office, 'Enforcing the UK Bribery Act – The UK Serious Fraud Office's perspective' www.sfo.gov.uk/2014/11/17/stuart-alford-qc-enforcing-uk-bribery-act-uk-serious-fraud-offices-perspective/ Accessed 6 December 2016.

Serious Fraud Office, 'LIBOR: SFO to investigate' www.sfo.gov.uk/2012/07/06/libor-sfo-to-investigate/ Accessed 25 February 2014.

Serious Fraud Office, 'Oxford Publishing Ltd to pay almost £1.9 million as settlement after admitting unlawful conduct in its East African operations' 3 July 2012 www.sfo.gov.uk/2012/07/03/oxford-publishing-ltd-pay-almost-1-9-million-settlement-admitting-unlawful-conduct-east-african-operations/ Accessed 6 December 2016.

Serious Fraud Office, 'Serious Fraud Office successfully obtains first ever Civil Recovery Order involving major plc' http://webarchive.nationalarchives.gov.uk/20110704124145/http://www.sfo.gov.uk/press-room/latest-press-releases/press-releases-2008/balfour-beatty-plc.aspx Accessed 6 December 2016.

Serious Fraud Office, 'SFO obtains Civil Recovery Order against AMEC' http://webarchive.nationalarchives.gov.uk/20110704124145/http://www.sfo.gov.uk/press-room/latest-press-releases/press-releases-2009/sfo-obtains-civil-recovery-order-against-amec-plc.aspx Accessed 6 December 2016.

Serious Fraud Office, 'The Serious Fraud Office and Vincent Tchenguiz announce settlement of civil claims' www.sfo.gov.uk/press-room/latest-press-releases/press-releases-2014/the-serious-fraud-office-and-vincent-tchenguiz-announce-settlement-of-civil-claims.aspx.

Serious Fraud Office, 'The Serious Fraud Office and Robert Tchenguiz announce settlement of civil claims' www.sfo.gov.uk/press-room/latest-press-releases/press-releases-2014/the-serious-fraud-office-and-robert-tchenguiz-announce-settlement-of-civil-claims.aspx Accessed 18 October 2016.

Serious Fraud Office, 'LIBOR (Yen) Hayes' www.sfo.gov.uk/cases/libor-hayes/ Accessed 23 August 2016.

Serious Fraud Office, 'LIBOR (Yen) Interdealer brokers' www.sfo.gov.uk/cases/libor-interdealer-brokers/ Accessed 23 August 2016.

Serious Fraud Office, 'LIBOR US dollar (Barclays)' www.sfo.gov.uk/cases/libor-barclays/ Accessed 23 August 2016.

Serious Fraud Office, 'Speech to Cambridge Symposium 2013' www.sfo.gov.uk/about-us/our-views/director's-speeches/speeches-2013/cambridge-symposium-2013.aspx Accessed 27 August 2014.

Serious Fraud Office, 'Forex investigation' www.sfo.gov.uk/press-room/latest-press-releases/press-releases-2014/forex-investigation.aspx Accessed 18 October 2016.

Serious Fraud Office, 'Speech to Cambridge Symposium 2013' www.sfo.gov.uk/2013/09/02/cambridge-symposium-2013/ Accessed 17 January 2017.

Serious Fraud Office, 'SFO confirms DPA in principle with Rolls-Royce PLC' www.sfo.gov.uk/2017/01/16/sfo-confirms-dpa-in-principle-with-rolls-royce-plc/ Accessed 20 March 2017.

Sinha, G, 'Post-crisis Regulation and Prosecutions in Financial Crime: Progress or Paradox?' in N Ryder and others (eds), *The Financial Crisis and White Collar Crime – Legislative and Policy Responses. A Critical Assessment* (Routledge 2017).

Smith, R G, 'Fraud and financial abuse of older persons' (2000) 11 *Current Issues in Crim Just* 273.

Sorensen, T C, 'Improper payments abroad: Perspectives and proposals' (1976) 54 *Foreign Aff* 719.

Squire, R, and S Ostlund, 'Racketeer influenced and corrupt organizations' (2012) 49 *Am Crim L Rev* 1211.

Staple, G, 'Serious and complex fraud: A new perspective' (1993) 56(2) *MLR* 127.

Stefanuc, R, 'Corruption, or how to tame the shrew with the European Union stick: The new anti-corruption initiative of the European Commission' (2011) 12 *ERA Forum* 427.

Stern, W E, 'Impact of the Volcker rule and related Dodd-Frank Act requirements on fund sponsors affiliated with non-US banking organisations' (2013) 4 *JIBFL* 229.

Stokes, R, 'LIBOR Manipulation: The Limits and Potential of Corporate Criminal Liability' in N Ryder, U Turksen, and S Hassler (eds), *Fighting Financial Crime in the Global Economic Crisis: Policy, Trends and Sanctions* (Routledge Cavendish 2014).

Strader, J K, *Understanding White Collar Crime* (LexisNexis 2002).

Strader, J K, 'White collar crime and punishment: Reflections on Michael, Martha and Milberg Weiss' (2007) 15 *Geo Mason L Rev* 94.

The Sunday Times, 'FCA ignored warnings of false market' 6 April 2014 www.thesundaytimes.co.uk/sto/business/Finance/article1396697.ece Accessed 18 October 2016.

Suskind, R, *The One Percent Doctrine* (Simon & Schuster 2006).

Sutherland, E H, 'White collar criminality' (1940) *Am Soc Rev* 1.

Sutherland, E H, 'Crime and business' (1941) 217 *Annals Amer Acad Pol & Soc Sci* 112.

Sutherland, E H, *White Collar Crime: The Uncut Version* (Yale University Press 1983).

The Sydney Morning Herald, 'Senate launches enquiry into ASIC' www.smh.com.au/business/senate-launches-inquiry-into-asic-20130620-2oksh.html#ixzz2l6sZzgpo Accessed 8 December 2016.

Tarun, R W, and P P Tomczak, 'A proposal for a United States Department of Justice Foreign Corrupt Practices Act leniency policy' (2010) 47 *Am Crim L Rev* 153.

Taylor, M, *'Twin Peaks': A Regulatory Structure for the New Century* (Centre for the Study of Financial Innovation 1995).

Taylor, M W, 'The road from "Twin Peaks" – and the way back' (2009) 16(1) *Connecticut ILJ* 61.

The Telegraph, 'Soaring ambitions of OFT get shot down' 11 May 2010 www.telegraph.co.uk/finance/comment/damianreece/7707709/Soaring-ambitions-of-OFT-get-shot-down.html Accessed 24 November 2016.

The Telegraph, 'W, for FSA?' 17 March 2011 www.telegraph.co.uk/finance/newsbysector/banksandfinance/8386709/What-next-for-the-FSA.html Accessed 18 October 2016.

The Telegraph, 'Director speaks out over plan to strip Serious Fraud Office of prosecution powers' 19 March 2011 www.telegraph.co.uk/finance/businesslatestnews/8392895/Director-speaks-out-over-plan-to-strip-Serious-Fraud-Office-of-prosecution-powers.html Accessed 24 November 2016.

The Telegraph, 'Russian officials told bribes are not tax deductible' 4 September 2012 www.telegraph.co.uk/finance/financial-crime/9519292/Russian-officials-told-bribes-are-not-tax-deductible.html Accessed 8 December 2016.

The Telegraph, '"BAE" documents lost by SFO found at cannabis farm' 13 September 2013 www.telegraph.co.uk/finance/financial-crime/10307238/BAE-documents-lost-by-SFO-found-at-cannabis-farm.html Accessed 24 November 2016.

The Telegraph, 'Fresh reversal for SFO as £40m bribery trial collapses' 10 December 2013 www.telegraph.co.uk/finance/financial-crime/10509552/Fresh-reversal-for-SFO-as-40m-bribery-trial-collapses.html Accessed 24 November 2016.

The Telegraph, 'SFO plans fightback in 2014' 28 December 2013 www.telegraph.co.uk/finance/financial-crime/10540905/SFO-plans-fightback-in-2014.html Accessed 24 November 2016.

The Telegraph, 'JP Morgan's "London Whale" trader breaks his silence' 23 February 2016 www.telegraph.co.uk/business/2016/02/23/jp-morgans-london-whale-trader-brea ks-his-silence/.

The Telegraph, 'Firms face EU blacklist in bribery law change' www.telegraph.co.uk/fina nce/financial-crime/10613645/Firms-face-EU-blacklist-in-bribery-law-change.html Accessed 11 March 2017.

The Times, '£2½m trial ends with fees inquiry' 2 May 1981*The Times* Digital Archive 1798–1985 http://find.galegroup.com/ttda/infomark.do?action=interpret&tabID=T003&prodId=TTDA&userGroupName=uwesteng&docPage=article&searchType=AdvancedSearchForm&docId=CS174020188&type=multipage&contentSet=LTO&ver sion=1.0&finalAuth=true Accessed 18 October 2016.

The Times, 'Financial Services Authority: Can it be saved after the election?' 26 March 2010 www.thetimes.co.uk/tto/law/article2467878.ece Accessed 12 August 2016.

The Times, 'Right to jury trial faces axe in post-riot reforms' 16 January 2011 www.thetim es.co.uk/tto/news/politics/article3287652.ece Accessed 18 October 2016.

The Times, 'Stanford's bank "made up the numbers for more than 20 years"' 4 February 2012 www.thetimes.co.uk/tto/business/industries/banking/article3309416.ece Accessed 14 November 2016.

The Times, 'UBS trader was only "a gamble away from destroying Switzerland's biggest bank"' 14 September 2012 www.thetimes.co.uk/tto/news/uk/crime/article3538412.ece Accessed 14 January 2017.

The Times, 'Banks lose bid to dismiss Libor claims' 9 November 2013 www.thetimes.co.uk/tto/business/industries/banking/article3916826.ece Accessed 18 October 2016.

The Times, 'FCA to punish bankers involved in Libor scandal' 4 February 2014 www.thetimes.co.uk/tto/business/industries/banking/article3994517.ece Accessed 24 November 2016.

The Times, 'Fraud Office gets £19m bailout after misleading taxman' 1 March 2014 www.thetimes.co.uk/tto/news/uk/article4019911.ece Accessed 24 November 2016.

The Times, 'Bond trader fined and banned for attempt to manipulate stimulus plan' 21 March 2014 www.thetimes.co.uk/tto/business/industries/banking/article4039438.ece Accessed 18 October 2016.

The Times, 'Ian King: Business editor's commentary: Market abusers on every side' 21 March 2014 www.thetimes.co.uk/tto/business/columnists/article4040153.ece Accessed 18 October 2016.

The Times, 'Hosking on Monday: Waiting for the watchdog to fall' 31 March 2014 www.thetimes.co.uk/tto/business/columnists/article4049293.ece Accessed 18 October 2016.

The Times, 'Settlement keeps Diamond and Ricci out of court' 8 April 2014 www.thetimes.co.uk/tto/business/industries/banking/article4057124.ece Accessed 18 October 2016.

Tomasic, R, 'Governance and the evaluation of corporate law and regulation in Australia' (2001) 1(3) *Corporate Governance* 24.

Tomasic, R, 'The financial crisis and the haphazard pursuit of financial crime' (2011) 18(1) *JFC* 8.

Trace International, 'Trace Compendium – Securency' www.traceinternational.org/TraceCompendium/Detail/162?class=casename_searchresult&type=1 Accessed 4 January 2017.

Trace International, 'The high cost of small bribes' 7 www.traceinternational.org/Uploads/PublicationFiles/TheHighCostofSmallBribes2015.pdf Accessed 6 December 2016.

Transparency International, 'Exporting corruption: Progress Report 2014: Assessing enforcement of the OECD Convention on Combatting Foreign Bribery' 4 www.transparency.org/whatwedo/publication/exporting_corruption_progress_report_2014_assessing_enforcement_of_the_oecd Accessed 6 February 2017.

Transparency International, 'Exporting corruption 2015' www.transparency.org/whatwedo/publication/exporting_corruption_progress_report_2015_assessing_enforcement_of_the_oecd Accessed 4 December 2016.

Transparency International, 'The European Union integrity system' www.transparencyinternational.eu/wp-content/uploads/2014/04/EU_Integrity_System_Report.pdf Accessed 18 October 2016.

Transparency International, 'GlaxoSmithKline – A wake up call for the pharma sector' www.transparency.org.uk/glaxosmithkline-a-wake-up-call-for-the-pharma-sector/ Accessed 10 November 2016.

Transparency International, 'Missing the point on facilitation payments' www.transparency.org.uk/missing-the-point-on-facilitation-payments/ Accessed 2 January 2017.

Transparency International, 'Corruption Perceptions Index 2015' https://issuu.com/transparencyinternational/docs/2015_corruptionperceptionsindex_rep?e=2496456/33011041 Accessed 3 November 2016.

Transparency International, 'Corruption Perceptions Index 2016' www.transparency.org/news/feature/corruption_perceptions_index_2016?utm_medium=email&utm_campaign=CPI%202016%20General%20Mailer&utm_content=CPI%202016%20General%20Mailer+Version+A+CID_310d39acff23636ebb54eda828e1e89d&utm_source=Email%20marketing%20software&utm_term=SEE%20RESULTS Accessed 25 January 2017.

Transparency International, 'Stop watering down anti-corruption legislation' www.transparency.org/news/feature/stop_watering_down_anti_corruption_legislation Accessed 14 November 2016.

Transparency International, 'How effective is the UK Bribery Act?' www.transparency.org.uk/how-effective-is-the-uk-bribery-act/ Accessed 20 March 2017.

Transparency International, 'Countering small bribes' www.transparency.org.uk/publications/countering-small-bribes/ Accessed 20 March 2017.

Transparency International Australia, 'A ten-point integrity plan for the Australian government submission by Transparency International Australia on the proposed National

Anti-Corruption Plan' May 2012, 9 http://transparency.org.au/wp-content/uploads/2012/07/2012-TIA-NACP-Subv2-FINAL.pdf Accessed 4 January 2017.

Turner, J W C, *Russell on Crime*, 12th edn (Stephens & Sons 1964).

UNCAC, 'Executive summary', UNCAC Implementation Review Group meeting on 18 June 2012 www.ag.gov.au/CrimeAndCorruption/AntiCorruption/Pages/Globalleadershipincombatingcorruption.aspx Accessed 8 December 2016.

United Nations, 'At a glance' www.un.org/en/aboutun/index.shtml Accessed 3 November 2016.

United Nations, 'United Nations Convention against Corruption: Background of the United Nations Convention against Corruption' www.unodc.org/unodc/en/treaties/CAC/index.html Accessed 8 December 2016.

United Nations, 'United Nations Convention Against Corruption' www.unodc.org/documents/treaties/UNCAC/Publications/Convention/08-50026_E.pdf Accessed 8 December 2016.

United Nations, Joint Inspection Unit, 'Fraud prevention, detection and response in United Nations systems organizations' www.unjiu.org/en/reports-notes/JIU%20Products/JIU_REP_2016_4_English.pdf Accessed 17 October 2016.

United Nations Office of Drugs and Crime, 'Legislative guide for the implementation of the United Nations Convention against Corruption' www.unodc.org/pdf/corruption/CoC_LegislativeGuide.pdf Accessed 8 December 2016.

United Nations, Office of Iraq Programme, 'Oil-for-food' www.un.org/Depts/oip/background/index.html Accessed 8 December 2016.

University of Portsmouth, 'Annual Fraud Indicator 2016' www.port.ac.uk/media/contacts-and-departments/icjs/ccfs/Annual-Fraud-Indicator-2016.pdf Accessed 12 September 2016.

US Department of Commerce, International Trade Administration, www.trade.gov/goodgovernance/adobe/bem_appendices/appendix_f.pdf Accessed 14 November 2016.

US Department of State, 'President freezes terrorists' assets' http://2001-2009.state.gov/s/ct/rls/rm/2001/5041.htm Accessed 14 January 2017.

US District Court, 'Hon. Jed S Rakoff' www.nysd.uscourts.gov/judge/Rakoff Accessed 18 October 2016.

US Federal Sentencing Guidelines, 'Chapter eight – part b – Remedying harm from criminal conduct, and effective compliance and ethics program' 2016 www.ussc.gov/guidelines/2016-guidelines-manual Accessed 6 December 2016.

US Legal.com, 'Definitions' http://definitions.uslegal.com/t/tolling-agreement/ Accessed 14 November 2016.

Veljanovski, C, 'Introduction' in Arthur Seldon (ed), *Financial Regulation – or Over-Regulation* (The Institute of Economic Affairs 1988).

Wainwright, E, 'Our failing neighbour Australia and the future of Solomon Islands' 16 www.aspi.org.au/publications/our-failing-neighbour-australia-and-the-future-of-solomon-islands/solomons.pdf Accessed 8 December 2016.

Warren-Smith, C, 'Regulatory: The year ahead' (2011) 161 *NLJ* 358.

Welu, C M, 'A brave (but scary) new world: Why private equity is not exempt from US and UK anti-corruption laws' 2 February 2011 www.squirepattonboggs.com/~/media/files/insights/publications/2011/02/china-outbound/files/squiresandersnewschinaoutboundenglishpdf/fileattachment/squiresandersnewschinaoutboundenglishpdf.pdf Accessed 6 December 2016.

The White House, 'Reforms for American homeowners and consumers: President Obama signs the Helping Families Save their Homes Act and the Fraud Enforcement and

Recovery Act' 20 May 2009 www.whitehouse.gov/the-press-office/reforms-america n-homeowners-and-consumers-president-obama-signs-helping-families-sa Accessed 14 November 2016.

Wilson, G, and S Wilson, 'The FSA "credible deterrence", and criminal enforcement – A "haphazard pursuit"?' (2014) *JFC* 4.

Wilson, J, 'The Day We Sold the Rule of Law' in *Halsbury's Law Exchange* www.halsburyslawexchange.co.uk/?s=the+day+we+sold+the+rule+of+law Accessed 24 November 2016.

Wilson, S, '"Collaring" the crime and the criminal? "Jury psychology" and some criminological perspectives on fraud and the criminal law' (2006) 70(1) *J Crim L* 75–92.

Wilson, S, *The Origins of Modern Financial Crime* (Routledge 2014).

World Bank, 'Helping countries combat corruption: The role of the World Bank. 2 Corruption and Economic Development' www1.worldbank.org/publicsector/anticorrupt/corruptn/cor02.htm

World Bank, 'GDP ranking' http://data.worldbank.org/data-catalog/GDP-ranking-table Accessed 20 March 2017.

World Trade Organization, 'Table A6: Leading exporters and importers in world merchandise trade, 2015' www.wto.org/english/res_e/statis_e/wts2016_e/wts16_chap9_e.htm Accessed 12 December 2016.

Wright, R, 'Keynote address to the 17th International Cambridge Symposium on Economic Crime' (2000) 9(4) *JFC* 304–307.

Wright, R, 'Fraud after Roskill: A view of the Serious Fraud Office' (2003) 11(1) *JFC* 10.

Xanthaki, H, 'What is EU fraud? And can OLAF really combat it?' (2010) 17(1) *JFC* 133, 138.

Yeager, F, and others, 'US legislation designed to improve corporate governance: An exploration' (2010) 33(1) *Co Law* 25.

Zelcer, A, 'Mail and wire fraud' (2012) 49 *Am Crim L Rev* 985.

Zucker, K D, 'Cautionary tale for corporate whistleblowers: Lessons from federal courts' decisions on Sarbanes-Oxley employee retaliation claims' (2011) 62(2) *Labor Law Journal* 81.

Index

For Product Safety Concerns and Information please contact our EU
representative GPSR@taylorandfrancis.com
Taylor & Francis Verlag GmbH, Kaufingerstraße 24, 80331 München, Germany

www.ingramcontent.com/pod-product-compliance
Ingram Content Group UK Ltd.
Pitfield, Milton Keynes, MK11 3LW, UK
UKHW010957180926
475701UK00004B/410

9780367594503